There's a good reason why the nation's capital has been called

"America's most haunted city."
—*The Washington Star,* 1891

THE ANSWERS ARE HERE

. . . in Nixon's troubled spirit still pacing the halls of the White House.

. . . in the terrifying—and true—premonitions of our chief executives.

. . . in a videotape that captured the ghostly image of Theodore Roosevelt.

. . . in Jacqueline Kennedy's chilling encounter with Lincoln's spirit.

. . . in the confidential revelations and predictions of Nancy Reagan's personal astrologer.

THE HAUNTING OF THE PRESIDENTS

Joel Martin is an ACE-winning cable television host who gained notoriety when he exposed the Amityville Horror hoax. The coauthor of the national bestsellers *We Don't Die, We Are Not Forgotten,* and *Our Children Forever,* Joel Martin has more than one million copies of his books in print and his works have been translated into five languages.

William J. Birnes is the *New York Times* bestselling author of *The Day After Roswell* and the publisher of *UFO Magazine.*

THE
HAUNTING
OF THE
PRESIDENTS

A PARANORMAL HISTORY
OF THE U.S. PRESIDENCY

JOEL MARTIN &
WILLIAM J. BIRNES

A SIGNET BOOK

SIGNET
Published by New American Library, a division of
Penguin Putnam Inc., 375 Hudson Street,
New York, New York 10014, U.S.A.
Penguin Books Ltd, 80 Strand,
London WC2R 0RL, England
Penguin Books Australia Ltd, 250 Camberwell Road,
Camberwell, Victoria 3124, Australia
Penguin Books Canada Ltd, 10 Alcorn Avenue,
Toronto, Ontario, Canada M4V 3B2
Penguin Books (N.Z.) Ltd, Cnr Rosedale and Airborne Roads,
Albany, Auckland 1310, New Zealand

Penguin Books Ltd, Registered Offices:
Harmondsworth, Middlesex, England

First published by Signet, an imprint of New American Library,
a division of Penguin Putnam Inc.

First Printing, February 2003
10 9 8 7 6 5 4 3 2 1

PUBLISHER'S NOTE
While the authors have made every effort to provide accurate telephone
numbers and Internet addresses at the time of publication, neither
the publisher nor the authors assume any responsibility for errors, or for
changes that occur after publication.

*This book is dedicated to the memory of
my mother, Sadie, always my first lady.*
                                    J. M.

*And to the memories of Abie Kaplan,
Velvel Katz, and Lolly Bruni—now forever young*
                                    W.J.B.

"We meet so seldom by stock or by stone."
                        Pearl

ACKNOWLEDGMENTS

I extend my special thanks and deepest appreciation to the following individuals, whose assistance and contributions to this book were invaluable:

- Gaylon Emerzian, who thoughtfully brought Bill Birnes and me together to write this book.
- Bill Birnes, for coauthoring and representing this immense project, and whose skill and knowledge made writing it a lot easier than it should have been.
- Kristina Rus, reference librarian, East Meadow (NY) Public Library, whose enormous reference and research skills were outstanding and tireless, and who amazingly located many unique and out-of-print materials for us.
- Alex Oberman, for sharing his vast metaphysical knowledge.
- Thomas Santorelli, with gratitude for contributing historical materials.
- Cecilia Oh, our editor, for her constant support and encouragement.
- Evelyn Moleta, for myriad clerical tasks.
- Elise LeVaillant, for her love, spirituality, constant support, knowledge, and computer skills.
- The late Stephen Kaplan, who first started me on my paranormal journey long ago.
- And of course, Christina Martin, without whose help and encouragement this book would not have come to fruition. Thank you for your loyalty, patience, and belief in me.
- Alan and Lucinda, for many reasons—all of them good.
- Tommy Rao.

—Joel Martin

Why shouldn't truth be stranger than fiction?
Fiction, after all, has to make sense.

—Mark Twain

Contents

FOREWORD   xi

AUTHORS' NOTE   xv

CHAPTER ONE
The Haunted White House   1

CHAPTER TWO
George Washington at Valley Forge and
Gettysburg   16

CHAPTER THREE
Presidential Prophecies, Predictions, and Curses   48

CHAPTER FOUR
FDR, Jeane Dixon, and the
Kennedy Curse   77

CHAPTER FIVE
Ghosts of Presidents Past   98

CHAPTER SIX
Presidential Birthplaces: When Presidents'
Spirits Go Home   139

CHAPTER SEVEN
The Ghosts of the First Ladies   173

CHAPTER EIGHT
The Presidents at the Séance Table in the
Age of Spiritualism   201

CHAPTER NINE
Abraham Lincoln: The Most Psychic President   227

CHAPTER TEN
Recent Hauntings   273

CHAPTER ELEVEN
The Reagans   299

CHAPTER TWELVE
Eleanor and Hillary 322
CHAPTER THIRTEEN
The Haunted Capital 337
CHAPTER FOURTEEN
The Channeling of the Presidents 367

APPENDIX A
Presidential Haunted Places: A Travel Guide 402
APPENDIX B
Presidential Terms of Office and Dates
of Births and Deaths 411
APPENDIX C
Presidential Wives 414
BIBLIOGRAPHY 416

Foreword

No doubt you learned in school about George Washington's bitter winter at Valley Forge during the American Revolution. But it's unlikely you were ever taught General Washington was guided by an angelic vision during his terrible ordeal.

Of course you learned that President Lincoln signed the Emancipation Proclamation. Did you also know that Lincoln may have been advised to do so from the spirit world? If you were told Lincoln was our greatest president, were you also informed that he was our most psychic and that sightings of his ghost have been reported in the White House countless times?

In all, the spirits of more than two dozen presidents, their wives, and other family members have been seen in the White House and elsewhere.

Although ignored in schools and rarely if ever touched upon in so-called "traditional" history books or biographies, the paranormal has played a part in nearly every administration—thirty-nine of forty-three—since George Washington was our first president to the present. It is a remarkable, if virtually untold, story. And it is a *true* story. Hundreds of psychic incidents involving the presidency have been uncovered. How many others were lost or never recorded? Which brings us to *The Haunting of the Presidents.*

In the course of researching the paranormal, my curiosity was often piqued by an occasional mention or brief anecdote about a president or first lady who had some type of supernatural experience. But never was I able to locate a central source to the psychic encounters of first families. Frustrated that the stories were scattered or largely omitted from "serious" histories, first families being largely precluded in the public consciousness and mainstream media from any involvement with the paranormal, I decided to gather them together in one book.

Locating credible accounts and documentation became a vast search through hundreds of books, magazines, newspapers, Web sites, personal interviews, and visits. Both Bill Birnes and I approach the paranormal seriously, and that is the way we've treated the subject here. We wanted this book to be more than merely a collection of anecdotes about a haunted house—even if it is the White House. Thus, we've made every effort to explain the meaning of presidential psychic experiences, as well as biographical data about the first families.

Allow me to be personal for a moment. I began my involvement with unexplained phenomena in the early 1970s when I hosted a late-night radio talk show in the New York area, which continued for more than twenty years. At first I was so blasé about the entire subject that I was less than skeptical. I was proud to help expose as a hoax the infamous haunted house story detailed in *The Amityville Horror*. Then something changed. I began to see displays of psychic ability that were so stunning they could be nothing less than genuine. Was I being tricked? No. I'm a hard person to trick. I lived and worked as a teacher in some pretty tough neighborhoods of New York City. That'll give you eyes in the back of your head, as they say.

After more than twenty-five years of studying and observing paranormal activity, my thinking has evolved. I know the subject is genuine. We all have psychic experiences—presidents and their wives included—while professional naysayers and debunkers have their own agenda. Too many of us have been intimidated from talking openly about our psychic experiences, fearing ridicule or criticism, although happily that attitude is slowly changing.

Do you believe in ghosts? Actually it's not a belief system or some article of faith. Either there are spirits walking the earth or there aren't. Until 1997, I would have not been able to give you a definitive answer. In October of that year, I was in Bonn, Germany, visiting a friend who was hospitalized. One day, my companion and I went to the Bonn Basilica, a beautiful Catholic church, to offer prayers for our ailing friend. The magnifcent building dates back nearly a thousand years and contains bones and relics of martyred saints. As we sat in a pew, I noticed the silhouette of someone walking toward me. As it moved closer, I realized it was not a person but rather an apparition. The shadowy form approaching on my right side was that of a small woman in a nun's habit. As she walked behind me, she placed a shawl over my shoulders. Of course, not an actual shawl, but one that, like her, was apparitional. Then she vanished past my left side. I felt strangely comforted and, at the same time, slightly stunned by the encounter. No, I was not dreaming, and this was not my imagination at work. I was fully awake. Nor would I dare invent the incident.

Later I shared my experience with my companion, who is Roman Catholic. She explained the symbolism, which she called "a shawl of protection," something I'd never heard of. I'm certain my experience was genuine. Ghosts are a form of energy that survive physical death and return to earth for any number of reasons.

Interestingly, millions of people—in and out of the White House—have told of encountering apparitions. Yet traditional science regards ghosts as something imaginary at best, delusional at worst, and believes countless witnesses as having no credibility. Yet a single eyewitness to a crime is sometimes sufficient to convict a suspect. It's a strange contradiction. The fact that we cannot "prove" many paranormal experiences doesn't mean they should be disregarded. Psychic events are a normal and natural part of human functioning, not some occult or magic "power."

It is important that this hidden side of the lives of our presidents and their families be told. No matter one's status in life, we all share similar experiences, questions, and concerns about life and life after death. Learning how first families used their psychic gifts is as much a part of the history of the presidency as any other detail in their lives.

—Joel Martin

Authors' Note

Because this book contains many historical facts, we discovered in the course of researching and writing that different sources sometimes varied in details such as dates, locations, events, dialogue, and even spellings of names and places. To the best of our ability, we have checked several authoritative references to provide the greatest historical accuracy possible. However, certain variations proved unavoidable and are a reflection of incomplete, inadequate, or contradictory historical record-keeping.

CHAPTER ONE

The Haunted White House

Why would they want to come back here I could never understand. No man in his right mind would want to come here of his own accord.
　　　　　—President Harry S. Truman,
　　　　　talking about the appearances
　　　　　of ghosts in the White House

The White House, at 1600 Pennsylvania Avenue in Washington, D.C., is the nation's most celebrated address. Without question, it is unequaled as the most important residence in American history because, far more than just another government building, the White House has come to symbolize the prestige and power of the United States over the course of two hundred years. No matter who its occupants have been through war and peace, depression and prosperity, triumph and tragedy, these first families have wielded more power than almost all other families in the world. Yet, ironically, because the public successes and scandals of the White House residents have commanded the attention of the world's press and the American people, precious little is known about the strange paranormal events—many of which have been documented and substantiated—that have taken place over the years behind the building's stately columns and porticos. Within the White House, first

1

families, staff and personnel, and parapsychologists and other psychic experts have discovered there are things that go bump in the night.

The million tourists who come to the nation's capital to visit the home of every chief executive since John Adams, our second president, and his wife, Abigail—the first first family to take up occupancy in 1800 when the building was still incomplete and officially called the President's House—see only the eight rooms and hallways that comprise the public tour. Few who visit the 132-room mansion realize that the White House has been, and continues to be, a home to the spirits and ghosts of a number of former presidents and their family members, who, even after they passed on from this earthly existence, were unable or unwilling to depart the mansion. These ghosts continue to inhabit the halls and rooms of the White House, appearing and reappearing to startled witnesses and coexisting with the living residents.

To most of us, the presidency and the paranormal may seem worlds or even galaxies apart. But, in fact, they have coexisted from the very beginning of our nation, often uneasily and surreptitiously. You won't read about this on the first page of the *New York Times*, but apparitions and visions of ghostly entities inside the White House are real and have been a part of the building's history ever since the first residents, President and Mrs. John Adams, moved in at the beginning of the nineteenth century.

Spirits and Ghosts

What explanation can there be for these presidential apparitions? How can anyone account for the existence of apparitions in general? Parapsychologists sometimes disagree, but conjecture that some component or aspect of the human being—most likely a form of energy we do not yet understand—survives the body's physical death. Although this component is not corporeal, as we have come to understand the word, what survives has been called "the soul" or "the spirit," an aspect of the deceased person, which is sensed or even witnessed by the living.

Parapsychologists also explain that the human soul is composed of energy, which often assumes the shape of the physical being it once inhabited, except that it is almost always either transparent or translucent. There are some religions that have asserted that the essence of the individual is immortal and is simply reincarnated into another physical being. Other religions say that the soul lives forever. And still others, including many spiritualists, suggest that the spirit of the deceased often remains among the living, either unable or unwilling to make the transition to the next phase of its existence because an event or tragedy during the decedent's life has bound its spirit to a specific place. Thus, Abraham Lincoln's spirit may forever haunt the White House because of his untimely death by assassination while Richard Nixon's troubled spirit may show itself from time to time because of his untimely departure from office by resignation in the face of the Watergate scandal and his all-but-certain impeachment.

When we talk about ghosts and spirits, we're using the terms interchangeably when, in actuality, there is a technical difference between the two phenomena. Many psychic researchers technically define a ghost as a soul who has remained on earth and refused to move on to the Other Side. In other words, ghosts are trapped within this earthly dimension. A spirit, on the other hand, is a soul that has successfully made the transition to the next stage of its existence. However, it returns to the physical world to visit and observe, but is free to return to the Other Side to resume its spirit existence and soul growth. It is not trapped in our dimension.

Ghosts, perhaps because they are earthbound entities, seem to have their own agendas, often oblivious to the living people around them. That's why, sometimes, people who claim to have seen ghosts remark that the ghosts don't interact with them, which can make them even more frightening. Moreover, because there is no concept of time in the afterlife, ghosts may remain affixed to a specific room or location, haunting even many years after they have passed on, frequently in the same repetitious pattern. This, too, can be a terrifying sight to any living person who sees a ghost.

Presidential spirits, on the other hand, seem to have returned to complete a specific task or piece of business. Maybe they returned to offer advice to the living, "clairaudiently" or telepathically. This, as we will see, was probably the case when the spirit of General George Washington appeared to the Union's 20th Maine Regiment at Gettysburg to direct them to head off a desperate Confederate assault that could have turned the tide in the opening hours of the historic battle. Here was a spirit with a specific agenda who, if the official army report that was filed after the battle with Secretary of War Stanton can be believed, returned at the head of American troops to save the Union.

Ghosts Inside the White House

We think of the President of the United States and, by extension, his family as grounded in reality and committed to the hard facts of running an administration. The last thing anyone would associate with the White House or the president is a ghostly visitation. The White House itself is covered by news teams twenty-four hours a day with reporters on hand for breaking stories whenever they happen. With all this surveillance and protection by the Secret Service, wouldn't stories have long since got out about hauntings at 1600 Pennsylvania Avenue? Couldn't the Secret Service at least keep the ghosts out?

The fact is, however, that presidents and their families are people just like the rest of us, and some of them have psychic powers they don't even realize. After all, it takes a special person to overcome the arduousness of a presidential campaign and a prescience to make the right choices, sometimes by sheer instinct. Maybe it's that instinct that allows a person to become more in touch with his psychic abilities or his intuition. Maybe that's what it takes to be president. Nevertheless, most people would be very surprised to learn that a president or one of his family members has encountered a ghost, had a dream premonition, experienced some form of ESP, or actually consulted with a psychic, medium, or astrologer, especially inside the White House. To accept that some of our presidents have been influenced by their paranormal involvement seems beyond the comprehension of many people, but it's true, and the astrologers themselves have talked about it. Professional mediums and parapsychologists aren't the only people capable of experiencing paranormal phenomena. Ghostly apparitions can appear to any one of us because we all have some psychic ability.

We've found that people also tend to think that all accounts of supernatural activity in the White House are relegated to the nineteenth and early twentieth centuries. Ghosts are old, haunted houses are old, and therefore, any apparitions and accounts of paranormal happenings at 1600 Pennsylvania Avenue must have taken place centuries ago. But that's a false assumption. During the so-called Great Age of Spiritualism from the 1850s through the 1920s, interest in communication with the deceased was immensely popular before it declined in the years leading up to World War II. However, some psychics have described hauntings and experiments in spiritualism that continued right through the end of World War II to the present. There are intriguing anecdotes of paranormal incidents in what historians sometimes refer to as the "modern presidency," dating from Dwight Eisenhower in 1952 to George W. Bush today. In fact, bestselling author Whitley Streiber in his book *The Key* reports that experiments in quantifying and qualifying the existence of an alternative set of parallel realities, where what we call the "paranormal" is as objectively substantive as anything in our frame of reality, are only a few years away from a series of successful conclusions.

Thus, there is a direct line of paranormal activity among America's historic families from the framers of the Constitution and our first president to the twenty-first century, including and especially the first ladies. Martha Washington was a spiritualist, as were Jane Pierce, Mary Todd Lincoln, and Eleanor Roosevelt. Many séances were conducted at the White House during the nineteenth century, and just twenty years ago, Nancy Reagan herself, much to the frustration of White House Chief of Staff Michael Deaver, asked astrologist Joan Quigley to conduct readings for President Ronald Reagan so that his policy decisions might be in accord with the ascending and descending planets.

Did Nancy Reagan's consultations with an astrologer turn President Reagan into our first New Age president? Not necessarily. But then again, we shouldn't forget that it was Ronald Reagan, who as the Governor of California ordered his pilot on a flight back to Sacramento to chase a UFO across the desert skies. Years later, in his second term as president, Reagan predicted to the startled delegates in the United Nations General Assembly how quickly their respective countries would resolve the differences among themselves if the earth were faced with a threat from hostile extraterrestrials from outer space bent on an invasion of the planet or the destruction of the human race. The evidence is clear: the normal and the paranormal coexist very easily in the White House and among the families who have lived there.

The Paranormal Presidency

The numbers of psychic or paranormal experiences are themselves very telling. Ghosts of no less than twenty presidents have been witnessed in various locations around Washington or at historic sites, and seven ghosts have been witnessed inside the White House itself. From Washington to Bill Clinton, paranormal or supernatural experiences occurred in at least twenty-five presidential administrations, many of which directly involved the chief executives. Seven first ladies are known to have returned in spirit form to haunt the White House as well as other places, and we can count no fewer than fifteen presidents' wives who've had a range of psychic experiences. Add to these numbers the ghostly apparitions of other presidential family members, including children of first families, and you have enough anecdotal evidence to argue that there are bizarre things going on inside the Beltway. In addition, at least three presidents and six first ladies privately consulted at one time or another with a psychic, medium, astrologer, healer, or New Age advisor while in the White House. This list includes not only Nancy Reagan, but also the former first lady and now the junior U.S. Senator from New York, Hillary Clinton, who channeled the spirit of former first lady Eleanor Roosevelt.

Maybe the White House doesn't look like the stereotypical, creaking old haunted house or even the now-famous "Amityville Horror" location but the presidential mansion is probably the most haunted house in America, the site of countless visions, apparitions, ghostly sightings, dream premonitions, spirit phenomena, mystical séances, and other supernatural occurrences. You won't hear about this on CNN or watch a member of the first family give a news conference about a spiritual visitation, but ask those who've worked there or someone no longer in the public eye and you'll find out that over the years many of the historic rooms and hallways inside the White House have been touched by the unexplained.

There's a great irony to all of this. Even though some presidents themselves have encountered their predecessors late at night on the second floor or in the West Wing and ample numbers of credible witnesses over the long history of the building have told stories of the ghosts of Lincoln and Andrew Jackson haunting their favorite rooms, presidential spokespersons have consistently denied rumors that the White House is haunted. Yet, in the years following World War II and right through the 1980s, while presidential press secretaries remained officially silent on the subject, declassified records revealed that covert psychic experiments in remote viewing and out-of-body projection were actively conducted by the CIA and three branches of the military. And at least three former presidents—Gerald Ford, Jimmy Carter, and Reagan—claimed to have witnessed unidentified flying objects. Carter even filed a report on his Georgia UFO sighting and promised the American people that he'd tell them the truth about UFOs. But a visit from a member of the National Security Agency to the Oval Office put a stop to that revelation even before Carter spent his first month in office. Nixon, one story goes, invited his good friend Jackie Gleason to a secret US military installation to see what was left of an extraterrestrial spacecraft and its alien inhabitants. And even John F. Kennedy once reportedly told the press that he would love to discuss the subject of UFOs but "my hands are tied."

The paranormal experiences of the presidents, their family members, administrative and personal staff, and White House guests generally fall into two categories: (1) The presidents and those related to them who have witnessed or experienced various psychic and unexplained events during their lifetimes. (2) The presidents and those related to them who have *been* seen or witnessed by others as apparitions or visions or who have been sensed in other supernatural ways by the living after they have passed on. Thus, living presidents and their families can be observers of psychic events, but after they pass on, they become the ghosts or spirits that are perceived by others.

A Roster of Spirits

The presidential ghosts that have appeared to witnesses in the White House make a stately list, beginning with the spirits of both George and Martha Washington. Perhaps our first president's apparition returned for a glimpse of the magnificent building that owes so much to his perseverance and foresight. Washington chose the architect who designed the White House, was present for the laying of the cornerstone when construction began in 1792, visited the site while the mansion was being built, and even suggested the location for the East Room. This was the same East Room where the ghost of our second first lady, Abigail Adams, has repeatedly materialized.

While the presidential ghosts themselves seem to be nonpartisan in their appearances, periods of national crises seem to have produced more hauntings in the White House. (While there have been no public reports of psychic activity in connection with the September 11, 2001, terrorist attacks on the World Trade Center and Pentagon, that does not preclude the possibility that there was such activity.) Notably, the spirits of presidents Washington, Jackson, Lincoln, and Lyndon Johnson have all been reported during times of war or national calamity. Are these remarkably strong presidents still haunting the Executive Mansion because the consistent air of crisis pervades not only the building but also the institution of the presidency itself? Or are the ghosts still the reflections of the men themselves whose respective grips on power were so intense that even in death they can't be broken and are only enhanced during periods of national crises?

Who, or what, were some of the other spiritual presences that manifested themselves to witnesses in and around the White House over the years in addition to George and Martha Washington? First, there was the spirit of our third president, Thomas Jefferson, who has been heard playing violin in the White House, the eerie sound of his eighteenth-century melodies floating from out of nowhere through the corridors at night. Then there was the scent of lilac perfume, a bouquet associated with the spirit of Dolley Madison, who called the White House home during the War of 1812. A physical manifestation of her presence—a ghost—was witnessed in the White House Rose Garden more than a hundred years later, during the administration of President Woodrow Wilson.

The restless ghost of President Andrew Jackson has been seen and heard storming about his former White House bedroom by several witnesses during the Lincoln and Eisenhower years. The spirit manifested itself again as recently as the middle 1960s after Johnson was re-elected president. Another presidential ghost, William Henry Harrison, has been heard rummaging through the White House attic. Years later, President John Tyler's ghost was recognized in the White House by startled witnesses, who reported the incident.

In addition to the premonitions of US presidents that predicted their untimely deaths in office—William Henry Harrison, Zachary Taylor, and James Garfield—President Tyler's second wife, Julia, had private visions of what fate would befall her husband. And Lincoln, arguably our most psychic president, had the most famous premonition in American history, which predicted his own assassination. In a dream, Lincoln actually claimed to have seen his own corpse lying in a coffin. Our sixteenth president may also have secured help from the spirit world for important political decisions he made during the Civil War. Was this similar to Ronald Reagan's scheduling the invasion of Granada upon the advice of Nancy Reagan's astrologer, Joan Quigley?

But premonitions and prophetic dreams are only part of the paranormal picture in the White House. The Executive Mansion has also hosted many formal and informal séances over the years. In the 1850s, during the great Age of Spiritualism that swept across the United States and Europe, First Lady Jane Pierce, wife of President Franklin Pierce, sought communication from the couple's deceased son through a medium. Mary Todd Lincoln, an ardent spiritualist, sought messages from her two departed children, Willie and Eddie. She also reported to her friends that she had seen the apparitions of Willie and Eddie Lincoln appearing before her eyes in her White House bedroom at night. And on different occasions, she saw the ghosts of presidents John Tyler and Thomas Jefferson.

Willie Lincoln seems to have become a fixture at the White House, becoming visible during the administrations of Ulysses S. Grant and William Howard Taft in the room he once occupied. Willie was also said to have continued his haunting into the twentieth century, appearing before President Lyndon Johnson's daughter Lynda. President Lincoln himself haunted a number of presidents, including Teddy Roosevelt (who admitted to friends that he'd confronted the ghost of Lincoln in the White House), Lyndon Johnson, and first ladies Grace Coolidge, Lady Bird Johnson, and Jackie Kennedy.

In fact, so many sightings of Lincoln's ghost have been reported that it is, without question, the most frequently seen apparition in White House history. Grace Coolidge once insisted to disbelieving friends and the wives of influential senators that she witnessed Lincoln's spirit roaming through a doorway on the second floor of the White House. This is the section most tourists never see because it's where presidential families have their private quarters and the public is not permitted to visit. It was also on the second floor, in the dead of night, where President Herbert Hoover described to friends "fantastic" strange noises that he heard coming from the other side of the door to the Lincoln bedroom.

There were several significant sightings of Lincoln's ghost during the administration of Franklin Delano Roosevelt. Among the witnesses were not only Eleanor Roosevelt, but also several members of her staff. World-famous dignitaries visiting the White House also reported encountering a vision of President Lincoln. Although President Harry Truman would not acknowledge a belief in ghosts, he never denied that something inexplicable was present on the White House second floor. However, it was Truman's daughter, Margaret, who left no doubt that it was Lincoln's specter she saw in the corridors of the second floor. President Eisenhower also admitted confronting Lincoln's ghost one day in a White House hallway.

It didn't end with Ike, JFK, or Johnson, all of whom had brushes with Lincoln's ghost. Nor did it end with George H. W. Bush, who had his suspicions about Lincoln's ghost, even though he denied ever seeing it. Perhaps his son President George W. Bush, Laura, or one of the twins might expect to see Lincoln now that the family has taken up residence in the White House. Maybe, since his inauguration, they've seen him if they hadn't already encountered him while visiting the White House during the term of President Bush's father. The first children are particularly receptive to ghosts in the White House. In recent administrations, the daughters of presidents Johnson, Nixon, Ford, and Reagan all reported seeing or sensing Lincoln's spirit while in various White House rooms. As recently as the Clinton years, a White House staff member believed he sensed Lincoln's presence.

But Lincoln wasn't the only psychic president in the White House. Other presidents and their families also had psychic experiences and have returned to this life, quite possibly to finish whatever it was that prompted their psychic visions in the first place. Frances Cleveland, for example, the wife of President Grover Cleveland, made a remarkable psychic prediction about her husband's political future while in the White House, and years after her passing, her invisible ghost was heard crying along the second-floor corridors. President Garfield reported that his late father's spirit visited him in the Executive Mansion, appearing in dream visions. Even Johnson, whose entire immediate family had encountered ghosts in the White House, confided to a staff member that he once had a significant psychic dream while president. And more recently, a report claimed that, despite protestations to the contrary from President George H. W. Bush, the spirit of LBJ was discerned after the Bush administration took office in 1989.

In addition to the first families, many White House employees have reported encounters with ghosts and other supernatural phenomena. Not surprisingly, some of them admitted to being frightened by the unexpected experiences, although there is no evidence that any of the apparitions of former presidents ever reappeared with the intent of causing any harm. But it wasn't only presidents who haunted employees and staff members. The ghost of David Burns, the man who originally owned the land on which the White House was built, returned to haunt, as did a British soldier responsible for setting fire to the White House during the War of 1812 when James and Dolley Madison were forced to flee for their lives.

Divinations at the White House

From the time of Martha Washington, first ladies and their husbands have had flirtations with psychics, mediums, and other purveyors of the paranormal. Traditional historians have pointed to the reliance that the Lincolns placed on paranormal consultations during the Great Age of Spiritualism during the middle to late nineteenth century. But what's interesting is that George and Martha Washington held spiritualistic beliefs even though the founders and framers of the United States and its government were mostly products of the eighteenth-century Age of Reason.

The first families' interest in the paranormal continued well after the turn of the twentieth century, however, extending, as reports have indicated about Hillary Clinton, right to the turn of the twenty-first century. More than a hundred years ago, Florence Harding, wife of President Warren Harding, sought advice from mediums, as did Mrs. Calvin Coolidge. President Woodrow Wilson was believed to have had secret consultations with famed American psychic, healer, and seer Edgar Cayce. Presidents Franklin Delano Roosevelt and John F. Kennedy both met with psychic and astrologer Jeane Dixon, who ultimately became one of the most famous and popular psychics not only for official families but also for the American public at large. During the Reagan years, First Lady Nancy Reagan depended heavily on the counsel of

White House astrologer Joan Quigley, who ultimately detailed much of the nature of her relationship with the Reagans in her book, *What Does Joan Say?* And more recently, Hillary Clinton admitted that she'd had "conversations" with the spirit of the late First Lady Eleanor Roosevelt, which some psychic experts regard as a form of "channeling."

Psychic Presidents

In addition to official psychic sessions to contact spirits or summon ghosts, residents of the White House have often exhibited great powers of intuition. Often misunderstood or joked about as the provenance only of women, intuition is actually a real phenomenon that has been studied not only by researchers in the paranormal, but also by clinical and research psychologists as well as neurologists. Intuition has not been dismissed as some unquantifiable and subjective experience, but is coming to be accepted as a valid and measurable form of perception that could be based on the ability of the individual to perceive or sense real indicators of reality going around him or her or the ability of an individual to react honestly to his or her own logic. Accordingly, it's not surprising that intuition has accounted for many presidential decisions. Those who've studied it in the form of a psychic ability say that intuition is often an instinct, thought, or idea that seems to emerge from nowhere, but whose source is actually within the psychic realm. Andrew Jackson is a notable example of a president who heeded his intuition just as Lincoln will go down in history as a president who abandoned his exceptional intuition by denying the reality of his psychic dream premonitions. Throughout history, many scientists, inventors, military and political leaders have credited their successes and victories to intuitive abilities.

Intuition and psychic abilities have even been reported to include the pets of presidents. Was President Clinton's first dog, Buddy, an intuitive focus that allowed Clinton to steer a brilliant political course through the shoals of impeachment? What role did Checkers play in Nixon's public appeal to the American people to keep him on the Republican ticket in 1952 when his nascent political career could have been all but extinguished? It has been reported that the pet dogs of Lincoln, Franklin Delano Roosevelt, and Reagan all sensed the presence of extranormal spirits around them. In the cases of Lincoln and Roosevelt, their animal companions exhibited strange behavior associated with the supernatural, and barked at the ghosts of their deceased owners. Presidential pets, as is true for many animals, have a distinct advantage in witnessing ghosts. No one has told them it is impossible to do so, as humans are too often taught. Did Buddy, in the waning days of the Clinton administration, stir in the middle of the night at the presence of a Lyndon Johnson, Abraham Lincoln, or Andrew Jackson and bark into the darkness as the graveyard team of Secret Service agents on duty in the family quarters shot knowing looks at each other across the hall as if they had a private joke they could never ever share with anyone else?

CHAPTER TWO

George Washington at Valley Forge and Gettysburg

Be not forgetful to entertain strangers,
for thereby some have entertained angels unawares.
—Hebrews 13:2

It's not surprising that some of the most incredible stories grew up around, and continue to circulate about, President George Washington. The story of Washington's vision at Valley Forge is one of the greatest tales of prophetic visions in modern history, and the documented story of the general's appearance at the Battle of Gettysburg to rally a Union regiment and encourage them into a daring charge that carried the day is still inspiring. Like Abraham Lincoln, Washington was a man who believed in his prophetic visions and predicted his own death in a harsh Virginia winter just as the last hours of the eighteenth century ticked to a close. In describing the paranormal aspects of our nation's first president, it is fitting that the story begins in what had to be the darkest days of America's embryonic beginnings: as the Continental Army wintered in Valley Forge mere miles away from the powerful British Army occupying Philadelphia. It was at Valley Forge, if the story is true, that a new era in modern history began when Washington was visited by an angel prophesizing the victory of

16

America and establishment of a new moral force in the world.

George Washington at Valley Forge

The biting wind drove the freezing rain like nails rattling against the sides of General George Washington's forlorn Valley Forge headquarters, bleeding through the sagging canvas into icy rivulets that froze into stalactites along the walls. The ground, deeply rutted from wagon wheels and artillery tracks, was also hard frozen, covered by sheets of ice that cut into the frostbitten feet of the sentries standing guard by the general's tent. Even if the Continental Army could have requisitioned adequate supplies, the troops couldn't have moved to warm and secure quarters because of the British garrison wintering in nearby Philadelphia and blocking their escape routes to the Delaware Bay. Washington was alone in his command. His own staff had become demoralized, adding to the misery he and his tattered and hungry soldiers were suffering. Since his forced retreat from New York, Washington had not experienced a darker hour as commander of the American Continental Army in the War for Independence.

The general, painfully aware of the wretched plight of his beleaguered troops, desperately needed help. His army was all but out of provisions, unprotected against the harsh Northeast winter wind that rolled out of the upper Delaware and Lehigh River valleys, and without the hope of reinforcements. Driven across central New Jersey and out of Philadelphia, Washington looked for anything that would keep his army together. But from where would aid come? Publicly stoic, he agonized privately for his men in their seemingly hopeless circumstance. He implored the Almighty for help and comfort. Often his prayers were offered secretly in a thicket, where, with bowed head, he appealed for strength and guidance.

Our citations as to what Washington wrote about the

winter at Valley Forge and the recollections and memories of others are drawn from a wide variety of sources. We used biographies of Washington, letters and journals of both officers and enlisted personnel at Valley Forge, and the writings of those who spoke to Washington about his experiences as General of the Continental Army and later recorded their conversations. The result is a depiction of the winter at Valley Forge drawn from the descriptions of the very people who witnessed it with their own eyes.

Washington himself wrote, "To see men without clothes to cover their nakedness, without blankets to lie on, without shoes—by which their marches might be traced by the blood from their feet—and almost as often without provisions as with, marching through frost and snow, at Christmas taking up their winter quarters within a day's march of the enemy, without a house or hut to cover them until they could be built . . . in my opinion can scarce be paralleled."

The general was hardly alone in his assessment of the dire situation. On December 19, 1777, the American troops arrived at Valley Forge to camp for the winter. Lt. Col. Henry Dearborn wrote in his journal, "This is Thanksgiving Day . . . but God knows we have very little to keep it with, this being the third day we have been without flour or bread . . . in huts and tents, lying on the cold ground."

"Poor food—hard lodging—cold weather—fatigue— nasty clothes—nasty cookery—vomit half my time— smoked out of my senses—the devil's in it—I can't endure it. . . ." wrote one officer.

Still another witness grimly observed, "There comes a soldier, his bare feet are seen through his worn-out shoes, his legs nearly naked from the tattered remains of an only pair of stockings; his breeches not sufficient to cover his nakedness; his shirt hanging in strings; his hair disheveled. . . . His whole appearance pictures a person forsaken and discouraged. He comes and cries with an air of wretchedness and despair, 'I am sick, my feet lame, my legs are sore, my body covered with this tormenting itch . . . and all the reward I shall get, will be—"Poor Will is dead." ' "

There was little food to be found. Supplies of beef and pork were nearly depleted. In addition, the American soldiers had not been paid for several months. Conditions grew so severe that pieces of clothing from those who died of illness and disease were reissued to the living.

There would eventually be four thousand soldiers living—if "living" it could be called—in that deplorable condition. With sickness, disease, and death increasingly rampant, the men continued to huddle against the bitter cold, ice, sleet, and snow. And conditions for officers were hardly better. General Washington, to his credit, assured his men he would "share in the hardship and partake of every inconvenience."

Against the background of this desperate situation, General Washington was prepared for his soldiers to desert or even mutiny. After all, they were, in the words of historian James Thomas Flexner, "unpaid, unfed, naked . . . suffering to protect fat civilians, who either criticized or ignored them." Even worse, the cause of liberty was by no means unanimous among Americans. The Tories and British loyalists lived secure and comfortable in British-occupied cities, where the Revolution, for them, was as troublesome as it was for the English. Approximately one-third of the American Colonial population favored independence, one-third opposed breaking ties with England, and another one-third appeared not to care one way or the other.

In fact, General Washington's complaints to the Board of War largely fell on deaf ears. On December 31, 1777, Washington wrote to Governor William Livingston: "A dreadful year. Our sick naked, our well naked, our unfortunate men in captivity naked."

Washington angrily called upon Congress for help or he predicted, "This army must inevitably be reduced to one or other of these three things: starve, dissolve, or disperse in order to obtain subsistence." But Congress, which had criticized General Washington's leadership, had fled from the nation's capital in Philadelphia before the advancing British, apparently unable or unwilling to provide any meaningful aid.

Despite his devotion and respect for the troops, Washington feared that even the strongest of his men at Valley Forge would waver or fail. His army, he told himself in his darkest moments, was on the verge of collapse. To his surprise and relief, however, the men remained steadfastly loyal, despite grumbling and some angry chants. They neither mutinied nor deserted, and their devotion in the face of terrible deprivation brought tears to Washington's eyes. He thanked them for their unswerving loyalty, and was moved to write, "Naked and starving as they are, we cannot enough admire the incomparable patience and fidelity of the soldiery."

By February 1778, Major General Nathaniel Greene implored, "God grant we may never be brought to such a wretched condition again."

Given their predicament, what would be the future of the American fight against the British? What would be the future of the American dream of independence? Could it surmount these crushing obstacles?

Throughout the misery at Valley Forge, George Washington maintained his composure and steellike courage. Remarkably, he was described by his officers as "calm and firm," despite the brutal conditions, the indifference of the Continental Congress, and the hostility of his political enemies and adversaries. These were, by some accounts, his finest moments and his greatest battles where his bravery in the face of seemingly insurmountable danger helped him face the hardships of the winter with the rest of his army.

During this period, Washington often called upon his deep faith in God, which he viewed "as an overruling providence, conceived as the power that sustains and guides human destiny." Washington believed that the American people were under the direct protective care of God, and that he had been personally directed and shielded by the Almighty. He had spoken of "the miraculous care of Providence that protected me beyond all human expectations."

The general looked the part of someone who had been blessed with enormous power and endurance. He had already proven himself to be a man of remarkable vitality. He was, at six-two, an imposing figure, unusually tall for his time, strong and vigorous. Lesser men would surely have died from the litany of diseases he had suffered and overcome. During his lifetime Washington endured dysentery, influenza, malaria, mumps, pleurisy, pneumonia, rickets, smallpox, staph infections, tuberculosis, and typhoid fever. That did not include his having survived the time he rode through a volley of enemy fire only to have two horses shot from under him and four bullets rip through his coat. Miraculously none of the bullets struck his body although other soldiers immediately around him had been cut down and killed in the fusillade of artillery and rifle shot.

One cold gray day in 1778, when all seemed lost, General Washington sat in his headquarters at a crude wooden table that served as his desk. He was preparing a dispatch, when he glanced up. To his surprise, before him was, according to his own description, an "apparition of a beautiful woman."

"I would have risen but the riveted gaze of the being before me rendered volition impossible," Washington later recalled in telling of his visionary experience. "My thought itself became paralyzed! A new influence, mysterious, potent, irresistible, took possession of me! All I could do was gaze steadily, vacantly at my unknown visitant!"

"I do not know whether it is owing to the anxiety of my mind or what," Washington later wrote, "but this afternoon, as I was sitting at this table engaged in preparing a dispatch, something seemed to disturb me. Looking up I beheld standing opposite a singularly beautiful female.

"So astonished was I that it was some moments before I found language to inquire the purpose of her presence, for I had given strict orders not to be disturbed. A second, a third, and a fourth time I repeated my question, but received no answer from my mysterious visitor, except a slight rising of her eyes.

"I felt strange sensations spreading through me. I assayed once more to address her, but my tongue had become useless!

"Gradually the surrounding atmosphere seemed filled with sensations, and grew luminous. Everything about me seemed to rarefy; the mysterious visitor herself becoming more airy and yet more distinct to my sight than ever.

"I next began to feel as one dying, or rather to experience the sensation which I have sometimes imagined accompanies dissolution. I did not think, I did not reason. I did not move. All that was impossible. I was conscious only of gazing fixedly, vacantly at my companion."

Washington continued, "Presently I heard a voice saying, 'Son of the Republic, look and learn!' while at the same time my visitor extended her arm eastwardly. I now beheld a heavy white vapor at some distance rising fold upon fold. This gradually dissipated, and I looked upon a strange scene. Before me lay spread out in one vast plain all the countries of the world—Europe, Asia, Africa, and America.

"I saw rolling and tossing between Europe and America, the billows of the Atlantic. And between Asia and America lay the Pacific. 'Son of the Republic,' said the mysterious voice, as before, 'look and learn.' At that moment I beheld a dark shadowy being, like an angel, standing or rather, floating, in midair between Europe and America.

"Dipping water out of the ocean in the hollow of each hand, he sprinkled some upon America with his right hand, while with his left hand he cast some on Europe. Immediately a cloud arose from those countries, and joined in midocean. For a while it remained stationary, and then it moved slowly westward, until it enveloped America in its murky folds.

"Sharp flashes of lightning gleamed through it at intervals; and I heard the smothered groans and cries of the American people. A second time the angel dipped water from the ocean and sprinkled it as before. The dark cloud was then drawn back to the ocean, in whose heaving bellows it sank from view. A third time I heard the mysterious voice say: 'Son of the Republic, look and learn.' I cast my eyes upon America and beheld villages and towns and cities springing up, one after another, until the whole land is dotted with them. Again I heard the mysterious voice say: 'Son of the Republic, the end of the century cometh, look and learn.'

"And with this the dark shadowy figure turned its face southward, and from Africa I saw an ill-omened specter approaching our land. It flitted slowly over every town and city of the latter. The inhabitants presently set themselves in battle array against each other. As I continued looking at the bright angel, on whose brow rested a crown of light on which was traced the word UNION, I saw the angel place an American flag between the divided nation, and say, 'Remember, ye are brethren.' Instantly, the inhabitants, casting from them their weapons, became friends once more, and united around the National Standard."

Washington described his angelic encounter further. "And again I heard the mysterious voice saying, 'Son of the Republic, look and learn.' At this, the dark shadowy angel placed a trumpet to his mouth and blew three distinct blasts; and taking water from the ocean, he sprinkled it upon Europe, Asia, and Africa. Then my eyes beheld a fearful sight: From each of these countries arose thick, black clouds that were soon joined into one.

"And throughout this mass there gleamed a dark red light, by which I saw hordes of armed men, who moving with the dark cloud, marched by land and sailed by sea to America; which country was enveloped in the volume of clouds. And I dimly saw these vast armies devastate the whole country and burn the villages, towns, and cities that I beheld springing up.

"As my ears listened to the thunder of the cannon, the clashing of swords, and the shouts and cries of millions in mortal combat, I again heard the mysterious voice saying, 'Son of the Republic, look and learn.' As the voice ceased the shadowy angel, for the last time, dipped water from the ocean and sprinkled it upon America. Instantly the dark cloud rolled back, together with the armies it had brought, leaving the inhabitants of the land victorious.

"Then once more I beheld the villages, towns, and cities springing up where I had seen them before; while the bright angel planting the azure standard he had brought in the midst of them, cried with a loud voice: 'While the stars remain in the heaven send down dew upon the earth, so long shall the Union last.' And taking from his brow the crown on which was blazoned the word UNION he placed it upon the standard, while people, kneeling down said, 'Amen.'"

Finally, General Washington concluded, "The scene instantly began to fade and dissolve, and I at last saw nothing but the rising, curling vapor I at first beheld. This also disappearing, I found myself once more gazing upon the voice I had heard before, said, 'Son of the Republic, what you have just seen is thus interpreted: Three great perils will come upon the Republic. The most fearful for her is the third; but the whole world united shall not prevail against her. Let every child of the Republic learn to live for his God, his land, and his Union.'

"With those words, the vision vanished. I started from my seat, and felt I had seen a vision wherein had been shown to me the birth, progress, and destiny of the United States."

Could George Washington actually have had an encounter with an angel? Might a messenger of God have come to Washington to help him survive the miseries of the terrible winter at Valley Forge? Why was the language of the apparition, consistently referring to Washington as the "Son of the Republic," so reminiscent of the language in the prophetic vision of Ezekiel where, after seeing the "fire in the sky," he was referred to as "Son of Man" before being shown visions of the future?

Did Washington in his reporting of the incident deliberately see himself in the role of the Old Testament prophet Ezekiel? Had the angelic being truly provided the general with a vision of America's future?

Washington certainly thought so. Some time after his remarkable encounter, he shared the experience with his close friend and young aide Anthony Sherman, who many years later, in 1859, retold the account to reporter Wesley Bradshaw, who then published it in the *National Tribune* in 1880.

Portions of Washington's prophetic vision seemed to refer to slavery in America, the divided opinion Americans had about the insidious issue, the eventual Civil War, and the ultimate reuniting of the nation as one. Remember that the apparition indicated "three great perils" would befall the Republic. The most fearful, the angel warned, would be the third, "but the whole world united shall not prevail against her." Were these references to future wars that America was destined to win? Which wars? Though there have been different interpretations, the likeliest is that the apparition predicted the outcome of the American Revolutionary War, the Civil War, and World War I.

Washington told confidants he was deeply inspired by the angelic visitation, whose appearance restored his faith in the cause for American independence. He was certain the angel's message had meant he would see victory. Despite the hardships, Washington's despair had lifted and he had the spiritual resiliency to make it through the Valley Forge winter. Spring soon arrived, and the muddy, impassable roads dried, allowing for the delivery of fresh supplies. The troops who remained so courageous in the face of terrible deprivation had survived not only with a special bond of camaraderie, but also emerged a stronger and better-organized Continental Army more ready to face the British and their paid Hessian confederates.

Help had also come to the American cause from two renowned European military experts: the skilled Prussian Baron Von Steuben, who molded the ragtag soldiers into a strong fighting force, and the brilliant young Frenchman the Marquis de Lafayette, who ultimately convinced France to send troops and supplies to aid the Americans. Eventually Washington led his troops to ultimate victory over the British at the battle of Yorktown, Virginia, in 1781, where the surrender of British general Lord Cornwallis effectively ended all hostilities. It was an astounding turnabout of events for Washington who, in his darkest hour of despair, had his faith renewed by the appearance of an apparition. Was this purely a supernatural vision or, in fact, a messenger of God in answer to Washington's devout prayers? Angel or apparition, the vision comforted and inspired Washington when his situation seemed absolutely hopeless. Thus, even before there was a President of the United States, even before there was a United States, the supernatural had already intervened.

Experts say every person on earth has a guardian angel charged with the responsibility to watch over and protect. It is a belief as old as humankind. But whose guardian angel actually appeared? Was it Washington's own angel answering his prayers amid the snows, bitter cold, and starvation at Valley Forge, or was it the guardian angel watching over the United States?

Washington's angelic visitor, of profound importance to the destiny of the new nation, may have altered the course of events. However, angelic encounters were not new, even in George Washington's time. Such visitations have been reported throughout history, in virtually every culture and religion, and centuries before the birth of Christ. Millions of people have experienced the effects of angelic interventions. It has been said that "through angels, God guides humanity and plans its destiny."

It is a common practice during wartime for soldiers to accept a deeper connection with religion and God, because of their proximity to battle and potential death. Paranormal researchers have also noted that psychic experiences are more frequent in times of war. Thus it is not unusual for soldiers to claim they have witnessed angelic beings or other apparitions, which often provide protection in the face of combat. Photographs of American GI helmets from the Vietnam War have on more than one occasion shown crosses or religious icons attached to the helmet, as if the religious symbol itself conferred protection on the wearer.

Protective "angels on the battlefield," as they have been called, have played a significant role in many struggles throughout history, most notably in the case of Joan of Arc, who claimed that "holy voices," which only she could hear, led her and the French forces under her command to an unexpected victory over the English at the Battle of Orléans in the fifteenth century. George Washington's vision at Valley Forge and subsequent battlefield experiences also qualify as a meeting with an "angel on the battlefield."

Although some skeptics would argue that "angels on the battlefield" are a product of stress or hallucination produced by the dangers of war, there is ample evidence to suggest otherwise. In many instances, angelic visitations have communicated information unknown to the recipient at the time of the encounter. Thus, soldiers in battle learned of events to come, or incidents that had not yet occurred, only because apparitions accurately prophesied or predicted them. As well, in some experiences, there have been multiple witnesses, suggesting that hallucination or imagination is an unlikely explanation.

Some find it easier to debunk or dismiss angelic encounters, rather than believe the countless number of credible individuals who *know* that what they felt, saw, or heard was genuine. Rather than disregard these often profound and moving experiences out of fear, doubt, or disbelief, we need to accept and understand them for the messages they bring and the positive purpose they serve. George Washington was one of numerous individuals throughout history who had met and been guided by angels.

One question asked by some is why no mention is made of the angelic vision by Washington in his well-known diaries. Although Washington kept diaries for many years that reveal much about his activities and private thoughts, he did not keep a journal during most of the Revolutionary War. His necessary preoccupation with the demands of war made it difficult to maintain a diary. Thus, with no personal written record for the period from June 19, 1775, to January 1780, we have no entries about the angelic visitation at Valley Forge. Washington did not resume his diary until 1781. Also, after his death, Martha Washington destroyed the majority of her husband's private letters. It is only speculation, of course, but there is a strong possibility that if anything had been written by Washington about the vision, it might have been lost.

Although George Washington was nominally an Episcopalian, he was more a man of deep personal faith than a blind follower of organized religion. He also had some familiarity with mystical subjects. From conversations with his friend and fellow patriot Benjamin Franklin, who had a deep interest in the occult and supernatural, including beliefs in an afterlife and reincarnation, Washington was exposed to Franklin's opinions about the paranormal. At one point, when Franklin was a Philadelphia printer, he worked for the cloistered religious community at Ephrata, Pennsylvania, whose zealous teachings combined Christianity with mysticism. With access to the sect's library, Franklin learned some of the occult concepts he later shared with Washington, who was in contact with the sect's leaders as well.

Also, both Washington and Franklin were Freemasons, a secret brotherhood that counted as its members many of the Founding Fathers. Freemasonry had its beginnings during the early Renaissance, founded by the builders of some of the great cathedrals of Europe, who required the knowledge of Euclidean geometry in order to develop the plans and engineering for the structures they were building. However, Euclidean geometry, because it was developed by a pre-Christian Greek, was regarded as a taboo subject by the Church, which had rejected the science and philosophy of pre-Christian societies. Therefore, the Masons had to study geometry secretly if they were to employ the skills necessary to build the structures for which they had been contracted. Out of this secret study grew the society of Freemasons. Freemasonry became a highly organized and structured society of like thinkers that grew over the centuries and attracted a wide membership. Eventually fourteen presidents of the United States, many signers of the Declaration of Independence, and nearly half of all officers who served in the American Revolution were Freemasons. Masons believe they are "divinely ordained guardians of democracy." Perhaps, then, an angelic vision was less a surprise to General Washington than it might otherwise have been.

In recent years, many have confused angelic beings with visitations from deceased loved ones. However, George Washington's description was clearly that of a messenger from a celestial realm, rather than the ghost or spirit of a departed person whose countenance he would have readily recognized. General Washington carried an enormous responsibility as commander of the American army; thus it is likely he had one or more guardian angels protecting him, for his monumental role was to lead an entire new nation. Washington seemed to recognize this because in August 1778, with the bitter winter of Valley Forge behind him, Washington corresponded with Thomas Nelson, a friend in Virginia, reflecting on the trials he and his men survived and suggested that a supernatural force had saved them: "The hand of Providence has been so conspicuous in all this that he must be worse than an infidel that lacks faith, and more wicked that has not gratitude to acknowledge his obligations. . . ."

Was Washington reflecting on his angelic encounter when he wrote those heartfelt words? Had divine intervention, in fact, been responsible for Washington's survival at Valley Forge? Did the mysterious apparition so profoundly affect Washington that the experience influenced his thinking, even his future political philosophy? Indeed, there is evidence that is exactly what occurred. In fact, while still at Valley Forge, on May 2, 1778, only months after the angel appeared to him, Washington issued the following general order to his soldiers and the American people: "While we are zealously performing the duties of good citizens and soldiers, we certainly ought not to be inattentive to the higher duties of religion. . . ."

Again, it seemed that Washington could not dismiss the impact of the angel's visit. On December 4, 1783, General Washington met with his troops for the last time at Fraunces Tavern in New York City, where he bade them a grateful and emotional farewell, saying, "With a heart full of love and gratitude, I now take leave of you." As one historian noted, "George Washington was an answer to America's prayers."

By Christmas, Washington was home at his estate in Mount Vernon, Virginia, with his wife, Martha. Washington's well-deserved retirement, which he hoped would be peaceful, proved short-lived, however. Four years later, he reluctantly agreed to preside over the Congressional Convention in Philadelphia and helped to shape the new nation's Constitution. The new Constitution designated that the head of the national government be a "single chief executive" known as "president." There was little argument about who was best qualified for that task: George Washington, patriot and war hero. Washington was unopposed when the Electoral College unanimously chose him as the first President of the United States, a country with just thirteen states and a population of approximately four million.

In the early afternoon of April 30, 1789, George Washington, at age fifty-seven, took the oath of office. He had previously rejected the suggestion made by some that he assume the title of king. "Banish these thoughts from your mind," he had answered. He did not wish, he said, to exercise such sovereignty. The ceremony, before a huge and enthusiastic crowd, was held on the balcony of Federal Hall in New York City. Washington, dressed in a handsome deep brown suit, wore a steel dress sword for the special occasion. To the brief oath of office, he added his own words, "So help me, God." Then he leaned forward with humility and kissed the Bible, which had been held for him. Historians have often noted the pious and earnest tone with which Washington repeated the oath of office. Might memories of the unforgettable vision at Valley Forge have coursed through his mind at that moment?

Celebrations resounded throughout the city and the nation in the new president's honor. Church bells rang, cannons boomed, soldiers and exuberant civilians filled the streets. Washington, accompanied by dignitaries and guests, walked victoriously among the adoring to attend church services. There was no mistaking the admiration, love, and respect Americans had for their first president.

After serving two successful terms, and refusing to consider a third, Washington left office on March 3, 1797. Shortly before his departure as president, Washington wrote a farewell address, his last thoughts as he prepared to leave office, after a long and distinguished career in service to his country. Some writers have suggested that the memory—and influence—of the angelic vision at Valley Forge remained with George Washington when he wrote the farewell address in 1796. The address was never actually delivered to Congress, but it was published on September 19, 1796, by a Philadelphia newspaper, the *American Daily Advertiser*. It is regarded by historians as one of the "classic statements of American political philosophy," and seems to offer guidance and caution for the new nation's future.

In his farewell address, Washington warned against "permanent alliances with foreign powers," urging instead neutrality for America. He wrote of the importance of "a government for the whole," suggesting that only then could there be an effective and lasting union. He called religion and morality "two great pillars of human happiness." He warned against "the insidious wiles of foreign influence . . ." and entreated Americans to "renounce party spirit and sectional passions and to avoid involvement in the wars and domestic affairs of other nations." He also cautioned against "big public debt and too large a military." And he added, "I shall carry to my grave the hope that your Union and brotherly affection may be perpetual; that the Constitution may be sacredly maintained; and that free government . . . the ever favorite object of my heart . . . will be the happy reward of our mutual cares, labors, and dangers."

Even though historians argue that the farewell address is contradictory in places, thus open to interpretation, it does offer something of a guide from Washington as to how the country should conduct itself in the years ahead. Washington was deeply concerned about the future unity of America.

We can only speculate about how many ideas conveyed in the farewell address were influenced by the prophetic messages offered by the "beautiful female figure" who visited Washington at Valley Forge. It appears the angel had considerable influence on Washington's political thinking, and gave him a unique sense of the future of America.

With service to his country completed, Washington was able to return to Mount Vernon, where since boyhood he had enjoyed a reputation as an excellent horseman. He rode his favorite horse almost every day, presenting a commanding figure in the saddle as he made the rounds of his estate.

On Thursday, December 12, 1799, Washington wrote in his diary: "Morning cloudy. Mercury 33. At about ten o'clock it began to snow, snow after to hail, and then to a settled cold rain. Mercury 28 at night."

Despite the inclement weather, he rode on horseback from ten in the morning until three in the afternoon, inspecting his farm. He returned wet and chilled, snow dripping from his white hair, and warmed himself before the fire. By the time dinner was served, Washington was still chilly, but he dined with his wife without bothering to change from the damp clothing he had worn outdoors. That evening he complained of a sore throat and hoarseness, but declined any medication, insisting the cold would go as it had come. But during the night, Washington awakened Martha. He complained that his throat hurt badly. He had difficulty breathing, his body shook with chills, and he could barely speak. Martha immediately sent for a longtime friend Dr. William Clark. Meanwhile, a Mount Vernon staff member, as was the practice of the day, bled Washington at his wife's request.

The next day, Friday the 13th, Washington managed one last diary entry: "Morning Snowing and about three inches deep." Now two more physicians arrived. Their diagnosis was quinsy, today known as strep throat. The doctors continued "bleeding, blisterings, and purges with laxatives," which were typical, if ineffective, medical treatments in Washington's time. Ironically, George Washington did not believe in the effectiveness of bleedings and blisterings, fearing them as more harmful than beneficial. He protested the medical treatment, but it did him little good because the doctors persisted. Would Washington's condition have worsened had the doctors not, literally, bled the life out of him? We do not know because, as the eighteenth century drew to a close, Washington was already an old man by the standards of that time. He was vigorous, but in all likelihood, pneumonia and congestive heart failure were already settling in.

Martha was called to her husband's bedside, for he knew he was dying: "I find I am going, my breath cannot continue long; I believed from the first that the disorder would prove fatal. . . ."

To his doctor he whispered, "I die hard; but I am not afraid to go. . . . My breath cannot last long." His final words, " 'Tis well."

On December 14, 1799, just two days after becoming ill, George Washington, with Martha by his side, died at the age of sixty-seven. News of his death sent the country into a state of deep mourning.

With the passing of her husband, Martha withdrew from public life. "All is now over. I shall soon follow him! I have no more trials to pass through!" she said. Three years later, in 1802, Martha followed her husband to the next stage of life. But their deaths, witnesses from the period reported, did not mean that they disappeared from view.

After the great patriot died, there were many reports from witnesses who claimed they saw his specter riding his favorite horse around the plantation and to the stables at Mount Vernon, just as he had on that cold, snowy winter day in December, 1799, when he'd become ill for the last time.

George Washington left this earth only nine months before John Adams, the second president, moved into the newly built Executive Mansion. Although the Washingtons never lived in the White House, as it was later called, their spirits have been reported, likely visiting the presidential residence they helped inspire and plan.

Many ghostly sightings have also been witnessed in what was once known as the Old Pension Building in Washington, D.C., built in 1885. In the early decades of the twentieth century, apparitions began making their presences known. Among them were the visions of George and Martha Washington. One theory to explain their materializations in the huge brick edifice is that hidden in the building's onyx columns were a number of invaluable papers, documents that belonged to the Founding Fathers. The papers were believed jammed into the hollow pillars by the building's designer, General Montgomery Meigs, as retaliation for being directed to construct hollow rather than solid columns.

George Washington's ghost has also been witnessed at Old Fort Monroe, on Virginia's Chesapeake Bay, an army post built in the early 1800s. The heptagon-shaped stronghold surrounded by a moat has been the site of a number of Civil War–era apparitions as well. Some psychic researchers have claimed that Washington's ghost later returned to Valley Forge.

George and Martha were not the only members of the Washington family to revisit earth as spirits. Apparitions of the family of George Washington's adopted son, George Washington Parke Custis, have been witnessed in a handsome Virginia home known as the Arlington Mansion, where Custis once lived and which became federal property after the Civil War, when the government confiscated the stately mansion. The hauntings, including the mysterious sounds of children playing, the ghost of a cat, inexplicable footsteps, and candles that snuff themselves out, may be attributed to the spirits of the Custis family members who, even now, probably still regard the home as their own property.

In 1789, George Washington's mother, Mary Ball Washington, passed on from breast cancer at the age of eighty-one. After her death, Mary's restless spirit was observed in the kitchen of her home in Fredericksburg, Virginia, where she lived for the last seventeen years of her life, and her ghost has also been seen on a pathway in back of the house. Among witness accounts have been reports of the swishing sound of Mary's skirts as her spirit passed between rooms, shutting doors.

Throughout her life, Mary was a domineering mother; her overbearing personality greatly aggravated her son. Although he contributed to his elderly mother's financial support so that she would live comfortably in the lovely house in Fredericksburg, Mary remained a difficult woman to please and continually pressed economic demands on her famous son even as she constantly complained that he neglected her. Despite George's attention to his mother's needs, she was never satisfied, and even let it be known publicly, a source of embarrassment to her son. As well, she would neither acknowledge nor compliment his remarkable military successes, including his personal victories over the British at Trenton and Yorktown. The reality of Mary Washington's personality was that she actually resented any achievement by her son that did not go to her care and support. In fact, she often spoke vehemently against his accomplishments. Not surprisingly, as a result, mother and son long held misunderstandings toward one another.

Perhaps, as is common with spirit presences, Mary Washington's ghost returned to her home in Fredericksburg to recall memories of her last years, or her restless haunting is a reflection of guilt and remorse at having treated her son with far less gratitude and respect than he deserved. Typically, in the afterlife, the souls of loved ones reunite, dissolving earthly animosities and the emotional differences or arguments that separated them in the physical world. We can only hope that George Washington and his mother, Mary, have both finally found peace, understanding, and forgiveness toward each other on the Other Side.

The Civil War and Gettysburg

In life, George Washington had rightly earned the title "Father of His Country." Now in death, as a benevolent spirit, Washington continued to behave as a protective entity, watching over, guiding, and advising the prominent leaders of the country he so loved and tenaciously fought for.

One evening in early 1850, John C. Calhoun, long one of America's most prominent and influential southern politicians and at the time in his late sixties and ailing, glanced up from where he sat in his Washington, D.C., home, known at one time as the Old Brick Capitol building, to notice a visitor standing before him. In the glow of lamplight, Calhoun blinked in surprise as he gazed at what he soon realized was an apparition. It was clearly the spirit countenance of George Washington. The old politician leaned forward in his chair to be certain this was not his imagination at work or his tired eyes playing tricks. He stared at the ghostly image floating before him. There, hovering in the air was George Washington's apparition. What had momentarily been trepidation of an unexpected intrusion turned to a sense of calm when Calhoun realized who his visitor was. But why would Washington appear now to John Calhoun?

A native of South Carolina, Calhoun had become an influential and controversial figure in American politics in the first half of the nineteenth century, serving at various times as a South Carolina state legislator, congressman, senator, secretary of war in President Madison's cabinet, vice president to President Andrew Jackson, and later secretary of state in the administration of President John Tyler.

As the antislavery movement gained momentum in the North, Calhoun unfortunately maintained that slavery was "a positive good," especially for Southern planters for whom he became their official spokesman. As the debate over slavery became more intense, Calhoun stepped up his defense of the so-called "Southern way of life," and what he viewed as Northern hostility and disdain toward the South and slavery. But even as Calhoun stubbornly defended the evils of slavery, he worried openly about secession as a result of the divisive issue.

Calhoun soon learned the purpose of George Washington's ghostly return. The "Father of His Country" had come to warn Calhoun about the danger to the nation of secession. Calhoun, a man who believed he had psychic ability and was open to such experiences, heeded the apparition's unequivocal message, which was communicated telepathically. Shortly after the visitation, Calhoun accurately predicted that secession would occur in the next decade, based on the spirit's caution to him. "The dissolution of the Union is the heaviest blow that can be struck at civilization and representative government," Calhoun cautioned ominously in an emotional address to Congress. Unfortunately, his admonition was ignored and a decade later, the United States was in the throes of the bloody Civil War.

Many criticized Calhoun for his dire prediction. Some even blamed him as one of the causes of the devastating War Between the States. However, there were others who had words of praise for Calhoun's efforts to avoid secession and the resulting Civil War. But few likely realized that Calhoun's warning to Congress in early 1850 had been inspired by the vision of George Washington. Obviously, ever the patriot, Washington's spirit remained worried about the future of the United States, concerned about the horrible effect secession would have on the nation. It was not unlike the counsel Washington himself received at Valley Forge nearly seventy-five years earlier when the angelic apparition emphasized the importance of preserving the Union. Now Washington's spirit was communicating to later political figures the same advice offered to him by an apparition.

Shortly after his futile plea to Congress, John Calhoun lay on his deathbed at home, where George Washington's ghost had so recently appeared. On the day he died, March 31, 1850, Calhoun's last words were: "The South . . . the poor South." But even after death, Calhoun found no peace.

For years after his passing, Calhoun's restless spirit was often seen wandering in his former residence. Some psychic researchers have speculated that Calhoun's ghost was unable to find peace because he remained distressed by the Civil War and the dissolution of the Union a decade after his death. His refusal to recognize the sins of slavery and his frustration that his impassioned warning to Congress had gone unheeded still plagued him. Now Calhoun's spirit was linked inextricably to Washington's spirit as a result of the visitation he received from Washington when he was still alive. This linking of spirits in the afterlife who had been joined together by an event during their lives is not an uncommon phenomenon.

A decade after Calhoun's death, there is no question George Washington's spirit was deeply troubled as he watched the Union dissolve into Civil War. Perhaps it was the nation's karma or destiny that no amount of warnings, admonitions, or divine prophecy could have prevented the terrible War Between the States. But that was small comfort to the restless spirit of the first president and proved insufficient for Washington's soul to find peace. He certainly could not rest when his country was at war. And it was time for his next visitation, this time to inspire Lincoln's army and its commanding officer General George McClellan.

General McClellan, only thirty-four and a West Point graduate, had just arrived at his Washington, D.C., headquarters three days earlier to take charge of the Union Army when he had his first encounter with the otherworld. The handsome and confident general, who had already distinguished himself as an engineer and soldier when President Lincoln appointed him Union commander, was deeply engrossed in his maps and reports, planning military strategy late into the night. He grew weary at his desk as the clock struck two in the morning, yet he still could hear the sound of military wagons rolling and artillery rumbling through the streets. The republic, not even a hundred years old, was preparing for a war to determine its very survival as a single nation, and McClellan, despite President Lincoln's urgings, had not gotten his army into the field to defend Washington in the event of an attack from the South.

McClellan moved the maps and reports aside, and placed his head on his arms. In moments he was asleep. He estimated his brief nap could not have lasted longer than ten minutes when he was awakened by the door to his room suddenly opening, although he was certain he had earlier locked it. Then the general felt a hand on his shoulder, although he did not yet see his unexpected visitor. Next he heard "a solemn voice" say, "General McClellan, do you sleep on your post? Rouse you, or ere it can be prevented, the foe will be upon Washington."

McClellan recalled, "Never before in my life had I heard a voice possessing the commanding, and even terrible tone of the one who addressed me those fateful words; nor felt the sensation that passed through me, as it fell upon my ears; and I instinctively shrunk into myself at the thought of my own negligence.

"I could not move, however, although I had tried hard to raise my head from the table as a sign of willingness to make my answer to the unknown intruder. I once more heard the same low solemn voice repeat: 'General McClellan, do you sleep on your post?' "

McClellan was not certain whether he was awake or asleep, typical of a hypnogogic waking sleep state of temporary paralysis. However, as he shook himself out of sleep and looked about him, there inexplicably appeared what he described as "a living map." On it he saw the United States, as far as the Gulf of Mexico, and from the Atlantic Ocean on the east to the Mississippi River on the west. It was, McClellan thought, "an immense scene."

The general turned in the direction of the mysterious voice. Before him stood an apparition. However, he was unable to recognize any features beyond "the general outline of a man." Once more he heard the same low solemn voice: "General McClellan, your time is short. Look to the southward."

McClellan obeyed by turning his eyes toward the living map. He described his observation: "Out on the Atlantic I saw various vessels of the blockading squadron looming up in the bright moonshine that illuminated everything with a strong but mellow light. I saw Charleston harbor, its forts, with their pacing sentinels and sullen looking barbette guns." McClellan also saw on the map every military fortification along the Gulf and the Mississippi. Then the maps became even more detailed and McClellan could see "every mountain range, hill, valley, forest, meadow, river, city, village, camp, tent, body of men, sentinels, cannons," among other details.

McClellan interpreted the vision to mean that he was being given knowledge that "would insure a speedy and happy termination of the war."

But then the voice said: "General McClellan, take your map and note what you behold. Tarry not, your time is short." The apparition next pointed to the southern portion of the map. McClellan felt a chill as he realized he was seeing "masses of enemy's forces being hurried to certain points. . . ."

"Ruin and defeat seemed to stare me in the face," McClellan reflected.

Again he heard the "slow solemn voice" warn, "General McClellan, you have been betrayed, and had not God willed otherwise, ere the sun of tomorrow had set, the Confederate flag would have floated above your own grave. But note what you see. Your time is short. Tarry not."

McClellan described his experience as "mysterious

and unearthly" and noted that a "shining light" had accompanied the apparition.

"Quickly I raised my eyes and never, were I to live forever, should I forget what I saw," recalled McClellan. "The dim shadowy figure was no longer a shadowy one . . . but the figure of George Washington, father of his country."

McClellan added, "It would be utterly impossible for me to describe the majesty of that returned spirit. I can only say that Washington, as I beheld him in my dream, or trance, as you may choose to call it, was the most God-like being I could have ever conceived of."

The voice concluded, "General McClellan, while yet in the flesh I beheld the birth of the American Republic. It was indeed a hard and bloody one, but God's blessing was upon the nation . . . and brought her out triumphantly. She shall be saved. Then shall peace be once more upon her, and prosperity shall fill her with joy. Let her in prosperity, however, remember the Lord her God. Let her trust in him and she shall never be confounded."

Then, as McClellan watched and listened in awe, "the heavenly visitant ceased speaking." McClellan could not stop gazing as the apparition of George Washington placed his raised hands above McClellan, who felt he had been blessed by Washington, himself.

There followed peals of thunder and McClellan awoke; the apparition was gone. He noticed the maps he had been working on before the spirit appeared were now "literally covered with a net of pencil signs and figures" as if McClellan had completed them with detailed information that would have taken years to gather and record.

McClellan interpreted the message from George Washington's spirit to mean: "The American Union is saved."

While that communication proved to be prophetic for the nation, McClellan's personal fortunes were not as successful. McClellan failed to heed the apparition's warning, "Tarry not, your time is short." For within a year of his appointment as commander of the Union Army, President Lincoln realized he had "badly overestimated" McClellan's abilities to lead the Northern Army to victory. In November 1862, Lincoln finally frustrated by McClellan's hesitant approach to battle, and his unsuccessful attacks on Richmond and Petersburg, removed him from command.

What is to be made of McClellan's visionary encounter? Psychic experiences often occur in a state that is somewhere between sleeping and awake. Parapsychologists point out that this hypnogogic state—also a typical experience of many UFO abductees—is a transient neuropsychological event when many visions occur, including those that provide glimpses of future events or places. Such precognitive experiences typically reveal themselves through clairvoyance or psychic sight. While the dream state provides a convenient conduit for visionary experiences, it does not imply these psychic events are merely dreams or hallucinations. Far from it. Another paranormal theory is that McClellan astral-traveled, meaning his spirit left his physical body during the time he was asleep, and thus witnessed details that he could not otherwise have known about. Today we call this an "out-of-body experience," and also refer to it as "lucid dreaming" or "remote viewing."

McClellan's detailed description of his experience leaves no doubt that his encounter with George Washington's spirit was meant as a warning to him personally, and a prophecy about the future of the Union. It is interesting that Washington's spirit admonished McClellan several times, "Tarry not, your time is short." McClellan's procrastination is precisely what caused his removal as Union commander. Had McClellan, a man of enormous ego, been willing to recognize the warning to him, might his military career have taken a different and more successful path?

The larger and more important message was the reassuring prediction that the Union would be preserved in spite of the terrible and divisive Civil War. That was the overwhelming concern of George Washington's spirit, even if General McClellan proved not the man who could lead the North to victory. The responsibility ultimately fell to General Ulysses S. Grant who was ultimately elected president.

George Washington had been gone from earth's plane for nearly sixty-four years when, on the morning of July 1, 1863, the Battle of Gettysburg, "the greatest battle ever fought on the North American continent," commenced with Confederate cavalry confronting Union soldiers northwest of Gettysburg, a small Pennsylvania town of some 2,400 people located at the confluence of ten important roads, all from different directions.

By July 2, 85,000 Union troops faced 75,000 Confederate soldiers. Eventually the two armies amassed more than 170,000 men in and around Gettysburg. The Union Army's 20th Maine Regiment, under the command of Colonel Joshua Chamberlain, a thirty-three-year-old former college professor with a theology background but no prior military leadership experience, had been ordered to march to Pennsylvania from Maryland in advance of what he knew was to be a major battle to turn back a force of Confederate troops led by General Robert E. Lee near Gettysburg. Although exhausted, his men continued through the dark, foggy, and dismal night, uncertain they were even traveling in the right direction since they had no exact maps of the area. Chamberlain rode ahead of his men as they marched silently through woods and over fields. These were not professional soldiers, but workers: farmers, fishermen, shopkeepers, and backwoodsmen.

Eventually they came to a fork in the road, where Chamberlain and his men were uncertain which path to take. Their choice would prove to be crucial. While they considered which direction to follow, the clouds inexplicably broke, and by the light of the moon, the men saw the outline of someone on horseback. The figure, dressed in a bright coat and tricorn hat, sat atop an imposing light-colored horse. The horseman galloped in the direction of one of the two diverging roads, waving for Chamberlain's soldiers to follow.

Colonel Chamberlain later recounted what had occurred: "At a turn of the road, a staff officer, with an air of authority, told each colonel as he came up, 'General McClellan is in command again, and he's riding up ahead of us on the road.' Men waved their hats, cheered until they were hoarse, and wild with excitement, followed the figure on horseback. Although weary, they marched with miraculous enthusiasm believing their beloved general had returned to lead them into battle."

However, the figure the soldiers saw was not General George McClellan, former commander of the Union Army, who they realized was nowhere in the vicinity of Gettysburg. When Chamberlain's puzzled men grasped that the horseman could not have been McClellan, one of them recognized the mysterious figure as none other than George Washington!

Word quickly spread through the troops that Washington's spirit had returned to lead them in the right direction. Despite their exhaustion and understandable fear, the sight of Washington's apparition seemed a divine intervention. Uplifted, the men marched with renewed confidence along the unlit road, although at that moment they were unsure where they were being led.

Once they arrived at the scene of the battle in Gettysburg, the 20th Maine Regiment received orders to defend a rocky hill known as Little Round Top, which they were instructed to hold "at all hazards" even though the Union forces were outnumbered by the Confederates. But Little Round Top was considered critical to a Union victory, and Chamberlain's men were in the best position to defend the unimposing but strategically important hill. Not at all hesitant in the face of enemy fire, they eventually managed to scramble up to the top and take defensive positions. Meanwhile, all around them were the concussions of groundshaking artillery explosions, while above them blasts of smoke and fire mushroomed over the treetops, creating an eerie and frightening sight.

The three-day battle with the Confederates, which began on July 1, 1863, was ferocious. The Rebels, from the 4th Alabama Regiment, on the offensive, overwhelmingly outnumbered the 20th Maine at Little Round Top. Making a bad situation worse, Chamberlain's soldiers were appallingly low on ammunition and, from the direction of the incoming artillery and small-arms fire, believed they were surrounded by Confederate troops. There were frantic cries from the men for more bullets. Colonel Chamberlain believed that it was only a matter of time before his unit would have to forfeit their position and give up the hill. Faced with this extremely grave and dangerous situation, the men were understandably frozen with fear.

But rather than retreat, Chamberlain made a bold decision. He bellowed above the sound of exploding shot, "Fix bayonets. Charge!" Almost incomprehensibly he'd ordered his soldiers to advance, a command tantamount to virtual suicide given the dwindling supplies of ammunition and the superior number of Confederate troops arrayed on the hillside below. Would the men even obey?

Then something that can only be described as miraculous or supernatural happened. The same enigmatic specter on horseback, which led the men on the road to Gettysburg, again inexplicably materialized. Glowing and with raised sword, the specter urged the soldiers to follow him into battle. The sight of the ghostly figure on horseback inspired the 20th Maine to attack. Charging down the hill into the teeth of enemy fire, but with a madness in their eyes and the blood of victory in their mouths, they completely surprised and overwhelmed the Confederates who weren't expecting so bold an action from a group of defenders they knew were outnumbered, outgunned, and possibly very low on ammunition. Although both sides suffered heavy casualties—Chamberlain lost 130 of his 386 men—the bewildered Confederate defense lines were overrun, and the enemy fell into a frantic rout. Survivors broke and ran for their lives, slipping and sliding along ground drenched with the blood of the dead and wounded. Confederate survivors from the 4th Alabama Regiment, who had faced Chamberlain's men at Little Round Top, later said, "They never were whipped before, and never wanted to meet the 20th Maine again."

Little Round Top proved to be one of the most unexpected victories of the Civil War and one of the most important at Gettysburg. Chamberlain's daring attack saved Little Round Top and helped maintain the Union defense. Many considered his accomplishment nothing short of a miracle—and perhaps it was. The Battle of Gettysburg raged for three days in the searing summer heat. Considered a major turning point of the Civil War, the Union victory thwarted a Confederate effort to penetrate the North.

After the Battle of Gettysburg, accounts of Washington's apparition witnessed by hundreds of soldiers resulted in Secretary of War Edwin Stanton's asking the Union Army to investigate the incident. At least one general, as well as other officers, swore the ghostly image was that of George Washington's face.

Chamberlain later achieved the rank of general, and was awarded the Congressional Medal of Honor. He also served as president of Bowdoin College, where he had once taught. Afterward, he became governor of Maine, and the incident of Washington's appearance seemed to fade into memory.

Many years after Gettysburg, he was asked by a reporter about the story of George Washington's ghost leading his troops at Gettysburg. Upon hearing the reporter's question, Chamberlain grew pensive, then answered, "Yes, that report was circulated through our lines, and I have no doubt that it inspired the men. Doubtless it was a superstition."

Then after a pause, the elderly soldier added, "Who among us can say that such a thing was impossible? We have not yet sounded or explored the immortal life that lies out beyond the Bar. We do not know what mystic power may be possessed by those who are now bivouacking with the dead. I only know the effect, but I dare not explain or deny the cause. I do believe that we were enveloped by the powers of the otherworld that day and who shall say that Washington was not among the number of those who aided the country he founded?" Chamberlain added a final thought, "You could not say from what world they came, or to what world they go."

Indeed, why shouldn't George Washington, Father of His Country, have returned in spirit to lead the Union soldiers to an important victory at Gettysburg, the Civil War's greatest battle? After all, it was an angelic vision at Valley Forge, years earlier that guided and inspired Washington through his darkest hours. The ghost of Washington had materialized at a time when the United States was on the brink of dissolution. The preservation of the Union remained of paramount concern for George Washington in spirit, as it had been when he was on earth's plane. Might the outcome at Little Round Top been different if Washington's spirit had not returned to lead?

Gettysburg, where more than 50,000 men lost their lives, and many more were wounded in three days of brutal and bloody fighting, has been called the most haunted battlefield in the nation. The ghosts of soldiers who fell there still march in phantom formations across the field to this very day. And George Washington, it seems, who himself was inspired by an apparition at his army's darkest hour, was its most celebrated and important ghost at what could have been the darkest hour of the Union Washington fought so hard to defend.

CHAPTER THREE

Presidential Prophecies, Predictions, and Curses

There is destiny that shapes our ends, rough hew them how we will.

—William Shakespeare, *Hamlet*

Prophets and prognosticators have predicted the fates of world leaders since the dawn of recorded history. From Joseph's interpretations of Pharaoh's dreams of feast and famine, to the dire warnings of Cassandra, to Jeane Dixon's sad prediction to FDR in early 1945 that he had but a few months to live, prophets have foretold the future for leaders of nations. We owe the word "prophecy," which translates into "speaking before" or "spokesman in the name of a deity" to the Greeks. Although we use the words "prophecy" and "prediction" interchangeably here, technically, they are not identical. Prediction is "a learned ability," more the domain of psychics and mediums, while prophecy is "an inspired phenomenon."

Among history's most famed prognosticators were the highly regarded oracles of Delphi in ancient Greece, mediums who drew monarchs from all over the known world for what was believed to be divinely revealed and unalterable prophecy. The Old Testament has a long tradition of foretelling the future through its prophets, the greatest of whom was Moses; in the New Testament, Jesus Christ remains the most gifted of all prophets.

Prophets traditionally spoke only to pharaohs, kings, or the powerful leaders of nations or city-states. Thus, it is no surprise that those who reach the American presidency, the most powerful office in the world, have been the subjects of predictions, and will probably continue to be for as long as there are presidents.

Perhaps no prophecy affecting U.S. presidents is better known, more ominous, and at the same time more hotly debated than the so-called "presidential curse," laid upon then-governor William Henry Harrison by the Shawnee medicine man and shaman Tenskwatawa, which predicted the death in office of the president every twenty years. The curse began in 1840, when Governor Harrison first sought the White House, as a direct result of his victory in a bloody military campaign—some would have called it a slaughter—against the Shawnee and their chief Tecumseh. Harrison became the victim of Tenskwatawa's curse, which very well may continue to this very day and has perhaps been among the discussions inside the administration of President George W. Bush, the most recent zero-year president.

"Tippecanoe and Tyler Too!"

William Henry Harrison's campaign slogan reminded potential voters that he had been a popular war hero years earlier and sought to turn that popularity into political victory. As Harrison stumped across the nation, his Whig Party catch-phrase attracted enormous attention, became wildly popular throughout the country, and ultimately proved to be an immeasurable help to Harrison in his presidential bid. Tippecanoe, in the Indiana Territory in 1811, was the site of a fierce battle between the Americans and Shawnee Indians, whose leader was the astute and charismatic chief Tecumseh. Harrison, then territorial governor, led American forces in repelling the Shawnee, forcing them off land Harrison wanted for new settlements.

Tensions between white men and Indians over the ownership of lands, long strained, had worsened as Indians increasingly found their territories encroached upon by white settlers. Angry and frustrated at Harrison's encroachments upon tribal lands, Tecumseh issued a warning to Harrison in 1810 that the Indians "were determined to make a stand where they were." To mount a united defense against the white men, he issued a call for a Western confederation of Indians both as a military force and a political front to deal with the U.S. government. But it was not to be. The loss at the Battle of Tippecanoe was particularly bitter and shattered Tecumseh's plans for the confederation, which died with him in 1813.

Tecumseh, one of the most famous of all American Indian leaders, and Harrison, a popular state politician, had become bitter enemies by the time the Battle of Tippecanoe was fought. For Harrison, a victory against the Shawnee was simply good politics, and he saw Tecumseh as a particularly good foil against whom he could vindicate his policies not just by a defeat, but by wiping out the Shawnee war parties completely and then inflating the body count, again, for political reasons. At the time and through much of American history, many Americans considered Harrison a hero for defeating what could have been a powerful tribal confederation led by the Shawnee. But from the Indians' perspective, Tippecanoe was no loss because the American losses exceeded those of the Shawnee. However, because the Americans had greater numbers of soldiers, they were able to drive the Shawnee off the field of battle and humiliate Tecumseh, destroying the Indian settlement at Tippecanoe, also called Prophetstown, in the process. By destroying Tecumseh's military prestige and reputation, Harrison all but ended the western migration of Indians in America. For Harrison, the victory became a stepping-stone to an ambitious political career, which he exploited as much as he could after he became known as the "Hero of Tippecanoe."

Tecumseh's younger brother, Tenskwatawa, widely known among the Shawnee as "the Prophet," was a religious leader and medicine man possessed with a remarkable gift for prophecy. His paranormal abilities intensified after he experienced a glimpse of a beautiful and peaceful heaven—the spirit world—following a serious bout of illness during an epidemic when he sunk into what doctors might today call a delirium, but which was probably a near-death event. The emotionally overwhelming out-of-body experience, which enabled him to reach a transcendental state, transformed him into a "holy man." Reacting to the encroachment of Indian lands by the Americans, Tenskwatawa admonished his followers to avoid contact with the white man, and pronounced Americans "the children of the Evil Spirit."

William Henry Harrison, however, branded Tenskwatawa an "impostor," and demanded that if he was a genuine prophet, to prove so. "If he is really a prophet, ask of him to cause the sun to stand still, the moon to alter its course, the rivers to cease to flow, or the dead to rise from their graves. If he does these things, you may then believe that he has been sent from God."

To Harrison's chagrin, Tenskwatawa proved ready for the challenge when he announced his powers would "darken the midday sun." To the absolute horror of his superstitious tribesmen, he then accurately, if inexplicably, predicted a solar eclipse and claimed he had darkened the sun. He followed one amazing prediction with another when on December 16, 1811, after pronouncing an angry threat to make the "ground shake," the most severe earthquake ever to strike the United States hit with such tremendous force over an immense Midwestern region that the Mississippi and Ohio rivers flowed backward, entire villages and farms vanished, and the skies darkened for two full days as the result of dust from collapsing homes and trees. Casualties likely numbered in the thousands. Now Tenskwatawa was taken seriously by his enemies.

The Presidential Curse

Tenskwatawa's best-known and most enduring prophecy was his infamous "presidential curse." Incensed by the defeat at Tippecanoe, Tenskwatawa invoked a curse on his archenemy, William Henry Harrison, and declared that the U.S. president elected every twenty years would die in office. "Harrison will not win this year to be the Great Chief. But he may win next year. If he does, he will not finish his term. He will die in office," Tenskwatawa proclaimed.

"No president has ever died in office," a visitor pointed out to the Prophet.

"But Harrison will die, I tell you," Tenskwatawa insisted. "And when he dies you will remember my brother Tecumseh's death. And after him, every Great Chief chosen every twenty years thereafter will die. And when each one dies, let everyone remember the death of our people."

Despite the Prophet's ominous forewarning, Harrison ignored the threat, and when it came time to run for president, he eagerly embraced the popular campaign slogan, "Tippecanoe and Tyler Too!" which ultimately helped propel him to the White House in 1840.

Harrison, who handily won the election, may have psychically sensed his fate when he said good-bye to friends and neighbors in Cincinnati, Ohio, on January 26, 1841. "This may be the last time I have the pleasure of speaking to you on earth or seeing you. I will bid you farewell. If forever, fare thee well," he told them. Harrison's words would quickly prove prescient.

Inauguration day, March 4, 1841, dawned cold, windy, and rainy in Washington, D.C. Harrison had made the grueling journey to the nation's capital from Ohio by stagecoach, boat, and train, and along the route stopped frequently to meet the throngs gathered to see and hear their new president. He arrived in Washington visibly tired and weak, but despite the ordeal of his trip, he gallantly rode with neither hat nor coat to his inauguration on a white horse, ignoring what was to be his peril the foul and blustery weather. After taking the oath of office, Harrison delivered the longest inaugural address in American presidential history, which ran an hour and forty-five minutes.

Later that bone-chilling day, Harrison was drenched by a heavy rainfall and soon after complained of chills and fatigue. It was obvious the new president had caught a severe cold, and during the next four weeks his health worsened. By April 3, Harrison was drifting in and out of consciousness. Then on April 4, 1841, after spending the previous eight days in bed, William Henry Harrison succumbed to pneumonia at the age of sixty-eight, becoming the first president to die in office, an office he had held for only one month. Tenskwatawa's prophecy had proven tellingly accurate.

Harrison's was the first presidential funeral to be held in the White House as the nation, stunned by his sudden death, deeply mourned the loss. The White House was draped in black crape, and black mourning silk hung everywhere on buildings and homes. Those who knew of Tenskwatawa's curse could only ask whether this was, indeed, the very fulfillment of the presidential curse, which, after Harrison's death, would continue every twenty years exactly as the Shawnee prophet predicted.

Abraham Lincoln, elected in 1860, was assassinated in 1865. Elected in 1880, James Garfield was assassinated in 1881. William McKinley, elected in 1900, fell to an assassin's bullet in 1901. Warren G. Harding, elected in 1920, died in office in 1923. Franklin Delano Roosevelt, elected for a third term in 1940, died in office in 1945, having survived one assassination attempt even before he was inaugurated in 1933 and an attempted military coup just two years later. John F. Kennedy, elected in 1960, was assassinated in 1963. Ronald Reagan, elected in 1980, barely survived an assassin's bullet in 1981, making him, at first glance, the first president to finally break the infamous curse 140 years later. Could it be argued, though, that Ronald Reagan began suffering from the effects of incurable Alzheimer's Disease during his term in office and actually began to die?

And finally, what will be the fate of George W. Bush, elected in 2000, with respect to the curse of Tenskwatawa? According to press secretary Ari Fleischer, who later seemed to retract the statement, George W. Bush, in September, 2001, narrowly escaped a double assassination attempt when a commercial jetliner hijacked by Middle Eastern terrorists became a cruise missile aimed first at the White House and then at the Pentagon, where it ultimately crashed. While President Bush was en route from Florida to New York, supposedly another hijacked plane was trying to collide with Air Force One. So the president's plane flew first to Louisiana and then to North Dakota, where, in secure communication with the White House situation room, President Bush and Vice President Cheney planned strategy on what was a day of tragedy for the United States. In some ways, like Harrison and Tenskwatawa, George W. Bush had an ironic relationship with his would-be assassin, Osama bin Laden. It was Bush's father, Vice President George H. W. Bush who helped elevate bin Laden as a guerrilla fighter during the Afghan war against Soviet occupation during the 1980s. Vice President Bush, who had been director of the Central Intelligence Agency, helped marshal the covert training, delivery of weapons, and support for the Afghan fighters, known as the mujihadeen, who took on Soviet troops and forced them to withdraw from Afghanistan. After the Russian Army's retreat, which ultimately helped erode the Soviet Union and precipitated the end of the Cold War, the United States terminated their aid for the Afghan fighters and the country descended into a bloody civil war.

Years later, when Vice President Bush succeeded President Reagan in the White House, he mustered support for a coalition against Saddam Hussein, whose Iraqi forces had invaded Kuwait in 1990. But it was that 1991 coalition, partly based in Saudi Arabia, which so incensed bin Laden that he focused his energies on seeking revenge against the United States for placing its troops and planes in Muslim countries. That revenge, many analysts have said, resulted in the bombings of U.S. embassies in Africa, attacks on American forces in Saudi Arabia, the destruction of the World Trade Towers in New York City on September 11, 2001, and, what many believed to be an assassination attempt on George W. Bush, son of President George H. W. Bush.

Is President Bush still in danger? Some think that he never was in danger, but even if he was, the danger has passed. Similarly, some parapsychologists speculate that Reagan's surviving John Hinckley Jr.'s attempted assassination may have been the result of First Lady Nancy Reagan's dependence on astrological charts for timing appointments. Others say that any subsequent threats to Ronald Reagan never materialized because Nancy's consultations with Joan Quigley made sure that Reagan always avoided travel and exposure to danger on days when his astrological chart said he was particularly vulnerable. These were conscious decisions the Reagans made during their White House years, although Mrs. Reagan neither confirmed nor denied an astrological connection may have saved her husband's life. For all anyone knows, Ronald Reagan's life might have been saved over and over again as a result of his wife's watchful concern.

Had Tenskwatawa made good on his threat to reach out from the spirit world to invoke a terrible curse on the presidents? Or had the Prophet displayed remarkable precognition by divining future events, which he cleverly declared to be of his own making rather than events already cast in the future? Whatever it was, coincidence, retribution from the spirit world, or a prediction of the future, Tenskwatawa's curse has lingered through the centuries and settled on all zero-year presidents in one form or another.

Of course, not all prophecy is pronounced in the form of a curse, and while skeptics may consider it an antiquated superstition, the concept of placing a curse on an enemy is regarded seriously even today by many scholars who have researched the field of the paranormal. For example, according to Dr. Larry Dossey, a leading authority on prayer in medicine, "Followers of Western religions tend erroneously to believe that sorcery, hexing, and cursing are engaged in only by 'uncivilized' peoples. But these activities permeate all religions and cultures."

The Curse on Yitzhak Rabin

In October 1995, the following prediction appeared in the magazine *Jerusalem Report*: "Yitzhak Rabin does not have long to live. The angels have their orders. Suffering and death await the prime minister, or so say the kabbalists who have cursed him . . . for his 'heretical' policies . . . [as] the . . . rabbi . . . read out the most terrifying of curses in the tradition of Jewish mysticism. . . ."

The curse, declared by a far-right religious sect, was proclaimed October 3. In just over one lunar month—November 4, according to the Roman calendar—Rabin was assassinated, fulfilling the ominous prophecy. But the question still remains, was the declaration of a curse really a prophecy or simply a death threat or warrant, an order proclaimed in public to be carried out by anyone who chose to do it? There are those who would argue that public pronouncements of death aren't really prophecies or divinations at all but simply orders to be carried out by those fanatically faithful to the group that issued the proclamation. A curse, on the other hand, is a "solemn invocation of supernatural wrath," and throughout history, there have been individuals who've claimed the power to invoke such maledictions and inflict evil on others who often seem wholly unable to protect themselves from the effects of curses. Tenskwatawa might just have been one of those individuals.

Prophecies and Predictions

While the "presidential curse" has fascinated generations of Americans, many presidential predictions were foretold with no malicious intent, so not every prophecy was issued as a curse even though the two have often been confused. Who doesn't want to know what will happen in the future? Through the ages foretelling the future has been the universal appeal of prophets and prognosticators, and the record of accurate predictions assures that prophecy is genuine. Precognition, the ability to see future events play out in one's mind, is actually very common even though we do not understand how it occurs. Precognition is what psychics and prophets call the supernatural ability to foretell events, which have not yet occurred.

Usually precognition or prophecy involves big things, such as wars, disasters, or sudden and dramatic changes in the leadership of cultures or societies. Accordingly, it's the leaders of countries or societies who are the subjects of prophecies even though you can look in any tabloid magazine and find an ad that announces a 900 number where you can find a fortune-teller willing to divine your private future. However, the broad range of mainstream diviners of the future, such as the late Jeane Dixon, usually focused their abilities on countries, heads of state, major celebrities and public figures, and the occurrence of natural disasters.

How are futures foretold? Some predictions are drawn using the tools of divination: horoscopes, tossing runes, scrying, tarot cards, or maybe even Ouija boards. Other prognosticators, traditionally called prophets or seers, claim access to information from a divine source. Old Testament prophets such as Isaiah, Ezekiel, Jeremiah, or Zachariah proclaimed that they obtained their messages directly from God. Psychics or mediums, however, may offer accurate predictions of the future by tapping into a supernatural realm or the spirit world. Today the term "remote viewing," another description for what our ancestors called prophecy, defines the ability to witness events from a distance or from a different time.

One attempt to explain how some are able to access the future is that time conceived in a linear sequence does not apply to prophecies and predictions. In other words, if past, present, and future are all one, are there individuals who can tap into time by traveling either forward or backward? Albert Einstein suggested "the distinction between past, present, and future is only an illusion, however persistent." Martin Ebon, a writer about the paranormal, offered this intriguing explanation for the ability to see into the future: "If you are in a helicopter, circling over a mountain, and can see two trains on opposite sides of the mountain . . . heading toward each other, you can then foresee a collision as if you had superhuman knowledge, at least in contrast to the passengers and engineers on the two trains."

As if to confirm what Ebon has written, many UFO abductees have reported that during the periods they were on board the spacecraft, they were able to see the present and future as if they were one and the same because the abductees were on a completely different plane. Abductees don't claim to be prophets or diviners of the future. They only maintain that extraterrestrials are able to see the future because they observe it from a vantage point out of linear time.

The future is uncertain, however, and those who prepare, warn, or otherwise enlighten when they reveal secrets that are locked in time are not always welcomed. Some were ridiculed, while others faced condemnation, persecution, or even execution. Superstitious people oftentimes confused the message with the messenger and believed that if the messenger were scorned, or even executed, the message would simply go away as if there were a cause and effect relationship between the message and the person who delivered it.

This superstition suggests the obvious question: are prognostications or premonitions the foretelling of events destined and immutable or only a possibility? It's the question that Scrooge begs the Spirit of Christmas Future to answer when he sees his own name on a desolate gravestone. In other words, for our own purposes, are psychics and seers revealing a future that is already written for some greater reason than the individual who acts out the circumstances? Might the karmic destiny of presidents be determined long before they are ever elected?

Was Abraham Lincoln fated to become, arguably, our greatest president? Was it his destiny to lead us through the Civil War, then be assassinated, only to return as a ghost to haunt the White House? Did Lincoln have the free will to alter his fate or were events beyond his control? Might Richard Nixon's downfall in the Watergate scandal have been karmically predestined? How was it possible for psychics to accurately predict the assassination of President Kennedy, unless it was preordained? Might presidents who heeded forewarnings have altered their destinies?

One can only wonder what might have happened in the minutes before the JFK motorcade began the drive through Dealy Plaza were Kennedy to have insisted upon having the bubble top on his limousine in place because of assassination rumors that had been circulating among the Secret Service. It was his vice president, Lyndon Johnson, who insisted that Kennedy not ride with the bubble in place because it would have been an insult to the citizens of Dallas. It was then JFK's successor, Lyndon Johnson, who told Chief Justice Earl Warren that it didn't matter who really shot JFK because he was only one man, a dead man, and not worth going to war over when all they needed was a guilty party, especially when the guilty party was already dead himself. Was Lyndon Johnson later haunted by the ghost of the assassinated president Abraham Lincoln as the reports say to remind him of guilt he may have borne for the Kennedy assassination? There are those, including Jackie Kennedy in interviews she gave to author William Manchester, who suspected Johnson's direct role in the assassination and subsequent cover-up.

Some presidents are not referred to in prophecy or predictions. Were their roles less critical or significant to the future or fate of the country? Some experts feel certain presidents were designated by God or a divine power to raise the nation's consciousness, and thus act as instruments to affect crucial change, often foreseen by prophets and psychics.

One theory postulates that God chooses particular individuals because they have the character and stamina to withstand the pressure of overwhelming negativity and crisis, and convert it into a positive force. In other situations, presidents fall under the influence of negative attack by evil spirits, and if they represent the power of good, the "dark side" attacks to prevent them from continuing and thus causes their assassinations or untimely deaths in office. It appears that certain presidents have had karmic lessons to learn from their transgressions, and ultimately they evolve into more spiritually developed people. The law of karma guarantees that "every good or bad action is eventually rewarded or punished, either in the present lifetime or in a future incarnation." So it seems that a divine or supernatural force has controlled or at least strongly impacted the fates of certain presidents and the destiny of the United States to a far greater degree than most historians will acknowledge.

When presidents pass from earth, their karmas extend into the afterlife, and their destinies transcend the boundaries of the physical world, which may be one explanation for why their spirits or ghosts materialize: to communicate positive advice and offer guidance to later presidents and other influential political and military leaders. A notable example is George Washington whose active spirit counseled and inspired future leaders and military commanders at key times throughout the nation's history. The spirit of President Kennedy once acknowledged through British medium Ina Twigg that "spirituality . . . extends into the afterlife."

"Old Rough and Ready"

Some presidents, as we will see in the story of Abraham Lincoln, have actually predicted their own deaths. One of the most well-known predictions came from

President Zachary Taylor, who, although he was never seen as a ghost, did seem to know that he was about to die. Zachary Taylor's military exploits earned him the nickname "Old Rough and Ready." After rising through the ranks and serving in several wars and key battles, Taylor emerged as a hero of the Mexican War. That success propelled him to the presidency in the election of 1848. He lived to serve just over a year in office.

July 4, 1850, was a mercilessly hot and humid day, typical of Washington, D.C., in summer. Despite exhaustion and discomfort from the sweltering weather, President Taylor sat for several hours under the blistering sun and participated in an Independence Day celebration, which included ceremonies for the laying of the cornerstone for the Washington Monument. Taylor also indulged heavily in refreshments that afternoon, enjoying several bowls of iced cherries in cold milk, not realizing the food he ate was tainted. Later in the day he complained of both the effects of heat and severe stomach pains. His doctors' efforts to relieve the effects of the food poison only made his condition worse. Then on July 7, three days after he became ill, Taylor made a startling prediction to those gathered at his bedside. "In two days I shall be a dead man," he said. They were incredulous upon hearing his words because no physician had made such a dire prognosis. How could President Taylor know what fate awaited him? Yet, exactly two days later, on July 9, just as he foretold, Zachary Taylor died at the age of sixty-five from a form of cholera. He had been President of the United States for only sixteen months.

Likely "Old Rough and Ready" experienced a premonition of the kind known to countless people throughout time, in which the spirit of a deceased loved one provided Taylor with the information, received clairaudiently, and possibly without even realizing it was a paranormal experience. Such precognitive psychic messages often prepare a dying person for the transition to the hereafter, and are a familiar form of afterdeath communication.

Prophets and Prognosticators

Famous prognosticators who are reinterpreted in a modern light are said to have predicted the rise and fall of nations and of despots thousands of years before the despots' countries ever existed. Other interpreters of ancient texts see all sorts of references to events taking place today. Could this be so? Could it be that an interpretation of the Old Testament might have predicted events involving U.S. history and American presidents such as Jack Kennedy and Bill Clinton? This is what is claimed in the controversial Bible Code, discovered by Israeli mathematician Eliyahu Rips.

In 1997, Michael Drosnin wrote the bestselling book *The Bible Code*, in which he claimed "there is a code in the Bible, and in a few dramatic cases it has foretold events that then happened exactly as predicted." Drosnin said, "All the assassinations that have changed the course of human history—the murders of Abraham Lincoln, Mahatma Gandhi, Anwar Sadat, Yitzhak Rabin, and both John and Robert Kennedy—were foreseen in the Bible."

He asked, "If the future can be foreseen, can it also be changed?" Could presidential assassinations have been avoided if we heeded prophecies about them? As Drosnin pointed out, "The question is whether the Bible code tells us what will happen or may happen, presents one predetermined future, or predicts all the possible futures."

How might it be possible that a code hidden in the Bible "recorded events" many centuries before they occurred? According to Drosnin, the great scientist Sir Isaac Newton was convinced that in the Bible was hidden a code that could disclose the future. Of course, that was in the seventeenth century, long before computers were able to implement a "sophisticated mathematical model" to decrypt elements of the code itself. Computer programs that analyzed the hidden code in the Bible determined the odds of such "encoded information" being a product of random chance were approximately one in ten million. Therefore, the encoded information discovered by Eliyahu Rips was there for a particular reason and not simply a figment of the decoder's imagination. Governments as well as data analysts for major industries took Rips' mathematical models very seriously. In fact, among the agencies around the world that reportedly studied the Bible code was the U.S. Department of Defense.

Drosnin concluded, "The Bible was encoded with information about the past and . . . future in a way that was mathematically beyond random chance," nor was it located in any other book or document. "The Bible is constructed like a giant crossword puzzle. It is encoded from beginning to end with words that connect to tell a hidden story," he explained. Thus, there is "a Bible beneath the Bible."

Who wrote the Bible code? Who had the capacity to look thousands of years into the future and encrypt information in the Old Testament, particularly within the first five books, which tell the story of the patriarchs and the prophet Moses? Since all of the prophets in the Old Testament derived their knowledge strictly from Divine revelation and from no other source, many believe that only a nonhuman intelligence, such as God, was responsible for creating the code within the Biblical texts.

About President John F. Kennedy, the Bible code indicates the phrase "to die" and the location "Dallas" is encoded in the same place in the text. Even the presumed assassin's name, "Oswald," appears, as does the exact means by which he carried out his murderous act. "He will strike in the head, death," the phrase indicates. The Bible code also mentions Robert F. Kennedy and predicted both his assassination and the name of his killer, "Sirhan."

Why does the Bible code contain the names of certain assassinated world leaders? Drosnin concluded, "There is a striking pattern to assassinations in the modern world. It is the leaders who bring hope who are killed. And each of the murders is encoded in the Bible."

President Abraham Lincoln's name has been located in the Bible code, encrypted twice in the Old Testament books of Genesis and Deuteronomy. "Booth" appears three times where the assassin's name crosses "Lincoln." And the word "assassinated" crosses the name "A. Lincoln." The Bible code reference to "Bill Clinton" crosses the word "president," thus predicting his election win in 1992. And presidential scandal is not forgotten, specifically "Watergate," which appears with the name "Nixon" and the year he resigned, 1974.

The decoders of the Bible have also discovered the words "America," "revolution," and "1776" together, as well as "President Franklin Delano Roosevelt" and "Pearl Harbor." "World War I" and "World War II" are encoded, as are "hundreds of other world-shaking events . . ."

Skeptics argue that the Bible code is possibly nothing more than a series or multiple patterns of words and terms that form coincidences. Skeptics also question why God would have hidden the code so well that it might have gone unnoticed forever, as it apparently had for many centuries. If the code were so important, why wasn't it decipherable centuries ago and why wait for the mathematical models of Eliyahu Rips? The mere fact that Drosnin has to argue for the code's existence suggests that it's more a perception than a reality.

The other problem with the encoded information in the Bible is the question of language. "Clinton," spelled out in Hebrew characters, is his name in English. Yet, reading the text as an acrostic, the English speaker recognizes the phonetic spelling as English, not a speaker of Hebrew or Greek or a reader of Aramaic. In other words, depending upon the language one speaks and the ways the Hebrew characters are read, an individual can interpret a multiplicity of meanings. Why would some names appear in Hebrew and other names in English? Does this mean the code has been intended for only certain individuals to eventually decipher?

Nostradamus

Another prognosticator whose predictions have gained fame over the centuries is Nostradamus. Born in 1503 in

St. Remy, France, Michel de Nostradame came of age at a time and place inhospitable for a psychic or seer to ply his trade. The mid-sixteenth century was dominated by the Church, which, at the dawn of the Reformation, controlled virtually every aspect of life. It was a dangerous time to stray from the orthodoxy of strict Catholic dogma, especially when people were terrified of witchcraft. Dabbling in the black arts of magic and the occult would have almost certainly been met with a charge of heresy, an accusation of consorting with the devil, torture at the hands of the Inquisitor, and a fiery execution at the stake.

Nonetheless, Nostradamus, a gifted physician, delved deeply into astrology and "magical studies," and his enduring fame came from his prophecies written in ambiguous four-line verses, or quatrains, first published in 1555 and open to multiple interpretations. In a set of ten books titled *Centuries*, Nostradamus compiled almost a thousand verses that looked into the future for the ensuing two thousand years, until the year 3797.

Nostradamus is perhaps the most recognizable name of any prophet or seer who ever lived. In the centuries since his death in 1566, which he also predicted, every generation has labored to decipher his cryptic verses, many written so obscurely that there are conflicting interpretations for them. Nostradamus admitted he purposely wrote in cryptic and difficult-to-understand language as a protection against those who might denounce him. He declared that his writings would be better understood after his death "and by those who penetrate my meaning." And indeed, centuries after his death, a mini-industry has developed in the publishing and exegesis of the works and predictions of Nostradamus.

To date, more than four hundred of the nearly thousand verses have, at least, according to interpreters, turned out to be true. In a number of quatrains, Nostradamus offered predictions about the United States and several presidents who would not be born until hundreds of years after his own time. For example, in a verse about President John F. Kennedy's assassination, Nostradamus predicted there would be considerable controversy surrounding the killing with "the guilty one hidden in a misty woods" and an "innocent would be accused."

One interpretation concluded the "misty woods" was actually the infamous grassy knoll from where some assassination researchers have suggested shots were fired at the presidential motorcade in Dallas on November 22, 1963. Was the "innocent . . . accused" a reference to Lee Harvey Oswald, who many felt was a dupe rather than the lone assassin? Does the Nostradamus suggestion that Oswald was the "innocent" contradict the Old Testament interpretation from the Bible code that Oswald was the assassin? Perhaps this contradiction is no contradiction at all but at most a difference in semantics. The Warren Commission concluded that Oswald was the lone assassin, and so it was officially recorded even though Oswald might have been, in his own words, a "patsy" set up by the conspirators to take the fall and Jack Ruby's fatal bullet.

Still another quatrain is thought to have foretold John F. Kennedy's murder: "The great man will be struck down in daytime by a thunderbolt./An evil deed, foretold by a bearer of a petition./Another is struck at night. . . ." President Kennedy was indeed murdered in the afternoon, "daytime," and Nostradamus may have clairvoyantly interpreted the bullet that struck Kennedy from the upper floor of the Texas School Book Depository Building as a "thunderbolt." The one "struck at night," according to other interpreters, may refer to Democratic presidential candidate Robert Kennedy, who was assassinated close to midnight almost five years after his brother was killed.

In a further verse, Nostradamus predicted, again, a presidential assassination: "The sudden death of the leading personage/Will make change and put another to rule./Soon, but too late he comes to high position, of young age./By land and sea it will be necessary to fear him."

John Kennedy was the youngest president ever

elected, during a time of international tensions, particularly the Cold War with the Soviet Union, and was thus feared on land and sea as one of the two world leaders who could have launched a nuclear attack.

Nostradamus prophesied the arrival of Abraham Lincoln in the following quatrain: "The sacred pomp shall bow down her wings/At the coming of the great lawgiver,/He shall raise the humble and vex the rebellious,/ No emulator of his shall be born." Researchers in the paranormal have strongly suggested that the ability of Nostradamus to predict the arrival of President Abraham Lincoln centuries into the future points to the prognosticator's ability to enter a psychic database, a kind of collective consciousness of the entire human race—living, dead, or yet to be born—so as to encounter the presence of Abraham Lincoln. The power of that presence, the sheer energy of his life force, not only announced his appearance hundreds of years before his birth, but also explains why his ghost still lingers in the White House.

In what is considered one of Nostradamus' most remarkable prophecies concerning a U.S. president, the name Roosevelt was actually given. "In the middle of the great field shall be the rose . . ./Then at the time will be the one long looked for." Nostradamus predicted the emergence of a great world leader whose name is decoded by a play on words in line one of the quatrain: "rose" and "field" (in Dutch, *veldt*) when combined become the name Roosevelt.

Nostradamus also foretold Richard Nixon's resignation from the presidency and, in the following verse, predicted the friendship between President Reagan and Soviet president Gorbachev, the latter responsible for the end of the Soviet totalitarian system: "One day the two great masters shall be friends,/Their great powers shall be increased. . . ."

Arguably, his most calamitous portent foretold the coming of Adolf Hitler, who Nostradamus called "Hister," also an early name for the Danube River, which flows from Germany: "Liberty shall not be recovered,/

A black, fierce, and wicked villain shall occupy it. . . ./ The republic of Venice shall be annoyed by Hister."

The most recent working out of a Nostradamus prophecy might have involved the destruction of New York City's World Trade Center. Nostradamus wrote, "At forty-five degrees the sky will burn,/Fire approaches the great new city,/Instantly a great scattered flame shall leap up." In another verse, there is a line that reads, "two brothers torn apart by chaos," although that line has sometimes been interpreted to foretell the assassinations of President John Kennedy and his brother Senator Robert Kennedy.

Did Nostradamus predict the destruction of the two World Trade towers and the coming of what might be a Middle Eastern war to destroy the terrorist network of Osama bin Laden and the countries that shelter him? The "great new city" has been identified as New York because the city sits between the fortieth and forty-fifth parallel. And the verse itself is in a section of the manuscript that continually references a great war between Christians, Moslems, and Jews. Other scholars have often said that the writings of Nostradamus consistently point to an ultimate war, an Armageddon in which the final battle is a precursor to the coming of the Messiah. Maybe that was why, in the hours after the attack on the World Trade Center, an ominous psychological cloud hung over the entire country as if it were a warning of things to come.

The World Trade Center and Pentagon attacks by terrorists occurred during the first year of the presidency of George W. Bush, who was elected in a zero year, 2000. Bush claimed through press secretary Ari Fleischer that he, too, was one of the targets of the terrorists, an assassination attempt that also marked the first time since 1814 that the nation's capital had been attacked. This was more than just an attempt on the president; it was, some people believed, the beginning of a new and calamitous war, one predicted centuries ago by Nostradamus.

Nostradamus did not believe his prophecies foretold

an immutable future. "The one who is reasonable can learn from my prophecies how to find the right path to take as if he would have found footprints in the sand from someone who has gone before," he wrote. Therefore, perhaps by studying the quatrains for their hidden meanings, we may find messages that predict the destinies of future presidents.

Although Nostradamus was, by far, the most celebrated prophet to emerge after the Middle Ages, he was not the only one in history whose predictions touched upon the fates of presidents. Other prognosticators have come after him and have made similar, powerful predictions about the individuals who would occupy the Oval Office. For example, during the period known as the Great Age of Spiritualism (the mid-nineteenth century) Daniel Dunglas Home became the most renowned medium of his time here and abroad, and his psychic gifts allowed him to predict future events. In 1863, while in France, Home accurately predicted that President Abraham Lincoln would be assassinated. Such "precognitive visions" had been a part of Home's life since boyhood.

Edgar Cayce

Twentieth-century American psychic, healer, and seer Edgar Cayce is perhaps one of the best-known prognosticators whose relationships with U.S. presidents and other powerful individuals helped to make him famous. Cayce writes in his memoir, *My Life as a Seer, The Lost Memoirs,* how he was secretly called to Washington, D.C., to consult with the ailing President Woodrow Wilson, who had suffered a debilitating stroke toward the end of his second term in office. The self-taught Cayce and Princeton-educated Wilson formed a strange dichotomy.

Born in 1877, Cayce, despite little formal schooling, demonstrated a remarkable faculty with complicated medical terminology while in a trance state. His reputation grew until he was known nationally as a clairvoyant, healer, and seer. In a trance state, Cayce diagnosed and prescribed unique remedies to treat a wide range of ailments and diseases through a combination of herbs, psychic techniques, and chiropractic manipulation. But what circumstances led Cayce to meet President Wilson?

By the time Wilson was elected President of the United States in 1912, his accomplishments included serving as the governor of New Jersey and the president of Princeton University. A deep believer in prayer, he felt strongly that God personally guided and even chose him to be president. With the campaign slogan "He kept us out of the war," Wilson was reelected to a second term in 1916. Although the United States entered World War I the next year, Wilson worked his way to the forefront of leaders who forged the Armistice to end the war, conceived the idea for a League of Nations, and ultimately won the Nobel Peace Prize.

But close to the end of his final term in office, in October 1919, calamity struck when Wilson suffered a disabling stroke that rendered him virtually paralyzed for no less than six weeks. The press falsely reported that he'd suffered "a complete nervous breakdown." There were also widespread rumors that his second wife, Edith Wilson, assumed many responsibilities of the presidency—a role no first lady ever found herself in before—while the truth about the dire circumstances of the president's health was kept hidden from the American public. Mrs. Wilson remained in charge of the executive branch for the last seventeen months of her husband's second term because he was never well enough to regain full command of the presidency. If Wilson's health was shrouded in secrecy, it would make sense that when Edgar Cayce was summoned to the White House to help the ailing president, it also was handled surreptitiously. Cayce's relationship with Wilson would remain a secret for more than a decade.

In 1932, eight years after Wilson's death, Cayce wrote that he was once ". . . called to Washington to give information for one high in authority. This, I am sure, must have been at least interesting, as I was called a year or so later for the same purpose." According to David E. Kahn, long a friend to Cayce, "At one time we were asked to give a reading [for] President Woodrow Wilson. I believe this was during the time that he was in the wheelchair and incapacitated and Mrs. Wilson was looking after his affairs."

Kahn wrote that the meeting between Wilson and Cayce was arranged by a Secret Service official who'd known Cayce from their childhood years in Kentucky. Kahn explained that, although he was not present for the psychic reading with Wilson, he learned that Cayce psychically determined the gravity of Wilson's health, then predicted the president would not recover and would not have long to live.

There was another aspect to Cayce's work that intrigued Wilson. Cayce, an avid reader of the Bible, had earned a reputation as a seer or prophet, albeit somewhat reluctantly. Some years ago in an interview, Cayce's son, Hugh Lynn, reported that his father "disliked making predictions" because he believed in free will and preferred not to influence anyone who might be vulnerable to suggestion. Nonetheless, behind his gentle countenance and rimless spectacles, Cayce did offer predictions about world events and disasters, both natural and man-made, including coming wars, conflicts between nations, and earth changes. Wasn't Edgar Cayce the perfect person to provide Wilson with a look into the future, especially as it concerned the president's all-consuming dream for a League of Nations?

Other books allude to psychic readings by Cayce for Wilson. In *Edgar Cayce, Mystery Man of Miracles*, author Joseph Millard said that Cayce was "mysteriously summoned to Washington" on two occasions. In *A Seer out of Season*, author Harmon Bro maintained that Cayce was invited to give psychic readings in the White House twice to President Wilson on the future of the League of Nations. Although no written documentation of those psychic readings has ever been found, there is a record of Cayce's readings for a cousin of the president, a man identified as Major Wilson.

No doubt, the famed psychic was warned in no uncertain terms to maintain silence—a White House position consistent with the veil of secrecy that concealed details about Wilson's health and Mrs. Wilson's role as de facto president. There was fear that political and public reaction to meetings between a psychic and the president would raise uncomfortable questions about Wilson's religious beliefs and mental stability, and further complicate his tenuous situation. When one considers the derision Nancy Reagan and Hillary Clinton faced because of their consultations with practitioners of the paranormal, one can only imagine what a scandal would have erupted had Wilson's relationship with Cayce been reported in the press.

Woodrow Wilson lived for three years after he left the White House in 1921, although he never fully recovered. Unfortunately, Edgar Cayce had been unable to help Wilson's condition. Most likely, it was already too late to cure the president, whose neurological impairments were quite severe. Or perhaps Cayce's unorthodox remedies could have helped, but they were ignored by Wilson's own physician, who, trained in late-nineteenth-century medicine, might have been afraid that he would harm his patient.

Wilson left this world for what Cayce called "God's other door," the afterlife, a bitter and disillusioned man whose intractable idealism remained unfulfilled. He never was able to garner Senate support for the League of Nations, and his dream to advance peace in the world or prevent future wars proved unattainable. Cayce's pessimistic—albeit accurate—prediction that the League was doomed to failure only deepened Wilson's disappointment that he could not fulfill his God-ordained mission to "save the world from war."

Warren Harding and the Curse of the Hope Diamond

In the story of President Warren G. Harding, there is another curse—a curse that, to this very day, lingers around the mysteries of the infamous Hope Diamond and even frightened former first lady and New York senator Hillary Clinton. We know about the story of the curse of King Tut and the spate of untimely deaths among those who broke into the cursed tomb. But can a person as powerful as the President of the United States become the unintentional victim of a dark prophecy whether he realizes it or not? That's the question raised by the effect the infamous Hope Diamond had on President Harding.

The "largest blue diamond in the world" began its strange journey in the seventeenth century when French trader Jean Baptiste Tavernier carried the gem from India. The magnificent stone, which weighed 112.5 carats, was believed stolen from a statue of a Hindu goddess in an Indian temple, where, it was said, the goddess would take vengeance on anyone who dared to possess the pirated jewel. Tavernier sold the diamond to King Louis XIV of France, who ignored the curse, wore the diamond once, then died of smallpox. Tavernier died suddenly after losing all his money. The diamond next became the property of King Louis XVI. He gave the jewel to his wife, Queen Marie Antoinette, and even if she had wanted to wear it around her neck, she would never have the opportunity. Both monarchs were beheaded on the guillotine in 1793 during the Reign of Terror that marked the beginning of the French Revolution. Princess de Lamballe, Marie Antoinette's dear friend who frequently borrowed the jewel, was also beheaded under the guillotine's blade.

But the story of the Hope Diamond didn't end with the deaths of the original owners. The diamond was later stolen, recut, and reduced to 44.5 carats, although no one knew where the rest went, and a string of its subsequent owners met untimely deaths or tragedies. In 1830, British banker Henry Thomas Hope acquired the gem. It remained in his family for the next seventy years and became known as the Hope Diamond. A kind of trophy within the family, the diamond continued to curse those who possessed it. Several family members met unexpected deaths, which were blamed on Hope's acquisition of the deep blue stone.

The diamond continued its travels from owner to owner around the world, all of whom met disastrous fates, such as murder, fatal accident, suicide, insanity, and bankruptcy. At least eleven owners of the diamond were reported to have fallen victim to the diamond's curse before the stone made its way to the owner who was to take possession of it in the United States. Unfortunately, in order to get to the United States from England, the buyer took passage on the doomed ocean liner the *Titanic*. He never took possession of the stone.

After the *Titanic* tragedy, the Hope Diamond was bought by wealthy American newspaper magnate Edward B. McLean. By then, of course, the curse of the Hope Diamond was already well-known, and people waited to see whether ill fortune would befall its new owner. It did, and the McLean family suffered a number of ill-fated accidents and deaths. But even as Evelyn McLean publicly scoffed at the idea of a curse, she forbade family and friends to touch the diamond. The ultimate tragedy occurred when the McLeans' ten-year-old son was struck and killed by an out-of-control automobile right in front of their home.

One of Edward McLean's dearest friends was Warren G. Harding, for whose election in 1920 McLean had worked tirelessly to secure with "the greatest majority given a president in a hundred years." Harding displayed a flash of prescience when a friend wished him "Godspeed" on his election victory. He answered, "Yes. God help me, for I shall need it."

But after Harding touched the Hope Diamond, his life turned upside down. His health failed from a combination of heart, lung, and abdominal problems, and he was involved in several extramarital affairs, including one in 1922 that produced a child. Also, two members of his troubled administration, both accused of corruption, met violent deaths. One of them committed suicide and the other was murdered.

On August 2, 1923, after less than 2.5 years in office,

Harding died mysteriously, presumably of a stroke, at the age of fifty-seven, fueling rumors that he'd been murdered. Only months after his death, the infamous Teapot Dome scandal broke. Among those involved was Edward McLean, who was accused of paying $100,000 in bribes to the U.S. interior secretary. McLean's reputation was destroyed.

Whether the Hope Diamond curse is to blame for Harding's unhappy legacy can be debated. However, in 1931, President Herbert Hoover acknowledged that "we saw [Warren Harding] gradually weaken, not only from physical exhaustion, but also from mental anxiety." Hoover described Harding's fall as a "tragedy."

Were the disastrous circumstances surrounding Harding related to the prophetic curse of the infamous, and ironically named, Hope Diamond? Not only was he possibly a victim of the diamond's curse, but he was also the fifth president in a row to succumb to the prophecy of doom pronounced by Tenskwatawa. It seemed Warren Harding's fate was sealed before he became president, locked in a wretched and unalterable confluence of two destinies: the curse of Tenskwatawa and the curse of the Hope Diamond.

After the death of President Harding, the diamond continued to wreak havoc upon the McLeans. Their marriage failed after Edward began to drink heavily and became mentally unstable. He finally died in 1941 while confined to a mental institution. The McLeans' only daughter, who'd worn the Hope Diamond at her wedding, subsequently died of a drug overdose. A few years later in 1947, sixty-year-old Evelyn McLean died as the result of a fall. Shortly after her death, a *Washington Daily News* headline asked, "Who'll Be Next to Risk Wearing 'Unlucky' Diamond?"

Eventually New York jeweler Harry Winston bought the troubled gem for one million dollars, displayed it for some years, and then donated it to the Smithsonian Institution for public exhibit. But the curse continued unabated. The mailman who delivered the diamond in 1959 met tragedy when his leg was crushed in a truck accident. Several months later, his wife died suddenly of a heart attack, his dog was strangled on its leash, and the mailman's home was lost to fire. Wisely, First Lady Hillary Clinton avoided coming into contact with the Hope Diamond when she visited the Smithsonian.

But what of President Harding, who became the victim of a double curse? He seems not to have returned to haunt the White House. Perhaps because all his trials and tribulations were completed on earth, President Harding's spirit has never been witnessed in the Executive Mansion. Maybe he has simply moved on with no need or desire to return to this physical world.

CHAPTER FOUR

FDR, Jeane Dixon, and the Kennedy Curse

A greater power than mine has willed it. I only saw it.

—Jeane Dixon

Despite his own objections and those of his doctors, President Franklin Delano Roosevelt was drafted by the Democratic Party to run for reelection in 1944. His health, compromised decades earlier when he was stricken with polio and mostly confined to a wheelchair, had dramatically deteriorated since his 1940 election victory for a third term. Fighting to drag America out of the Great Depression for nine years and then leading America and its Allies through a bloody war fought simultaneously across two oceans had taken its toll on the paralyzed FDR. His doctors had told him that his weakened body would not hold out much longer. They advised him in the most urgent language they could to retire from the presidency and relocate to a warmer climate in order to buy a few more years for himself. But the country, the party, and the Allies all needed FDR's leadership, he was told, and he reluctantly acceded to his party's drafting him to run for a fourth term. He won the election on November 7, 1944.

As President Roosevelt took the oath of office in January 1945, it seemed to many who listened to him on the radio that he'd always been the president. Since 1933, he had survived one assassination attempt and a near coup d'état and guided the people of a fearful nation through the darkest days of the Great Depression. Then, during the horrific early years of World War II, when it looked like all of Asia and the Pacific world would fall prey to the Japanese Empire and Europe and Africa would be crushed under the hobnailed boots of Hitler's goose-stepping *Wehrmacht,* President Roosevelt was America's beacon of hope. Who could imagine the White House without FDR? Didn't it seem he would be there forever? But by February 1945, as he began his fourth term, Roosevelt's demeanor clearly revealed the strain of twelve years in the White House. He was pale, worn, and gaunt-looking, and he'd noticeably lost weight.

That same year, in Washington, D.C., a well-manicured and confident young woman named Jeane Dixon, who'd moved with her husband to Washington in 1942, was attracting attention for her psychic abilities and predictions. One Thursday morning in November 1944, Dixon received a phone call inviting her to the White House. When she arrived, she was quietly ushered into the Oval Office, where President Roosevelt sat behind his desk. He smiled, greeted her, and thanked her for coming. However, he carefully avoided using the term "psychic." The president wheeled himself around his desk to where he could shake Dixon's hand. He held her hand for a moment and, after a brief exchange of pleasantries, asked her, "How much time do I have to finish the work I have to do?"

With FDR's permission, Dixon placed her hand on his so that she might sense his "vibrations," as she called them. She was hesitant to say aloud what she felt, but the president insisted, so Dixon answered, "Six months or less."

Roosevelt said nothing for several minutes. When he spoke again, he asked Dixon her thoughts about dealing with Russia, a U.S. ally during the War, and what Russia's role would be when the War ended. Dixon explained that her visions showed the United States and Russia would not be allies in the postwar years. However, she added, the two nations would someday, far in the future, again be friendly.

The president asked again, "How much longer in years do I have to complete my work?"

"Mr. President, you cannot measure it in years, only in months. There is less than six months," Dixon repeated.

Curiously, Roosevelt never specifically asked Jeane Dixon how long he had to live. Rather, his concern was for the time remaining to complete his work. The president, who some may have considered immortal, in fact knew the somber truth about the limits of his mortality. A short while later, the remarkable meeting between the psychic who could see into the future and the President of the United States was over. Years later, Dixon reported that during her meeting with Roosevelt she felt the president had a premonition that he would soon die.

Dixon's next call from the White House came in January 1945, again inviting her to visit President Roosevelt. Looking at FDR, she thought how his health had deteriorated in just the past two months, for the president looked even more haggard than when she had first met him in November. After greeting her, Roosevelt wasted no time asking, "How much time do I have now?"

Dixon held her thumb and forefinger up so that there was perhaps an inch of space between them. "This much," she answered, looking at her hand.

The president nodded, but he didn't seem startled or visibly upset by Dixon's pessimistic prediction. "The time is short," he agreed, seemingly at peace with himself.

"Yes, the time is shorter than we want to think it is," Dixon answered.

Roosevelt then abruptly changed subjects, returning to questions about America's postwar policy and ways to handle Russian demands for carving up Nazi-occupied Europe. Dixon advised FDR not to give anything to Russia that the United States had a right to. As their meeting ended, Roosevelt warmly clasped Dixon's hand and thanked her for her time and advice. It was the last time Jeane Dixon ever saw the president.

In February 1945, an ailing Roosevelt attended a secret conference at Yalta with British prime minister Winston Churchill and Soviet dictator Joseph Stalin, in which FDR, against Churchill's advice, agreed to giving the Soviets control over the eastern half of Germany. Worse, the clearly weakened American president, now in the last months of his life and no longer capable of conducting the difficult negotiations that clearly lay ahead, allowed Eastern European and Balkan nations to be carved up and handed over to the Communist puppet governments the Soviets were putting into place, thus singularly determining their futures for the next forty years. Roosevelt had not listened to what Dixon had warned. And as she'd predicted, FDR's time was very short. The president was at Warm Springs, Georgia, when he died suddenly of a cerebral hemorrhage on April 12, 1945. The tasks of winning final victories in Europe and in the Pacific, dropping the top-secret atomic bomb, and dealing with a pro-Soviet Eastern European bloc were left to Vice President Harry S. Truman. Jeane Dixon's predictions had come true because her warnings had been neglected.

Jeane Dixon had made other significant presidential prophecies, the first of which, forecast in 1928 when she was still in school, predicted Herbert Hoover would be elected. Twenty years later, in January 1948, against virtually the opinion of everyone else including the professional pollsters, Dixon foretold the outcome of the next November's election: "Harry Truman will be elected." The prediction flew in the face of every political prognostication, because the Republican candidate New York governor Thomas E. Dewey, the popular former racket-busting prosecutor who'd put away Lucky Luciano and mob killer Louis Lepke, was overwhelmingly favored to win. Moreover, Truman's base in the South was seriously eroded when, after a powerful speech by Hubert Humphrey at the Democratic National Convention, the president approved the inclusion of a strong civil rights plank in the Democratic platform. When Strom Thurmond led the Dixiecrats out of the Convention, Truman's fortunes looked grim indeed. Yet, in November 1948, in one of America's greatest political upsets, Truman proved Dixon's predictions to be accurate when he beat Dewey for the presidency. It was just as Dixon had said, and her own fortunes rose.

In 1952, Dixon predicted Dwight Eisenhower would be elected president, first defeating Dewey, who entered the national convention as the front runner for the Republican nomination, and then Democrat Adlai Stevenson. In 1955, Dixon said Ike would be reelected the next year. However, when she made that prediction, Eisenhower had not yet announced he would seek office for a second term because he was still recuperating from a severe heart attack. In fact, just prior to his coronary, Dixon predicted that Ike would become "seriously ill." Eisenhower recovered, ran for reelection in 1956, and easily won a second term.

During the late 1950s and early 1960s, Dixon was also asked to consult on what would become the CIA's remote viewing program. Because she had powerful psychic abilities, the managers of the program thought she could be beneficial to the assembly of the theoretical components of the remote viewing project. Dixon sought advice from Lt. Col. Philip Corso, one of her old friends in the army intelligence community, who advised her against working with the CIA, and she ultimately declined to participate.

When Lyndon Johnson was still vice president, Dixon accurately forecast that in the future he "would withdraw from the presidential race. He's going to quit. He's going to be a victim of circumstances." Although Johnson staged a landslide defeat over Arizona senator Barry Goldwater in the 1964 election, he withdrew from contention in 1968 after the North Vietnamese Tet Offensive. Johnson was indeed a victim of "circumstances," the domestic political fallout due to the widely unpopular and divisive Vietnam War. Years later, in a series of recorded audiotapes made from the Oval Office and released by Ladybird Johnson after her husband's death, Johnson revealed that he was pushed into the war in Vietnam by the military, against his better judgment. It was a war he knew the United States could not win, and it was the war issue that forced him out of office after a dangerously weak showing in the New Hampshire Democratic primary against Senator Eugene McCarthy, the antiwar candidate challenging LBJ's incumbency.

All the way back in 1949, nearly twenty years prior to Richard Nixon's election, Dixon predicted Nixon would eventually become president. What made her later Nixon predictions controversial was that long before the Watergate scandal Dixon spoke of his "excellent vibrations." What was her reaction to Nixon's ignominious fall? She stubbornly insisted he would someday be considered "a great president." At the time he resigned in 1974, her prognostication seemed ludicrous. Dixon's prediction was viewed differently twenty years later, when many historians and political analysts, in spite of Watergate, became more generous in their praise of Nixon's contributions, especially in foreign policy.

Dixon was not the only psychic or clairvoyant to predict events for ill-fated President Nixon. Several years before Watergate toppled the Nixon administration, well-known British psychic Malcolm Bessent predicted: "Starting with 1972–73, it will be a critical year for the United States. Water everywhere, resulting in social upheaval, anarchy, and political confusion. The American people will be looking for a new leader." Psychics often experience visions as symbols, much the way we dream, and then must logically translate what the dream metaphors represent or signify. Obviously Bessent's reference to "water everywhere" was a psychic symbol that represented the Watergate scandal.

Jeane Dixon's most famous prophecy foretold the assassination of President John F. Kennedy. The first time she told anyone about the fate of the president who would be elected in 1960 was in 1952 when she predicted that Kennedy, then a Congressman, would achieve political victory at the highest level, but would die violently. Dixon even foresaw that the presidential candidate elected in 1960 would have blue eyes.

Her 1952 prophecy, she said, was based on a vision of the White House and the numbers 1-9-6-0 over it, which then were blotted out by a "dark cloud that dripped onto the dome." Dixon explained that she psychically witnessed JFK in a doorway while a clairaudient voice impressed her that Kennedy would be elected president, then be assassinated in office.

Although witnesses heard Dixon's prediction as far back as the early 1950s, it was not published until 1956, when columnist Jack Anderson interviewed Dixon for *Parade* magazine. The publication had asked her to predict the future with such questions as who would win the presidential election in 1960: "As for the 1960 election, Mrs. Dixon thinks it will be won by a Democrat. But he will be assassinated or die in office, though not necessarily in his first term."

Denis Brian in his book *Jeane Dixon: The Witnesses* corroborated Dixon's prophecies through witness accounts and other documentation. Brian learned that Dixon told several friends in 1963 that President Kennedy would soon die in office, the result of an assassination that would occur "down south." One friend confirmed that Dixon said, "All I can see is the casket over the White House." To another Dixon predicted, "What I see is going to happen to the president himself and he cannot avoid it. It won't be long now." In January 1963, Dixon made the same prediction, privately, to a skeptical New York radio talk show host and eventual target of the CIA's domestic MK Ultra operation, Long John Nebel, who asked her not to repeat it on the air. Brian also discovered that Dixon attempted to communicate warnings to President Kennedy, through intermediaries, but to no avail.

On November 22, 1963, Dixon lunched with two friends in Washington, D.C., to whom she'd already predicted, "Someone is going to shoot the president," when an acquaintance approached to tell her President Kennedy had been shot at 12:30 P.M. in Dallas, Texas, as he rode in a motorcade. While some early news reports said Kennedy might live, Dixon psychically knew the outcome. "No, he's dead," she said sadly, the color drained from her face. Dixon made clear that Kennedy's murder was destined, and the outcome could not be changed despite her efforts to warn him.

There were many predictions and premonitions prior to the assassination of President John F. Kennedy on November 22, 1963, from both professional psychics and mediums, as well as from ordinary private citizens. Some reported dream visions; others simply experienced a "sensation" that tragedy surrounded Kennedy. By various estimates, there were at least fifty thousand predictions of JFK's death. Even Edgar Cayce predicted that a future president, after FDR, would not survive his term in office, a prophecy that aptly applied to President Kennedy's fate.

Another renowned psychic who predicted President Kennedy's murder was trance-medium Arthur Ford, whose controversial séance to receive messages from the spirit of the late magician Houdini is still being debated. In 1962, at a séance attended by U.S. senator McClellan of Arkansas, Ford experienced a vision that Kennedy would be assassinated. Ford also foresaw Lyndon Johnson's presidential win in 1964.

Five years after JFK's assassination, Dixon experienced visions that Senator Robert Kennedy would suffer the same fate as his brother. She told friends that he, too, would be assassinated, but that it wasn't completely predetermined. She felt that, unlike John Kennedy, Bobby's life could be saved if he was cautioned in advance. Brian reported that Jeane Dixon did everything humanly possible to forewarn RFK by contacting anyone who had access to him. Although she did get a personal message to Bobby Kennedy, it was apparently ignored, and history, again, proved her warnings to have been accurate.

On several earlier occasions, she'd predicted that RFK would not become president, and each time Dixon was asked, she gave virtually the same answer, "He will never become President of the United States." In early 1968, Dixon also foretold the murder of the Reverend Martin Luther King, Jr., and added the warning, "Robert Kennedy will be next." But Jeane Dixon was not the only one to predict Robert Kennedy's fate. Prior to his murder, an organization called the British Premonitions Bureau was sent four precise predictions foretelling the assassination.

RFK's death was foretold by other seers as well. *We Don't Die*, for example, told the story of America's most gifted psychic-medium, George Anderson, who when he was eleven was enveloped by a sense of dread shortly before President Kennedy was assassinated. He experienced the same feeling just prior to the murders of Martin Luther King, Jr., and Robert Kennedy. In 1980, he also warned of danger to President Ronald Reagan. In March 1981, shortly after Anderson's prediction, Reagan survived an assassination attempt.

On May 28, 1968, Dixon attended a conference at the Ambassador Hotel in Los Angeles and repeated her prediction that Bobby Kennedy would be assassinated. One week later, on June 5, he was murdered in that same hotel on the night of his California presidential primary victory. Without doubt, the course of American history had been altered by the tragedy, just as John Kennedy's murder unquestionably changed the direction of the country.

Jeane Dixon's career stretched successfully on for the next thirty years until her death in 1997 from a heart attack. Despite ongoing skepticism and criticism, she continued to advise people in power, taking on and ultimately confounding her critics, and later used her psychic and astrological skills to advise First Lady Nancy Reagan.

Other Prognostications and Curses

Jeane Dixon made her living as a psychic and author. But not all forewarnings come from professional psychics or seers. A clinical psychologist who asked the authors not to use his name said that during World War II, his mother had a fascination with the Ouija board. One day in 1944, she and a friend were startled when the board spelled out that President Franklin Roosevelt would soon die in office. Sometimes it's not uncommon for what some people might call "random psychic messages" to turn up on a person's Ouija board or even in a dream. It's as if the energy ripples from an event that has either just taken place or will occur in the immediate future are so strong that, like waves traveling across the ocean of the time continuum, they intrude upon the psychic awarenesses of individuals who just happen to be tuning in at that moment. This is the power and fascination of the occult.

The Nazis also took a keen interest in the study of the paranormal even before they came to power. During World War II, they employed seers to help them discern the outcome of future events. Hitler, himself a strong believer in the occult and a follower of the Abraxis Society, employed mediums and astrologers until they foresaw Germany's inevitable defeat. John Toland, author of a critically acclaimed biography of Hitler, said the Nazi dictator also claimed to have possessed personal "occult powers," including clairvoyance. When British prime minister Winston Churchill discovered Hitler's use of a personal astrologer for "making military decisions," Churchill also engaged astrologers to forecast Hitler's strategies. According to author Craig Hamilton-Parker, Churchill "believed in destiny and that an invisible power guided his life." Looking at the evidence of what happened during World War II and how much the world leaders of the Allies and the Axis had relied on a belief in the occult, one wonders whether much of what happened might have been mapped out and predicted long before the events occurred. Could World War II and the death and destruction have been prevented?

Modern Curses and Prophecies of Doom

The stories of how curses of doom might have influenced the U.S. presidency continue right through to the present. For example, the story of President Jimmy Carter, a deeply religious man who fought for human rights all over the world, and Haitian dictator François ("Papa Doc") Duvalier is instructive. Papa Doc was furious with President Jimmy Carter whose anti-Duvalier policies threatened to erode the dictator's power over the island. It was no secret to the Haitian people that Papa Doc never hesitated to summon the "darker side of voodoo" as a means of maintaining tyrannical control over his impoverished nation. In fact, Papa Doc was himself a "houngan," a high priest of voodoo, the Haitian religion that mixes magical practices and Catholicism. To influence Carter's fate by placing a curse on him, an enraged Duvalier invoked chants and engaged in the rituals of black magic.

Did the hex against President Carter alter his destiny? Consider that soon after Papa Doc's evil invocation, Carter's presidency took some unexpected and unfortunate turns. Fifty-two Americans were taken hostage in Iran, and Carter proved unable to secure their release. The nation's economy was in trouble as inflation and interest rates soared. There was even a gas shortage that for a few desperate weeks caused long gas lines at gas station pumps all across the country. Carter's popularity plummeted as the American economy seemed to collapse before his very eyes. Even Carter's desperate top-secret attempt to free the hostages by force ended up in flames in the Iranian desert, lost amid confusion and, what some would later say, was a compromise in security.

In 1980, Jimmy Carter, the first president ever to promise that he would tell the truth about UFOs to the

American public, was defeated for reelection by Ronald Reagan, who also tried to warn Americans about UFOs. Was this the result of the Duvalier curse or the set-up and actual conspiracy of soon-to-be vice president and later president George H. W. Bush, as Gary Slick has suggested in his book *October Surprise?* Bush, a former CIA director, was well-connected within the American intelligence community and, some have said, peripherally involved in the Kennedy assassination, as well as more directly involved in the Iran-Contra conspiracy during the Reagan administration years later. Bush was no stranger to conspiracy, nor was his father, Senator Prescott Bush, who, with his father-in-law George Herbert Walker, had his property seized on October 20, 1942, by President Franklin Roosevelt's Alien Property Custodian, Leo T. Crowley, in Vesting Order Number 248 under the Trading with Enemy Act. The order had to do with the involvement of Senator Bush and George Herbert Walker with the Union Banking Corporation, which was run by the "Thyssen family" of "Germany and/or Hungary"—"nationals . . . of a designated enemy country." Prescott Bush was one of the directors of the UBC, which was run for the Thyssen family, who had helped to finance Germany's rearmament. In his book, Fritz Thyssen had bragged that he was "Hitler's banker."

The Kennedy Curse

Perhaps no presidential curse is more talked about than the curse on the Kennedy family, which began in the Middle Ages and continues to this very day. When President John F. Kennedy was assassinated in November 1963, his grief-stricken brother Robert wailed in agony, "Why, God?"

Why, indeed, has so much tragedy haunted America's most famous political dynasty? On the first anniversary of the 1999 death of John Kennedy, Jr., in a plane crash, a History Channel TV documentary asked, "Did the gods conspire against the Kennedys?" Was the Kennedy family afflicted with a terrible curse that originated centuries ago and destined their tragic fates? Are recent generations of Kennedys still repaying the karma of their forefathers' transgressions?

The infamous "Kennedy curse" was believed to have originated in Ireland sometime during the Middle Ages—the result of a bitter dispute between Kennedy ancestors and an individual so incensed at being wronged in a transaction that he made a terrible prediction in the form of a curse, which ordained that male members of the Kennedy family would meet ill-fated deaths and tragedies in future generations. For those skeptical of such supernatural afflictions, consider the disproportionate—and unnatural—calamities that have befallen Kennedy family members. In recent years, no less than fifteen tragedies have struck. Earlier generations of Kennedys also met with an unusual number of tragic and inexplicable deaths.

The Kennedys' rise to fame, fortune, and political influence has been recounted many times and is the subject of a number of books, including the excellent *The Kennedys: Dynasty and Disaster* by John Davis. Joseph Kennedy, Sr., married wealthy and pretty Rose Fitzgerald, daughter of a colorful and powerful Boston mayor and machine politician nicknamed "Honey Fitz." Joe, Sr., a charmer who loved the company of beautiful women, consorted with notorious underworld characters like Murder, Inc.'s Meyer Lansky and Sam Giancana and was not above cheating to get where he wanted. He believed he could buy anything and anyone. "Everything has a price," he declared.

With money he stashed away from the profits of bootlegged liquor he smuggled in from Canada with partners Meyer Lansky, Benny Siegel, and Charlie Luciano, and with some smart Wall Street investing, Joe, Sr., amassed his fortune, then invested in commercial real estate and other businesses. With wealth and the influence of the politically powerful and well-connected Fitzgeralds came the prominence and influence Joe craved, including an appointment as the U.S. ambassador to England. However, as Europe girded itself for war, Joe Kennedy favored appeasing Hitler and strongly advised the Roosevelt administration not only to stay out of the war but also, if necessary, to become an ally of Nazi Germany.

Joe, Sr., was not alone in his insistence that the United States had no business going to war with Germany. He was part of an immensely powerful Wall Street clique, actually popular among powerful American industrialists during the 1930s, which believed Hitler was the best defense against the worldwide Communist conspiracy led by Joseph Stalin. This group of industrialists, bankers, and international investors—including Pierre DuPont; Henry Ford; E. Roland Harriman and his investment firm Brown Brothers Harriman; UBC banker and author of *I Paid Hitler,* Fritz Thyssen; brothers John Foster Dulles and Allen Dulles and their law firm Cromwell and Sullivan; and George Herbert Walker and his son-in-law, and President George W. Bush's grandfather, Senator Prescott Bush from Connecticut—had helped finance and facilitate the reindustrialization and rearmament of Germany and then sought to keep the United States out of World War II. All this lobbying took place even as the *Wehrmacht* marched across Europe, invaded France, unleashed the most intense aerial terror bombing in history against the civilian populations of British cities, and carried out an ongoing continent-wide campaign of genocide unparalleled in human history. For more than two years, as Europe pleaded for help against the Nazi menace, Kennedy, Bush, and the other industrialists along with their allies in Congress forced Roosevelt to keep the United States neutral. It was no surprise, therefore, that after the Japanese attack on Pearl Harbor and Germany's declaration of war against the United States, Joe Kennedy's political aspirations simply evaporated.

Does a child pay for the sins of the father? Joe, Sr., and Rose Kennedy's nine children were fated to pay karmic debts accumulated by their ancestors over the centuries. The Kennedy family had been gripped by a disastrous and unrelenting curse that systematically played itself out on successive generations of Joe, Sr.'s children and their children's children, continuing to this very day.

First there was Joe, Jr., the shining star of the family, in whom the elder Kennedy had resided all his hopes for the Kennedy dynasty to rise to the U.S. presidency. But it was not to be. In 1944, twenty-nine-year-old Joseph Kennedy, Jr., while flying a military mission in World War II, was killed when his bomber mysteriously exploded over the English Channel. With his tragic death, the legacy Joe, Sr., sought would have to be fulfilled by his second son, the dashing and handsome John Fitzgerald, who was carving out his own heroic legend as a fearless navy lieutenant commanding PT 109 in the South Pacific.

In 1941, Kennedy's daughter Rosemary, mentally underdeveloped, was hospitalized, during which stay Joe, Sr., ordered her lobotomized, leaving her with the functional ability of a four year old and requiring that she be institutionalized for the rest of her life. In 1948, twenty-eight-year-old Kathleen was killed during a storm in a plane crash with her new husband of six weeks. He was her second husband. Her first husband had been killed only four months after the couple married.

Now it was John F. Kennedy's turn. The politically gifted JFK had staged a dramatic rise to power from his first election to the House of Representatives in 1948 and then as a U.S. senator from Massachusetts in 1952. After a masterful withdrawal from the balloting for the vice presidential nomination at the 1956 Democratic Convention and Adlai Stevenson's second loss to Eisenhower, Kennedy emerged as one of the leading candidates for the party's presidential nomination in 1960. With his father brokering deals and pulling strings—some of them very dangerous strings with his old acquaintances in organized crime families—JFK ran roughshod over Hubert Humphrey in the Democratic primaries and won the nomination on the first ballot. Then, running against Vice President Richard Nixon,

JFK reached the pinnacle of power, and his father's dream, when he was elected president in 1960, the first Roman Catholic and, at age forty-three, the youngest man ever to achieve the office. The next year, Joe, Sr., suffered a paralyzing stroke. In August 1963, First Lady Jacqueline Kennedy gave birth six weeks prematurely to a son, Patrick, who died just two days later. JFK was now at the center of the family's curse and with his enemies all around him, including his own vice president.

It was then, in November 1963, that a history-changing crisis struck when the first successful coup d'état in U.S. history was carried out by a highly organized conspiracy of JFK's enemies. This group of like-minded conspirators included:

1. The CIA, whose protection of drug lords in the Southeast Asian golden triangle had come to JFK's attention via his brother Robert, who brought him secret Senate Judiciary Committee testimony about the CIA's activities—testimony subsequently declassified by Senator Strom Thurmond—and whose role in Southeast Asia was about to be terminated along with American military involvement in South Vietnam.

2. Members of organized crime families in Chicago under boss Sam Giancana, in New Orleans under Carlos Marcello, and in Miami under Santos Trafficante.

3. A group of powerful Texas businessmen, which may have included dissident members of the Cuban community still angry over JFK's refusal to back the Bay of Pigs invasion.

4. And perhaps even the Vice President of the United States himself, who was not only about to be thrown off the 1964 ticket by Jack and Bobby Kennedy but was in danger of going to jail as a result of the Bobby Baker scandal in the U.S. Senate.

Even Jackie Kennedy believed that Lyndon Johnson was either a member of the conspiracy before the fact or participated in it after the fact through his assembly of the Warren Commission. Jackie made these assertions during recording sessions with William Manchester, author of *The Death of a President*, but according to Manchester in a newspaper interview, the tapes were sealed by court order.

LBJ's own words, recorded on tape in the Oval Office days after his taking the oath of office in November 1963, and published for the first time in *Taking Charge* by Michael Beschloss, connect him to the conspiracy when, in a conversation with FBI Director J. Edgar Hoover, the two men share knowledge that there were actually two Lee Harvey Oswalds, a fact deliberately kept out of the investigation by the CIA and Allen Dulles. This was a conspiracy of mammoth proportions that left Lyndon Johnson not only sitting in the Oval Office but now responsible to those who plotted and carried out the assassination and who wanted the American military to pursue what President Johnson believed to be an unwinnable war in Vietnam.

The meticulous plans for the assassination and the subsequent cover-up were carried out with a terrible precision. With Lee Harvey Oswald set up by Texas right wingers, Dallas mob associate Jack Ruby ready to silence Oswald the moment the opportunity presented itself, and LBJ poised to control the investigation via a special commission, the operation was set into motion. While riding in a motorcade in Dallas, Texas, on November 22, 1963, President John Fitzgerald Kennedy was assassinated, the seventh president afflicted by the Indian prophecy, and a victim of the Kennedy curse. Perhaps even worse than the double-cursed assassination of Warren Harding, JFK was at the center of a triple curse. The first curse reached all the way across the Atlantic and into the twentieth century from the Middle Ages. The second came in the form of a death warrant pronounced by both the intelligence community and their allies in the Cosa Nostra as a result of broken promises made by Joe Kennedy, Sr., to Sam Giancana and JFK's proposed legislation to eliminate the paramilitary wing of the CIA so as to stop opium production in Southeast Asia. And the third curse was a deadly prophecy laid upon a modern president from the lips of a Native American shaman after the collapse of the Shawnee confederation of Indian tribes in the wake of Tecumseh's loss of the battle of Tippecanoe.

The curse of Tenskwatawa might have been satisfied for the next twenty years, but still the scourge upon the Kennedy family would not release its insidious hold. In June 1964, Senator Edward M. Kennedy of Massachusetts, JFK and Bobby's younger brother, was seriously injured in a plane crash that also killed an aide. Robert Kennedy remarked afterward, "Somebody up there doesn't like us."

After John was assassinated, Robert desperately attempted to make some meaning of the tragedy. *Newsweek* reported that Bobby ". . . read and reread sagas of Greek gods and mortals whose pride led them to tempt fate. When [he] read . . . from Aeschylus' *Agamemnon* it seemed as if he could feel, personally, the curse on the House of Atreus."

In June 1968, Robert Kennedy, on the wings of victory after his successful campaign in the California Democratic primary, was shot down in a corridor of the Ambassador Hotel in Los Angeles as he made his way from the ballroom to the kitchen. With Bobby's death, coming as it did only a few short months after the assassination of civil rights leader and anti-Vietnam war activist Dr. Martin Luther King, Jr., in Memphis, died the hopes of an entire generation for whom the war in Vietnam would linger on for the next five years. Years later, one of Bobby and Ethel Kennedy's ten children, Robert, Jr., admitted, "When Daddy died, there were some feeling [among certain family members] of 'What the hell, we're all marked by a curse.' "

Then, on July 18, 1969, tragedy struck Ted Kennedy again when he drove his car off a bridge on Chappaquiddick Island, Massachusetts. His aide, Mary Jo Kopechne, was killed in the accident. The resulting damage to Ted's presidential ambitions was fatal, and he became the first family member to publicly mention a "Kennedy curse." In speaking to the nation following the tragedy at Chappaquiddick, Ted attempted to explain what occurred there, and raised the question about "some awful curse that hangs over all the Kennedys." Does Ted Kennedy, one of the deans of the U.S. Senate, whose own campaign for president against incumbent Democrat Jimmy Carter in 1980 died before it really began, still believe in the power of the curse today, particularly after he officiated at the funeral of his nephew John F. Kennedy, Jr.?

In 1973, Bobby Kennedy's son Joseph ran his car off the road, and a passenger was permanently paralyzed in the accident. That same year, Ted's son Ted, Jr., had his right leg amputated, the result of bone cancer. In 1984, the late Robert's son David died of a drug overdose. The following year, Ted's son Patrick sought treatment for cocaine addiction.

Even Jackie Kennedy Onassis suspected a curse on the family, an uncomfortable feeling, which she admitted she could not dismiss. In fact, when her second husband, Greek shipping magnate Aristotle Onassis, lost his son in a plane crash, he also blamed the Kennedy curse.

In 1991, Ted Kennedy's nephew William Kennedy Smith was charged with raping a woman at the Kennedy's Palm Beach estate. Smith was acquitted later that year, amid a torrent of embarrassing tabloid headlines and media attention. Currently William Smith is exploring a run for a seat in the House of Representatives.

In 1997, another son of Senator Robert Kennedy, thirty-nine-year-old Michael, was accused of having an affair with a fourteen-year-old baby-sitter. The scandal forced Michael to relinquish plans to run for Congress in the district his late uncle John once served. Then, on New Year's Eve, that same year, Michael was killed in a tragic skiing accident in Colorado when he crashed headlong into a tree at dusk during a family football game on the icy slopes.

In July 1999, the family—and the nation—were stunned once again as another highly visible young Kennedy met a tragic and untimely death. *George* magazine publisher John F. Kennedy, Jr., the popular thirty-eight-year-old son of the late president, was killed, along with his wife, Carolyn Bessette Kennedy, and her sister, Lauren, when the private plane John, Jr., was piloting crashed off Martha's Vineyard, Massachusetts. Ironically, John, Jr., was wearing his late uncle Joe's World War II military insignia at the time, and in another strange synchronicity, his plane crashed into the Atlantic Ocean the same weekend that marked the thirtieth anniversary of his uncle Ted's automobile accident on Chappaquiddick.

In *The Day John Died*, author Christopher Anderson said, "Jackie had a recurring premonition that John would be killed piloting his own plane. She pleaded with Maurice [Tempelsman, her longtime companion] to do whatever it took to keep John from becoming a pilot." Jackie had also revealed to friends that thirty-six years earlier she'd had another premonition, this time in a waking dream state, when she actually saw her husband covered with blood while riding in a car.

The major media has long since taken note of the curse. A *New York Post* story titled "Carolyn's Terrible Premonition," reported that John, Jr.'s wife, Carolyn, on the day before her death, experienced ". . . a frightening sense of foreboding."

CBS television anchorman Dan Rather acknowledged "the alleged Kennedy curse" when he reported John, Jr.'s death. *U. S. News & World Report* ran a July 26, 1999, cover story titled "The Kennedy Curse." In 1998, after Michael's death, *Newsweek* wrote of "The Camelot Curse." Four years earlier, the magazine had called the Kennedy family "a star-crossed dynasty." Michael, once reflecting on Bobby Kennedy's death, commented grimly, "It was as if fate had turned against us. There was a pattern that could not be ignored." And nearly a year after John, Jr.'s death, the FBI finally released documents that revealed he had been "the target of . . . at least three kidnapping threats between 1972 and 1995."

Will the curse ever relinquish its terrible hold on the Kennedys? Not every tragedy can be foretold, so we are left to wonder who the Kennedy curse will strike next. Many experts suggest that prayer can offer protection from an evil affliction. Only time will tell if the tragic fates visited on Kennedy family members in the past can be broken in the future.

CHAPTER FIVE

Ghosts of Presidents Past

Be sure you're right. Then go ahead.
—Davy Crockett

Although the Executive Mansion itself is the most intensely populated location in Washington, as far as presidential apparitions are concerned, it isn't the only place where witnesses have spotted the ghosts of presidents past. Spirits may revisit any location with which they were either familiar or had an emotional connection in this physical world. Accordingly, presidential ghosts have been seen at places other than the White House, such as public buildings, monuments, and even their birthplaces in different parts of the country. Thomas Jefferson roams Monticello, Teddy Roosevelt's image can be seen floating in the window of his Long Island mansion, and Richard Nixon's ghost haunts his Yorba Linda birthplace. Why have the ghosts of presidents reappeared and what binds them to specific places? Maybe it all has to do with unfinished business here on earth that forces spirits to linger on centuries after they've passed.

John Adams

The White House was still a work in progress when John and Abigail Adams became the first residents, on

November 17, 1800, of the new President's House, as it was then called. Adams, a prominent Boston attorney, had been George Washington's vice president and had proven himself a fierce patriot for the cause of American independence. But patriot or not, he and his wife were just like any family of today when they first pulled up to their brand-new home.

First Lady Abigail Adams was appalled at the ongoing construction site that greeted her when her carriage rolled to a stop at the front door of what was supposed to have been a fully completed executive mansion. Abigail, used to the finer things in life, found the unfinished building cavernous, dank, chilly, and remarkably uncomfortable. Technically, the builders told them, the mansion was ready to be occupied, but in reality, it was far from live-in condition because only about half of the building was completed and construction materials lay everywhere, even in the front yard. Yet here is where Abigail was expected to perform her duties as first lady and the official hostess of the new republic.

The Adamses' front door opened onto Pennsylvania Avenue, itself a far cry from today's busy thoroughfare. In 1800, it was really little more than a muddy, unpaved road, like most of the streets in the young nation's new capital city, which were, in truth, barely passable foot and cow paths. And when it rained, which it does quite a bit in Washington, the paths turned into marshy wetlands through which only horse-drawn carriages could travel. In fact, Washington, D.C., then called Federal City, was actually a small village of only a few thousand people built in the swampy wilderness along the Potomac River flood plain at the border of Maryland and Virginia.

The Adamses were only moving into the White House for the sole purpose of completing the final six months of his term, although President Adams didn't know it at the time (since he expected to be reelected). For the first 3.5 years of his administration, the rotund Adams and his tall, slender wife lived in a well-appointed residence in Philadelphia, the temporary capital of the

United States. During the summer of 1800, Abigail remained at the couple's comfortable home in Quincy, Massachusetts, known then as Braintree. John, meanwhile, had been in Federal City since June. He very much wanted his wife to join him as soon as the presidential home was habitable and after the oppressive summer heat and humidity eased.

Abigail made the long journey by coach from Massachusetts, eager to join her husband by November 1800. Her last rest stop before arriving at her new home was stately Montpelier Mansion in Maryland, just outside Federal City, where her husband and other prominent American political figures often visited. Abigail Adams described Montpelier as "a large, handsome, elegant house, where I was received with what we might term English hospitality." Built in 1783, the mansion played host to several of the Founding Fathers, including Washington, Adams, and Jefferson. The gracious congeniality of the owners, Major Thomas Snowden and his wife, made the attractive estate a frequent stop for many dignitaries of the day. Therefore, imagine Abigail's shock when she moved into the new presidential mansion, which had only six livable rooms, all poorly heated, none complete, with two of them set aside for presidential offices.

John and Abigail Adams shared the discomforts of the chilly and damp mansion for less than four months. Then the vain, aloof, and cautious John Adams left office in March 1801, a bitter man, after serving a single term as president before being voted out of office in a hotly contested election against Thomas Jefferson. But even though the second first family moved out of the White House, Abigail returned. Nearly a hundred years after her passing, Abigail Adams's ghost remembered her difficult experiences in the White House and came back to haunt the now-completed mansion during the administration of William Howard Taft.

Thomas Jefferson

Thomas Jefferson, our third president, had defeated the unpopular Adams for reelection in 1800. The animosity between the two men was so great that Adams refused to participate in Jefferson's inauguration. Their political differences were vast and their relationship, during the administration of President Washington when Adams was vice president and Jefferson was a member of the Cabinet, was tenuous at best.

Tall, slim, and sophisticated with striking red hair, Thomas Jefferson was a man of extraordinary intelligence and enormous curiosity, interested in a wide range of subjects: agriculture, architecture, history, music, political philosophy, religion, and science. In only a few days when he was just thirty-three years old, Jefferson wrote the Declaration of Independence, the document that charted the course for American independence and has remained a principal statement of the rights of individuals for 225 years.

Jefferson was not yet forty, in 1782, when his cherished wife, Martha, still quite young at thirty-three, died after childbirth. Afterward, a grief-stricken Jefferson wrote, "I rested all prospects of future happiness on domestic and literary objects. A single event wiped away all my plans and left a blank which I had not the spirits to fill up." He vowed never to marry again. But he went on to serve President Washington as the new nation's first secretary of state, in which post he became one of Washington's most trusted advisors. During the Washington administration, Jefferson and Vice President Adams competed for influence in the new government and their personal rivalry flared when Jefferson ran against the incumbent Adams and defeated him. After two successful terms as president, Jefferson returned in 1809 to his handsome home at Monticello, Virginia, which he had designed and built, and where he devoted his time to reading, writing, and farming.

Once Jefferson and his predecessor John Adams both retired from public life, they mended their political differences and began a remarkable correspondence, exchanging countless letters and becoming the closest of friends. The communications were often deeply personal and even included each man's religious ideas and concepts. The letters between Adams and Jefferson are regarded as among the most "interesting and intelligently written correspondences in American history" and have been combed over by hundreds of scholars, each more impressed than his predecessor by the intensity of the personal feelings each former president had for the other.

Jefferson was a spiritualist who shunned the dogma of specific religions because he thought them too limiting. However, although Jefferson never identified a religious denomination to which he could subscribe, he did believe in the afterlife. He reminded Adams in a series of letters that they not forget that soon both would depart their earthly bodies and "ascend in essence to an ecstatic meeting with the friends we have loved and lost and would never lose again." John Adams answered his friend, "I do not know how to prove physically that we shall meet and know each other in a future state. . . . My reasons for believing it, as I do most undoubtedly, are that I cannot conceive such a being [as God] could make such a species as the human merely to live and die on this earth. And if there is a future state, why should the Almighty dissolve forever all the spiritual dendrites which unite us so delightfully in this world and forbid us to see each other in the next?" Clearly, both former presidents had faith in a life after death, and the relationship between them endured in the hereafter, for each reappeared as an apparition.

One location where the spirits of Washington, Adams, and Jefferson have been seen is the lovely Montpelier Mansion. Witnesses reported that the presidential apparitions of Jefferson and Adams returned to Montpelier, sometimes together, still brothers in spirit. Those who've seen their ghostly countenances described them as cordial to each other, dressed in Colonial finery and sporting hairstyles of the period, and apparently oblivious to the living around them. So entwined were their lives and careers with the founding of the United States, it is no surprise this duo of famed American patriots remained friends on the Other Side, and materialized in a place they especially enjoyed and shared on earth.

Nor has Thomas Jefferson forgotten his years in the White House, for his spirit has been witnessed there, too. Jefferson had called the presidency "a splendid misery." Nonetheless his ghost returned to the Yellow Oval Room on the second floor of the White House, adjacent to the Lincoln Bedroom. As Mary Todd Lincoln, who moved into the White House fifty-five years later, once told a friend, "My, my, how that Mr. Jefferson does play the violin."

Indeed, it was in the Yellow Oval Room that President Jefferson years earlier received guests and relaxed with a favorite pastime, playing violin, an instrument at which he was quite accomplished. Mrs. Lincoln, an avowed spiritualist and quite sensitive to paranormal events, was certain she psychically detected Thomas Jefferson's spirit still enjoying his violin, just as he had from the time he was a young attorney when he and fellow patriot Patrick Henry played duets during the heady days during which the Virginia colony rose against the Crown. Ironically, Jefferson's spirit returned to that same Yellow Oval Room, which he favored when he was president, and a room with a commanding view of Washington, D.C., including the dome of the Jefferson Memorial beyond the famed Japanese cherry blossom trees. One can only speculate what Thomas Jefferson's spirit thought in recent years if he revisited and peered at the monument built in his honor, in one of his favorite styles of classic architecture.

James Monroe

Fredericksburg, Virginia, a charming city, has a rich history of haunted houses, many dating back to the earliest days of Colonial America. Spirits or ghosts are said to appear in almost every structure, one of which is the building that housed the law office of James Monroe, our fifth president, elected in 1816.

The tall, gaunt Monroe had studied law under Thomas Jefferson, already an attorney and Governor of Virginia at the time. The two quickly became close friends. The elder Jefferson advised Monroe throughout his life and career, and Jefferson appointed Monroe to several notable diplomatic assignments.

In the late 1960s, the specters of both Jefferson and Monroe, dressed in Colonial garb, were witnessed as they entered Monroe's old law office, where he practiced from 1786 to 1789. The apparitions occurred at a time when a sizable crack appeared in the building's front door. Perhaps the two close friends returned to earth concerned about Monroe's former office, or their apparitions reappeared for the same reason people on earth visit places that hold fond memories or reminiscences.

Carter's Grove Plantation

Can unrequited love play a role in the return of a presidential ghost? Near Newport News, Virginia, is a beautiful mansion called Carter's Grove Plantation, where the restless spirits of two presidents, George Washington and Thomas Jefferson, have materialized. On the downstairs floor of the mansion is a drawing room. There, in the mid-1700s, an attractive young woman named Mary Cary received a bouquet of white carnations and a marriage proposal from an eager young officer named George Washington, but Mary rejected his hand. Years later, in that very same room, a young woman named Rebecca Burwell turned down an offer of marriage from none other than Thomas Jefferson. Thus the room was dubbed the "refusal room," where inexplicable paranormal occurrences later became manifest.

The most curious phenomenon in the refusal room has been witnessed sightings of white carnations torn into small pieces and thrown about the floor, always at night. No other flowers are found on the floor, only the petals of white carnations. Flowers elsewhere in the house are never disturbed. A nationally reported news story in 1939 quoted the owner of Carter's Grove confirming that "something" occurred in that room late at night to "blight her blooms." Tour guides in the house also admitted finding torn petals of white carnations strewn about the room.

One explanation is that the ghost who tore the petals was one of the young women who later realized she had turned down someone who achieved great fame and fortune. Spirits will sometimes cling to earthly discontents or regrets. Thus it is not unheard of for an angry ghost to make its presence known on this plane by causing destruction or mischief as a poltergeist or by manifesting psychokinetic energy. Perhaps that is why some think Mary Cary's unhappy specter returned to vent displeasure for rejecting George Washington's bouquet and his marriage proposal. How different a turn her life would have taken had she accepted his offer to wed and one day become the First Lady of the United States.

Or could the ghosts of the two rejected suitors, George Washington and Thomas Jefferson, be responsible for mysteriously tearing the carnations even though both men had been happily married during their lifetimes? It is possible their spirits returned to earth because of frustration or pique after being spurned by the pretty young women they once wished to marry.

James Madison

The administration of President James Madison, who succeeded Thomas Jefferson in 1809, became mired in a dispute with the British over American shipping rights, which Britain had openly violated on the high seas by boarding American vessels and impressing seamen they selected—whom they claimed were British deserters—into the British Navy. When an ultimatum to the British failed, Madison asked Congress for a declaration of war, and the growing conflict became known as the War of 1812. This was a rash war for the United States to have entered into and, as might be expected, went very badly for the United States both at sea and on land. The U.S. Navy was no match for the British and couldn't protect the Atlantic coast. Consequently, in August 1814, American forces couldn't protect Chesapeake Bay from an invading British force, which sailed up the Potomac to Washington, D.C. On August 24, the British force overpowered the ill-prepared and outnumbered Americans, captured the city, and forced many government officials to flee. President and Mrs. Madison also made preparations to leave.

British troops quickly set the Capitol on fire, as well as other government buildings. Next they torched the White House. President Madison, who had personally taken charge of some of the American militia, watched in horror from a distance as flames lit the night sky in what proved to be one of America's most embarrassing military defeats. Only rain and the eventual withdrawal by the British troops, who had no plans to occupy the United States capital for any great length of time, prevented further destruction to the defenseless city.

First Lady Dolley Madison had been left in charge of the presidential mansion, where some of the nation's most valuable documents, including the original drafts of the Constitution and the Declaration of Independence, were stored. With remarkable presence of mind and courage, Dolley fled the White House, saving the priceless papers as well as a portrait of George Washington by the well-known artist Gilbert Stuart. She even managed to carry her pet parrot to safety.

Dolley Madison was safe from the conflagration. However, the presidential home, its furnishings, and other contents were lost, victims of the British torching, and the mansion's interior was completely ruined. All that remained was the exterior of the building. Nothing more than a shell was left standing, and the Madisons were unable to return to the White House.

While the British occupied the capital, the Madisons were invited to reside in a mansion in the city known as the Octagon House, built by Colonel John Tayloe, a wealthy Virginian and friend of George Washington. The residence had been spared by the British because it flew the French flag. It became a temporary White House until the original could be reconstructed. Years later the Octagon became the site of several notable and legendary hauntings, many involving members of the Tayloe family who met with tragedy.

Despite its name, indicating eight sides, the Octagon was actually a six-sided house. Inside the three-story mansion, a stately spiral staircase wound its way from a downstairs rotunda to the third floor of the house. That staircase has been the location of several apparitions. Other inexplicable supernatural occurrences have been reported elsewhere in the house, even in recent years. Tourists, visitors, and employees in the Octagon were among the many witnesses to the ghostly sightings, which have been reported since the mid-1800s.

One night in the 1950s, Octagon House caretaker, James Cyprus, called a doctor for his wife, who had been taken ill. After treating the woman, the physician asked the caretaker a peculiar question. The doctor wanted to know if a costume party was under way. No, Cyprus answered, puzzled at the query. The doctor explained he had just seen a man on the staircase costumed in the style of the early 1800s. In fact, the doctor said, he had to move to one side of the stairs in order to allow the man in nineteenth-century attire to pass by.

It is likely the physician witnessed the apparition of the diminutive President James Madison, whose spirit materialized in the Octagon many years after he departed this earth in 1836 at the age of eighty-five. Perhaps his ghost returned to visit the building that had been the temporary White House, the location of intense activity and excitement in his life at a tumultuous and unsettling time in American history. It was in the Octagon that Madison signed the Treaty of Ghent, which ended the War of 1812, and it had also been the scene of many extravagant parties hosted by First Lady Dolley Madison.

Dolley Madison also returned as a spirit. In the years after her death, Mrs. Madison's ghost was witnessed in several locations, once in very dramatic fashion on the grounds of the White House when Woodrow Wilson was in office.

In the late-nineteenth century, long after the Madisons both passed on, there were newspaper reports of apparitions of footmen dressed in early 1800s uniforms, flagging down carriages of guests who attended the Madisons' Octagon parties. Witnesses also told of hearing the noises of carriage wheels bumping along stone roads, doors of ghost carriages opening and closing, and horse-drawn coaches driving away. Perhaps the phantom footmen materialized to recall a long-gone era when the Octagon, serving as the Executive Mansion, was at the pinnacle of Washington society.

Spirits often assume the physical characteristics by which they can be recognized when they return to earth. Once on the Other Side, a spirit form sheds the physical being. If a spirit wishes to be seen, it must materialize in a way that can be identified by the living, such as by facial features and some distinctive characteristic, especially clothing or hairstyle from the time or era he or she lived in. The ghosts of the Madisons and their guests haunting the Washington buildings where they celebrated in life are no exception.

Andrew Jackson

Andrew Jackson was one of our country's most colorful presidents. He had a keen sense of intuition and often let his instincts guide him in making decisions. Many experts regard intuition as a form of psychic ability. Was Jackson psychic? Given his uncanny military skills during the War of 1812, when he assembled a coalition of the most improbable allies to fight the British at the Battle of New Orleans, it almost seemed as though he could read people's minds. In combination with his natural political survival skills during a period when our nation was experiencing its first growing pains, his ability to outwit his political adversaries inside his own party, and his ability to marshal his allies to work for him, people believed he really must have been psychic. But Jackson was also destined to have several significant paranormal experiences before he entered the White House, particularly his encounter with the infamous Bell Witch of Tennessee.

Old Hickory and the Bell Witch

Adams is a tiny town on the banks of the Red River in north-central Tennessee. In 1817, it was home to a wealthy farmer, John Bell, his wife, Lucy, and their children. The Bells were God-fearing people, well-liked and respected in the small Baptist community, where they lived comfortably on their thousand-acre farm in the peace and prosperity that followed the Treaty of Ghent that ended the War of 1812.

One especially hot summer day in 1817 as Bell walked through his cornfield, rifle in hand to warn off wild animals, he was stopped short by the sight of a strange creature that he first mistook for a dog. However, after a closer look, he realized that he'd never seen anything like it before. The animal just sat there motionless and calmly stared at him. When the farmer gazed at the creature's face, he was taken by its unusual, almost human-looking eyes. Slowly, he raised his rifle ready to shoot the beast before it could attack him. Then, unbelievably, the strange creature began to dim until it disappeared. There wasn't so much as a single animal track remaining on the ground after the creature dematerialized. Bell was incredulous. However, despite the disturbing nature of the incident, he decided not to tell his family so as not to alarm them.

Several days later, Bell cautiously returned to his cornfield, and warily searched the area where he'd earlier encountered the odd creature. To his relief, it was gone. Suddenly Bell caught sight of a large bird perched on a split-rail fence. He stared in astonishment at the gigantic fowl. It wasn't a crow after his crops. It wasn't a hawk after his chickens. And it wasn't a bird of prey after downed carrion. He'd never seen a bird that size before. Bell realized the bird's strange eyes were identical to those of the bizarre-looking animal he'd witnessed days earlier. Frightened, he wasted no time bringing his rifle to bear and firing a round at the horrifying creature. The shot missed. Instantly the bird spread its massive wings and flew overhead, casting an enormous shadow on the ground below as Bell shivered in terror.

Never again, from that moment, did the Bell family have any peace. For the next three years, they were haunted and cursed by a sinister and demonic spirit, an evil force that came to be known popularly as the Bell Witch. Actually, its behavior suggested that it was not a witch at all, but rather a poltergeist or noisy spirit, capable of moving objects and people, even sending them flying. However, unlike most benign or only marginally mischievous poltergeists, the Bell Witch proved to be an angry and dangerous force.

Shortly after the encounters in the cornfield, the Bells heard outside their home an inexplicable noise that sounded as if an animal were scratching at the door. Then the noise grew louder. Someone, or something, was banging on the doors and windows, causing a horrible fright. The Bells typically went to bed nightly at nine o'clock, but every night at about ten an incessant thumping commenced. When Bell sleepily made his way to the door and opened it, the terrible banging ceased, but it resumed when he returned to bed. Usually it ended around midnight. Not surprisingly, the Bells became frazzled.

One day, the inexplicable noises moved indoors. It sounded as if hundreds of little animals were scratching on every surface of the house. There was no wall or floor free from the vexing and ceaseless noise of whatever invisible force was responsible for the nerve-racking clatter. Sometimes it sounded as if rodents were gnawing; other times there were choking noises, and the sound of lips smacking. Family members heard chains being dragged, furniture moved about, and invisible stones pelted at the roof. Might it have been the work of a prankster bent on mischief? Bell and his sons kept watch at night, but found no prowlers or anyone lurking about. Bell demanded that family members keep their supernatural experiences a secret, no matter how frightened or disturbed they were.

A year later, the events grew worse. The scratching noises were gone, but the entire house shook on its foundation as if struck by an earthquake. There were nights when the evil force tore covers from the beds as family members slept, striking terror into the children, who could not see the invisible forces pulling at the bedspreads. The Bell family found it increasingly difficult to live normal lives with the presence of this force in and about the house. Then, incredibly, the witch became even more aggressive and cruel. One night, something struck seven-year-old Williams Bell, and the child screamed in pain from blows by the unseen force. He later described the attack as if someone was trying to tear his head off.

The witch seemed angriest with thirteen-year-old Betsy Bell, the only daughter of the eight Bell children still living at home. At first, the poltergeist dragged the terrified child out of bed by her hair. Then the demonic entity cast spells on the pretty little girl, which sometimes lasted as long as thirty minutes. With each attack, Betsy momentarily lost her breath. The episodes became so severe that she gasped for air, then fainted. On other occasions, the invisible force smacked Betsy's face hard enough that red marks mysteriously appeared where she'd been struck.

Finally the Bells realized they could not keep their encounters with the sinister being secret. Clearly they needed help, so Bell shared his family's troubles with a trusted friend and lay preacher, James Johnson. Johnson's concern for their safety and well-being increased after he also heard the unearthly noises with his own ears. This was no tall tale; it was a real demonic possession. His immediate advice was to call upon God's help, so he conducted an exorcism, read from the Bible, and commanded the evil entity, "Stop, I beseech you, in the name of the Lord!"

The exorcism appeared to work. Incredibly, for a time, the commotion stopped. Relieved that their home was peaceful once again, the Bells gave thanks to God. For the next several weeks, they savored the calm and quiet, free from the frightening and relentless tumult of the past year. The Bells assumed the witch was gone from their lives.

Unfortunately they were wrong. When the unseen entity returned, it was even more enraged. The Bells again called upon the preacher for assistance, and once more, the witch seemed to respond. It was as if the demonic spirit calmed when prayers were offered. However, the poltergeist soon resumed its incessant noises and assaults, particularly against young Betsy Bell. In one incredible incident, Betsy threw up after she drank a foul medicine given her to combat the witch's spells. The child's vomit contained sharp needles and pins. Mrs. Bell and the family's physician, who both witnessed the event, were appalled and repulsed. The witch, however, laughed and goaded Betsy to consume more of the putrid tonic so that she might retch again. Lucy Bell gathered the needles and pins, placed them in a closed glass jar, and kept them the remainder of her life.

The Bells' next plan of action was to organize a committee of local citizens to visit and witness the terrible incidents for themselves, and perhaps suggest a solution to free the family from their affliction. The disapproving witch grew even more incensed. And again, the attacks were stepped up, the harshest against Betsy. Eventually, fearing they were unable to protect their daughter, the Bells sent her to live with neighbors. However, wherever she went, the persistent spirit followed. There seemed no escape from the relentless being, who continued to also harass other family members, even as it tormented Betsy.

Eventually as news of the entity spread, the Bell house attracted the curious from throughout the region, who, not surprisingly, came in droves hoping to observe for themselves evidence of the witch. There were times when the spirit complied. One night it whistled and then began to speak in a whisper that became a low female voice. At first, the words were inaudible; then they became clearer. The entity even debated the Bible and scripture with visiting clergy, but when asked about its identity and purpose, the witch refused to answer. To be sure, there were skeptics, some of whom blamed Betsy, claiming the entity's voice was really manufactured by the child. Was Betsy capable of ventriloquism? When a visiting doctor placed his hand firmly over the child's mouth, the witch's utterings could still be discerned.

By the summer of 1820, the story reached all the way to Nashville and newspapers told of the family's troubles. One of those who heard about the witch was none other than General Andrew Jackson, hero of the Battle of New Orleans. Like many others, he was curious about the tale of the elusive and troublesome spirit. After defeating the Creek Indians, facing down the Seminoles, swapping tall tales with Colonel Davy Crockett, and driving the invading British through the briers and the brambles to the Gulf of Mexico, General Jackson thought himself well-equipped to face the Bells' witch.

Jackson, joined by several friends, one of them a self-proclaimed "witch-layer" or exorcist, set out on the forty-mile journey from the Hermitage to the Bell plantation to personally witness the bizarre events. Jackson, however, was initially on the side of the skeptics. The outspoken general wagered a gallon of "good Tennessee whiskey," insisting the witch did not even exist, let alone engage in the terrible acts of which it was accused. Jackson reasoned the entire story was either a hoax or a result of some perfectly rational and natural phenomena. Events soon challenged Old Hickory's opinion.

Jackson's wagon was within one mile of the Bell home when inexplicably its wheels locked. The wagon stopped dead in its tracks and would not move so much as an inch. The men attempted to get the wagon going again, but they could not budge it or force the horses to advance although the road was smooth and dry. Jackson even personally inspected the axle and wheels. The men again struggled to push the wagon, but it still refused to move. Jackson found the predicament amusing. "What else could it be but the Bells' witch?" he asked. Then the group was surprised by a female voice that seemingly came from nowhere. "I'm glad you understand, General. Now you can go on. I'll speak with you again tonight," the disembodied voice snickered.

Jackson immediately knew he'd heard the entity. "By the Eternal, boys, it's the witch!" he exclaimed. Then, as suddenly and incomprehensibly as the wagon wheels had frozen, they unlocked. Jackson and his band continued their ride to the Bell home, wondering if the witch would be waiting there as she promised.

John Bell played host to Jackson and his party that evening. The men sat around the fireplace talking, telling stories, and drinking rum, as they nervously anticipated the arrival of the witch. One especially brazen member of the group who fancied himself a witch slayer claimed he could rid the house of the noxious entity. To prove it, he took his pistol, loaded with a silver bullet—which, legend says, is one way to kill a witch, ghost, or devil—then screamed at the Bell Witch, demanding it show itself.

Jackson was unamused by his boastful crony. "I wish the spirit would appear to show this braggart's true colors," he declared. Moments later, the stunned group heard heavy footsteps, and a voice announced, "Here I am as promised, General, and ready for business."

Jackson and the others were speechless as the spectral voice turned to the boaster and declared, "And that business would be this bag of hot wind." The man fell silent. But the entity continued. "Here I am. Go on and shoot. I'll make it easy. Go on and shoot, for Christ's sake!" The others moved cautiously aside. The braggart pulled the trigger of his pistol, but the weapon wouldn't fire. "I can't wait forever. Try again. Hurry up!" the Bell Witch demanded. Once again, the gun refused to fire. "Now it's my turn," the entity angrily retorted.

Within the next moment, the boastful witch slayer was lifted off his feet by an invisible force, and as he fell, the unseen spirit slapped and dragged him by one leg, crashing him into furniture, walls, and dishes. Then the witch grabbed the horrified man by the nose, causing him to scream in pain. Amused by her accomplishment, she began laughing, and her eerie cackle filled the room. The man who'd experienced the unearthly wrath fled screaming in terror and never again returned to the Bells' house.

Jackson had watched the remarkable supernatural demonstration in rapt attention, and when it concluded, he laughed. "Double-dee-damned, that was the most fun I've had in my life. I'm glad I said nothing against the witch!" he exclaimed. "I vow I'd rather fight the entire British Army single-handed than face this witch."

The witch also chuckled. "I'm pleased to entertain you, General," she declared. "I'll wager this is the last we will see of that coward. But there is another in your company who is a fraud. I will attend to him tomorrow night, as the hour is getting late."

But the entity could not depart without a swipe at Rachel Jackson. The witch howled, "How's that fat old wife of yours? Think you'll ever get Rachel's swollen carcass into the White House?" A stunned Jackson claimed he felt the witch brush his chin. Then the evil being vanished into the night, leaving Jackson, who'd once shot and killed a man for insulting Rachel's name, angered by the unexpected and vulgar outburst.

Despite the spirit's promise, the next morning Jackson was convinced by his men to leave the Bell farm. Although several insisted the witch could not go beyond her chilling demonstration of the night before, likely they were frightened about what she might conjure next. Jackson appeared exhausted as he and his group departed and headed back to Nashville.

Curiously, in future years, Jackson said little if anything to others about his encounter with the witch. If he ever spoke publicly about facing the entity, there is no record. Nor did he ever again visit the Bell farm or urge others there. His last known words on the subject were: "I wish no more dealings with that torment."

After the personal display the general witnessed, it's conceivable that he did not doubt the witch's warning that it could wander anywhere it wished or taunt anyone it chose. In fact, the entity did visit others in Robertson County, Tennessee, from time to time, often spewing crude and obscene remarks. Despite his bravery in battle, perhaps Jackson did not want to chance becoming its next target. There is no question, however, that the visit to the Bell farm by the famed general added to the notoriety and veracity of the story. That Jackson, a respected national figure, witnessed the haunting added immensely to the credibility of the Bells' claims.

What eventually happened to the witch? Her malevolent and demented antics continued unabated. She especially despised John Bell, although curiously, she never bothered Mrs. Bell. The entity finally revealed itself to be someone named Kate Batts. There were various theories about who she might have been, but her identity was never determined with any certainty. Old Kate, as many called her, promised to haunt John Bell until he was "dead and buried."

In the autumn of 1820, John Bell took ill. He'd felt a strangeness in his mouth. Then his tongue stiffened and became badly swollen, and he was unable to speak or eat for hours at a time. He also developed an uncontrollable facial twitch. He knew the cause of his affliction. "This terrible thing, the witch, is killing me," he told his son.

Finally, on December 19, 1820, Bell lapsed into a coma, and the vindictive entity was ecstatic. "It's useless to try and revive Old Jack," the witch said. "I've got

him this time. He'll never get up from that bed again!"
She even bragged that she'd converted a tonic he was
prescribed into poison. When a cat was given a taste of
the medicine, the animal quickly dropped dead. The next
day, Bell died. The witch, who could not contain her joy,
was heard laughing and singing, even as family members
grieved and buried John Bell.

The Bell Witch pronounced her work done. She
threatened to reappear in future years, but one later
visit, in 1827, was brief, inconsequential, and largely ignored. However many Bell descendants met violent or
untimely deaths.

True to the behavior of most poltergeists, the "witch"
had centered her attention on a child, Betsy Bell. While
ghosts generally cling to a single location, poltergeists
are capable of attaching to a person or family, and they
even have the ability to move with them from one place
to another. Unlike ghosts, who often remain for years
in a familiar earthly haunt, poltergeists seem transient
and ultimately dissipate and leave.

Was young Betsy the "poltergeist agent" whose own
telekinetic energy caused the horrific activity in her family's home? Some researchers have theorized that Betsy,
under emotional stress, may have acted out a subconscious resentment of her father that manifested itself in
the form of psychic energy responsible for creating the
poltergeist's havoc. Skeptics blamed Betsy, accusing her
of fabricating the Bell Witch phenomena. However, no
one ever proved that and Betsy never again spoke of
her family's "troubles."

Once the Bell Witch left as mysteriously as it first
arrived, people were left to wonder why she'd so vehemently attacked the Bell family. No definitive answers
have ever been established. Although poltergeist phenomena have been reported since ancient times, the Bell
Witch holds the distinction of being the only poltergeist
to ever speak to—and kill—someone. Poltergeist activity
typically results in mischief, rather than serious harm.
The Bell Witch proved the exception to that rule. Andrew Jackson had been one of the best-known and most

credible witnesses to America's most infamous ghost story.

Eventually the Bell house was torn down. However, some believe the area remains haunted. There have been reports of "ghostly lights" where once the entity made her vengeful presence felt, and a cave on the former Bell property is said to be plagued by strange sounds of rattling chains, unearthly screams, and the sight of mysterious apparitions.

On U.S. Highway 41, a marker placed by the Tennessee Historical Commission briefly tells the story of the infamous haunting. Close by is a monument dedicated to the Bell family, the only official monument to a ghost in the United States.

Old Hickory in the White House

Following the Bell Witch incident, Andrew Jackson concentrated on his political ambitions. After a term in the U.S. Senate, he ran for president in 1824, but lost to John Quincy Adams—a one-term president like his father—after a hotly disputed contest in which Jackson won the popular vote, but lost in the House of Representatives as the result of back-room power brokering. However, in 1828, after a ruthless campaign filled with personal attacks and acrimony, Jackson won the election. Among the charges made during the bitter campaign were accusations about his marriage to Rachel, specifically the three years the legal status of the union was in question due to the unintentional oversight about her divorce. That was sufficient for Jackson's political enemies to malign Rachel's good name and accuse her of bigamy for marrying Andrew when technically she was still wed to her previous husband. Jackson, himself, was branded a liar and "wife stealer."

Rachel was a gentle, hospitable, and religious woman, and the vicious allegations so deeply shamed and humiliated her that she did not wish to be first lady. And the political slander exacted its toll on Rachel's health, emotionally and physically. On December 17, 1828, she suffered an apparent heart attack. Andrew kept vigil at her bedside. On December 22, only a little more than a month after he won the election, she collapsed and died at the age of sixty-one. Jackson was devastated by Rachel's death. They'd been happily married for nearly thirty-eight years. "Heaven will be no heaven to me if I do not meet my wife there," he lamented.

Several days after her funeral, Jackson, grief-stricken, visited her grave and cried, "She was murdered by slanders that pierced her heart! May God Almighty forgive her murderers as I know she forgave them. I never can." As far as he was concerned, Rachel had died of a broken heart. Despite his anguish, only ten weeks after Rachel's death, Jackson, gaunt, pale, and dressed entirely in black, was inaugurated our seventh president on March 4, 1829. Hot-tempered and as controversial as ever, Jackson ran for reelection in 1832 and won in a landslide.

In 1835, an unemployed, mentally disturbed house painter named Richard Lawrence attempted to shoot Jackson as he stepped outside the Capitol building, but the gun, a single-shot derringer, misfired. Jackson lunged at the would-be assassin with his cane when Lawrence suddenly pulled a second derringer and fired point-blank. Again the gun did not fire. Bystanders threw the man to the ground and held him for police.

Following the assassination attempt, the derringers were found to be in complete working order. Incredibly, the odds of two such guns consecutively failing to fire were estimated at 1 in 125,000, and many Americans interpreted Jackson's narrow brush with death as a sign of "divine protection." Jackson agreed with the mystical reasoning, and it added greatly to his stature and popularity.

Could a guardian angel or spirit have intervened on Jackson's behalf to block the shooting attempt by disengaging the gun's firing mechanism? Such PK, or psychokinetic, effects have been reported in paranormal research. Might it have been Rachel's spirit that acted to protect her husband?

His two terms in office took their toll on Jackson, who was tired, frail, and in failing health when he left office in 1837 to return home to the Hermitage in Tennessee. Now seventy, he'd never remarried and was in constant pain from old war injuries and a variety of ailments. "Death has no terror for me. I am ready to depart when called," he said. His dying wish was to again meet friends on the Other Side. On June 8, 1845, at the age of seventy-eight, with his family at his bedside, Andrew Jackson said, "Do not cry. Be good children, and we shall all meet in heaven." Then he left this world for the next to join his beloved Rachel.

The Ghost of Andrew Jackson

President Andrew Jackson's spirit first returned to the White House in 1865, twenty years after he passed on. First Lady Mary Todd Lincoln said she confronted Jackson's cantankerous ghost in his former bedroom, the Rose Room, where Mrs. Lincoln insisted she heard Jackson's spirit "stomping about" near his canopied four-poster bed. His fiery personality, which in life resulted in a number of altercations, even duels, must have remained intact because Mrs. Lincoln also claimed she heard Jackson's spirit swearing and "cussing" as it loudly stamped and stormed around the room.

One paranormal theory for the obstreperous behavior is that Jackson's ghost continued to be disturbed by political scandals that consumed his time and energy on earth. Another theory concerns his run-in with the infamous Bell Witch of Tennessee. Might Andrew Jackson's spirit have remained troubled even years after he departed this physical existence? On earth, Jackson was not one to forgive or forget a hurt or slight. More than likely in the afterlife, Jackson was unable to release his enmity toward old political adversaries, some of whom he blamed for viciously insulting his beloved wife Rachel years earlier. Following Mrs. Lincoln's account of Jackson's ghost, Old Hickory's spirit quieted for many decades.

In the 1950s, Andrew Jackson chose to make his spectral presence known to a longtime White House seamstress, Lillian Rogers Parks, in the room that had been his as president. Mrs. Parks, who walked on crutches after being stricken with polio as a child, had been a maid and seamstress in the White House for thirty years, succeeding her mother, who also served through several administrations.

By the 1950s, the Rose Room had earned a reputation as one of the most haunted locations in the White House because of frequent reports of an unexplained cold spot and the sound of loud laughter emanating from what had been Jackson's bed. One day, Mrs. Parks was alone in the Rose Room sewing when with no warning she felt someone's staring eyes boring into her from behind. The presence leaned over as she sat in a chair near Andrew Jackson's bed. Years later in her autobiography, *My Thirty Years at the White House*, Mrs. Parks described her experience:

"I remember that when I was working at the bed in the Rose Room, getting a spread fixed for Queen Elizabeth, I had an experience that sent me flying out of there so fast I almost forgot my crutches. The spread was a little too long, and I was hemming it as it lay on the bed. I had finished one side, and was ready to start the other, when suddenly I felt that someone was looking at me, and my scalp tightened. I could feel something coldish behind me, and I didn't finish that spread until three years later." Mrs. Parks concluded that the spirit presence in the Rose Room was none other than Old Hickory himself.

Years earlier, another White House maid who had worked with Lillian's mother also experienced a ghostly encounter in the Rose Room. Katurah Brooks was busy with her chores when inexplicably she heard laughter in the room, which she said had a "hollow," or otherworldly, quality. Was it Andrew Jackson's spirit?

In 1964, Jackson's ghost made its most recent White

House appearance when an aide to President Lyndon Johnson reported he heard shouting and expletives that he believed were Old Hickory's still restless spirit.

Apparently, Andrew Jackson has had a difficult time finding peace in the hereafter, and his ghost has maintained definite elements of his earthly personality: restless, raucous, and coarse. As noted earlier, spirits who display earthly traits are more easily identified by those who encounter their ghostly presences. Jackson's spirit was drawn to the White House Rose Room, home for the eight years of his presidency, where he felt comfortable expressing a range of emotions.

Why did Jackson's ghost return at the times it did? His first reported appearance in 1865 came during the bloody and divisive Civil War, a time the general, a fierce fighter, would have been attracted to. Because Jackson was America's first president born in a log cabin, did he return to the White House during the administration of another frontier president, Abraham Lincoln? Had he felt a kinship with the burdens and travails of the Great Emancipator? Did Jackson's spirit feel the need to help or advise Lincoln? Who better to materialize to than Mary Todd Lincoln, a strong believer in communications with the spirit world and open to recognizing ghostly presences?

When Jackson's spirit returned in the 1950s, it was during the administration of President Dwight Eisenhower, who, like himself, had been a war hero and commanding general before assuming the presidency. Again, in the 1960s, when Jackson's ghost was last heard, it was at the time of the Vietnam War, another fractious national conflict.

It seems Andrew Jackson's restless spirit was drawn back to earth at times of war or to presidents with whom he felt an affinity. They were obviously eras that stirred up emotions and memories of battles and controversies, which the fiercely patriotic Jackson had been unable to forget in the hereafter. There are no reports on the record, at least, that Jackson's spirit ever attempted to offer guidance to future presidents. However, given his strong and passionate political opinions, some paranormal experts and psychics suspect Jackson did just that, clairaudiently and telepathically conveying advice to later chief executives, which could very well have influenced their thinking and decisions.

It has been more than thirty-five years since Old Hickory's last reported ghostly appearance in the White House. It is to be hoped that by finally learning to forgive, to release anger at long-ago political and personal battles and enemies, his soul has progressed in the afterlife.

William Henry Harrison

Several years following President William Henry Harrison's passing on April 4, 1841, after only thirty days in office, his ghost returned to the White House, which he'd known ever so briefly. One day workers reported hearing someone rummaging through the attic on the third floor of the Executive Mansion. When they searched, no one was found nor could the noises be explained.

At a later date, the puzzling noises recurred. It sounded as if someone were digging through an accumulation of possessions. White House staff members again thoroughly examined the spacious attic, used for storage and later as servants' quarters, but their investigations were fruitless. Then someone recognized the apparition of none other than William Henry Harrison with his distinctive long thin face. What might the ghost of President Harrison have been searching for?

Obviously he had an attachment to something in the White House attic: an article, object, or document. Had something he once owned been stored there? Perhaps he was looking for the hat and coat he should have worn at his inauguration to avoid exposure to the elements that cold and rainy day. His spirit may also have haunted because of frustration at his one month in office, the shortest time any President of the United States ever served. Perhaps Harrison is still ruing either his foolhardiness at ignoring the inclement weather on the day of his inauguration or his greater foolishness at provoking the Shawnee medicine man, Tenskwatawa, who pronounced the now-famous presidential curse upon him.

That same haunting pattern was repeated several times in the years after Harrison's passing in 1841. Each time White House employees heard the sounds of someone poking around the attic, they pursued the source of the noise. Each time, they discovered to their surprise the cause was the restless ghost of President Harrison scouring the third floor.

David Burns

William Henry Harrison was not the only apparition witnessed in the White House attic. When Harry S. Truman was president (1945–1953), his secretary of state was James Byrnes. One day, a White House guard heard someone calling, "I'm Mr. Burns. I'm Mr. Burns." The guard turned in the direction of the voice, which seemed to be coming from the attic above him. The officer, unclear why the secretary of state would be there, nonetheless felt a responsibility to check. However, he found the entrance to the attic stairway closed off. Furthermore, the guard discovered that Secretary Byrnes was not in the White House at the time.

Whose voice caught the guard's attention? The history of the White House held the answer. In 1790, the land upon which the White House was to be built was owned by a man named David Burns. President Washington had nicknamed him Obstinate Davy because of his initial resistance to selling the property where Washington wanted the presidential mansion erected. Finally, Washington's persistence won out. Was it the ghost of the unyielding David Burns who called to the White House guard? Had the restless spirit stormed through the attic, still believing it was his real estate? Some say David Burns's troubled ghost was also the cause of objects being thrown around, pictures falling from walls, and papers tossed about in the obviously haunted White House attic.

Mary Todd Lincoln

The second floor of the White House, where presidential families live, has been the scene of many ghostly sounds and sights. One day in the early spring of 1862, First Lady Mary Todd Lincoln walked by the Yellow Oval Room, next to the room where her husband held cabinet meetings to deal with the urgent and pressing business of the Civil War. Mrs. Lincoln paused when she heard an unfamiliar voice emanating from the Yellow Oval Room. Wondering who it might be, she looked in. This was the room her husband used as a library, and where he often stood at the window intently staring at the city of Washington as he contemplated the heavy burdens of the war. This was also where Mrs. Lincoln previously heard psychically the strains of Thomas Jefferson's violin.

However, when Mrs. Lincoln stepped into the Yellow Oval Room, no one was there. She thought perhaps it was her imagination at play or the voice of a White House servant from elsewhere. That spring Mary Todd Lincoln was consumed by the devastating grief of losing her favorite son, Willie, who had died from typhoid fever only months earlier on February 20, at the age of eleven. Had it been Willie she'd heard psychically? Whoever it was, the spirit's words were not sufficiently clear for her to discern. Mrs. Lincoln, sensitive to such psychic experiences as afterdeath communications, would certainly recognize her son's voice and that hadn't been it.

Several days later, Mrs. Lincoln once more passed by the Yellow Oval Room when, again, she was stopped by the same voice. If it was psychic in origin, the only one she prayed to hear from was the spirit of her dear departed Willie. She had already claimed the boy's spirit came to her on several occasions, appearing at the foot of her bed.

Her curiosity piqued, she turned to see the ethereal form of a tall, lean man whom she soon recognized as President John Tyler, although the apparition completely ignored her. There was no mistaking Tyler's Roman nose, which gave him a distinct patrician profile. She concluded it was Tyler's spirit she'd previously heard in the Yellow Oval Room. Mrs. Lincoln wondered why his ghost returned. Someone less sensitive might have dismissed the incident as a shadow or a reflection of light rather than an apparition. Mary Todd Lincoln knew better. She listened attentively to the words of the spirit presence: "Julia, marry me? Julia, marry me. Please be my wife! I offer you my hand."

Whether Mrs. Lincoln realized it or not, John Tyler's ghost was proposing marriage to Julia Gardiner, a pretty and vivacious young woman, thirty years his junior, who had become his second wife after he was widowed. He was reliving the touching moments when he offered his hand nearly twenty years earlier in that very same room in the White House. Julia had at first rejected Tyler's marriage proposal saying she had no interest in love, or him, although she admitted his attentions "amused" her. When finally she said yes, the love-struck president was overjoyed, and the couple wed.

Each time Tyler's ghost materialized, he repeated his marriage proposal to Julia Gardiner. Obviously it had been a deeply felt and extremely important occasion for Tyler—one his spirit could not dismiss. Thus he remained drawn to the location where the lovely young woman eventually accepted his hand. Such was President John Tyler's reason for returning to haunt the Yellow Oval Room nearly twenty years after he left office in 1845, and only months after he departed this physical world on January 18, 1862, at the age of seventy-one.

Whether psychically attuned Mary Todd Lincoln had literally heard Tyler's voice aloud or clairaudiently, and therefore telepathically, is unclear. But the experience with Tyler's ghost was one she shared with several close friends, even as her deep grief for Willie remained undiminished, as did her greater desire to receive messages from the boy rather than someone she barely knew.

Ulysses S. Grant

Another account of an apparition or paranormal incident involving a first family occurred when Ulysses S. Grant resided in the White House, and later when his spirit returned to his two favorite locations.

During the years of the Grant administration, spiritualism endured as a widespread belief in America. The popular interest in the occult, séances, mediums, and communicating with the Other Side had continued unabated for more than twenty years by the time Grant became president, just as it endured in England during the same period. Among the legions of faithful—and there were millions—were several members of Grant's family, who considered themselves believers in communicating with spirits of the deceased. Thus there was little amazement among the Grants when White House personnel breathlessly reported they'd witnessed the apparition of President and Mrs. Lincoln's young son Willie, who had died in the White House in 1862.

When Willie was taken gravely ill with typhoid fever, he was put to bed in what was then known as the Prince of Wales Room on the second floor of the White House. President Grant's staff members told of seeing Willie's ghost materialize in that room. This was the first time the boy's apparition was observed by someone other than a Lincoln family member. That Willie's apparition returned during Grant's presidency is not surprising, considering the close relationship between Grant and Abraham Lincoln years earlier. One of the witnesses swore he'd spoken with the child's spirit, now healthy and at peace in the afterlife. Willie's presence would again return to the White House some forty years later during the William Howard Taft administration, and in the 1960s when Lyndon Johnson was president.

Despite the corruption that permeated his administration, Grant himself remained a popular figure after he left office. Happy to be freed from the burdens of a presidency he hadn't sought, he tried to rediscover his life as a civilian in private business. But it wasn't long before professional and financial problems again plagued Grant after he invested all his money in a stock brokerage firm that failed. In 1884, only seven years after he had been President of the United States, Grant was overwhelmed by debt, with virtually no income, and deeply embarrassed by his circumstances.

Then, at nearly the same time economic woes bedeviled him, Grant was diagnosed with incurable cancer of the throat, probably the result of his smoking twenty cigars a day. What remained intact, however, was Grant's pride. Fearful that his family would be left penniless, he agreed to write his memoirs, notably about his Civil War years. Among his writings was a dire prediction: "A conflict between races may come up in the future, as did that between freedom and slavery before. . . ." His words, whether born of political acumen or intuitive insight, were to prove prophetic.

While the specter of death hovered, Grant stubbornly persisted despite torturous pain, depression, and fatigue. The cancer so destroyed the tissue lining the inside of his mouth and throat that in his last days on earth he could no longer eat or speak. Still, he sat and wrote in a cottage in the Adirondack Mountains of New York State, and refused to depart this world until his memoirs were completed, even as he endured enormous physical agony. On July 10, he wrote, "In two weeks the second volume [will be] ready to go to the printer. I will then feel my work is done."

Grant completed his two-volume autobiography, *Personal Memoirs*, only four days before his earthly suffering ended on the morning of July 23, 1885, when he died at the age of sixty-three in Mount McGregor, New York. His book became an immediate bestseller and was considered a classic. Published by the famed writer Mark Twain, it earned an astounding $500,000 in royalties, a huge sum in its day and not too bad for today, either, providing a very ample retirement fund for Julia Grant to live on comfortably for the remainder of her life. Grant's memoirs have been the only bestselling memoirs of any former president, even though many recent presidents have become accomplished writers after they left office.

While gravely ill in the months before he died, Grant could only communicate to his doctors and loved ones by scrawling notes. Following his passing, a letter was discovered that Grant had written privately and carried with him, knowing that death was imminent. It was addressed to his wife, reminding her: "Look after our dear children and direct them in the paths of rectitude." Grant concluded his letter with a hint that he believed in an afterlife: "I bid you a final fond farewell until we meet in another and, I trust, a better world."

During his presidency, Grant made a practice of walking nearly every evening from the White House to the Willard Hotel, two blocks from the Executive Mansion. There, in the lobby of the hotel, where he had often been a guest, Grant relaxed with glasses of brandy while he smoked his favorite cigars. After his passing, visitors and employees in the hotel claimed they could occasionally detect a whiff of President Grant's cigars. Spirits sometimes communicate or make their presence known through scents or smells that were associated with them when they were on earth.

When Grant's spirit returned to this physical plane, it materialized in a location that set in motion the defining moment of his career, Fort Monroe, Virginia, where he had planned much of his successful Civil War strategy. Grant's ghost's return to a military installation makes sense considering his achievements. Certainly the fort was a stronger pull for his spirit than the White House, which he had been only too happy to leave.

The heptagon-shaped Fort Monroe, with its seven sides and angles, had the distinction of being one of the very few Union military installations in the South not captured by the Confederates during the Civil War. Resembling a medieval fortress and surrounded by an imposing moat, Fort Monroe was considered in its day the nation's strongest bastion. In use as an army post since 1834, fourteen hundred soldiers resided within its walls during the Civil War. In later years, Fort Monroe became known as a site where the ghosts of many famous historical figures materialized.

Countless witnesses insist ghosts *still* haunt Fort Monroe. One particularly haunted location in the fortress is an area called Old Quarters Number One, actually a plantation-style house. Many ghosts have been reported in the Old Quarters, which was once used for visiting guests. First among the roster was the apparition of General Grant, whose spirit returned to the very place where he detailed the military tactics of his last Union campaign, which led to the defeat of the Confederates and Lee's surrender. Grant's specter has continued to haunt the building, unable to release the bonds of earthly triumphs and tragedies.

James Garfield

President James Garfield had a lifelong relationship with his father, Abram, who, according to James's own descriptions, often advised and guided his son. Nothing is unusual about this, except for the fact that Abram Garfield died before James was two years old. Garfield's mother was left to raise the boy alone in circumstances that bordered on poverty in a modest log cabin in Orange, Ohio, where he was born in 1831. Garfield never really knew his father when Abram was alive. However, when James was six years old, he began experiencing what he later described as "strange ghostly visitations" from his late father who continued to counsel his son throughout his life. Garfield never doubted the authenticity of the spirit communications, nor did he feel any conflict between his psychic experiences and deeply held religious beliefs.

To look at the tall, bearded, erudite Garfield, one

might not immediately think of his long-held belief in the paranormal. However, Garfield was not at all perturbed by his supernatural experiences, which continued in the White House. In fact, the vivid, lifelike visions, during which messages were communicated telepathically, became a source of comfort and strength for him. For Abram Garfield, the visitations were an opportunity to communicate with the son he barely knew in life. Physical death may separate us temporarily; it does not break the emotional connection between loved ones here and hereafter. The fact that as president Garfield was willing to admit to his psychic experiences and share them with confidants speaks to the power and importance of the contact he had with his late father.

As Garfield later confided to several close friends, his father's spirit advised him on the course of his education and career. Garfield heeded his father's messages. He attended Hiram College in Ohio and Williams College in Massachusetts, went on to a teaching career, and eventually became a college president, all of which were according to the psychically expressed wishes of Abram Garfield. The first documented reference by James Garfield to metaphysics, the philosophy of the mind, which can embrace both theology and parapsychology, occurred in his college commencement address, which was titled "Metaphysical Oration." This became a study, which the future American president practiced throughout the rest of his life.

After the Civil War started, Garfield was named commander of a regiment of volunteers, an appointment he had been encouraged to take by his late father's spirit. Garfield eventually rose to the rank of general. After his career in the army and his term as a college president, Garfield served in Congress for seventeen years. He was also an ordained minister in the Church of the Disciples of Christ, where he frequently preached.

Many historians believe that the deprivation Garfield knew in his youth spurred him to constantly strive to be the best at everything he attempted. He was fiercely ambitious throughout his life. Considering his admission to friends about frequent psychic advice from his departed father, is it also likely that Garfield was motivated toward success because of Abram's prodding from the hereafter?

On one occasion, Garfield attended a public appearance by Charles Dickens, who read from his widely popular book *A Christmas Carol*. As Dickens recited the words "Bless his heart: it's Fezziwig alive again!" a dog in the room suddenly moved as if aroused by something only it had seen. It was an ironic moment for the dog to react. Had the animal witnessed a ghost? Garfield did not rule out that possibility, especially when the dog barked vigorously and stared intently at one corner above where it sat. Was it mere coincidence or had the dog noticed a spirit undetectable to the human eye? For his part, Dickens later said he found the timing of the incident both curious and humorous.

After Garfield was elected the twentieth President of the United States in 1880, in the wake of the corruption of the Grant administration, he sought the reform of civil service laws so as to replace a patronage system with a merit-based system. This was ultimately a fateful policy, which antagonized many politicians in both political parties along with those who sought their patronage. Garfield's stance on the controversial issue, he privately admitted, was guided by psychic advice from his late father, who wanted him to reform government in the wake of the scandals of the Grant administration.

At some point during his short term in office, Garfield experienced a frightening premonition that he would be murdered. It is probable the information was also psychically communicated to Garfield by his father Abram. Unfortunately records do not exist to tell us the exact dialogue between Garfield and his father's spirit in the White House, although a presidential aide later confirmed the premonition. The warning, however, could not save Garfield from his appointed fate. Nor could an unusual meeting Garfield held with his Secretary of War Robert Lincoln, son of President Abraham Lincoln. At the end of June, Garfield called Lincoln to the White

House and asked him to describe in detail recollections of his father's assassination. Robert Lincoln, twenty-one when President Lincoln was shot and killed in 1865, spoke with an extremely attentive Garfield for more than an hour.

Only four months into his term of office, on July 2, 1881, and just two days after his conversation with Robert Lincoln, Garfield waited in the Baltimore and Potomac Railroad Station in Washington, D.C., to board a train for vacation when he was approached by a deranged, rejected office seeker named Charles J. Guiteau, who had stalked Garfield for several weeks. Guiteau had sought to be appointed the U.S. consul in Paris, but was spurned in his bid. The assassin, blaming the president personally for the political rebuff he had received, fired two rounds into James Garfield's back. As he collapsed on the floor and strained for breath, Garfield whispered, "My God, what is this?"

Ironically, President Garfield, who had openly talked about his acceptance of psychic phenomena, had been mortally wounded by a self-described spiritualist. In his own delusions, Guiteau was convinced he was fulfilling his role as "the hand of destiny." Several times the mentally troubled assassin rambled that his murderous act had been instigated by "spirits," and that he considered Garfield to be the personification of evil. Not surprisingly, those who abhorred spiritualism seized upon the shooting of Garfield as a means to discredit the belief. Others, more realistically, viewed Guiteau as a crazed religious fanatic.

Garfield did not die on the railroad station floor. In fact, he lingered on in terrible pain for several weeks while doctors tried to remove the bullets that had splintered his spine. Even the famed Alexander Graham Bell was called in to help locate one of the bullets with the use of an electrical device he'd invented. But the team of surgeons had made a grievous error when they failed to sterilize their medical instruments or sufficiently wash their hands before they probed the president's wounds. As a result, Garfield developed a serious infection that, likely in combination with blood poisoning caused by the bullets, proved fatal. Even though he was moved to the New Jersey shore in the hope that the sea air would be more healthful than the heat and humidity of Washington, D.C., it was too late. Despite the prayers of the nation horrified by the shooting, James Garfield became the second President of the United States to die at the hand of an assassin when he passed on September 19, 1881, with his wife, Lucretia, at his bedside. Garfield was not yet fifty years old. No doubt, the spirit of Abram Garfield was there to meet his son when the younger Garfield crossed to the Other Side.

Garfield once wrote, "My life has been made up of a series of accidents, mostly of a favorable nature." However, an assassin's bullets had intervened. Was it by chance? Or had James Garfield become the third president whose fate had been predicted by the Shawnee prophet's curse more than sixty years earlier, and first visited on President William Henry Harrison?

When President Garfield's spirit returned to Washington, D.C., just after the assassination, witnesses reported that he was observed haunting the halls of the Capitol Building at the very same time his body was lying in state.

A week after Charles Guiteau was hanged for murdering the president, in June 1882, a Capitol guard glimpsed Guiteau's ghost on a staircase going toward the Capitol basement. The guard, momentarily forgetting that Guiteau had been executed for his crime, gave chase. However, the apparition disappeared.

Woodrow Wilson

Obviously some accounts of paranormal events involving presidents and their family members are easier to document than others. One of the strangest incidents involving any U.S. president and the supernatural—and one of the most difficult to document—concerned President Woodrow Wilson, whose spirit many believed had materialized from a substance called ectoplasm exuded from a French-born medium known professionally as Eva.

The curious phenomenon known as ectoplasm was one of the more controversial aspects of physical mediumship, especially as it was practiced in the nineteenth and early-twentieth centuries. It was a milky-white substance, often described by witnesses as "lifelike," that could assume a solid form, manifest itself as a sticky material, or even float like a vapor or mist. Ectoplasm was believed to be secreted from the eyes, ears, nose, and mouth of mediums such as Eva, whose name was actually Marthe Béraud. When Béraud was studied by paranormal investigators and physicians, they observed a viscous phlegmlike composition exuding from her in the form of wriggling protrusions, which then took the facial appearance or shape of well-known deceased political or historical figures. One of them was none other than President Woodrow Wilson.

The Spirit of Franklin Delano Roosevelt

Although President Franklin Delano Roosevelt never acknowledged that he witnessed any spirits during his long White House tenure, he did concede he "was not surprised" when Queen Wilhemina of the Netherlands reported, with considerable consternation, that she'd seen an apparition during her visit to 1600 Pennsylvania Avenue. Mrs. Roosevelt also shared with her husband the fact that she experienced spirit phenomena in the White House, which she was unable to explain. Ultimately, Roosevelt's own passing would be the subject of paranormal speculation at the White House.

For President Roosevelt, Thursday, April 12, 1945, at his vacation home, dubbed the Little White House, in Warm Springs, Georgia, began normally. World War II still raged in both Europe and the Pacific even though an Allied victory, especially against the German army, which was at the point of collapse as the Allies advanced on Berlin, seemed within reach. In the afternoon, the president posed for a portrait being painted by one Madame Shoumatoff. Then he worked on his papers and handled war correspondence and other duties, all the while balancing his familiar cigarette holder between his clenched teeth. He looked pale and weary, not surprising for a man who had led the nation for twelve years through the Great Depression and war. Nearby stood Lucy Rutherford, Roosevelt's longtime clandestine romantic interest. All the while, Roosevelt's beloved black Scottish terrier, Fala, sat quietly and contentedly on the bedroom floor.

Fala had become a national celebrity in his own right. Roosevelt had been given the dog in 1940 by a cousin when it was just a puppy. He named the terrier Murray the Outlaw of Fala Hill. Asked about the unusual name, FDR explained it was in honor of a distant Scottish relative. But the public came to know the presidential dog simply as Fala, and he was FDR's constant companion, sleeping in the president's bedroom and accompanying the president when he traveled, even to critical wartime conferences with such world leaders as British prime minister Winston Churchill. Fala became so popular with the American people that once, when the president and Fala journeyed from California aboard the USS *Baltimore* during the summer of 1944, so many sailors snipped locks of Fala's hair to keep as souvenirs that poor Fala looked nearly bald.

That trip by President Roosevelt spurred criticism from Republicans who complained of the excursion during an election year in which Roosevelt was seeking an unprecedented fourth term. There were rumors that Fala had remained on the USS *Baltimore* in the Aleutians and that a destroyer was dispatched to return the dog to FDR, at a huge expense to taxpayers. That incident involving Fala became the subject of a famous Roosevelt speech. In September 1944, the president answered critics in a nationally broadcast address to the Teamsters Union. FDR explained that he bore no ill will toward those who criticized him. Then in a tone of mock indignation, the president said that when Fala heard the accusation, "His Scotch soul was furious. He has not been the same dog since." The audience roared its approval. FDR had defused a political flap with the help of his dog, something Richard Nixon would do less than a decade later in his famous Checkers speech.

So on this day in April 1945, like so many before, Fala sat faithfully while FDR went about his business. It was about 1:15 P.M. when the president lifted his left hand to his temple and applied pressure to his forehead. Then his hand seemed to jerk in a spasmlike motion and fall by his side. A moment later he again raised his hand and pushed his fingers against his neck. His eyes closed, and he said in a weak voice, "I have a terrific headache." Roosevelt's arm dropped once more. His head sagged to one side; his body slumped forward.

His physician was hurriedly summoned. The symptoms seemed obvious. The president had suffered a "massive cerebral hemorrhage." The doctor worked frantically to treat Roosevelt, who had broken into a cold sweat, was breathing with great effort, and had turned ashen in color. But despite the emergency medical attention, it was too late. Franklin Delano Roosevelt, the nation's thirty-first president, was declared dead at the age of sixty-three. The time was 3:35 P.M.

All the while doctors were doing their utmost to revive the unconscious president, Fala remained calm in a corner of the bedroom, ignoring the urgent medical efforts going on around him. However, the moment Roosevelt died, the dog sprang forward and vaulted for the screen door. He pushed it open and ran to a hill near the house, howling and crying as if he was in pain. Once Fala reached the top of the hill, the barking ceased, and the dog froze where he stood, as if he was keeping watch or observing something that no one else could see. He refused to leave the hill.

What had Fala seen or sensed? Had he witnessed FDR's spirit depart its physical body? Paranormal experts have long taken a serious interest in what some term "animal ESP," and psychic activity involving dogs and other animals is common. More specifically, in the case of Fala, many parapsychologists believe the dog undoubtedly detected Roosevelt's spirit. It is a fact that animals possess psychic senses or abilities lacking in humans. One of those appears to be a psychic link or bond between owner and animal, especially when the two have grown close, as in the case of FDR and Fala. Another is the ability of animals to witness ghosts, even when humans cannot perceive them. What explains this heightened sensitivity is open to debate. But it is clear that many animals can see, hear, and sense psychic phenomena beyond the range of human capability. The heartbroken dog had likely witnessed FDR's soul as it made the transition to the next stage of life.

Eventually Fala regained his composure, and on the day of Roosevelt's funeral, as a stunned nation grieved, the dog once again observed his owner's ghost. Mourners who watched Fala noticed that during the funeral services he rolled around on the ground and happily barked. At one point, Fala stared intently at a particular spot near the altar, and those gathered heard small yelps of delight. One witness, longtime White House employee Lillian Rogers Parks, heard an unusual cry from Fala. No doubt he was elated to see the president's spirit. "Fala was always my husband's dog. He merely accepted me," Mrs. Roosevelt frequently remarked. Seven years later, Fala joined Franklin Delano Roosevelt on the Other Side. No doubt it was a joyous reunion.

CHAPTER SIX

Presidential Birthplaces: When Presidents' Spirits Go Home

Mid pleasures and palaces though we may roam,
Be it ever so humble there's no place like home . . .
—J. H. Payne

Presidents and their families have to leave the White House when their terms of office are up, but for presidential ghosts, it's a different matter. Some presidents' spirits have remained in the White House and are there to this day, while others departed at the point of death, only to return years later. However, there have been those ghosts who've chosen not to linger at 1600 Pennsylvania Avenue at all, preferring instead to revisit their birthplaces, the locations of their greatest triumphs or failures, or in many instances, the private residences they once called home.

Thomas Jefferson

In 1769, when he was just twenty-six, Thomas Jefferson applied his deep interest and self-taught skills in architecture to the design and construction of his estate on a hill overlooking Charlottesville, Virginia, which he named Monticello, Italian for "little mountain." In 1773, just three years before he drafted the Declaration of

Independence, he moved into the mansion with his new bride, Martha, who gave birth to six children before she passed on at age thirty-three after ten years of marriage. Monticello with its distinctive domed roof and classic columns was finally completed in 1809. By then, Jefferson had devoted forty years to adding and renovating his beloved home in the Virginia countryside, which eventually had thirty-three elegantly furnished rooms bordered by meticulously landscaped grounds and gardens.

When Jefferson left the White House in 1809 after two terms in office, he returned to Monticello, where he enthusiastically pursued his studies into the sciences and new philosophies of the nineteenth century, entertained notable figures of the day, and began a remarkable correspondence with his predecessor in office, John Adams. After Jefferson had defeated Adams in a bitter presidential campaign, the two men, who had served in Washington's cabinet together, didn't even speak to one another at Jefferson's first inauguration. They had finally become friends, however, and engaged in a long correspondence with each other, touching on the great issues they shared as presidents and the issues that confronted the young United States.

In one of the most remarkable incidents of synchronicity in American history, John Adams died at the age of ninety at his Quincy, Massachusetts, home, on July 4, 1826, the fiftieth anniversary of the signing of the Declaration of Independence. Among his last words, "Thomas Jefferson still survives!" Unbeknownst to Adams, in an era that lacked instant communications, his dear friend Thomas Jefferson, at Monticello, on that very same day and only hours before Adams's passing, also departed this physical world. The man who'd written the Declaration of Independence fifty years earlier had asked on his deathbed, "Is this the Fourth of July?" Yes, he was told. Then he passed on, at the age of eighty-three.

Were the deaths of two of America's great patriots and presidents and, in retirement, close personal friends on the exact same day a coincidence or something beyond that? Carl Jung, founder of analytical psychology, espoused the theory of synchronicity to explain "meaningful coincidences," which are not obviously connected by cause and effect. An incident of synchronicity is a chance occurrence that is so unlikely it is reasonable to assume it is founded on some as yet unexplained precept. What might be responsible for synchronous events? Is there a supernatural component? Is there an element of premonition involved?

Adams and Jefferson had developed a strong emotional bond, the result of their long and close association and prolific exchange of many deeply felt thoughts. Therefore it is not unreasonable to conclude a psychic link or connection existed between them. So when Jefferson died, Adams witnessed his spirit in what is commonly known as a deathbed vision. This would account for Adams's remark about Jefferson surviving. Had Thomas Jefferson's spirit materialized to help his friend ease the transition to the afterlife? Had Adams chosen to make the transition to the next stage of life simultaneously with his esteemed friend? Far from coincidence, people on the brink of death often sense or experience visions of predeceased loved ones or individuals close to them.

When the nights are still and visitors have gone, security guards making their rounds at Monticello have told of hearing someone happily humming. The guards are certain it is Thomas Jefferson, who in life frequently hummed favorite tunes as he went about his activities from place to place along the grounds of the estate. Psychic historians are not surprised that the guards hear a ghost humming at night because if it's, indeed, Jefferson's ghost it means that his spirit has returned to his much-loved Monticello, where many of his prized possessions remain on display. Included in the museumlike setting are several of Jefferson's own inventions, which are probably the physical repositories of much of Jefferson's powerful creative energies.

But it's not only the sound of humming that permeates the night air at Monticello. Behind the main house is a two-story cottage, similar in style to Monticello's principal dwelling. Witnesses have reported sensing Jefferson's spirit in the vicinity of the cottage, a positive sensation of a soul that returned to a place teeming with memories. Perhaps mixed emotions tinged Jefferson's ghostly visits to Monticello, many happy reminiscences mingled with sadness and guilt concerning his infidelities and wife's death.

James Monroe

Only two miles from Monticello is Ash Lawn, the former home of President James Monroe. The proximity of the two estates is no coincidence because Thomas Jefferson himself chose the location of Ash Lawn as Monroe's residence, which Monroe purchased in 1793 when he was the American minister to France. Monroe moved to Ash Lawn, then known as Highland, in 1799, and it became his country home, which provided him much respite during his term of office from 1817 to 1825. Before and during his presidency, Monroe enjoyed lively and thoughtful conversations with his good friend and neighbor Thomas Jefferson at Ash Lawn, and Monroe would rock back and forth in his favorite chair in the largest room of what he fondly called his "cabin-castle." Monroe died at the age of seventy-three on July 4, 1831, the third president to die on Independence Day, five years after Thomas Jefferson and John Adams had passed on.

When Monroe's spirit returned to Ash Lawn, it was to sit in his favorite rocking chair. For many years, witnesses reported the chair would rock back and forth, without being touched, as though someone was still sitting in it. Objects such as furniture can be affected or influenced by ghosts or spirits, undetected by the human eye. Such psychokinetic activity gives the appearance of some invisible force at work. Actually the motion or movement of an object is driven by psychic energy generated by the spirit. Likely, the ghost of James Monroe returned to Ash Lawn, not to haunt, but rather to recall happy times when he and comrades such as Thomas Jefferson shared the hours, talking politics and the future of the young nation they both helped found.

Martin Van Buren, Lindenwald, and the Ghost of Aaron Burr

Kinderhook, a small community originally settled by the Dutch, is nestled along the Hudson River, south of Albany, New York. There, Martin Van Buren was born on December 5, 1782, in a modest apartment above his father's tavern. Because he was born after the Declaration of Independence was signed, Van Buren was the first president to have the distinction of being born a citizen of the United States of America, albeit one year before we had successfully fought our way out from under British rule.

His early life was centered in Kinderhook, where he attended school and the Dutch Reformed Church and then, in his teens, studied law with a successful attorney in the town. In 1807, Van Buren married his childhood sweetheart, Hannah Hoes, who died of tuberculosis in 1819 and left him with four sons to raise. He chose never to remarry.

A good-looking young man with red hair, who later in life grew distinctive muttonchop sideburns to frame his bald head, Van Buren earned the nickname the Little Magician for both his political leadership and his winning personality, which served him well by the time he became an attorney at age twenty-one. Van Buren gained political prominence through a succession of elected positions, and by the time he was elected to the nation's highest office in 1836, he'd held more public offices than any other president had. But after a largely undistinguished presidency, Van Buren, defeated in his bid for a second term, retired to Kinderhook, where he persuaded the son of the man under whom he'd studied law to sell him Lindenwald, an estate built in 1797. Once the brick Dutch Colonial farmhouse became his, Van Buren wasted no time having it remodeled and lavishly furnished, and the more than two hundred acres became a successful working farm with gardens and fruit orchards.

Van Buren lived at Lindenwald for the rest of his life and passed from this world to the next on July 24, 1862, at the age of seventy-nine. After a funeral at the Kinderhook Reformed Church, his body was laid to rest in the village cemetery, alongside his wife. Death, however, could not separate Van Buren from Kinderhook, especially his home at Lindenwald. For when his spirit returned, his apparition was first seen there, moving stealthily through an apple orchard. The Little Magician couldn't resist the lure of revisiting the place so much a part of his life on this plane. After he passed, witnesses reported hearing footsteps at Lindenwald untraceable to any earthly being or physical cause. Many insisted it was the ghost of Martin Van Buren back home again.

But Lindenwald's haunted history goes well beyond Van Buren's enduring spirit. The house has a reputation as one of the most frequently reported locations of spirit and other paranormal activity of any presidential home.

Aaron Burr, Thomas Jefferson's vice president and a close friend of the original owner of Lindenwald, was a bitter political enemy of the popular patriot Alexander Hamilton, who thwarted Burr's efforts to gain the presidency. Their bitter feud came to a head when Burr shot and mortally wounded Hamilton in their famous duel in July 1804. Dueling was then legal, and the daring and conceited Burr, faced with disapproving public reaction, retreated and spent the next three years at Lindenwald. After Burr's death, many believed his ghostly presence haunted Lindenwald because of the strange sounds that seemed to emanate from inside the walls. His repetitive footsteps were perhaps an indication that he had not forgiven himself for killing Hamilton. The mystery continued through the century until the early 1900s, when the owner of the house discovered a secret attic compartment. In that tiny windowless room was found a long-faded calling card bearing the name AARON BURR along with a rocking chair and a small whittled wooden pig. Could inexplicable noises emanating from the attic room be attributed to Burr's restless and troubled spirit?

Later residents, through the mid-1950s, also reported hearing footsteps and stirrings, certain they were ghosts. The large sturdy doors sometimes closed on their own, and dresser drawers opened and shut themselves. Former Lindenwald servants claimed they'd witnessed what they believed was Aaron Burr's ghost materialize near the house, wearing a handsome burgundy coat with lace cuffs. There has long been dispute about whether a ghostly presence at Lindenwald, often witnessed as a "white apparition," is that of Aaron Burr or Martin Van Buren. Perhaps the specters of both famed Americans returned to Lindenwald for their own very different reasons.

Finally, a frequent guest at Lindenwald was the noted author Washington Irving. It is no small irony that Irving was inspired to create his fictional characters, including Ichabod Crane for "The Legend of Sleepy Hollow," after a visit to Lindenwald, where he first learned the saga of the headless horseman, a widely told tale in and around Kinderhook. Perhaps it is fitting that one of America's most enduring fictional ghost stories was created in one of the most celebrated haunted houses in the country, formerly the home of a U.S. president and vice president.

Andrew Johnson

Is the small gabled-roof house in Raleigh, North Carolina, where Andrew Johnson was born in 1808, still haunted by the lingering spirit of the beleaguered president who succeeded Lincoln in the dark days following the assassination of the Great Emancipator? The only president before Bill Clinton ever to have been impeached by the House of Representatives, Johnson was raised in dire poverty by a widowed mother who could barely provide for his sustenance. Consequently, Johnson had no opportunity to attend school and was the only American president to grow up without a formal education or knowing how to read and write. Instead, after moving to Greenville, Tennessee, Andrew opened his own tailor shop and eventually learned to read and write on his own and with the help of his young wife, Eliza.

Motivated by burning ambition that belied his lack of formal education, Johnson became active in politics and was ultimately elected to the U.S. Senate, where, as a Southerner stubbornly in support of slavery, he, nevertheless, strongly opposed secession. As the only senator from a Southern state who maintained loyalty to the Union, Johnson was rewarded with the second slot on the 1864 national Republican ticket, which rode to victory even as the final battles in the Civil War were coming to an end. In March 1865, Johnson was inaugurated as Lincoln's vice president to the hoots and catcalls of a derisive press, who condemned the choice as a blatant attempt at political balance in the months before a defeated South would have to be reconstructed and amalgamated back into the Union. However, the Northern press believed that Johnson was the weakest choice Lincoln could have made. In an editorial that revealed an eerie prescience, the *New York World* wrote disparagingly about the vice president: "To think that one frail life stands between this insolent, clownish creature and the presidency."

Then fate cast Johnson into one of the most untenable circumstances any president ever faced after Lincoln was assassinated at Ford's Theater. He'd been vice president for barely six weeks and was also an intended assassination target himself because the conspirators saw him as a traitor to his own home state. However, a drunken coconspirator working for presidential assassin John Wilkes Booth never carried out the murder, leaving the ill-prepared and universally scorned Andrew Johnson at the helm to navigate a still bitterly divided United States of America through the postwar period history books euphemistically refer to as Reconstruction. In reality, depending upon which side one was on, Reconstruction was a period during which either the North exploited the South or the South systematically replaced slavery with a series of Jim Crow laws, which didn't begin to disappear until the 1950s. But it was during Reconstruction that Johnson was called upon to, in Lincoln's words, "bind up the nation's wounds" and restore the Union, a monumental task for any individual regardless of his abilities.

Historians still ask the question: "Was there any man capable of filling the shoes of Abraham Lincoln, whose leadership to preserve the Union was as monumental as it was difficult?" Most scholars agree that Johnson lacked the political skills, personality, and acumen to bring the different sides together, though few doubt his intent and sincerity. Despite his best efforts, however, the former tailor, now turned chief executive, was quickly overwhelmed by political adversaries, who bitterly opposed his efforts to continue Lincoln's policies of Reconstruction and reconciliation with the South. In 1868, led by the zealots in the radical wing of the Republican Party, the House of Representatives voted to impeach Andrew Johnson, making him the first sitting president ever to be impeached. Subsequently, he was spared removal from office by a single Senate vote, but his administration was crippled, and he simply became a caretaker president for the final months of his term. When he left the White House in 1869, at the end of what should have been Lincoln's second term, the office of the presidency was severely weakened and left in far worse shape than it was when Lincoln was first sworn in eight years earlier.

Andrew Johnson, who had faced scorn and embarrassment before in his life, was bitter and disillusioned at first but overcame the humiliation of impeachment and ran for the House of Representatives from his district in Tennessee. He won and redeemed both his political reputation and his place in history before he died in 1875. The example set by Andrew Johnson, a president targeted by overzealous Republicans angry at the loss of the White House, was frequently cited by Bill Clinton's supporters in the days after the latter's impeachment and his subsequent acquittal by the Senate in 1999. President Clinton himself often talked about Andrew Johnson's resiliency and the contributions Johnson made after he became a member of the House.

When Andrew Johnson's spirit returned, it was to his Raleigh, North Carolina, birthplace. Author Nancy Roberts told of visiting Raleigh in recent years, where she discovered a witness to ghostly phenomena in the Johnson home located within a group of historical buildings in a park known as Mordecai Square. Terry Myers, a former teacher familiar with North Carolina history who worked in one of the buildings in that historic cluster, reported that one autumn evening, after dark, she'd left her office as usual but, unlike other evenings, felt that "something" was different as she passed the nearby Johnson birthplace. Then she noticed an unfamiliar light. Myers considered that someone might have left a light burning in one of the buildings. Maybe it was a reflection from an automobile's passing headlights or perhaps someone had walked by with a flashlight or lantern that had reflected off the windowpanes.

She glanced into the only window on the first floor of the little house where the seventeenth president was born, and to her surprise, she saw a single candle burning brightly. Despite her nervousness, Myers couldn't help but think that the candle looked as if it were being held aloft by some "invisible human hand." She stared at the dangling light, although certain no one was in the building. Then the candle slowly but steadily moved away from the window until it disappeared. Moments later, the flame was again visible, this time in an upstairs window. Myers was as alarmed as she was curious about who—or what—was in the pitch-black house. A while later, from the street, she watched the candle abruptly wink out "as if it had been extinguished with an old-fashioned candle snuffer."

Had Myers unwittingly witnessed the lonely spirit of

Andrew Johnson? Did his ghost illuminate the single candle, while he lingered in the house where he was born, still longing to restore his tarnished reputation and place in American history as if in response to the old saying that it is better to light one candle than curse the darkness?

Theodore Roosevelt

Even if we can't see them with our naked eyes, can the spirits of the departed be captured on motion picture film or videotape? Most people think not, although many ghost hunters claim that the energy signatures of earthbound or trapped spirits can indeed be picked up on electronic or photo media. And this might very well be the case with the spirit of President Theodore Roosevelt, which was spotted by Janet and Peter Edstrom sitting in the window of the Roosevelt house in Oyster Bay, Long Island. The Edstroms live on Long Island, where Janet maintains her psychotherapy practice and Peter works as an electronics engineer. One warm, sunny day in July 1996, the Edstroms and another couple drove to one of Long Island's best-known and loveliest historical sites, the towering twenty-three-room Victorian mansion named Sagamore Hill, built by Teddy Roosevelt in 1884 to 1885 overlooking Long Island Sound and called the Summer White House. T. R. adored the house, where he and his wife lived from 1886 until his death in 1919, and today the Sagamore Hill National Historic Site, restored to look as it did when Roosevelt was president from 1901 to 1909, is open to the public.

"I love the history of the house. You feel a sense of the Roosevelt family when you go through there," Janet said. "We had no other objective in going to Sagamore Hill except to enjoy seeing the house. We'd been there only once before."

As they always did when they traveled, the Edstroms carried their video camcorder. "I thought we'd have some videotaped memories of the day and Teddy Roosevelt's home," Janet explained. "I love the porch at Sagamore Hill. It's that famous porch I've seen in old newsreels where Teddy Roosevelt is seen talking to dignitaries."

The Edstroms and their friends toured the house with its comfortable and attractive period furniture. Janet was especially impressed by the room that contains Teddy Roosevelt's hunting trophies, big game mounted and hung on walls. Later, walking around the grounds, Janet readily agreed when her friends asked to use the camcorder, which they pointed toward the second-floor window of the house. It was now late afternoon, the public tours were over, and the house was locked and empty. They'd already taken video of the house, so what was there left to shoot? Janet, curious, asked her friend, "What do you hope to see in the window?"

The answer startled her and Peter. "Spirits sometimes are seen on film or videotape that you can't see with the naked eye."

Janet and Peter had not even remotely considered anything paranormal occurring at Sagamore Hill, let alone the possibility the house might be haunted. She was a psychologist, not a parapsychologist, and more than skeptical about the existence of noncorporeal spirits let alone the capturing of those spirits on a piece of videotape. Nevertheless, Janet gazed intently at the window as her friends videotaped it, but she saw nothing unusual in the old panes of glass. Peter agreed. "It's just a window," he dismissed. The Edstroms doubted the videotape would reveal anything supernatural, although they decided not to express their incredulity aloud even as their friends panned the entire house and zoomed in and out on the second-floor bedroom window.

That evening, the four returned to the Edstroms' home to watch the tape, more out of curiosity, Janet explained, than with the expectation they'd see anything inexplicable. Perhaps the absence of any spiritual images on the video would dispel the nagging doubt that Janet had that perhaps her friends had seen something after all. The video rolled on for several uneventful minutes, playing back the scenes of the Roosevelt house and grounds in a slow pan across the screen. Then, as the camera moved in for a close-up of the second-floor window, the four gasped at sudden, fleeting appearances of images of several young children and also teddy bears, which Janet was certain they'd not seen in the window earlier that day. Here they were on video even though they had been invisible to the naked eye. Moments later, as the tape continued to roll, the Edstroms and their friends were further astonished to see a face, unmistakably Teddy Roosevelt with his distinctive pince-nez eyeglasses and full mustache, in the same window where the children had appeared. It was as if the video camera had captured images from a century earlier.

But it wasn't just the mysterious demeanor of Teddy Roosevelt that stunned Janet Edstrom. The psychotherapist, now staring at images that defied what all of her professional training had taught her, wondered why she was seeing the ethereal faces of little children floating in the window. Was someone else haunting Sagamore Hill? Whose ghosts were the astonished foursome witnessing on the videotape?

What the Edstroms and their friends did not know, as they sat there in front of the television in stunned silence, was that Teddy Roosevelt's first wife, Alice, died in childbirth on the same day his mother died in another room of their house. He was grief-stricken, and three years later, in 1886, he remarried lifelong friend Edith Kermit Carow. The Roosevelts raised six children, Alice, Teddy's daughter by his first wife, then four sons and another daughter born to Edith. These children had turned the Roosevelt household into a lively place, indeed. But had the restless spirits of the children returned to revisit their playroom with toys and dolls, and its memories of an idyllic life at Sagamore Hill? Were the teddy bears at the window psychic symbols of the many pets the Roosevelt children kept as well as of the famed toy bear affectionately named for Teddy Roosevelt?

The Edstroms and their friends knew they were seeing something on the video, but whether these were actual ghostly images or reflections of light or shadows of leaves dancing on the panes of glass was not immediately obvious. After replaying the video several times and debating at length, they decided they'd captured on tape something they couldn't explain. From the angle of the late-afternoon light and the angle of the camera, which was shooting up, they believed it couldn't have been a reflection, but they couldn't rule it out for sure. Then Peter, the most skeptical of the group, by virtue of his technical background, studied the tape, frame by frame.

"I never saw anything like that," Janet exclaimed. "We felt someone—or something—was up there in that window. But it didn't look human. The faces had a transparent quality and they seemed to float. Honestly, they looked like spirits."

The video ran for a total of several minutes. "We would have recorded more," but as Janet explained, "we didn't expect to see anything like this." The four friends concluded they'd "seen something supernatural."

Despite his inherent skepticism, Peter thought "it definitely looked like faces with features, moving around, and changing shape. I don't believe we saw leaves or shadows from light. What we saw looked like children and teddy bears."

The Edstroms, later shared their experience with the authors, for whom they played their videotape. Remember these Sagamore Hill videos were shot, not by professionals with special equipment, but with a home camcorder subject to all kinds of distortions of light and resolution. Who could figure out what the camcorder actually caught? However, within a few moments of Peter's cueing up the tape, just as the Edstroms had promised, a close-up could be seen in the second-floor window. It was the distinctive face of Teddy Roosevelt floating, it looked like, behind the glass with an ethereal rather than a human quality.

The tape continued to roll, coming in tighter on the images and then panning back. It was replayed several times, with each frame examined closely in stop motion. Ultimately, the tape was shown to a number of people, some quite skeptical, even disdainful, of psychic phenomena. All seven who viewed the videotape arrived independently at the same conclusion. Ruling out reflected light in the room or mistaking shadows or other reflected light off the Sagamore Hill glass windowpanes for Theodore Roosevelt's image, they reached the consensus that the mysterious images were of the president himself, somehow trapped in time's window.

Janet summed it up for all of us: "The experience took me aback, especially when everybody saw the same thing. We really thought they were spirits. Since nobody was in the building either time we were in there, Pete and I thought they couldn't have been living people. The way the faces, eyes, and features moved and changed, they weren't human. But they definitely weren't the shape leaves take. They definitely looked like faces of children, teddy bears, and Theodore Roosevelt, himself."

We have no way of knowing how many others have witnessed apparitions of T. R. and his family, or whether their spirits had manifested themselves to others but had been overlooked by those less observant. Maybe one could only capture the images on video because the spirits were invisible to the naked eye. Perhaps the Edstroms and their friends stumbled upon the ghostly presences quite inadvertently. Neither the Edstroms nor their friends know the answer or can even hazard a guess as to why something they did not see with their own eyes was apparent to a video camcorder. Although it is considered relatively rare, genuine spirit images can be captured on videotape, film, or photographs. After all, why should we be surprised that the ghosts of Teddy Roosevelt and his large and exuberant family returned home to Sagamore Hill where they'd known such happy and fulfilling years?

James Garfield

When Bruno and Dorothy Mallone purchased a lovely two-story Greek Revival home in Hiram, Ohio, in 1961, they knew they were moving into the house James Garfield and his young bride, Lucretia, lived in a hundred years earlier. What the Mallones didn't know was that the Garfields still called it home. James Garfield had moved there in 1856 while still a teacher and principal at Western Reserve Eclectic Institute, later called Hiram College. Originally built in 1826, the house was converted to a faculty boardinghouse. Garfield, who became president of Hiram College in 1857, lived at the Hiram College house with his wife until 1861 when he left to fight in the Civil War. He wasn't to return to Hiram until twenty years later, and then again after his physical death.

After the Mallones renovated the house and relocated it from the Hiram College campus to its present location, they settled in with their family in the fall of 1962. Shortly before Christmas that year, Dorothy's family visited, and soon they were chatting about the history of the house. Dorothy's sister jokingly asked if the old house was haunted. Dorothy laughed, "Oh yes, every once in a while James walks around." She wasn't serious, but, at that moment, unexpectedly and inexplicably, a lamp on the dining room wall turned itself on, the first of many supernatural incidents the Mallones would experience in their new home.

"It shook all of us up," Dorothy remembered, "because we were in the living room, and nobody was in the dining room."

From then on, lights and lamps seemed to have minds of their own. Finally, one day, Dorothy, irked and tired of turning off the light that repeatedly switched itself on, scolded, "Well, that's enough of this!" Whoever—or whatever—was responsible took the hint. Never again did the dining room lamp turn itself on of its own volition. However, that didn't stop other lights from behaving strangely.

"The lights in the living room just turned on," Dorothy said. "You could hear the snap as they went on. We usually had to turn them off. We thought it was James

Garfield because I'd say his name every once in a while, and that's when the lights turned themselves on."

The Mallones had had the house rewired when they moved in, but to be certain there were no lingering wiring problems responsible for the mysterious activity, they called back the electrician to make another check of the house circuitry. He ran tests on all the power supply lines that fed the lights, but could find nothing wrong. He also checked the wall lamp in the dining room again, just to make sure, but found nothing out of the ordinary.

Bruno Mallone, a teacher, was initially skeptical about any supernatural goings-on in the house and insisted there was a perfectly natural explanation for the electrical anomalies in the house. Whatever was wrong, they'd find it, he believed. However, after he personally experienced strange occurrences, his opinion began to change, especially when the events didn't involve a light turning itself on. One day, he recalled, as he sat in the dining room grading papers, he heard the unmistakable sound of the family's melodeon, an old-fashioned parlor organ they'd set up in the living room, strike three chords all by itself. Bruno got up from the dining room chair to see who was playing with the melodeon, but the room was empty. Then, astonished, he watched as the chair in front of the melodeon rocked itself. Standing there, he waited until the rocking stopped and examined the chair from every side. He could find no rational explanation for what he had just seen. Nor could he explain what happened, days later, when he sat down to watch an afternoon football game on TV, and placed a can of soda on a table near him. As he reached for it, the can slid forward, eluding his grasp, until it finally slid all the way over the edge of the table and spilled on the floor in front of the TV set.

This was only the beginning. As the weeks went by, it seemed as if more items in the house took on lives of their own. Trays, cans of food, dishes, and even furniture moved about, seemingly under their own power. One afternoon, for example, when the Mallones hurried to investigate a loud crash they heard coming from the living room, they discovered that several items on a cabinet—a plant, a glass lamp, a candlestick, and a dish of candy—had inexplicably fallen to the floor, neatly piled together. But to the family's amazement nothing was broken. The items were simply arranged at the foot of the cabinet by an unseen hand. Plumbing was also affected. "The faucets would turn themselves on. We'd have to go turn them off in the kitchen and bathrooms," Dorothy recalled.

The Mallones, in spite of the unexplained activity, were not frightened. "We would have been if everything happened at once. But things happened gradually," Dorothy said. And they became accustomed to the events, which became just another part of their lives.

For ten years the Mallones kept quiet about the mysterious incidents. "We thought people would think we were odd. They'd think we were crazy," Dorothy explained. Nonetheless, word of the unusual events became known, told by visitors to the Mallones, who'd witnessed disturbances they couldn't explain, and the story of the haunted house was reported in the *Akron Beacon-Journal*. One evening, a friend came over, hoping to witness the incidents he'd heard about. However, when nothing happened, he was disappointed. Then the Mallones' daughter, Pamela, who'd grown up with the strange phenomena, asked whatever invisible force or being might be present, "Do you want to communicate with us?" Suddenly, a candlesnuffer on the fireplace mantel flew halfway across the room. The company quickly left.

Oftentimes at the dining room table, Pam detected the strong aroma of cigar smoke, then heard footsteps going through the living and dining rooms. "We thought it probably was James Garfield because he smoked cigars," Dorothy said. The family also reported that they smelled the same aroma of cigar smoke on the anniversary of Garfield's assassination. Because of this cigar phenomenon, one of the Mallones' guests left an unopened cigar on the fireplace mantel, curious to find out whether anything unseen would affect it. Nothing did. The cigar remained there, forgotten, gathering dust behind some candlesticks for about a year and a half. One evening, however, as the family finished their supper in the dining room, they heard cellophane rattling. "When we looked for the source of the sound, there was the cigar with the cellophane completely off, lying in the middle of the living room floor," Dorothy recalled.

The mysterious presence also interfered with the children's electrical devices and toys. On one occasion, Pam recalled, she was playing an audiocassette, enjoying the music, when the machine suddenly stopped. Both Pam and her mother tried to figure out what had stopped the tape player when they heard a male voice they could not identify announce that he had shut off that infernal noise maker. Whose voice was that?

The paranormal occurrences in the Hiram house continued over the ensuing months and involved a variety of devices. It was as if whoever was responsible for the phenomena was becoming proficient at a variety of skills, not the least of which involved taking apart various appliances. For example, despite its newly installed water pump, the Mallones' washing machine suddenly stopped working. Luckily it was still under its warranty, Mrs. Mallone recalled, a fact she reminded the repairman about when she tried to explain the problem. It wasn't just that the machine was making odd sounds, she told him; the washer simply wouldn't work at all. "The repairman came back," Mrs. Mallone said, "and turned the machine over. Underneath, he found all the screws he'd soldered in now removed and placed neatly in a row on the floor. Startled, he said he'd never seen anything like this." There was simply no way these screws could have fallen out of the machine randomly and wound up as an organized row on the floor. This was sabotage.

Once the unexplained phenomena became publicly known, a local psychic, recommended by two colleagues of the Mallones, was invited to the house to inspect the premises and to discount any natural causes for the phenomena. Finding nothing out of the ordinary in the natural world, the psychic utilized a technique called automatic writing, "a form of mediumship in which the writer records information from sources other than her own mind." There are different techniques of automatic writing, some of which may involve self-hypnosis or writing with one's opposite hand so as to draw on information from the nondominant brain hemisphere. Many paranormal researchers, however, theorize that automatic writing, popularized in the nineteenth century, may be a direct method of spirit communication that bypasses the brain's logical filters and is reported by the medium as pure, unedited text from a source beyond the world of normal experience.

"As she started writing," Dorothy recalled, "a candle flamed up, twelve inches or more, just going up and down. Then the psychic read back what she wrote. 'This is James Garfield.' He was upset about being murdered by so-called friends. They'd conspired to kill him." Was the medium tapped into a piece of history through a murder victim's own spirit?

On another occasion, two young women acquaintances visited. "One girl got real pale and was shivering. She said she felt cold and someone behind her," Dorothy explained. "The other girl said, 'Let's go try the Ouija board.'" Dorothy thought it would be a good test to ask the Ouija board Garfield's wife's name, a piece of information she was certain neither young woman knew. "Well, that pointer [the Ouija board's planchette] immediately spelled out C-R-E-T-E, Garfield's nickname for his wife, Lucretia." Whatever was directing the planchette, Dorothy realized, certainly couldn't have been the hands of her two friends because there was no way either could have known Mrs. Garfield's nickname. Whether the presence in the Hiram house was a spirit, ghost, or something else, the Mallones believed it was benevolent, not malicious, and certainly worthy of continuing study. In fact, the family was fascinated by the invisible inhabitant who rocked in its chair, smoked cigars, played the organ, and knew how to take apart a washing machine.

As the years went by, the incidents continued. One evening, Bruno Mallone brought home a local newspaper with plans to complete the daily crossword puzzle. He never got to it that night, and left the newspaper on a table. The next morning, the puzzle was completed in a handwriting he didn't recognize. He asked Dorothy and Pamela if either was responsible. No, they assured him. "The one thing we noticed that was particularly odd was the letter E. We checked a copy of Garfield's diary and compared the handwritings. His E looked like a backward three—same as in the puzzle," Dorothy said. Had the spirit identified himself through his own handwriting?

When the psychic returned to the Mallones just before the next Christmas, she performed more automatic writing and, in addition to James and Lucretia Garfield, sensed several other spirits present. One of them was a sickly child named Andrew, whose father was a friend of Garfield's and the town doctor. Another spirit, Marsha Henry, once lived in the house, and her father was also a Garfield friend and government official in Washington when Garfield was assassinated. Marsha communicated, through the psychic, that she remembered, as a small child, sitting on Garfield's lap. "So you see, all the spirits in the house have some connection to Garfield," Dorothy explained.

In 1979, nationally known ghost experts Ed and Lorraine Warren, at Hiram College for a seminar, asked if there were any haunted houses in the area, and were told that the Mallone home was an area of some kind of supernatural presence. But the individual who suggested they visit the Mallones at home was careful not to tell the Warrens anything about the red-painted house with white shutters, other than to say it had "activity." Thus, with no advance information about the nature of the supernatural presence and with no stories about the history of the Hiram house or its relation to President

James Garfield, Ed and Lorraine Warren visited the
Mallones and attempted to make a psychic connection
with whatever spirits were visiting the house.

"The Warrens found no evil in the house," Dorothy
said. "We were visited by good ghosts." Lorraine reported that she psychically detected two presences, one
a large man, the second, a small woman, who were a
couple, but who did not seem to be emotionally close.
Lorraine wasn't certain of the relationship between the
two spirits. However, from her descriptions, Dorothy
was certain Lorraine had discerned the Garfields. Lorraine also identified each room and what it had been
used for years earlier. The large room the Garfields lived
in had become Pamela Mallone's bedroom.

"Lorraine also psychically sensed a cradle in the living
room, by the fireplace," Dorothy explained, an interesting psychic experience because, unbeknownst to Lorraine, the Garfields had lost two children when they
lived in Hiram. The future president's firstborn likely
died in the house and that may well have explained the
presence of the cradle and spiritual energy that ema-
nated from it. "Lorraine also said our living room was
just full of Christmas. She said there was Christmas everywhere, even the smell of Christmas," Dorothy said.
"That's when we have the most activity, every year. I
guess the spirits just love the holiday and cluster around
the living room, where we put up the tree. We've even
seen ornaments twirl on the tree."

Dorothy and Pam have attempted to tape record
noises, curious to see whether any unusual sounds would
be captured. "We heard rapping," Pamela said. "You
turn on the tape, ask questions, then wait a little bit.
When you play back the tape, you get responses. Many
times we'd hear lots of rappings. One time we played it
back and there was a lot of banging, as if someone was
standing next to the tape recorder and pounding his fists
around the machine. Right after that, we heard a sigh
on the tape. It was a man's deep voice. But you only
heard it when you played the tape back." This is not an

uncommon phenomenon. It was similar to the Edstroms having been able to capture the image of Teddy Roosevelt on videotape when none of those present at the taping could see the image in the window through the naked eye.

Dorothy Mallone reported that the spiritual manifestations at the house intensified after the two psychics tried to make contact. Once, months after her attempts to audiotape the sounds of the spirits, Dorothy walked into her living room and she saw a large man standing right in front of her. At first she thought it was her husband, Bruno, but she suddenly realized that she didn't recognize the man at all. Ultimately she came to believe the figure was likely the apparition of James Garfield, and although Dorothy could not discern any facial features, the size and heavy build of the specter matched Garfield, who was over six feet tall. But President Garfield wasn't the only specter who appeared to the Mallones. Pamela Mallone, in particular, recalled the time a girlfriend saw the specter of a small woman in long skirts, typical of mid-nineteenth-century dress. "The apparition made its way downstairs from the second floor and walked to the front room door." Could this have been Lucretia, the person the Ouija board's planchette spelled out years earlier?

Remarkably, the Mallones never expressed any fear of the spirits who live with them, nor do they want them to leave. "We were told by psychics, they are not earthbound," Dorothy said. "They know they're dead. They just enjoy coming back. They enjoy the house. Lorraine Warren also said they were protecting us." The spirits of President Garfield and his wife visit any time they wish, often calling attention to their presence. "We'll hear the lock snap, and the door will open on its own," Dorothy explained. "Once a health aide we had here to care for my mother thought someone was coming up the driveway. She walked into the dining room. Our dogs were barking. Then the aide sensed someone behind her. She turned around and right there in the doorway, between the dining and living rooms, was the figure of that same large man. The aide was really frightened. She never came back."

Pamela Mallone explains that she will talk to the spirits as if she can communicate with them across the divide between life and death. "Sometimes the door will open or close, and I'll ask, 'Well, are you coming or going?' Another time a minister stopped by for a visit one day. As he was getting ready to leave, the lock snapped and the door opened. It was as if they opened it to let him out. The minister said, 'I must not have snapped the door shut.' We didn't say anything. That was on Garfield's birthday."

On other occasions, rooms will feel unnaturally cold. "My grandson said one room was like a freezer. And it was a warm day," Dorothy recalled.

"We've seen the dogs, who greet anybody who comes in the house, just stop at the dining room door and not go any further," Pam explained. "My nephew was here one day. He was very young, but old enough to talk. He looked into the kitchen and said, 'Look at that ball. Bouncing here. Bouncing there.' We didn't see it." One night, around the same time, Pamela also witnessed a floating ball of light, which her dog growled at, until the psychic energy that comprised the light dissipated and the light disappeared.

James Garfield last visited Hiram College to deliver a farewell address on February 4, 1881, and recalled warm memories of his life there more than twenty years earlier. "Never despise the days of Hiram life and childhood," he told the members of the student body. "The associations that you are now forming, your lessons, your thoughts, and your deeds from day to day, are what go to make up your life here. And this is the foundation of your afterlife. Be wise now, and when you live over again, the life you live here, may it be such as you could wish." Seven months later, James Garfield, open to spiritualism all his life, was dead. But his spirit still rejoices in visits to his old home in the small college town of Hiram, Ohio.

Woodrow Wilson

Among the issues that bind the spirits of the deceased to this earth and prevent them from passing on are the pieces of unfinished business that may have frustrated them in life. The more powerful the individual, or the greater the individual's agenda, the more likely that spirit is to remain here to finish the business that was started. This describes the spirit of President Woodrow Wilson, probably, along with Jimmy Carter, one of the most idealistic presidents America has ever had, yet at the same time one of the most frustrated in his endeavors. Not only did Wilson see his plan for the League of Nations fail, but he had to spend the final years of his life between his wheelchair and his cane, watching while his dreams for a world union of free nations dissolved into chaos.

When President Woodrow Wilson's term in office ended in 1921, he—already sick and partially disabled—and his wife moved into a comfortable redbrick Georgian house they'd purchased in Washington. There, the former president, unable to recover from the effects of a stroke he'd earlier suffered while still in office, lived for the remaining three years of his life. Wilson died in 1924, bitter and disillusioned, having failed to "make the world safe for democracy." Edith Wilson remained in their home until her death in 1961. But after Edith Wilson's passing, strange things began to take place behind the stately brick walls of the Wilson house, events that were reported by the staid *Washington Post*, an unlikely source for news about psychic phenomena.

On May 4, 1969, the usually skeptical newspaper ran a story about the presidency and the paranormal titled "Playing Host to Ghosts?" by reporter Philip Casey, which told of a Wilson house caretaker who said he'd heard the sound of someone shuffling with the help of a cane. "The Woodrow Wilson house . . . is a quiet and serene place most of the time . . . but sometimes at night there's more noise than José Vasquez, the house man, can stand. Vasquez has been hearing queer, and sometimes loud, noises in the night. Vasquez doesn't believe in ghosts, but he's finding it hard to hold that position. . . ." Vasquez said that one night while alone in the Wilson house, playing piano, "I felt that someone was behind me, watching me. My neck felt funny. But there was no one there. I looked."

The article continued, "Later [Vasquez] was walking up to his fourth floor apartment when he heard something behind him on the third floor, near the bedrooms of [President Wilson and his wife]. Vasquez said, 'The steps were loud, and heavy, like a man. The footsteps went into Mrs. Wilson's bedroom.' " The caretaker entered and "kept hearing the steps in the room. . . . 'I go to this corner, and I stand here and wait. I waited a long time and then I hear the steps again, going into the hall and to Mr. Wilson's bedroom. I follow.' " Hearing "the heavy footsteps at the foot of the president's four-poster bed . . . [Vasquez] decided to hurry upstairs." When he did, " 'the steps they come running behind me, and they follow me, bump, bump, bump, up the stairs. I am very nervous.' "

When President Wilson lived in the house, he could only move about with the help of a cane and an elevator, which carried him to his upstairs bedroom. Ghosts do not need the assistance of elevators, even though a cane, used in life, can become an accessory after death. If the spirit that frightened Vasquez was, indeed, Woodrow Wilson, it might well have been able to navigate the stairs, pushing the cane along as if it were a symbol of the frustration the spirit experienced in life.

On another occasion, "Vasquez was in his tub when he heard some knocking noises. 'I knock right back, like this,' he explained, thumping the tub, 'and the noise stops.' " Vasquez said his wife also "hears occasional noises and sometimes wakes up in the night under the impression that someone is standing at the foot of the bed. There never is anyone she can see." Other employees in the Wilson house have also told of hearing inexplicable noises, especially at night.

Mediums who've visited the house have confirmed the

presence of Wilson's ghost, unsettled and frustrated by his failure to achieve his vision of world peace. Psychic researcher Bryce Bond reported he visited the Wilson house accompanied by a medium who received a message from Wilson's spirit that the former president harbored intense disappointment about his fervent but failed efforts to vanquish wars. The communication he received from President Wilson's spirit included a prediction that by the end of the 1980s there would be "a major development toward world peace between former enemies." Bond did not know it then, because his visit to Wilson's home occurred several years before the Soviet Union was dismantled in 1989, but the collapse of the Berlin Wall, which had yet to occur, would pave the way for the end of the Cold War. Perhaps that history-changing development brought Woodrow Wilson's restive spirit a measure of peace in the next stage of life, although who's to say whether he still haunts on nights when his former home is empty and there are no living beings there to interfere with his shuffling up the stairs to his old bedroom.

Harry S. Truman

Blunt-speaking Harry S. Truman never had a problem telling people what he thought of them, often in very colorful language as reporters escorted him on his morning "constitutionals." So when someone shouted, "Give 'em hell, Harry," as he campaigned for the presidency in 1948 from the back of his private railcar, the phrase stuck. Even though Truman was a feisty man who professed not to believe in ghosts, his nature continued in the afterlife.

Born in 1884 in rural Lamar, Missouri, the child of a farmer, Harry was six years old when his family moved to the big city of Independence. Limited by poor eyesight, which necessitated his wearing thick glasses, Harry grew into adolescence a shy, bookish stay-at-home who enjoyed playing piano. After serving in World War I, he opened a haberdashery, but his store in Kansas City failed and he was forced to close its doors. Even though he was unsuccessful as a shopkeeper, he pursued a career as a politician, working inside the Missouri state Democratic Party ranks at first until he began winning elected offices. Still more a local politician than a national figure, he was rewarded for his party loyalty in 1944 when the Democrats drafted Franklin Delano Roosevelt to run for an unprecedented fourth term. Truman, popular within Democratic Party circles and a strong FDR supporter, accepted the second spot from party leaders on what was considered to be a shoo-in national ticket. No one actually thought he'd wind up becoming president, least of all Harry Truman himself.

But only three months after his inauguration, Franklin Roosevelt died on April 12, 1945. Vice President Truman, told by Mrs. Roosevelt, "Harry, the president is dead," was sworn in that evening to a job for which, he readily admitted to anyone who asked him, he was ill-prepared. When reporters congratulated him, Truman asked for their prayers, then said he "felt as though the whole universe had fallen on [him], the sun, the moon, and all the stars." The daunting tasks ahead were made far more difficult by his succeeding one of the twentieth century's towering political figures at a time when there was still a war to be won and difficult negotiations ahead on the status of the liberated European countries and the future of Japan. It was Harry Truman who, shortly after he assumed the presidency, was faced with the decision to drop the atomic bomb on Japan.

In 1948, Truman pulled off one of the greatest upsets in American politics, leading a badly splintered Democratic Party and running on the nation's first civil rights platform to defeat the heavily favored Republican candidate, Thomas Dewey. But burdened by the responsibility of the fall of China to Mao Tse-tung, the beginning of the Cold War with the Soviet Union, the North Korean and Chinese invasions of South Korea, an openly hostile Congress, a virulent Republican Party angry at losing the presidency for the fifth time since Hoover, and an antagonistic press eager for a Republican victory, Truman was glad to leave the White House to Dwight Eisenhower in 1953. He and his wife returned home to Independence, where he wrote his memoirs, remained interested in politics, helped plan the future Truman Presidential Library, and became nothing less than the dean of the Democratic Party when, in 1960, he conferred his blessings on the JFK candidacy. On December 26, 1972, Truman died of natural causes in Kansas City. He was eighty-eight years old. Bess Truman followed her husband to the Other Side ten years later, at the age of eighty-seven.

During his presidency, Truman never admitted to witnessing any apparitions, although he didn't deny their presence, and insisted he had no fear of running into ghosts in the White House. However, once when traveling, he said his late mother appeared to him in a dream vision moments after she died. It was a way, he was certain, of her saying a final good-bye. Although Truman claimed he never really believed in the presence of actual ghosts, his acceptance of the appearance of his mother's spirit might have been a precursor to his own later appearance at his Independence home, where the Trumans lived from the time they were married in 1919 until their deaths.

The Truman house on North Delaware Street had been in Bess's family since 1867 and was considered one of Independence's finer residences. Bess had been the rich girl from one of Independence's better families who surprised the entire town by allowing herself to be wooed by a local farm boy. Bess always said that when she first met Harry she knew he was destined for great things. The Trumans always kept the house on North Delaware Street, and during Truman's presidential years it became the Summer White House and the center of the Trumans' close family relationships in Independence. It was to this lifelong home that Harry Truman's spirit returned and that Truman still visits to this very day.

Employees at the house, now open to the public, have reported on several occasions that they've seen President

Truman's apparition in the living room, sitting in a favorite chair with a glass of his favorite bourbon filling the room with its unmistakable bouquet. It is certain that for Harry Truman, his home in Independence held fond reminiscences because it was a haven from the political hounds in Washington that the plainspoken farm boy often complained about. Truman's spirit has visited from time to time to observe and to savor the feeling of the old home, but not to haunt it. His is not an earthbound ghost trapped in this physical dimension by his own frustration and anger. Having made his peace with both his achievements and shortcomings in life, and having accepted the destiny he fulfilled as President of the United States, Harry Truman's soul is free to come and go as he chooses. Because in life he believed in the existence of the spirit world, he may happily be a member of that world in death.

Internationally celebrated medium and author Kenny Kingston tells the story of how he first met Truman in the flesh in 1948 in San Francisco, where he was campaigning for president. Truman wanted "to talk to the spirits," mainly to learn if they saw him being elected. Kingston assured him of victory. When Kingston next met Truman three years later, the president quipped that he'd requested "to be buried on the grounds of the future Truman Library" in Independence, so that he'd be able to "get up now and then and stroll in my office there!" Obviously, Harry Truman was good to his word.

Not all apparitions in presidential homes are ghosts of presidents and first ladies. At the Key West, Florida, home the Trumans visited, which became known as the Little White House, caretakers reported "inexplicable dark shadows" moving about the house. According to paranormal researcher Dennis William Hauck, "several employees," unnerved by sights of the specter, quit their jobs. Psychics who've investigated discovered the "restless" spirit was neither Harry nor Bess Truman; rather it was the angry ghost of a former housekeeper upset that the Little White House was permitted "to fall into disrepair."

Richard Nixon

As peaceful as the spirit of Harry Truman was after his death is as restless as the spirit of former president Richard Nixon, who has been seen haunting his grave site in Southern California. What is the nature, observers have asked, of the "luminous green mist" that has been seen floating above Richard Nixon's grave in Yorba Linda, California, where he was born? Is this his troubled ghost now returned home, still trapped by the very emotional forces that unraveled his presidency in 1973?

According to *Haunted Places: The National Directory* by Dennis William Hauck, Nixon's ghost has been observed at the front door of the small frame house built by his father. When Nixon was born there in 1913, his maternal grandmother accurately predicted he would grow up to either be a lawyer or preacher because his crying was unusually loud. Today, Yorba Linda is the site of the Richard M. Nixon Library and Birthplace, open to the public since 1990. The Yorba Linda Library is a haunted place where "strange tapping sounds" have been heard emanating from the Watergate Display Room, as if someone or something is in there ruminating and fussing over the evidence of Nixon's disgrace. There have also been accounts of inexplicable malfunctions in the machines on which visitors play the infamous Watergate tapes surreptitiously recorded by Nixon during his White House years.

Nixon's ghost is an example of what paranormal researchers and psychics term an "earthbound" spirit. While souls may return to the places and possessions they knew on earth, for a variety of reasons, most eventually accept death and their exit from this life, release their personal emotional attachments to the physical world, and successfully make the transition to the nonmaterial dimension, the Other Side. This act of release and acceptance marks the growth of the soul to the next stage of being. One can call it surrender, but it's a surrender to the irrevocability of death that releases the soul from the restrictions of the corporeal concerns that vexed it during life. Nixon's spirit doesn't believe in surrender. He didn't believe in it during life, even after it was forced upon him as a result of the Watergate impeachment hearings, and he certainly doesn't believe in it after death.

Earthbound spirits like Nixon's, therefore, whether through a remorse of conscience or a lingering shame or anger, cannot accept death and are thus unable or unwilling to make that progression to the afterlife, sometimes for many decades. Such disturbed entities cannot release themselves from the events they regard as unsettled in this realm and are tied to the event and the places that troubled them. For these reasons, earthbound ghosts do not advance to the Other Side, but deliberately remain bound to the physical world, trapped and tortured by themselves, unable to satisfy the unresolved conflicts or traumas that have held them back. That is the predicament Richard Nixon's unhappy ghost finds itself in.

Earthbound spirits, rightly or wrongly, feel they yet have a mission to complete in this world, and will not surrender to the next stage of life until that which they believe is incomplete or needs correction is resolved. Earthbound ghosts, such as Nixon's, can be obsessive in this regard, and exist in the spiritual hell of torment and misery, unlike most spirits who return here to visit in a more positive state. Nixon's spirit has remained earthbound since his death in 1994, because he has one overriding purpose: to clear his politically disgraced name and reputation.

In life, Richard Nixon was one of this country's most complex, enigmatic, and controversial presidents. During his career, he rose to towering achievements, then fell to the depths of crushing defeat. Like Lyndon Johnson, his presidency was ultimately undone by the Vietnam War and his reactions to his enemies. His departure from the White House in August 1974 marked the only time a United States president ever resigned from office. Nixon was brought down by the weight of the Watergate scandals that overshadowed his accomplishments as chief executive. When he realized he faced certain impeachment, Nixon's only choice was to leave office, in disgrace, on August 9, 1974. Privately, his mood was accurately captured by Nixon's Secretary of State Henry Kissinger, who explained, "Nixon was a man awake during his own nightmare."

Shortly before noon on that last day, the public saw Nixon on the steps of the presidential helicopter. There he turned, raised his right arm "in a sweeping gesture and awkwardly waved good-bye." Then, accompanied by his wife, Pat, and daughter Tricia Cox and her husband, Richard Nixon retreated to exile at his San Clemente, California, estate, reportedly in a deep state of physical and emotional depression.

During the next twenty years, Nixon devoted himself to primarily one cause: the repair of his badly damaged reputation and tarnished place in American history. Granted a full pardon by his successor, President Gerald Ford, for his Watergate crimes, Nixon traveled and wrote extensively. He became a bestselling author and a foreign policy scholar in his own right. He advised presidents Carter, Reagan, and Bush and was Bill Clinton's foreign policy tutor in the early weeks of the Clinton administration. Nixon also attempted, unsuccessfully, to gain possession of the secret White House tapes, but was rebuffed by Congress. Nixon was ceaseless in his efforts to restore what he believed was his rightful status in the chronicles of American presidential achievements. Nixon often explained that one of his favorite presidents was Teddy Roosevelt because T. R. never gave up and never gave in no matter what his enemies threw at him. And since his death in April 1994 from a massive stroke at the age of eighty-one, he has continued to do just that. Richard Nixon's earthbound spirit is no less bitter and obsessed with his legacy, hoping to erase the stain of scandal that marred his reputation and became synonymous with his name. In his afterlife, Richard Nixon is doing exactly what he preached in life, fighting for his name and reputation.

In 1974, Richard Nixon said, "We think that when someone near us dies, we think that when we lose an election, we think that when we suffer a defeat that all is ended. Not true. It is only a beginning, always." Ironically, Nixon's own death may have been just such a beginning of the next stage of his quest. Now, as Nixon's earthbound spirit struggles to release itself from the emotional agony brought to bear by his errors and misdeeds on earth, we can only ponder whether, in his mission to restore his reputation, he has learned from the mistakes he made, the disgrace he suffered, and the upheaval he caused the American political system. We now know that Watergate was not Richard Nixon's end. But does he know it? Does his spirit not know that history has already subordinated his tarnished political reputation to the now commonly accepted prescience of his statesmanship? Or does he still seek a second chance in the spirit world? If that is the case, Nixon was correct when he said defeat is not the end. Whether it was his fate or his own free will to be caught in a monumental political scandal, perhaps for Richard Nixon the next stage of life is truly a new beginning.

CHAPTER SEVEN

The Ghosts of the First Ladies

I hope that someday someone will take the time to evaluate the true role of the wife of a president and to assess the many burdens she has to bear and the contributions she makes.

—President Harry S. Truman

From Abigail Adams, the first first lady who took up residence in the White House, to Laura Bush, the current resident, one of the primary roles of the first lady has been to turn the "House" into a home, even if it's more in the perception than in the deeds themselves. This was one of the difficulties that Senator Hillary Clinton struggled with as first lady in the early months of the Clinton administration when she was perceived by the partisan Republicans as pursuing her own agenda. This was also one of the difficulties faced by First Lady Betty Ford, who was struggling with addiction and all the problems associated with it.

The Nature of a First Lady

Who were the women who became the first ladies of the nation? Each was "an ordinary woman, who stepped onto an extraordinary stage," wrote Cheryl Heckler-Feltz in *Heart and Soul of the Nation*. Their interests, personalities, educations, and beliefs varied greatly. Many were bereaved parents or widowed, several of them in the White House, their spirits tested by life's tragedies. Some loved their roles as first ladies; others intensely disliked it. Most were long-suffering women, as political spouses frequently are, in love with their husbands but not with their jobs. Five first ladies were daughters of clergymen, but almost all presidential wives were politically astute and often confidantes to their husbands on matters of state.

It is not surprising that of all the first ladies in the two centuries of the presidency—in all, there were forty-five presidential wives—nearly half had contact with the supernatural. Likely, there were many more psychic incidents than those reported since relatively few were publicly revealed. Based on the number of paranormal incidents reported by the population at large, which are in the tens of millions, certainly many more experiences occurred to first ladies, including afterdeath communications, dream visitations from deceased loved ones, premonitions, and the witnessing of apparitions. And many first ladies have returned as ghosts to haunt the locations they inhabited in life with their husbands.

The religious beliefs of first ladies appear to have no relationship to their supernatural encounters. Rosalynn Carter's comment "You seek guidance from God to do what's right and best" has consistently been the prevailing attitude of presidential wives, most of whom were spiritual women. However, there is no record that any first lady ever indicated a conflict between her religious or spiritual beliefs and her psychic or mystical experiences.

Accordingly, the lives of our first ladies are intimately connected to their years at the White House, and it's no surprise, therefore, that their spirits return to visit the house they managed. It all began during the final year of the administration of John Adams, the first occupant of the new Executive Mansion.

Abigail Adams

Abigail Adams could barely contain the anticipation and excitement she felt on that chilly day in November 1800, as her carriage bumped along the muddy and unpaved streets of the small and swampy village called Federal City, on her way to the President's Palace, as the White House was then known. John Adams, America's second president, had been elected to succeed George Washington in 1796, and for the first 3.5 years of his presidency, John and Abigail had lived in a fashionable Philadelphia residence. Now, in the waning months of John's term, they would call the President's Palace on Pennsylvania Avenue their official home.

Her excitement dissipated immediately, however, when, after all the months of expectation, the carriage pulled up the drive. What greeted her shocked her very sensibilities as a lady and hostess. After a lifetime in comfortable homes, here she was at the doorstep of a mansion that was still partially a construction zone. Tools and materials were scattered everywhere. She was appalled when she realized she had to squeeze the family into only four rooms in the living quarters, even though the mansion promised someday to be a structure of immense grandeur. In a letter to her daughter, Abigail was at no loss for words to describe what she saw:

"The house is upon a grand and superb scale, requiring about thirty servants to attend and keep the apartments in proper order . . . an establishment very well proportioned to the President's salary. The lighting of the apartments, from the kitchen to parlors and chambers, is a tax indeed, and the fires we are obliged to keep to secure us from daily agues is another very cheering comfort. . . ."

Abigail immediately began the task of making the half-built mansion as agreeable as she could. When she discovered that the not yet completed East Room was the driest part of the building, it became her choice as the place to hang the family's laundry. In fact, she spent a considerable amount of time in the East Room during her nearly four months in the President's Palace, until John's term in office expired in March 1801. The discomfort of the White House notwithstanding, Abigail loved her role as first lady and was saddened when it came time to leave. Her attachment to the Executive Mansion must have been fond indeed because there were stories during the nineteenth century of the return of Abigail's ghost to the White House. However, the first officially recorded appearance of Mrs. Adams wasn't until the twentieth century during the administration of Ohio's William Howard Taft.

By the time President Taft moved into the White House more than a hundred years later in 1909, the official and state functions in the East Room had long replaced Abigail's family laundry. However, spirits often remember certain emotional or traumatic moments of their lives on earth regardless of the passage of time or new uses put to original locations. Thus, Abigail returned to the East Room, a place for which she had a strong attachment. And what task did the ghost of one of our most celebrated first ladies repeat? Witnesses during the Taft years say they saw the specter of Mrs. Adams, in her familiar "cap and lace shawl," float through the unopened doors of the East Room, her arms extended and laden with heaps of laundry. Some claimed they knew when Abigail's spirit was present, for it was accompanied by the slight scent of soap and wet laundry. The "oldest ghost" in White House history, Abigail Adams had not forgotten her makeshift laundry room, and even one hundred years after she left the White House, she still continued to do the family's laundry.

Dolley Madison

In the years after her death, Dolley Madison's ghost was witnessed, sometimes under very dramatic circumstances, in several locations both inside and outside the White House. A charming and accomplished hostess who dressed in elegant satin gowns accompanied by lovely accessories, First Lady Dolley Madison was hugely admired and emulated. Her distinctive headdress was typically "a turban . . . of velvet and . . . satin with two superb plumes, the bird of paradise feathers," a friend admiringly observed. It was that headdress that helped identify the spirit of Dolley Madison to observers when she appeared in the early twentieth century.

The first lady enjoyed her life in the White House and had a unique attachment to it. She not only helped in the design of the exterior landscaping of the grounds, but she also helped preserve the historic treasures of the White House in the desperate hours when she and her husband were forced to flee the city as invading British forces advanced on Washington, intent on destroying as much of the new nation's capital as they could. Under the command of Sir Alexander Cochrane—uncle to Captain Lord Thomas Cochrane, the British sea captain author Patrick O'Brian used as his model for Captain Jack Aubrey—the British troops set fire to the mansion on August 24, 1814, destroying large parts of the structure. But because of Dolley Madison's prescience, many important items, such as the portrait of President George Washington, were removed before the English arrived.

Dolley especially loved the White House's enormous lawn, and there, behind the mansion, she patiently planted her garden, a gift to future first ladies. In the wake of the torching by the British, the Madisons, unable to return to the presidential mansion, took up residence in two other locations. While the White House was being rebuilt, Dolley attentively watched over the reconstruction of the building and, of course, the restoration of her beloved garden, which over the years and through every subsequent administration continued to bloom.

Some one hundred years later, First Lady Edith Wilson, President Wilson's second wife, decided to make changes and instructed White House gardeners to dig up and relocate the garden. Mrs. Wilson's plans did not escape Dolley's vigilant spirit, which became enraged that another first lady would undo what she'd so affectionately planned and tended. Unable to bear the affront to her landscape design, Dolley's specter materialized before the gardeners could touch so much as one flower or clump of earth with a shovel or spade. There was no mistaking the apparition, for Dolley was dressed in her familiar early-nineteenth-century attire.

Dolley's ghost wasted no time angrily confronting the gardeners, and as the terrified men watched, her apparition stomped about wildly, her arms furiously gesturing them away. Then she scolded them in no uncertain terms. That was enough. The gardeners, sufficiently frightened and intimidated, tossed aside their tools and quickly fled, no match for the infuriated ghost of the first lady. According to White House legend, "hundreds of roses" were planted to calm Dolley's anxious spirit, and the garden was never again tampered with. Today the famed White House Rose Garden continues to flower, just as Dolley Madison wished it, and in exactly the same place.

After the Madisons fled the blazing White House during the British attack, they were forced to take up residence in the Octagon House, a stately Georgian mansion, home of Colonel John Tayloe and his family who'd invited the Madisons to make it their temporary White House until the original could be rebuilt. The Octagon has a long history of hauntings, and many ghosts have been reported there, among them several members of the Tayloe family, President Madison, and his ubiquitous wife. Dolley's ghost has been seen passing through the well-appointed rooms of the Octagon. As recently as the 1960s, witnesses reported the apparition still wore her familiar plumed turban and her favorite lilac perfume, and was often detected in the Octagon's drawing room accompanied by a cold spot.

Not surprisingly, Dolley's ghost returned to the house she lived in during her last years, on Lafayette Square in Washington, the city she adored and where she remained socially active until her death in 1849, at the age of eighty-one. When guests left the exclusive Washington

Club at night, a short distance from Dolley's home, they often reported seeing her apparition seated in a rocking chair on the porch adorned in her favorite turban. Many of the men passing by politely tipped their hats to the ghost of one of the country's best-liked and most popular first ladies, who always enjoyed the company of men. In life, Dolley Madison was a vivacious and vigorous woman, and her spirit has been among the most energetic and lively in the nation's capital.

Abigail Adams and Dolley Madison were two of the strongest and best known of our first ladies. Had their earthly exuberance translated into psychic energy that better enabled their spirits to materialize?

Martha Jefferson

Hans Holzer, the author of many books about hauntings, once visited Thomas Jefferson's home Monticello accompanied by a psychic who was especially drawn to the cottage behind the main house. The psychic's impression was that Jefferson's young wife, Martha, had been unhappy living in the small cottage when the couple first married in 1772, and hoped for a larger and better-appointed residence. Martha's spirit communicated that she'd been uncomfortable with her husband's associations, especially his relationships with other women. The psychic sensed Martha's distress and anxiety that long ago became attached to the cottage. Had she lived, Martha, who died in 1782 when she was just thirty-three, would have been President Thomas Jefferson's first lady.

Letitia Tyler and Julia Tyler

John Tyler assumed the presidency unexpectedly in April 1841, upon the sudden death of William Henry Harrison in the weeks after his inauguration, the first victim of the curse of Tenskwatawa. Six feet tall, thin, with a prominent nose and high cheekbones, the principled and honorable Tyler had enjoyed a long and distinguished political career when fate elevated him to the nation's highest office, affording him the historic distinction of becoming the first Vice President of the United States to ascend to the White House upon the death of the president. His first wife, Letitia, thus became the first first lady who had ascended to her office upon the death of a sitting president and the first first lady to die in office as well.

Although Letitia was a quiet and devoted spouse who'd given birth to nine children, seven of whom survived, her health worsened after the loss of two infants. Then in 1838, at the age of forty-eight, she suffered a debilitating stroke, and her deteriorating condition prevented her from carrying out the duties of first lady after her husband's inauguration. When Letitia died in 1842, at the age of fifty-two, President Tyler and the entire nation mourned her death. Hers was the shortest tenure in office of any first lady.

For John Tyler, life in the Executive Mansion became increasingly depressing and lonely, overshadowed by his wife's "wretched health" and subsequent passing. Letitia's death marked another dubious distinction for Tyler, whose elevation to the presidency was the result of death: he also became the first president to be widowed in office.

Tyler's period of loneliness lasted little more than a year when his head was turned by the lovely Julia Gardiner, the daughter of the U.S. Senator from New York, whom he met at a Washington reception she'd attended with her wealthy and socially prominent family. The widowed president was clearly smitten with the beautiful and lively young woman from New York, who, thirty years younger than Tyler, was affectionately dubbed by the social columnists in the New York newspapers the "Rose of Long Island." With her "large gray eyes, raven hair, and clearest olive complexion," she attracted attention and suitors wherever she traveled and was certainly used to fending off advances. Although Tyler delicately flirted with Julia, she resisted his entreaties. This was not the Washington, D.C., of today, and Tyler got nowhere. Adding to his frustration, being the President of the United States made it all the more difficult to court her in the open, so he cleverly found other ways to remind Julia of his affections. On one occasion when she visited New York, Tyler ordered the U.S. Marine Band to play for her. However, it would take a tragic twist of fate, tinged with the power of the supernatural, before Julia would draw closer to him.

That event happened on February 28, 1844, when a public presentation was held for a new type of naval cannon aboard the steamer *Princeton* anchored in the Potomac River. Among the hundreds invited were President Tyler, many government officials, military figures, other dignitaries, and their wives. One of the guests was former first lady Dolley Madison, then a spry seventy-seven years old. All of those gathered on board the *Princeton* were in a festive mood with the exception of Ann Gilmer, the wife of the secretary of the Navy, who'd experienced a terrifying premonition in which she envisioned her husband's death right there on the deck of the war ship. Another person who admitted to a frightening dream premonition the night before was Julia Gardiner, who wasted no time sharing with her father, Senator David Gardiner, the chilling specifics that she said were more realistic than any other dream she ever had. Julia described in detail the deck of the *Princeton*, although she had never been aboard it. In her disturbing vision, she saw two white horses galloping toward her across the ship's deck. As they came closer, she could see that the riders were skeletons, death itself. Then one of the skeletons turned to look at Julia. It was the face of her father staring directly at her.

Julia was so alarmed by the macabre vision that she pleaded with her father not to attend the ceremonies on the *Princeton*, fearing for his life. But Gardiner dismissed his daughter's concern, thinking it humorous that she would take seriously what he discounted as "a silly bad dream." He asked her instead, "And you would give up for that the President's reception?" Senator Gardiner was adamant in his insistence that he was not going to miss such a special occasion, particularly because his daughter had suffered a foolish nightmare. Julia pleaded, but to no avail, and ultimately agreed to attend with him.

Once aboard the *Princeton*, Julia was shaken by how precise her vision of the ship's deck had been. How could her nightmare have been so accurate if it were only a "silly bad dream," as her father had said? Julia's mood darkened, lifted only slightly when the ardent President Tyler approached, smiling warmly, obviously happy to see her. A short while later, Julia noticed Ann Gilmer looking deeply troubled.

"What can be the matter with her?" Julia inquired of a friend.

"Oh she has had a dreadful dream, the silly. She's a perfect killjoy. Look at her moping about!" the friend answered.

Julia, understandably shaken by the explanation, was still worried about the impending events from her own dream the night before. However, she tried her best to dismiss any uneasiness and, relying on the logic of her father, enjoy the festivities and the persistent attention she was receiving from President Tyler. She partook of the light refreshments and mingled with the crowd. Then she enjoyed the luncheon served to the guests below-decks and waited while the crew prepared the cannon for its next demonstration. The big cannon, which had been successfully test-fired earlier, was to be set off again, this time for the assembled dignitaries to witness the awesome destructive power of the weapon. As Secretary of the Navy Gilmer joined the group to be assembled up on deck, his sobbing wife pleaded with him to remain below. She tried to hold him back, but he broke free of her grasp and she was left there, crying. Although it would still be a few more minutes before the test was ready, Secretary Gilmer wanted to make sure he was getting a good view of the gun's performance, so he took his place early.

President Tyler, however, had decided to forgo the

demonstration. He'd already seen all the cannon he needed to see that day and he wanted only to spend a few minutes with Julia. So the president quietly retreated from the crowd to a private room belowdecks from where he discreetly sent a message for Julia to join him. Julia, flattered by the invitation, went downstairs, accompanied by her father, and met the president for champagne. A short while later Tyler was informed by an aide, "Come, Mr. President, the gun is about to be fired." But the president was far more interested in the delightful young woman than in hearing another loud blast from the big gun. Julia's father, despite Julia's premonition and warnings, left for the deck and the demonstration.

As President Tyler pressed his intentions, and Julia bantered with him, the two of them heard a deafening explosion from above them and smelled the acrid clouds of smoke that billowed through the deck. Even the president was startled at the intensity of the explosion. But Julia instantly knew something was terribly wrong. Then a voice shouted, "The Secretary is dead!" This was her terrible vision suddenly come true.

"Let me go to my father!" she pleaded.

However as Julia reached the top of the stairway, someone physically restrained her from going topside. "My dear child, you can do no good," the person told her. "Your father is in heaven." Instantly the shock overwhelmed her, and she fainted.

Julia's premonition had been chillingly accurate. The big gun had breachfired, exploded, broken apart, and killed those observers closest to it, including Senator David Gardiner and Secretary of the Navy Gilmer, just as his wife predicted. In all, five people were killed, many more seriously injured, while others suffered less critical burns and shattered eardrums. One of the first people to brave the smoke and burning ash in her rush to bring aid to the wounded was the elderly, ever courageous former first lady Dolley Madison.

Julia Gardiner remained unconscious while the dead and wounded were taken from the deck and did not come to until after she was gently carried from the doomed ship by none other than President Tyler, himself. Holding the beautiful Julia Gardiner in his arms, the president knew that if he'd gone on deck with her father he certainly would have been among those killed. But fate had intervened, he realized, because his dalliance belowdecks with Julia had unquestionably saved his life. He cradled the woman in his arms, knowing that his infatuation for her was somehow meant to be. Meanwhile the grief-stricken Mrs. Gilmer stumbled amid the smoke and debris, crying in vain, "I knew it. I knew it! Why would no one listen to me?"

In the days that followed, as Julia mourned her father's shocking and ill-fated death, which her premonition had been unable to prevent, the president was concerned and caring. He ordered the victims to be laid in state in the Capitol. And while preparations for the funeral proceeded, the president and Julia became closer to each other until, finally, before the funeral, Tyler said that he was not just engaging in an idle flirtation—he deeply cared for the young woman. At the funeral service, Julia approached her father's coffin, gazed lovingly at him lying there, and asked softly, "Father, shall I marry him?"

She said later, "Father seemed to smile, and I took that to mean yes."

When Tyler formally proposed to Julia in the Yellow Oval Room of the White House, she accepted, and four months later, after a brief engagement, the couple quietly married in a New York City church on June 26, 1844. The romance and marriage were not without controversy, however, for many thought Julia too young to be first lady at the age of twenty-four. Others were more scornful of the president and openly laughed at the thirty-year age difference between the two. Notwithstanding the criticisms, their romance blossomed and endured, and Julia, who relished her role as first lady, entertained lavishly. Finally, John Tyler left office in 1845 and returned to Virginia with Julia and their family.

He was seventy when the couple's last child was born in 1860.

In January 1862, Julia experienced a vision of frightening clarity in which she saw her husband lying close to death in a bedroom in Richmond, Virginia. He had gone there to ready himself for a seat in the Confederate Congress to which he'd been elected after throwing his support to the South. Julia had no doubt what the premonition meant; so she rushed from their Virginia plantation, Sherwood Forest, to be by his side. Tyler did not expect a visit from his wife and was quite surprised when she arrived at the Exchange Hotel, where he was staying.

"Are you well?" she asked urgently.

"Perfectly, my dear. Had you heard that I was ill?" he replied.

Julia was at a loss for a comforting explanation. However, when she looked into the room she immediately recognized the same bed she'd seen her husband in during the dream. Sadly, it wasn't long before her premonition proved accurate. That night Tyler unexpectedly collapsed as a result of what his doctor called "bilious fever." Although his doctor hoped Tyler would recover and return home, it was not to be. On January 18, 1862, at the age of seventy-one, John Tyler died in the very same bed Julia had seen in her foreboding vision.

The psychic bonds between the Tylers certainly endured because it seemed that Julia remained in contact with her husband after his death. Psychics have said that Julia Tyler experienced afterdeath communications from her late husband, in the form of dream visitations, visions that continued until her death in 1889 at the age of sixty-nine. Perhaps the most ironic dream she had as a widow was the one that encouraged her to visit the exact same Richmond hotel where her husband died in 1862, for it was there that she, herself, died of natural causes. The dream visions that she had, predicting both her father's and then her husband's deaths, indicate that Julia must have possessed a psychic ability. Yet she probably wasn't unique. Psychics report that throughout history as many as seventy percent of widowed people have experienced some form of contact with their deceased spouses.

Jane Pierce

First Lady Jane Pierce, the wife of President Franklin Pierce, turned to spiritualism during her tenure in the White House after she lost her young son, Bennie, to an accident shortly after her husband's inauguration. Mrs. Pierce was, in the words of author Cheryl Heckler-Feltz, "completely broken by life's events" and became a tragic figure in the White House during the bloody and tumultuous years leading up to the secession of the South. Jane had a psychic premonition, when Franklin was elected president in 1852, that a tragic event would befall her family. Her premonition was proven true in 1853 when her son, eleven-year-old Bennie Pierce, was killed in a freak railroad accident. Mrs. Pierce was plunged into a permanent state of mourning that no amount of care or attention could release her from. She became fixated on attempts to reach Bennie via a spiritual medium. In addition to holding séances to communicate with Bennie's spirit, Jane Pierce also experienced several afterdeath communications with her three other deceased children. As a mother who had lost so many children to accidents and disease, she herself became a tragic death-in-life figure, perpetually seeking solace from her constant state of grief and bereavement.

Even years after Bennie's death, Mrs. Pierce spent most of her time secluded in the White House writing letters to him as if he could actually receive them. She was also heard playing and talking with her departed sons, causing some friends and family to fear that she'd withdrawn into a world of delusional fantasies that her children were still with her. However, psychics have written that grieving mothers often report spirit materializations of their deceased children even years after they have departed. Perhaps, rather than a grief-induced hallucination, Mrs. Pierce genuinely witnessed her sons' apparitions and was addressing them as if they were in the same room. On one occasion, for example, Mrs. Pierce wrote her sister to share with her the recollection of a dream visitation she'd had: "The last two nights my dear boy has been in my dreams with peculiar vividness. May God forgive this aching yearning that I feel so much. . . ."

Dream visitations, such as those Mrs. Pierce experienced, are genuine opportunities to communicate with deceased loved ones. It bears reporting that paranormal research has found a marked difference between ordinary dreams and those we define as a dream visitation. The latter are extraordinarily vivid or hyperreal experiences in which a deceased loved one appears so lifelike that the bereaved is left with little or no doubt that the departed genuinely communicated from the spirit world. Sometimes just after someone has died, the person's spirit appears to loved ones, often in dreams or often in a waking state, to let them know that the spirit has, indeed, moved on. Likely, there were other afterdeath communications experienced by Mrs. Pierce, which have been lost to history.

Mary Lincoln

Like Jane Pierce, her predecessor in office, First Lady Mary Lincoln experienced the untimely deaths of two of her young children, Eddie and Willie. For Mary Lincoln, who may have suffered from a bipolar personality condition, her son Willie's death was an unbearable tragedy that filled her with inconsolable grief. "She could not bear to look upon his picture," her maid and dressmaker Elizabeth Keckley said, and Mary's "voice shook and the tears came whenever Willie's name was mentioned." "When I bring myself to realize that [Willie] has indeed passed away, my question to myself is, 'Can life be endured?' " Mary once wrote a friend.

Again, like Jane Pierce, Mrs. Lincoln wrongly concluded that her son's death was "divine punishment" for her having been "so wrapped up in the world, so devoted to our own political advancement." In 1863, a year after Willie's death, Mrs. Lincoln experienced an afterdeath communication when Willie's spirit materialized. "He comes to me every night and stands at the foot of my bed, with the same sweet, adorable smile he has always had; he does not always come alone. Little Eddie is sometimes with him," she said to her half sister, who grew concerned that Mary was experiencing hallucinations because of her fragile emotional state. However, Mary assured her that seeing Willie's spirit was a great comfort and no cause for alarm.

To a friend she wrote, "A very slight veil separates us from the 'loved and lost' . . . [assuring us] that though unseen by us, they are very near."

By the time the Civil War ended, Mary Lincoln had lost two children. While the divided country was reeling from the war's devastation, Mary—and the nation—suffered another staggering loss when President Lincoln was assassinated. Mrs. Lincoln was now both a bereaved mother and disconsolate widow. Still, her faith in her ability to make contact with the spirit world remained largely intact, and she pursued her spiritualistic endeavors throughout the rest of her life. In 1869, she wrote to a friend, "I am not EITHER a spiritualist, but I sincerely believe our loved ones, who have only 'gone before' are permitted to watch over those who were dearer to them than life."

Just as she'd been desperate to hear from Willie at séances, so, too, did she ache for a message from her departed husband, a sign to skeptics that she'd become "unhinged." In fact, people believed that Mary Lincoln had lost her mind when, in reality, she'd retreated into herself as a refuge against the loneliness and bereavement she felt. Her grief would soon become exacerbated once again as a result of another personal tragedy in 1871 when Tad, who'd been his mother's nearly constant companion since his father's murder, fell ill with tuberculosis and died at the age of eighteen. "Ill luck presided over my birth and has been a faithful attendant ever since," Mary said bitterly. And again she found sanctuary in her long-held beliefs when she took up residence for a time in a "spiritualist commune" to develop her ability to see spirit faces and converse with Mr. Lincoln in the beyond. Mary later traveled to Boston, where, using an alias to prevent detection, she attended a séance, reported contact with her husband's spirit, and said she felt his hands on her shoulders. She also participated in one of spiritualism's more questionable practices: spirit photography.

In the 1870s, photography was still quite primitive, and few were sufficiently expert about taking pictures to recognize a fraud. Many other people, however, believed that if a camera could photograph a person, it could also capture the image of a ghost, apparition, or spirit. So it was that spirit photography became a popular fascination both in the United States and in Europe during the latter half of the nineteenth century. The concept was quite simple: the spirit photographer claimed he could take a picture—then known as a daguerreotype—of a live subject, and when the plate was developed, the apparition of a deceased loved one would appear behind the subject. Typically the spirit appeared ethereal or dreamlike so that it projected an otherworldly quality on the developed print.

Mrs. Lincoln yearned for her husband to be manifest in such a photo, and so under the assumed name Mrs. Tundall she visited William Mumler, the best-known spirit photographer of the time. From 1861 on, Mumler had pursued a lively and profitable business producing daguerreotypes that showed shadowy likenesses of deceased loved ones poised behind his customers. Wearing her widow's black, Mary Lincoln sat, her hands folded, her round face older, more tired, and heavier than only a few years earlier, while Mumler slid the photo plates into his camera and asked her to stay motionless so that he could expose the picture he was taking of her.

When the daguerreotype was developed, Mrs. Lincoln

was not disappointed because behind her she could make out the nearly transparent image of Abraham Lincoln's face, meant to seem heavenly, with his hand on his wife's shoulder. He was bathed in cloudlike fog and his body appeared as a white form. Many suspected an obvious double exposure, although Mumler had supporters who vouched for his honesty. Mrs. Lincoln was certain the picture was genuine and that Mumler had not recognized her. Mary Lincoln, with her husband's ghostly presence hovering over her, became Mumler's most famous spirit photograph.

Her joy in seeing the daguerreotype offered her only fleeting solace. She soon retreated into a deep depression. In fact, Mrs. Lincoln's final seventeen years were spent in such misery that she was briefly committed to a sanitarium in 1875 after her son Robert—himself an established lawyer and politician who could ill afford having to explain away a deranged mother running around New York and Boston seeking communication with her dead husband and children—had her declared legally insane. With the help of her sister, however, Mary was released four months later and eventually returned to Springfield, Illinois, where she died on July 16, 1882, at the age of sixty-three. When she was laid to rest, she wore her wedding band with the inscription that read: LOVE IS ETERNAL.

Mrs. Lincoln's many psychic experiences give her the distinction of being the first lady most involved with the paranormal, for better or worse. Despite her obvious spiritualist bent, however, there have been no substantiated reports of her ghost being sighted. Perhaps she has moved on, found peace in the next stage of life, became reunited with her beloved children, and, therefore, had no need or reason to return to the physical world even though her husband continues to haunt the White House. Or perhaps because Mrs. Lincoln was mentally ill, death became a release for her tormented spirit that struggled so desperately in life to find solace.

The nature of Mrs. Lincoln's psychotic depression was that it bordered on a constant paranoia that made her intensely jealous of her husband's attention to other women. Even the slightest kindness that Mr. Lincoln showed to another woman, no matter how insignificant, caused Mary Lincoln to fly into a rage when she and the president were alone. Sometimes she became so angry, she didn't wait until they were alone and her mood would darken even in front of their friends. Mary Lincoln also became violently jealous whenever she perceived that another woman was showing too much attention to her husband. Her rule was simple: "I never allow the president to see any woman alone."

Ironically, this jealousy, some historians have said, might have actually saved the life of General Grant and allowed him to become president years later. This all happened because toward the end of the Civil War, on a trip to inspect the Army of the Potomac, President Lincoln and General Grant were accompanied by their wives and General Edward Ord and his wife. When General Ord's wife made the mistake of riding horseback alongside the president, Mary Lincoln became infuriated "beyond all bounds" and accused Mrs. Ord of trying to flirt with her husband. When Mrs. Grant attempted to intervene on behalf of her friend, Mary's wrath turned on Mrs. Grant, and the rift between the two of them became irreconcilable. It was a rift that continued into Lincoln's second term.

Having promised, in the face of his own dire premonitions and nightmares, to attend Ford's Theater on Friday evening, April 14, 1865, the president invited the victorious General Grant and his wife to accompany the first family as they celebrated the end of the war. The two couples, Lincoln promised, would share the same box at Ford's, to the delight of the audience that night. The Grants, however, declined the invitation saying they had to return to their home in New Jersey, which was only partially true.

Actually, there were two explanations for why the Grants did not attend the theater with the Lincolns. First, and most obvious, Julia Grant flatly refused to be in Mrs. Lincoln's company after the incident involving General Ord's wife. Thus, Mary Lincoln's jealous rage spared the life of the future President Grant. But there was another more ominous but less obvious reason. That Friday morning Mrs. Grant awoke with a strong sense of uneasiness and impending danger. Troubled by a vague premonition that something was amiss, Mrs. Grant was unable to shake the feeling that either a tragic accident or terrible disaster was about to overtake her husband. Although unable to say with certainty what provoked her discomfort, she knew it concerned her husband's personal safety enough to the point where she demanded they leave Washington immediately.

General Grant protested, arguing he could not go because of scheduled appointments that entire day. But Julia persisted as her misgivings intensified, and she urgently pleaded for them to depart. So insistent was she that throughout the day she sent him messages until finally he yielded to her pleadings. Mrs. Grant's premonition had become too strong a force for her husband to resist. She was certain that danger would lie in wait if they joined the Lincolns for the theater, so the general made his apologies to the president and left Washington. When the Grants arrived in Philadelphia, they heard the terrible news that stunned the nation: President Lincoln had been assassinated. Julia's seemingly groundless prediction of a disaster had been completely validated.

Premonitions of impending danger are quite common. By heeding her foreboding, Mrs. Grant, who, like her husband, was open to and believed in spiritualism, saved his life. When John Wilkes Booth's papers were later found, a list of intended assassination targets on which the name General Ulysses S. Grant figured prominently was discovered. He was a prime candidate for assassination, it was later determined, because he had become the blood enemy of those seeking revenge for the defeat of the Confederacy.

Nell Arthur

The lovely Georgian-style mansion on Caroline Street in the heart of Fredericksburg, Virginia, built in 1770, with its two imposing chimneys, was the childhood home of Ellen Lewis Herndon, nicknamed Nell, born in August 1837, the daughter of a prominent senior naval officer. In 1859, the twenty-two-year-old Nell married thirty-year-old Chester Alan Arthur, who'd been a teacher and principal before he settled into a law practice in New York. The Arthurs were married for twenty years and had one daughter and two sons. But in January 1880, Nell died at the age of forty-two and, sadly, did not live to see her husband, then the vice president, become president the following year upon the death of James Garfield.

Over the years there have been persistent reports that Nell's ghost has returned to her childhood home in Fredericksburg. Whether there simply to enjoy the familiarity of her old surroundings or because she was looking for something there, Nell frequently appeared to startled witnesses. Visitors to the Fredricksburg home told of seeing the apparition of a young girl, of hearing inexplicable footsteps down a hall or in an adjoining room, of seeing empty chairs rocking of their own volition, and of watching as windows and doors opened and closed themselves. There has also been poltergeist activity in the house, including smashed glass, dishes dashed to the floor, and pieces of tableware that hurled themselves across the room. Was there a relationship between Nell and the young girl's ghost, or was Nell Herndon's spirit responsible for the frenzy of psychokinetic energy? Because spirits have been known to sometimes materialize as children even when they passed on as adults, could the apparition have been Nell Herndon herself? To this day, people still speculate about the nature of the mysterious and mischievous spirit.

Interestingly enough, Chester Alan Arthur never remarried after his beloved Nell's death, but throughout his presidential years, he claimed to draw "inspiration" from keepsakes that had belonged to Nell. Was her spirit presence close by, acting as a guardian angel, which spirits often do for loved ones who remain on earth?

Frances Folsom Cleveland

There had never been a wedding in the White House until President Grover Cleveland married a pretty, dark-haired young woman named Frances Folsom in the Blue Room on June 2, 1886. It was a grand affair, and every church bell in Washington rang in celebration. Frances was only twenty-one, while the president was forty-eight. He'd known her since her childhood, when she became his ward upon the death of her father, one of Cleveland's closest friends. At once, she was the youngest first lady ever, at the center of the nation's attention. In an eerie foreshadowing of today's Washington press corps, reporters afforded the first lady no privacy and wrote about her every move, a situation that angered the cantankerous president, who called them "those ghouls of the press."

Despite the intense scrutiny from the press, Frances became a gracious and popular first lady, well liked by White House staff. So when Grover Cleveland lost his bid for reelection in 1888 to Benjamin Harrison, there was much sorrow among the employees who had grown to love her. For her part, Frances Cleveland was no happier to leave the White House than the staff was to see her depart. However, Frances psychically knew something no one else could have predicted at the time, and she did not keep it secret. Calmly, reassuringly, and without hesitation, she told forlorn White House staffers, "I want everything just the way it is now . . . [for] . . . when we come back. Take good care of the house and furniture, for we are coming back exactly four years from today." Her staff was incredulous at Mrs. Cleveland's prediction, since no president had ever served nonconsecutive terms. Still, the endearing first lady sounded so certain of her conviction even the unhappiest of employees seemed heartened by her promise.

The Clevelands left the White House in 1889 when Benjamin Harrison took office, and Grover returned to his law practice. Four years later, in 1892, Cleveland again ran for president and won, exactly as Frances predicted it would happen. She knew she'd return because a strong premonition or precognition allowed her a glimpse of the future. Back, happily, in the White House, Frances gave birth to her second daughter, Esther, in 1893.

Following Frances's death in 1947, White House staff members reported hearing the sounds of a woman's cries emanating from the room in which Esther was born more than fifty years earlier. Lillian Parks, longtime White House seamstress, wrote: "Then there has been the ghost of Mrs. Cleveland, who gave birth to the first child of a president to be born in the White House. Some of the moaning . . . is supposed to be the echo of her childbirth pangs." Frances's spirit had returned to the location of one of the most meaningful experiences of her life.

Ida McKinley

First Lady Ida McKinley was a petulant woman who, an epileptic at a time when grand mal epilepsy was considered a taboo, was ever in frail health and falling victim to what her staff called "spells." She was, nevertheless, a possessive woman, always screaming at her husband, whom she called Major, and bringing him immediately to her side whenever she thought she was going to be sick. The emotional bonds between President William McKinley and his wife were strong, and her concerns for her husband's well-being were obvious to all who knew them. When he was elected in 1896, Ida made a blunt and ominous prediction, "Oh, Major, they will kill you. . . ." Although frightened by what she'd psychically sensed, she was unable to alter her husband's destiny. That destiny came to be in September 1901, the year of his inauguration for his second term. President McKinley, now a zero-year president and subject to the curse of Tenskwatawa, traveled to the Pan-American Exposition in Buffalo, New York, with First Lady Ida, who insisted on accompanying him. When told the news that the president had been shot and mortally wounded by an anarchist assassin, she accepted the terrible news with greater reserve than anyone thought she would. Mrs. McKinley's premonition could not change her husband's fate, although it better prepared her for the tragedy.

Julia Dent Grant

At the turn of the twentieth century, some fifteen years after President Ulysses S. Grant's death in 1885, his sisters, Mary Grant Cramer and Virginia Grant Corbin, living together in East Orange, New Jersey, shared a frightening premonition with each other. One morning in 1902, Mrs. Cramer awoke shaken, after she'd experienced a remarkably vivid dream. At breakfast she shared the details with her sister and an overnight guest, Katherine Lawrence. Mrs. Cramer said that in her dream she saw President Grant's widow, Julia, approach her bed and place her hand on her sister-in-law's shoulder. Then Mrs. Cramer heard Mrs. Grant say, "Mary, I have come to talk with you and to say good-bye, because I am not going to be with you much longer."

Mrs. Lawrence was astonished because she also had a disturbing dream the night before that seemed to involve the late president and Mrs. Grant. Mrs. Lawrence explained that in her dream both Cramer and Corbin were at the entrance to Grant's tomb in New York City, where the late President was laid to rest. Meanwhile, great numbers of people had gathered, apparently awaiting some sort of procession to arrive. At that point, Mrs. Lawrence's dream ended.

Sadly, true to the premonitions the two women had, just eight days later, Julia Dent Grant died of natural causes at the age of seventy-six. Her remains were laid to rest near her husband in Grant's tomb, which he'd chosen years earlier as their burial site. The dream premonitions Cramer and Lawrence experienced were considered interesting and provocative enough to be reported in newspapers at the time, including the popular *New York Sun.*

Florence Harding

First Lady Florence Harding was among the many wives of politicians in the 1920s who became attracted to the practice of astrology. Astrology was in fashion, and the wives of powerful men saw themselves as contributing to their careers by having their favorite astrologers cast divinations about upcoming events. As First Lady Nancy Reagan would do in the 1980s, Florence Harding relied on her astrologer, the popular Washingtonian Madame Marcia. Among the many observations that Madame Marcia provided was that Warren Harding, a Scorpio, had powerful sexual urges, and she warned the first lady that her husband would indulge in secret sexual liaisons with other women. In fact, Harding's constant gallivanting resulted in a number of clandestine affairs, ongoing relationships with mistresses, and even an illegitimate daughter.

At various times during her marriage, Mrs. Harding had been known to consult with mediums, although not all predictions ultimately proved accurate. While one Washington medium correctly predicted Harding's election, another claimed to see the "Star of Destiny" emblazoned over him, the beacon that would steer him to great prominence. In fact, Harding presided over one of the most scandal-ridden administrations in U.S. history.

Madame Marcia, upon whose observations Florence Harding relied the most, made another startling prediction after consulting her charts: President Harding, born on November 2, 1865, would not live to complete his term in office. The prognostication shook Mrs. Harding, but without specific details, Florence Harding could not alter her husband's fate. When he died under mysterious circumstances on August 2, 1923, only his wife was with him.

Immediately after his death, one night when all was

quiet, Florence Harding visited the White House East Room, where she instructed that her husband's casket be opened, and then was heard to say, "They can't hurt you anymore." Likely she was alluding to the revelations of corruption that were about to envelop him. Had Mrs. Harding engaged in an imaginary conversation, or was she spurred by seeing, hearing, or sensing her husband's spirit presence? Psychic experts say that when we communicate with deceased loved ones—as in prayer—they are able to hear us.

Grace Coolidge

Upon Harding's death in office, Calvin Coolidge, a taciturn Vermonter, became president. Immediately rumors started up that his wife, Grace, was consorting with mediums and astrologers just as Florence Harding had. Like Mrs. Harding, Grace Coolidge belonged to a circle of women married to Washington's political elite who sought guidance from the spirit world. Grace Coolidge, in fact, was the first person to report having witnessed the specter of President Lincoln roaming through the White House, an observation that assures her place in the paranormal history of the Executive Mansion. Also, at least one medium publicly announced that she'd given readings to Mrs. Coolidge at the White House, but later retracted the claim in the face of negative press and adverse political reaction. There were other conflicting and contradictory stories about the presence of spiritual advisors in Mrs. Coolidge's retinue, but none could be confirmed or denied. If Grace Coolidge was a consistent devotee of spiritual advisors, there is no documentation available to prove it, making for a particularly frustrating chapter in the elusive search for the truth about the paranormal and the presidency.

Eleanor Roosevelt

In 1944, *Chimes* magazine revealed that President Franklin Delano Roosevelt had attended séances with several gifted mediums, although the specifics were kept hidden from the public to every extent possible. But little was written about the paranormal interests of First Lady Eleanor Roosevelt, one of the most activist and controversial first ladies to ever occupy the White House. During the Great Depression and through World War II, Eleanor, who had rallied her husband's strength in the months after he contracted polio and challenged Roosevelt's own mother on her husband's behalf, had become her husband's eyes and ears as she traveled tirelessly on behalf of the mostly wheelchair-bound president. But she faced many uncertainties—in her marriage, the condition of the world, and her own future—so she journeyed to the modest Indianapolis home of one of the nation's most famed palm readers, Nellie Meier.

Mrs. Roosevelt was hardly the only well-known American to make the trek to Nellie's home, for many screen stars and celebrities also sought Mrs. Meier's advice. But the gossip that the First Lady of the United States was having the lines and features of her palm read by a person practicing an occult science was a jolt to people who knew about it, although it was kept out of the press. Mrs. Roosevelt also invited the skilled Nellie Meier to visit the White House, which the palmist did prior to her death in 1944. During the Clinton administration, stories appeared in the newspapers that said that the spirit of the deceased Eleanor Roosevelt returned to the White House at the urging of First Lady—now Senator—Hillary Clinton, who sought to channel her for guidance and inspiration.

The First Ladies and the Supernatural

What makes the supernatural experiences of America's first ladies different or unique? Psychic communications initiated or received by presidents' wives, in many instances, changed the course of history. Dream visitations from deceased loved ones, premonitions, precognitive, clairvoyant, or clairaudient incidents heeded by a president or his wife can have immeasurable impact on the lives of many people, even the entire nation. That so many first ladies listened to their inner voices and responded to, rather than denied, their intuitive or psychic sense has been for the better, notwithstanding the criticism of skeptics and naysayers. We share also the grief that first families experienced when a loved one passed on, for every person, famous or not, has known the pain of loss. The fact that several presidential wives sought counsel and comfort from psychics and mediums makes them not unlike millions of bereaved who seek contact with the beyond.

Did the first ladies each have a destiny to fulfill? Do we all? Are we listening to the psychic and intuitive experiences that connect us to the spirit world and God? Are we heeding the messages as many presidential wives have in the past and undoubtedly will in the future?

Finally, there is little evidence that first ladies feared their supernatural encounters. Perhaps the answer to that is in a comment from Teddy Roosevelt's outspoken daughter, Alice Roosevelt Longworth, who said she feared bad presidents in the White House more than she feared ghosts.

CHAPTER EIGHT

The Presidents at the Séance Table in the Age of Spiritualism

If the dead can come back to this earth and flit unseen around those they loved, I shall always be near you; in the gladdest days and in the darkest nights it shall be my spirit passing by.
—Sullivan Ballou, U.S. Major, Union Army, 1861

In 1847, famed American medium and clairvoyant Andrew Jackson Davis predicted that interest in spirit phenomena would "spread all over the world." The next year his prophecy came true, spurred into reality by the Great Religious Awakening of the early and mid-nineteenth century and the invention of the electric telegraph, which revolutionized communication around the world. After all, if messages could be sent from one location to the other invisibly over thin metallic wires by this mysterious new instrument, why shouldn't human beings be able to use their own forms of magnetic energy to receive communications from the spirit world? This led, from the middle of the nineteenth century right through the Fin de Siècle and into the early years of the twentieth century, an Age of Spiritualism that enveloped not only the rich and powerful in the United States, but the intellectual and social elite in Victorian England, France, and the rest of Europe. The Age of Spiritualism spawned not only an interest in astrological charting and palm reading, the practice of séances and mediumship, demonstrations of clairvoyance and prognostication, but a firm belief on the part of millions of people that there was an alternate reality, a world beyond the material through which individuals could communicate and the departed could return to inspire their loved ones among the living. Although the Age of Spiritualism dissolved into entropy and then licentiousness during the decade after World War I, and then a collective hopelessness and radical nationalism from the Depression to World War II, spiritualism became reincarnated in the latter half of the twentieth century, this time disguised as New Age science.

In the late 1950s, the U.S. government began its own investigation with an alternate reality. Drawn into it, perhaps, by Soviet experimentation with psychic phenomena, the U.S. military intelligence services and the CIA began their own serious experiments with chemically and psychologically altered states of reality both as nonlethal military weapons to pacify hostile civilian populations and disorient senior officers of opposing military forces and training "viewers" in the practice of out-of-body projection, as an active intelligence weapon to spy on the enemy's deepest held secrets. Former director of U.S. Army intelligence (G2) and later the commanding general of the army's Office of Research and Development Lt. General Arthur Trudeau wrote in his memoirs about the early army experiments with LSD 25 as a military weapon. And today, at the beginning of the twenty-first century, writers, such as Whitley Streiber in *The Key*, predict that within the decade science will establish a physical, quantifiable basis for the transmission and reception of psychic energy and that the existence of alternate dimensions and entire universes will become matters of fact. Similarly, television and telephone psychics, like Miss Cleo, practice their divinations to large audiences, and mediums, such as John Edward, have hit shows both on cable television and in syndication. In other words, the Great Age of Spiritualism's alternate reality will have been shown to have a physical reality.

The Great Age of Spiritualism was spawned in the mid-nineteenth century and became a movement that spread across the country like a wildfire that only fed on itself. By 1855, spiritualism had become a national craze attracting many notable figures of the day, who participated in séances with the famous Fox sisters, who had actually started the movement. Among the illustrious who attended mediumship presentations and demonstrations were William Cullen Bryant and James Fenimore Cooper. Also enticed into learning more about the movement was famed New York newspaper publisher Horace Greeley, who took the Fox sisters into his home to observe for himself their psychic abilities. Then he enthusiastically wrote about them in the *New York Tribune*, attesting to their veracity and thereby immensely boosting their credibility. By the end of the nineteenth century, writers such as H. G. Wells, Jules Verne, Bram Stoker, and George Bernard Shaw had been influenced by the philosophies of spiritualism, as was the notorious occult writer Aliester Crowley.

There were two notable figures who influenced the subject. Many spiritualists were inspired by the eighteenth-century Swedish philosopher Emanuel Swedenborg, who wrote of "journeys" to the spirit world. The other was Anton Mesmer, who gave public demonstrations of what came to be known as "mesmerism," the precursor of modern hypnotism, which led subjects into trance states of heightened concentration and was later adopted by mediums to receive spirit communications. Mesmer's experiments were popularized into parlor games and stage entertainment all across Europe, but they also attracted the attention of the medical community as well as the spiritual community because subjects seemed to be looking into another world. Because Mesmer's practice seemed to open up a direct channel into an entirely hidden area of the human mind, his work influenced Sigmund Freud and Carl Jung, the founders of modern psychotherapy, who claimed that much of human behavior was governed by the subconscious. This subconscious, Freud and Jung initially believed, could be reached directly through an induced state of mesmerism. There was even more fallout from Mesmer's theories because his students found that public demonstrations into these altered states of consciousness encouraged an investigation into the world of spirits and life in dimensions human beings could not perceive in their routine comings and goings. But the idea of an alternate reality that people could perceive in a trance state was both intriguing and, as it ultimately turned out, very lucrative.

Soon spiritualists even developed new terminology that redefined the whole idea of death into a transition to another life that, nevertheless, had an immediate presence for the living. "Dying" became "passing over," while heaven was known by many as "summerland." The dead were no longer unreachable, only waiting for those to whom they could speak. Now communication between the departed and the living was not only possible, it was simply a matter of finding the right transmitter and receiver: the medium.

By 1850, pamphlets about the "strange sounds or rappings" the famous Fox sisters had discovered were selling briskly. In 1851, New York City boasted no less than a hundred known mediums and forty thousand serious believers in spirit rappings. In Philadelphia, there were fifty to sixty private spirit circles and an unusually large number of mediums. Some two hundred spirit circles sprung up in Ohio. By 1855, the New England Spiritualist Association estimated some two million believers in America, and when spiritualism spread to Europe, it became even more popular in England than in the United States.

The interest in spiritualism in the United States corresponded with a fascination with otherworldly speculations in England. Important writers of the day, including Charles Dickens, experimented with Ouija boards and other occult paraphernalia and ultimately inspired a group of writers from the late nineteenth century to form their own societies to study the occult. Among these were science fiction writers H. G. Wells and Jules Verne; Bram Stoker, the celebrated author of *Dracula*;

the playwright George Bernard Shaw; and one of the most notorious occultists of them all, Aliester Crowley. However, as spiritualism became big business on both sides of the Atlantic, opposition to the movement began to develop.

In 1852, the *Spiritual Telegraph* began publishing, and a flood of books and magazines followed. More than two thousand so-called "writing mediums" throughout the country who wrote down, under spirit control, the messages they telepathically heard from the spirit world. Medium Isaac Post, in 1852, published a book that contained about forty spirit communications from such notables as George Washington and Thomas Jefferson. The messages from the two late presidents, at least as Post told it, revealed no startling wisdom and, to the dismay of many readers, appeared to be much of what they said on earth.

The growth of spiritualism was so phenomenal that in April 1854, Congress was presented with a "memorial" by Representative James Shields of Illinois requesting an "inquiry into the truth of spiritualism." It contained nearly fifteen thousand signatures. The opposition mobilized quickly to set limits on occult practices in all areas of the supernatural, especially mediumship. Alabama passed a law imposing a five-hundred-dollar fine on those who publicly demonstrated the phenomena, and other states eventually limited or banned performances by mediums. In 1857, the *Boston Courier* cast a skeptical eye when it offered five hundred dollars to anyone who could demonstrate genuine spiritualist occurrences.

But the spiritualism market continued to proliferate. Soon the Fox sisters found themselves among a crowd of psychics, all competing for recognition to service the forlorn, grief-stricken, and bereaved. Ultimately, as the Great Age of Spiritualism moved toward its conclusion after the turn of the twentieth century, women continued to dominate the movement. It had been three young women who started the movement in America, demonstrating their craft to a mostly female audience. This was by no means out of the ordinary because during the

Victorian period, mediumship was among the few outlets that permitted women unbridled recognition. By the time the Age of Spiritualism waned in the years immediately preceding World War I, few people remembered how it had all begun. And few people would have realized from the modest beginning of the Age of Spiritualism in America in upper New York State that the movement would grow to encompass the most powerful political elite in Washington, including President Abraham Lincoln himself and his wife, Mary. But that's exactly what happened as America got caught up in a craze that reached from the damp and drafty cellar of the Fox farmhouse to private parlors of palm readers and mediums in New York and Chicago to literary salons in London and Paris and all the way to the family quarters in the Lincoln White House.

The Fox Sisters

On Friday March 31, 1848, a cold and windy night in the tiny community of Hydesville in western New York State, the Great Age of Spiritualism was born. The Fox family—James, a farmer; his wife, Margaret, a devout Methodist; and their two young daughters, Margaretta, ten, and Katherine, seven—had moved into the small frame house only three months earlier. Although the house they'd moved into had a reputation for "mysterious rapping noises," which caused the previous tenant to move out, the Fox family experienced no upset until March, when they were disturbed by inexplicable jarring noises and mysterious footsteps. After they'd searched the entire house, Mrs. Fox concluded some "unhappy restless spirit" must be haunting the place.

Mrs. Fox wrote: "On Friday night, March 31, 1848 . . . [my] husband . . . heard the noises and helped in the search. It commenced as usual. I knew it from all the other noises I had ever heard before. The children, who slept in the other bed in the room, heard the rappings and tried to make similar sounds by snapping their fingers.

"My youngest child, Katie, said: 'Mr. Splitfoot, do as I do,' clapping her hands. The sound instantly followed her with the same number of raps." They'd given the invisible entity the name Mr. Splitfoot after Mrs. Fox's fear that the disturbances were 'the work of the devil.' Then Margaretta said, in sport, 'Now, do just as I do. Count one, two, three, four,' striking one hand against the other at the same time; and the raps came as before.

"Then Katie said, 'Oh Mother, I know what it is. Tomorrow is April Fool's day and it is somebody trying to fool us.' I then thought I could put a test that no one in the place could answer. I asked the noise to rap my different children's ages, successively." The answers were correct.

"I then asked: 'Is this a human being that answers my questions so correctly?' There was no rap. I asked, 'Is it a spirit? If it is, make two raps.' Two sounds were given as soon as the request was made. I then said, 'If it was an injured spirit, make two raps,' which were instantly made causing the house to tremble. I asked: 'Were you injured in this house?' The answer was given as before."

Through the code established by Mrs. Fox with whatever it was that the family believed came from the Other Side, the rappings communicated that the spirit in life had been a peddler, murdered and robbed in the house, then buried in the cellar. A search of the premises, including the dark cellar, proved inconclusive at first, although as the Foxes dug beneath the mounds of charcoal and quicklime in the cellar, they discovered human hair and bones. Someone, indeed, had been secretly buried in the cellar and covered with quicklime to speed up the corpse's decomposition process. Now the Foxes had a sense of who the spirit might be, and rumors about the paranormal presence in the farmhouse began to spread among the neighbors.

By the next weekend, news of the spirit rappings attracted so much attention that hundreds of visitors clamored for entry to the Fox house. "It caused a great deal of trouble and anxiety," Mr. Fox complained, adding, "I am not a believer in haunted houses or supernatural appearances." Still, for all of the hardheaded rationalism the Foxes brought to bear on the strange communication, they said they could not account for the noises, which not only grew worse, but were also transformed into other physical manifestations. In addition to the mysterious rappings, other inexplicable phenomena—including slamming doors, shaking beds, "etheric hands" seizing the girls, the ghostly sounds of a struggle, and someone being dragged down a flight of stairs—took place in the house, the gossip about which excited the neighbors even more.

The startling revelations spread quickly beyond the community, attracting curiosity from believers and skeptics alike. In an era before radio, telephones, television, and the Internet, the information spread so rapidly that it was as if there had been a discovery of another world, a world about which skeptics as well as believers wanted to know much more. It was as if the communication channel opened up between the Fox sisters and the unseen entity had touched a nerve in a population eager to look beyond the physical confines of the everyday world. With their ability to elicit a response from the unseen spiritual entity inhabiting their house, the young Fox sisters seemed to have tapped into the public's enthusiasm for the supernatural. Within a matter of months, starting gradually within the tiny community of Hydesville and then radiating out to the surrounding communities and from there, via newspapers, to the large cities, it was as if a new age were coming into being wherein people could find a seeming confirmation of the spirit world's ability to communicate with the physical world.

As the public fascination with the Fox sisters' paranormal experiences continued to grow, the girls' mother sent them to visit their older sister, Mrs. Leah Fish, in nearby Rochester. But if the Foxes thought that would end the tumult surrounding their house, they were mistaken. The rappings from the spirit world actually followed the two young sisters from Hydesville to Leah Fish's house, where the girls and their spirit friend attracted even more attention, and Margaretta soon became the nucleus of a faithful "spirit circle." Katie, meanwhile, was sent away to nearby Auburn, New York. There, her parents hoped, she would be free of the spirit who had followed them to Rochester.

Meanwhile, back in Rochester, many curious people who believed in what they called the "rapping telegraph" eagerly congregated at Leah's home to witness Margaretta's paranormal abilities for themselves. When Leah saw the effect her younger sister's communications with Mr. Splitfoot had on large numbers of people, she realized she was sitting on a gold mine. She told friends she had suddenly become aware of the financial possibilities inherent in Margaretta's talents because, she said, "all western New York was excited by the reports and doctrines of Spiritualism." At the same time, however, Leah realized she had to tread softly because Margaretta's spirit communications produced two sharply opposing positions. There were those who denounced her for "heresy and blasphemy" as well as those elated by contact with the spirit world. (In Hydesville, only the murdered peddler's ghost had imparted messages; now many other spirits allegedly came forth to rap out messages to the young girl.)

Leah moved quickly to capitalize on the public interest in Margaretta's abilities. She organized a public lecture and demonstration in Rochester's largest auditorium, Corinthian Hall, at one dollar a person, which, 150 years ago, was a whopping price for an admission ticket. An audience of individuals who ranged from the curious to those who thought they might be witnesses to the coming of a spiritual revolution filled the auditorium to capacity. By all accounts, the sellout crowd provided Leah with a huge financial success and launched the career of young Margaretta, whose performance received positive reviews in the local newspapers. Many of the people who attended were sure they'd witnessed genuine communication with the spirit world, while others were certain it was a fraud, although none could explain the cause of the rappings. All agreed, "the effect upon . . . guests was great."

The effect of the public demonstration of Margaretta's abilities prompted many of Rochester's most prominent citizens to form several committees to investigate and, if possible, determine the real source of the rappings by testing Margaretta. Perhaps if they could show the whole thing were a parlor trick, the public fascination would disappear. However, the investigators also ran the risk of not being able to debunk the events and thus reinforce the public's belief that Margaretta was a gifted spiritualist who could actually make contact with the Other Side. The investigators looked for, but could not find, any straightforward explanations for Margaretta's performance. They suspected that the girl was a ventriloquist who was simply answering herself, but a careful investigation of her proved fruitless. If she were using ventriloquism, she was very good at it. And if the rappings were a trick, no one on the committees could prove it. Accordingly, the investigation served to validate what Margaretta claimed. The spirit rappings were real.

Katie had now joined her sister, and the two quickly became the toasts of Rochester and were publicized throughout New York State. Soon the stories of what they were demonstrating reached newspapers in Boston, Washington, Chicago, and San Francisco, and the girls achieved national notoriety. After only a few months, the two were traveling the country, demonstrating rappings for huge audiences as well as offering exclusive private sessions for the wealthy and famous. The Age of Spiritualism had not only begun, but it had begun to make money. Soon the market for mediums and spiritualists would become very competitive, forcing the Fox sisters to vie for their piece of the Age of Spiritualism market. But for their immediate future, the Fox sisters had caught the attention of America's first lady.

The Fox Sisters and the First Family

In 1853, Jane Pierce, wife of President Franklin Pierce, was especially interested in the mediumship of the Fox sisters after the tragic death of her young son. A beautiful, quiet, frail woman who suffered from tuberculosis, Jane Means Appleton Pierce had been raised in a strict religious family imbued with Calvinist beliefs. Her husband was a dashing and popular political figure in his native New Hampshire, and later in Washington, but Jane had no affection for politics or life in the nation's capital. When Franklin was nominated for president in 1852, Jane promptly fainted at the news. Then Franklin's electoral victory was quickly overshadowed by the death of their young son.

On January 6, 1853, just months before Franklin's inauguration, the Pierces were aboard a train not far from Boston when the car they were riding in uncoupled and derailed, and the train car rolled over, split apart, and plummeted down a rocky ledge. Pierce and his wife were slightly injured. However, their eleven-year-old son, Benjamin, was killed instantly, the only fatality in the accident. Before the very eyes of his horrified parents, Benjamin's head hit a large rock with such a violent impact that his skull cracked and blood and tissue spurted from the resulting huge gash, entirely covering the boy's face in seconds. It was a gory sight so overwhelmingly traumatic that Mrs. Pierce was paralyzed with shock and became almost cataleptic in the weeks that followed the accident. The personal tragedy was made worse by the fact that the Pierces had earlier lost their firstborn son in infancy and a second son at age four.

While still in mourning, president-elect Franklin Pierce was inaugurated in March, 1853, but Jane, numb with grief, was too devastated to attend. The pall of gloom cast over the White House was palpable, and the effect of Benjamin's death diminished not only Franklin's ensuing presidential term, but also his entire capacity to enjoy life. Jane became "one of the most tragic figures" to ever occupy the White House, so seldom seen she was dubbed the "shadow in the White House." Someone who glimpsed her described her "woebegone face, with its sunken eyes and skin like yellowed ivory. . . . Her life was over . . . from the time of that dreadful shock of her son's death."

Jane shunned the life and formal obligations of the First Lady of the United States. The world went on around her, while she, in her cloud of grief, only thought about the child she had lost. She passed countless hours in complete solitude behind the walls of the White House family quarters writing long letters to her deceased son, whose loss she continually mourned. Sometimes she spoke aloud, calling out to the shadows of the dead as if they were within hailing distance. At other times, servants in the White House could hear her playing with her deceased children, whom she must have thought were in the room with her. The skeptics who heard these stories clucked their tongues and bemoaned the first lady's "fantasy." His own grief notwithstanding, Franklin Pierce tried to comfort his wife as best he could and humored her claims that she had made contact with their children. However, who's to say with certainty that she had actually not seen her beloved children's spirits materialize in the evening darkness of the family quarters?

In their sorrow, Franklin and Jane sought some form of logic in the deaths of their children, particularly Benjamin, who'd been the sole fatality in the train derailment. But there was no logic in that tragedy. However, the president and his wife soon arrived at their respective, though erroneous, rationales for their son's death. Jane drew the mistaken conclusion "that Bennie's fate was a divine punishment meted out for [Franklin's] political ambition," while Franklin believed Benjamin's death was "a judgment of God on him." Each parent was terribly mistaken, for neither traditional Christianity nor spiritualist belief teaches that God punishes parents by killing their innocent children. This was a message no legitimate medium would dare to offer.

Desperate to hear from Benjamin in the afterlife, Jane

invited the now-celebrated Fox sisters to the White House to demonstrate spirit rappings and conduct a séance, the first one ever held in the Executive Mansion. Unfortunately, no records exist to tell us what spirit messages were delivered, and the Fox sisters offered no details of their White House experience. However, whatever the Fox sisters did tell Jane in their rapping session was enough to console the first lady at the same time as it made her more anxious to receive more messages from her son Benjamin from the Other Side. The stories that circulated about the Fox sisters and their communication with Benjamin inspired other people to explore the possibilities that the spirits of the departed communicated with the living. In one of the strangest incidents of the era, after Benjamin was killed, a Kansas family named Eaton decided to "marry" his spirit to their daughter Katie, who died when she was just three weeks old. The unusual ceremony was held with much celebration at the Eaton home and served to underscore the public's fixation on the afterlife.

Jane's invitation to the Fox sisters to demonstrate their abilities to her also bestowed upon Franklin Pierce the distinction of becoming the president during whose administration spiritualism officially entered the White House. Although the president at the time the Hydesville rappings first began was James Knox Polk, there is no indication that either Polk, or his wife, Sarah, was interested in the supernatural save for Polk's premonition of his death in 1849. Pierce, however, may have been more open to the subject, influenced by Nathaniel Hawthorne, a close friend since their student days at Bowdoin College. Hawthorne, a believer in spirit communications, once experienced a ghostly sighting of a minister he'd seen every day in the Boston Library. After the minister died, Hawthorne continued to witness his specter sitting in his favorite chair, reading his newspaper.

Abraham Lincoln

In no administration were mediums and séances more prominent than in that of President Lincoln. Mary Lincoln's impetus, like Jane Pierce's, was personal tragedy: four-year-old Eddie Lincoln's death in February 1850 from tuberculosis, and eleven-year-old Willie Lincoln's death in February 1862, which plunged Abe and Mary Lincoln into deep grief. Mary Lincoln, a troubled woman from as far back as her early teens, was a borderline psychotic who found it difficult to cope under any set of conditions. But after her children died, Mary, who was almost catatonic at times, sought desperately to communicate with them through mediums who practiced within the growing spiritualist movement. The president, meanwhile, looked for more traditional comfort in the form of counsel from a Presbyterian pastor, the Reverend Phineas Gurley, who assured him Eddie and Willie were not dead, but in heaven.

By the time President Lincoln entered the White House in 1861, mediums, spirit circles, and séance rooms were familiar sights throughout the country, and bustling Washington, D.C., was no exception. The nation's capital had its share of spiritualist mediums. This was no surprise, considering that virtually everyone had a macabre preoccupation with death as the bloody Civil War dragged on. Women rushed for the latest newspapers and hurriedly turned to the lists of war dead, fearful that among the casualties were their husbands, brothers, and sons. The war "carried mourning into almost every home," President Lincoln said. Mediums capable of bringing forth messages from the departed to the bereaved were welcomed by many and eventually found their way into the White House.

President Lincoln, who, it is documented, suffered from bouts of depression throughout his life, was very much a spiritualist believer himself. He'd told friends he'd had numerous psychic experiences, such as strong premonitions that vividly manifested themselves in his dreams. Lincoln also attended séances, mostly at his wife's urging, and there is an overwhelming amount of documentation that survives to shed light on Lincoln White House séances and the influence spirit messages even had on presidential policy. Mary was the driving force behind these séances because "the death of her Willie was a sore deeper to the bone than the war had been," wrote Jim Bishop. Accordingly, she sought reassurance from mediums to help ease her numbing grief. The Lincolns' participation in paranormal and spiritualist ceremonies continued right up until the president's assassination—an assassination that the very spirits themselves foresaw and communicated to President Lincoln both through mediums and premonitions in the president's own dreams.

Believers and Hoaxers

At the end of the Civil War, interest in spiritualism increased among the many bereaved, who'd lost loved ones in the fight and yearned to hear from them. By now, along with spirit rappings, there were other "standard" phenomena, such as automatic writing, trance speaking, and table tipping. Physical mediums proliferated, demonstrating such baffling and theatrical spectacles as feats of levitation. There were mediums of many kinds: rapping, tipping, speaking, or mental mediums, and even those who chanted spirit messages from the Other Side. Some people actually celebrated the soul's survival by holding parties.

Among the many celebrity mediums who caught the public's attention during the latter half of the nineteenth century, no medium achieved the success and recognition of the charming D. D. Home, whose levitations, even in fully lighted rooms, astounded witnesses. Born in Scotland in 1833 and sent to live with relatives in the United States when he was thirteen, Home became internationally famous and demonstrated his abilities for royalty around the world. Adept at receiving spirit communications, he also had immense telekinetic abilities.

His most remarkable exploit was his ability to "rise in the air and float out through a window and in again through another window." No critics ever proved fraud on Home's part, and his seemingly supernatural abilities earned him a reputation as one of the period's great communicators with the spirit world.

However, in contrast to the mysterious gravity-defying Home, the Great Age of Spiritualism was also marred by many charlatans, who resorted to trickery to fake manifestations, such as causing musical instruments to fly through the air and materializing disembodied glowing "spirit hands." These were feats that entranced audiences and brought the true believers to their knees in awe. One of the strangest phenomena produced by some of these mediums was called "ectoplasm," a mysterious, supposedly otherworldly substance that exuded from the medium's body and was claimed to be the ultimate evidence of spirit contact. Upon examination by debunkers, though, it turned out to be a gauzelike material that the medium "self-induced," purely a product of deception.

There were even seemingly incredible spirit materializations bursting out of large cabinets during performances and demonstrations. However, the spirits were actually young girls and costumed confederates. The darkened séance room afforded the cover necessary to dupe the gullible during this period in which spiritualism actually had the ring of science. By comparison, mental mediumship, which only offered verbal messages from loved ones in the beyond, even when the mediums were honest and not charlatans, was simply not as flashy as spirit materializations, floating bugles, glowing lights, or masses of oozing ectoplasm.

Unfortunately, by seizing on frauds and ignoring those mediums who genuinely offered information, detractors and skeptics turned some of the public attention away from legitimate spiritual channelers, whose information could not have been obtained any other way but by supernatural means. Many negative stereotypes long associated with mediumship, which persist today, are traceable to the attacks against paranormal practitioners by debunkers of the nineteenth-century spiritualist movement.

Despite the attacks from skeptics, however, serious scientific interest in spiritualism did develop during the middle of the nineteenth century. In 1857, Charles Darwin's publication of his *Origin of Species* provided a purely materialistic theory of the evolution of human beings and opened up a debate between individuals who supported the creationist theories of the origin of humanity and those who argued for evolution. The debate, which continues to this very day in local school districts all across the United States, also pitted spiritualists against philosophical materialists in the nineteenth century and stimulated scientific research into the claims of believers of the paranormal. The strict religionists of the period, those who disputed Darwinism as well as spiritualism, argued that people could not possibly possess psychic abilities absent a Divinely inspired revelation because then the very nature of humankind, religion, even God would have to be redefined. This was a prospect that alarmed the traditional American clergy and helped garner support for the skeptics and debunkers, while at the same time it piqued scientists interested in discovering a physiological or materialistic basis for what they called an "alternate medium of communication."

While spiritualism for most people who believed in it, like any religion, was strictly a matter of faith, scientists serious about testing mediumship and other psychic phenomena quickly divided themselves between the "believers" or "debunkers." In 1882, the eminent scientist Sir William Crookes, who'd studied the mediums Katie Fox, D. D. Home, and Florence Cook, cofounded the Society for Psychical Research (SPR) in London with several other respected scientists and philosophers. Three years later, the American Society for Psychical Research began. When Sir William observed D. D. Home and then published a positive report about him, some fellow scientists concluded Crookes was "mad," or Home was a clever fraud. Unfortunately, while to the organized Church, séances, mediumship, and contact with the spirit world represented a belief in sorcerers, straight-out blasphemy, or the workings of the devil, many scientists took a different view. Rather than argue from a counterspiritualist or religionist point of view, scientific researchers reasoned that every psychic event was chicanery or slight-of-hand, the work of charlatans or a clever deception, even when the available evidence pointed to the contrary. One leading American figure who did study the paranormal carefully and brought as much scholarship to bear as was possible was the noted psychologist and philosopher William James, whose deep interest in survival of the spirit following physical death resulted in his study of the gifted Boston medium Leonora Piper and her substantial writings on the topic.

In 1872, presidential politics and spiritualism merged again as they had twenty years earlier, this time in the person of Victoria Woodhull, suffragist, feminist, and spiritualist. In 1868, at age thirty, she had come to New York, she said, "directed by a spirit guide." As a child, Victoria worked in traveling medicine shows demonstrating fortune-telling. Victoria, who said spiritualism "formed the core of her beliefs," claimed mediumistic, clairvoyant abilities and trance states. In 1872, she became the first woman nominated for the presidency when she ran against the main party candidates, Ulysses Grant and Horace Greeley. Hers was a radical and controversial move, especially in an age when women could not vote. Although Victoria did not expect to win, her candidacy called attention to the issue of women's suffrage years before the women's suffrage campaign began in earnest. But, notable for our purposes, all of the candidates in that election demonstrated the extent to which spiritualism was flourishing. Victoria was a professional spiritualist; Horace Greeley had publicly attested to the Fox sisters' abilities; and General Grant publicly attested that he believed in the power of spiritualism. Twenty years later, in 1892, Victoria again ran unsuccessfully for the presidency against Grover Cleveland and Benjamin Harrison.

The Fox Confession

In August 1888, spiritualism was rocked by an explosive admission when Margaretta Fox confessed her rappings had all been a fraud, and Katie corroborated her story. At the New York Academy of Music, while thousands watched, Margaretta demonstrated how she and Katie allegedly produced the rapping and knocking sounds by popping their joints or clicking the first joint of her large toe. It was an astounding admission before an audience of the faithful, who sat there utterly stunned. On October 21, 1888, the *New York World* published Margaretta's confession, which received wide publicity. Believers were crushed, many refusing to accept the revelation, while skeptics pronounced themselves vindicated and went on the attack against all practitioners of spiritualism. But there was more to the story about the confession because rumors began emerging that both the Fox sisters had been near penniless at the time and had been paid $1,500 for their admission.

The confession itself, Fox sister supporters contended, had been bought and paid for by promoters looking for a big story and anxious to capitalize on the physical and emotional condition of the Fox sisters. Both women were now widowed, clinically depressed, and poverty-stricken. Friends said the sisters drank heavily. Some people even said that Margaretta was an alcoholic and suicidal as well. However, Margaretta later recanted her confession, saying it was never true, and her spiritualist followers claimed that they, in turn, had been vindicated. Meanwhile their older sister, Leah, became wealthy from demonstrating psychic abilities for New York City's socially prominent and seemed unaffected by the Fox sisters' confessions and recantations. By 1893, Katie and Margaretta had passed on, but their confession mattered little because spiritualism had become so immense a movement by the turn of the century, it overshadowed any single detractor or denouncements by science and clergy. And finally, as if it were in epitaph, in autumn

1904, fifty-six years after the first spirit rappings, a nearly complete human skeleton was discovered in the cellar of the former Fox home in Hydesville. Near the bones was a peddler's tin box, which belonged to the murdered man. It was as if the entire story of the peddler, the spirit, and the murder were shown to be true at last.

The Great Houdini and Sir Arthur Conan Doyle

After the controversy over the Fox sisters had abated, the Great Age of Spiritualism moved into the twentieth century and what would become its most contentious public debate. This time it was an open feud between two of the world's most famous men: Houdini, the ostentatious master illusionist and magician, and Sir Arthur Conan Doyle, creator of Sherlock Holmes. The two larger-than-life celebrities were close friends until they collided over the legitimacy of spiritualism after Houdini's mother, Cecilia Weiss, died in 1913. Houdini had been on stage performing that night when he glimpsed his mother. What he did not know was that, moments before he believed he saw her, she'd passed on to the Other Side. Houdini was extremely close to her and was irretrievably bereft by the loss. Yet despite his hope that he could find a way for her spirit to communicate with him, it was not to be. For years he tried in vain, but never received what he considered to be a genuine message.

In 1915, when his son died, Doyle, who fervently believed in contact with the spirit world, formed a stronger bond with his good friend Houdini because of their mutual grieving for their loved ones. Eventually, however, Houdini became discouraged about the possibility of communication from his mother's spirit and stopped trying to reach the Other Side, while Doyle remained a staunch believer and continued his efforts. The breaking point between the two of them came in 1922 when Lady Doyle performed a séance for Houdini during which she claimed to have received messages from his mother.

However, the messages that Lady Doyle conveyed to Houdini, which were purported to have come from Mrs. Weiss, on the Other Side, were full of Christian allusions about the nature of the afterlife. Houdini exploded in rage when he heard the messages, screaming, "She's Jewish, you imbecile, as am I." Houdini, now convinced that Lady Doyle's mediumship was fraudulent and had packaged phony messages about life in the spirit world so as to gull unsuspecting clients, issued a torrent of insults upon the head of the now pale and weak-kneed Lady Doyle before turning his out-of-control wrath on Sir Arthur. Not only was Lady Doyle a fraud, Houdini thundered at his former friend, but also the entire mediumship movement was based on chicanery. There wasn't a shred of truth to it, Houdini screamed. Doyle, now on his tiptoes with his fists balled at his sides, sputtered in outrage, but what was said could not be unsaid, and the argument that ensued ended forever the friendship between Houdini and Doyle. In just a matter of months, the two famed, egotistical, and strong-willed figures became locked in a bitter public feud.

The two men even fought over the spiritualist legacy of Abraham Lincoln, who had been a lifelong hero for Houdini. The magician was angered "to have the great Abraham Lincoln known as a spiritualist when such is not the case." Doyle, on the other hand, wrote that Lincoln was "a convinced spiritualist," and this only added fire to the boiling feud between the two celebrities.

Increasingly frustrated and disappointed that he'd still not heard from his mother, and convinced he never would, Houdini changed course. Instead of seeking spirit contact, Houdini turned against spiritualism with a single-minded vengeance, determined to prove all mediums were frauds, whether they were or not. Not unlike today's debunkers, Houdini pursued challenges to mediums and their followers wherever he could, particularly against Lady Doyle. And Doyle's further public insistence that Houdini possessed psychic abilities, which he believed explained his amazing escapes, only made Houdini angrier because, Houdini said, his tricks were just that, tricks. And so the world-famous magician became the world's first publicly acclaimed psychic debunker, attracting wide attention for his vitriolic campaign against spiritualism.

Driven by a fury he could not control, Houdini, himself, also proved capable of deception. In 1924, *Scientific American* magazine offered a cash prize for anyone demonstrating mediumship to its satisfaction. After stringent testing, the prize was about to be awarded to Boston medium Mina Crandon. Houdini, outraged that science had not proved the medium to be a charlatan, resolved to do it himself by any means possible and so proceeded to test Crandon personally. He accused her of concealing a ruler to aid in moving objects during demonstrations of physical mediumship, thus denying her the prize. It appeared that Houdini had exposed another fraudulent psychic. However, many years later, Houdini's assistant confessed the magician actually planted the ruler when he found no other way to discredit Crandon's abilities. Despite the often-told tale that Houdini exposed *all* mediums as frauds, he did not, and actually used chicanery to discredit someone who otherwise would have been awarded a prize for legitimacy.

In his continuing fury, Houdini dismissed spiritualism as a "swindle," and those who believed in it, "poor misguided souls." All spiritualism was trickery, Houdini insisted, while Doyle's belief remained unshakable. "Spiritualism is the greatest revelation the world has ever known," Doyle said.

Houdini's relentless pursuit took him to the nation's capital, where he complained that the District of Columbia had no law against fortune-tellers and thus became a haven for the plethora of mediums that congregated there. Some of the mediums had become quite influential, counting as their clients senators and congressmen for whom spirit communications often influenced legislative decisions. Florence Harding visited mediums during her husband's presidency, and Houdini said he'd heard "on rather good authority that they did hold séances in the White House." "Worse," he said, "were the persistent rumors that First Lady Grace Coolidge consulted mediums." In the face of this quasi-official endorsement of mediums, Houdini sought a law against these practitioners of the paranormal, and called for President Coolidge to launch an investigation.

Receiving no response from the president to his continued call for a law banning the practice of mediumship, Houdini convinced a New York Congressman to introduce legislation to prohibit fortune-telling in Washington. The proposed legislation called for a two-hundred-fifty-dollar fine, six months in jail, or both for anyone convicted of passing himself or herself off as a professional medium offering services to the public. In February 1926, the bill was the subject of a House committee hearing, and Houdini was there to urge its passage. Also present were hundreds of angry mediums and other psychic practitioners. Although the legislation failed to pass, Houdini insisted he'd performed a public service by exposing fraudulent mediums who "preyed on the vulnerable, gullible, and bereaved." Actually, his campaign became an obsession, and in 1924, Houdini wrote *A Magician Among the Spirits*, in which he continued his relentless debunking.

Two years later, Doyle received a disturbing message at a séance: "Houdini is doomed, doomed, doomed!" Doyle knew it would be futile to warn Houdini, who would only scoff at him. So Doyle had no choice but to wait helplessly for the spirit prophecy to come true. It did, on Halloween 1926, when, after an accidental punch to his stomach that severely injured the muscles of his solar plexus, Houdini died of peritonitis at the age of fifty-two. How ironic it was that Doyle was probably the only person who could have warned his old friend to beware of crowds because the attack that took Houdini's life was entirely avoidable. Not only did Houdini's feud with Doyle force Sir Arthur to remain silent in the face of what he believed would come to pass, Houdini's public tirade against spiritualism would have forced him to debunk the very warnings that might have saved his life.

The Transformation of Spiritualism into the New Science

Toward the end of spiritualism's heyday, an unlikely voice emerged: the great inventor Thomas Edison, who'd long had an interest in mental telepathy, told *Scientific American* in 1920 that he hoped to "construct an apparatus" to communicate with "personalities which have passed on." Edison, the founder of General Electric, who'd already explored motion pictures, the transmission and recording of sound waves, and the transmission of electrical energy, wanted to explore the realm of psychic energy to see if he could invent a receiver that could pick up what he believed was just another form of electrical waves. Unfortunately, Edison, then seventy-three, never completed building his "electric medium."

The End of the Great Age of Spiritualism

The Great Age of Spiritualism's final burst of popularity occurred immediately after World War I when the bereaved sought comfort. But spiritualism was on the wane, no doubt hurt by fraudulent mediums and Houdini's campaign against them. Spiritualism was also forced off the stage by the development of new measurements of the "other world," psychology and physics. For Sigmund Freud, dreams and the messages they bore were not passageways to the world of the paranormal but into the individual's unconscious mind, where entire dramas played themselves out. For Albert Einstein, Karl Planck, and Werner Heisenberg, there were particles or waves that exerted strong and weak forces on all mass in the universe. Something could either be a particle or wave depending upon how it was observed, and even the observation changed the nature of what was being observed. The implications of relativity and quantum physics are only just being appreciated at the beginning of the third millennium, while the effects of Freudian psychology have transformed Western society.

When it was redefined in the later twentieth century, spiritualism had changed its name but not its spots. It would never again reach the fevered pitch that followed the Hydesville rappings, but transformed into a world of New Age beliefs, it would still hark back to its first flush of acceptance. Its golden age had lasted more than a half century and at its peak, there were nearly eleven million spiritualists in the country. Physical mediums and séances gave way to lower-key, less-flamboyant practitioners, the best of whom applied their gifts to communicate psychically with the deceased and bring messages of hope and comfort to loved ones on earth.

In its prime, spiritualism attracted many of society's elite and those at the highest levels of government. Abraham Lincoln, arguably our greatest president, sought advice from mediums at one of the most dangerous and divisive times in American history. Who knows if the spirit world did indeed help shape some of his important decisions and even change the course of American history. Today practitioners of New Age science are convinced that the ability to perceive now hidden forms of energy or the tools to measure psychic activity are just around the corner. Devices to measure low levels of electrical and magnetic waves are indeed already in use.

As the *Washington Post* reports, the FBI and some of our national intelligence-gathering agencies are now using electrical wave measuring devices so sensitive that they can pick up the energy generated by the closing of a specific key on a computer keyboard so as to decrypt encoded files. As ways of successfully monitoring the keyboarding of information from a remote location and retrieving the text of email messages a party sends, these measuring devices do prove that there are levels of energy that can be analyzed so as to pick up signals most people think do not exist. Aren't many forms of psychic energy simply other aspects of brain wave activity that can be measured as if they were being picked up by a very sophisticated and delicate EEG? If this is the case, we may already be proving that psychic energy fields are absolutely verifiable phenomena and can be measured scientifically, even though we're calling them by other names such as "low-energy magnetic fields." And with the advent of new energy detection and measurement tools, many believers in spiritualism are convinced that there will come a renewed interest in a science of spiritualism, a fourth culture, which will unite physical science with the paranormal and transform what was once myth into a quantifiable reality.

CHAPTER NINE

Abraham Lincoln: The Most Psychic President

I claim not to have controlled events, but confess plainly that events have controlled me.
                                        —Abraham Lincoln

"More than any other man in history, the foundation of his character was mystic," the poet Walt Whitman said of Abraham Lincoln. No one has ever established with certainty what caused Lincoln to be our most psychic president or why he has been, without question, the most evident ghost in the White House. What is indisputable is that spiritualism, precognitive dreams, visions, premonitions, and clairvoyance played important roles in Lincoln's life and decisions, and his spirit has long been resident in the White House, witnessed by presidents, members of first families, and the White House staff itself. Maybe it was the assassination, maybe it was the unfinished business of Reconstruction, or maybe it was Lincoln's connection to the spirit world through his séances and communication with the spirits, but Lincoln's restless ghost is the longest resident in the history of the White House.

Abraham Lincoln was born on February 12, 1809, in a one-room log cabin in Hardin County, Kentucky, to Thomas Lincoln (a farmer and carpenter) and his wife, Nancy. When Abraham was seven years old, the Lincoln family moved to Indiana, where his father continued to work and young Abe was old enough to take on chores. One chore in particular, milling corn into meal, might well have been the event responsible for what some say was his sudden acquisition of psychic abilities while he was still an eight-year-old child. It was the result of a frightening accident that happened at a local mill some two miles from home. Anxious to complete the task and return before sundown, young Lincoln hurried the horse by striking her with a whip each time she circled. But the mare struck back with a kick that knocked Abraham to the ground, where he hit his forehead and lay bleeding and unconscious until the miller discovered him and summoned his father, who hurried to the mill with his wagon and brought his son back to the house.

At first, the injury appeared so serious that Thomas Lincoln thought his son had been killed. Finally, after several hours during which he was unable to speak, Abraham appeared to recover. If there were lingering aftereffects or symptoms of brain damage, they were never reported. However, did the blow initiate psychic abilities? Some parapsychologists theorize that trauma to the head may cause a rerouting of neurological impulses in the brain, maybe even creating new circuitry loops and awakening a dormant area in the brain where psychic experiences can take place. If this happened to Abe Lincoln, the only evidence might be that his psychic abilities, and any accompanying emotional problems, didn't manifest themselves until he was older.

Another event that occurred a year after Abe Lincoln's accident at the mill also might have been responsible for the onset of his emotional problems later in life. In October 1818, nine-year-old Abraham was at his mother's bedside when she died of "milk sickness." Some historians suggest the loss of Nancy, whom the heartbroken child called his "angel mother," caused mood swings and bouts of depression and self-doubt that plagued him no matter how successful he became. However, other people suspect his melancholy was caused by some form of permanent brain damage as a result of the injury to his head, which was exacerbated by his emotional turmoil over his mother's death. Whatever the root cause, Lincoln suffered from moderate to severe melancholia throughout the rest of his life, which grew more intense after his marriage to the bipolar, severely depressed, and ultimately delusional Mary Todd and the subsequent deaths of his children.

In 1810, Thomas Lincoln married a tall attractive widow named Sarah Bush Johnston with three young children of her own. For Abraham, she became a guardian angel in whom he found lifelong love, support, and encouragement. The affection was mutual, for she loved him as much. "I never gave him a cross word all my life. . . . His mind and mine—what little I had—seemed to move together—move in the same channel," she said. Sarah encouraged her stepson to learn to read and find a profession for himself that would give him satisfaction.

His stepmother's encouragement worked because, despite less than a year of formal schooling, young Abraham developed a love for books and became a voracious reader. By the time he was sixteen, he was six foot two inches tall and with his physical strength and size became excellent at rail splitting as well as "farming, grubbing, hoeing, [and] making fences." But father and son grew apart because Abraham had no desire to make a career of farming or rail splitting. Finally, in 1831, when he was twenty-two, he left home forever, yearning for more than he believed he could get by working his father's farm.

He traveled to Mississippi and New Orleans, where, for the first time in his life, he witnessed large numbers of newly arrived African slaves under the brutal lash of taskmasters and overseers. This was profoundly disturbing for Lincoln, who had been raised by adamantly antislavery parents. Lincoln once said, in describing his passionate emotions against slavery, "I cannot remember when I did not so think and feel." He traveled back north and soon moved to the small village of New Salem, Illinois, on the Sangamon River, which he called home for the next six years even while describing himself as "a piece of floating driftwood." He struggled financially in the small community while first taking a job as a clerk in a general store and later as the local postmaster. He was a well-liked, hardworking individual who tried to help as many people as were in need.

After serving in the Black Hawk War, Lincoln returned to New Salem, ran his own general store, and worked as a surveyor. By now his lifelong belief in fatalism was firmly set, accepting the idea of predestination, that "events were ordained by immutable natural law." Although his parents were Baptists, Lincoln was never comfortable with evangelical belief. "Freethinkers" were more to his liking, and although scarce on the frontier, they found their way to his general store, where they debated and pondered such things as how literally the Bible should be taken, the likelihood of miracles, and the reality of free will versus destiny. Lincoln also displayed an introspective side, sometimes becoming so quiet as to appear as if he were in a trance, something not uncommon for individuals with a bent for the mystical or supernatural. He also developed a belief in dreams as well as "other signs and portents."

Lincoln ran for a seat in the Illinois State Legislature, studied law, and was admitted to the Illinois Bar. His prospects were rising. However, following a tragic love affair with a young New Salem woman named Ann Rutledge, who died of typhoid in August 1835, he fell into a deep and intractable depression. "Ann was the only woman he truly loved," said his law partner, William Herndon, who also claimed "her memory exerted a mystic, guiding influence throughout [Lincoln's] life." Lincoln's bouts of depression would continue to haunt him the rest of his life even as he navigated the country through some of its most perilous times. For most of his public life, the kindhearted Lincoln was able to temper his moods, revealing his dark side only during moments of deep personal tragedy. No doubt, had Ann Rutledge lived, she would have counterbalanced Lincoln. Mary Todd actually exacerbated his moods and needed her husband to counterbalance her.

Lincoln seemed to recover from the shock of Ann's death as his stature in Illinois politics rose. In 1837, he moved to the larger and more prosperous community of Springfield to practice law. There he soon met and wooed the pretty and socially prominent Mary Todd. The couple seemed odd to friends at first, the rough-hewn backwoodsman-turned-lawyer was an awkward-looking giant. But he was a gentle, courteous, and impeccably honest politician who had caught the eyes of the state power brokers. Mary Todd, on the other hand, was the high-spirited daughter of the city's most successful banker and merchant, whose family, ironically enough, had owned slaves, even though Mary Todd herself, though not an abolitionist, believed the ownership of slaves was wrong.

Lincoln's relationship with Mary Todd grew and flourished, and the two became what today we would call the "power couple" of Springfield. Would the improbable pair from so completely different backgrounds marry? Could Springfield's most successful new attorney tame the hot-tempered, moody Mary Todd? In 1842, notwithstanding Lincoln's trepidations about marriage and his year-and-a-half-long indecision about commitment, Lincoln and Mary Todd married. A year later on August 1, 1843, the Lincolns' first child, Robert, was born, but arguments, differences, and Mary Todd's explosive temper frequently marred the marriage. Today, Mary Todd might have been clinically treated for her bipolar personality with medication almost as soon as her postpartum depression after her first child was diagnosed. But in the middle of the nineteenth century, before the practice of modern psychiatry, Mary Todd's wild fluctuations between a manic frenzy that covered up her depression and her alternate states of deep melancholy, which required that she be constantly tended to, was not diagnosed as an illness but as her temperament. It was simply the way she was, and because she came from an affluent and powerful family, people accepted it as her eccentricity without question.

Mary Todd was eerily prescient, however, and endowed with psychic gifts. But she was emotionally very needy, suspicious of everyone and everything, utterly dependent upon others—her husband, in particular—for attention, and she could not tolerate being ignored. With his law practice now booming and exercising his new-found political power at the statehouse level, Lincoln could not tend to Mary Todd as much as she wanted, and, rather than do battle with his tempestuous wife, retreated deeper into himself during her bouts of depression. During these periods, Lincoln was usually slow, moody, painfully quiet, and submerged in his private melancholy thoughts. When one looks at the ways Mary Todd's and Lincoln's depressive personalities played off one another and the ways in which each sought solace, one might call their relationship essentially dysfunctional. But nobody knew what dysfunctional meant in the nineteenth century, so the Lincolns were just two unhappy people, paradoxically at the pinnacle of power in the White House during the darkest days of the young Union's existence. They had no idea they might have been among the functionally mentally ill; they simply tried their best to get along even during the worst of times.

Despite their blowups, they remained a couple devoted to each other, perhaps as much out of emotional insecurity as love. Their friends might have known about their domestic difficulties, but the sanctity of marriage was a far greater force in the mid-nineteenth century than it is today, and no one questioned it. In 1846, the Lincolns' second son, Edward, was born; his birth drew the soon-to-be first couple closer. But almost as quickly as they celebrated his birth and early years, they were again thrown back into grief and depression when Eddie, not yet four, died of tuberculosis in February 1850. Their third son, William Wallace, called Willie, was born later that same year in December. In 1853, a fourth son, Thomas, nicknamed Tad, was born.

As Lincoln's political stature grew in Illinois, the country slid toward a constitutional crisis over the issues of states rights and the demands to abolish slavery. In 1850, the Fugitive Slave Law that essentially allowed vigilante groups to seize free black citizens as runaway slaves without any due process of law was passed. Then in 1854, the Kansas Nebraska Act was passed, which held out the promise to Southern states that new Western states entering the Union would be slave states, not free states. These laws, meant to preserve the Union by granting the slave-holding states rights they already had, infuriated many Northerners and, during the 1850s, led to the formation of the Republican Party, whose platform was that slavery would not be expanded into the new territories and states. Thus, by 1855, the Union was divided into those Republicans who sought to prevent expansion of slavery without eliminating it in the Southern states, and thus preserving the Union; abolitionists who sought to impose the end of slavery on the Southern states, by force if necessary; and leaders of the Southern states who sought to bring slavery into the Western territories. Amid the bitter divisiveness and calls to arms, Lincoln sadly predicted, "There is no peaceful extinction of slavery in prospect for us." To this day, we don't know whether his prognostication was born out of prescience or political astuteness, or a combination of both, but about this he was clear: "No man is good enough to govern another man, without that other's consent."

By the beginning of 1860, Lincoln had concentrated a centrist group of leaders around him inside the Republican Party, most of whom sought a political solution to the issue of states rights by opposing the expansion of slavery in new states but not abolishing slavery in the South. This group turned to Lincoln, their moderate candidate in the 1860 presidential election, who counterbalanced the fiercely radical Northern abolitionists on the one hand, while running strongly on the issue of states rights. And in the campaign Lincoln promised not to interfere with the existing practice of slavery in the South while opposing the expansion of the institution. This was as tiny a center as any candidate, given the radical and violent opposition on both sides, could have defended. But, for Lincoln in 1860, it worked.

In a tough campaign that was narrowly focused on the issues of slavery, states rights, and secession, the tall, "sorrowful and sad," gaunt-looking candidate with black hair, gray eyes, and a high-pitched voice argued that he would preserve the Union at all costs. This was the platform that most Americans wanted, and they elected Lincoln as the sixteenth president by only thirty-nine percent of the raw vote. The self-taught son of a farmer, strangely psychic and still grieving over the loss of his second son, Eddie, prepared to take up residence in the White House. But even in early 1861, Lincoln's psychic visions invaded his consciousness.

In Springfield, shortly before his inauguration, Lincoln explained an unsettling premonition he had after the election. "I was pretty well tired out and went home to rest," he told friends. "Opposite where I lay was a bureau with a swinging glass, and looking in the mirror, I was astonished to see myself reflected, almost at full length, but with my face double. It had two separate and distinct images. . . . I was more than a little bothered, perhaps startled, and I got up and looked in the glass. But the illusion vanished.

"On lying down again I saw it a second time, plainer if possible, than before. Then I noticed that one of the faces was paler, much paler than the other. I got up and the thing melted away. Later in the day, I told my wife about it, and a few days later I tried the experiment again, when, sure enough, the vision came.

"My wife thought it was a sign that I would be elected to a second term of office and that the paleness of one of the faces was an omen that I shall not live through the last term. . . ."

Four years later, as Lincoln began his second term, the foreboding vision recurred. "I have seen this evening what I saw on the evening of my confirmation. As I stood before a mirror I saw two images of myself: a bright one in front and one that was pallid, standing behind. It completely unnerved me. The bright one, I know is my past, and the pale one my coming life. I do not think I shall live to see the end of my second term. . . ."

But his second term was still four years away while his first presidential victory brought no cheers from the Southern states, who, fearing the effects of a Lincoln presidency, began to declare themselves for secession. In his March 1861 inaugural address, Lincoln borrowed from the Bible when he said, without equivocation as he promised to preserve the Union, "A house divided against itself cannot stand." His words were put to the test one month later when Confederate soldiers fired on Union-held Fort Sumter in Charleston, South Carolina, igniting the Civil War and rejecting Lincoln's appeals to prevent bloodshed. Lincoln's daunting task was clear: to preserve a divided nation, an intractable commitment from which he never wavered.

Throughout his career, particularly his stewardship of the Civil War, Lincoln was a fatalist, seeing himself as destiny's tool rather than someone who shaped destiny. "I have been controlled by some other power than my own will," Lincoln once said, reflecting on the degree to which his fate and fortunes depended not on his own actions, but were instead determined by some greater power. "I frequently see my way clear to a decision when I am aware that I do not have sufficient facts on which to found the decision. I cannot recall one instance in which I have followed my own judgment, based upon such a decision, where the results were unsatisfactory; whereas in almost every instance where I have yielded to the views of others I have had occasion to regret it. I am satisfied that when the Almighty wants me to do or not do a particular thing, he finds a way of letting me know it. . . ."

Lincoln did not deny his psychic inclinations even though he did not publicly embrace them. However, he confided to friends that he was, indeed, a spiritual believer. As he once wrote to Joshua Speed, his friend from Springfield, "I always did have . . . a . . . strong tendency to mysticism." Nor was he alone given to psychic experiences. While president-elect, in January 1861, he traveled to Coles County, Illinois, to visit his beloved stepmother, Sarah. It was a moving experience for both, but when the time came to bid her farewell, she cried, fearful for his safety. Lincoln did his best to reassure her and ease her fears: "No, no, Mama. Trust in the Lord and all will be well. We will see each other again."

Years later she remembered, "I did not want Abe to run for president, did not want him elected, was afraid somehow or other . . . that something would happen [to] him . . . and that I should see him no more." Sarah Bush Lincoln outlived her stepson by four years.

From almost the time he was elected, there were threats to kidnap and murder him, but Lincoln, believing his life was in the hands of Providence, allowed few safeguards. Only when pressured by advisors did he concede to changes in travel routes or allow added protection. On Inauguration Day, however, extra precautions were taken to shield him as he rode down Pennsylvania Avenue to the Capitol to be sworn in. Advisors convinced him that even though he might believe his fate might be predetermined, a lucky shot from a crazed enemy would throw the country into chaos and change the course of the entire Union.

Shortly after his election in 1860, the *Cleveland Plain Dealer* published an article based on comments from medium J. B. Conklin, who asserted Lincoln was "a sympathizer with spiritualism," because Conklin claimed he'd seen Lincoln anonymously at several of his New York séances. The newspaper contended that Lincoln was a spiritualist, one who believes in communication with the deceased. The assertion gained further credence from a report in the *Spiritualist Scientist* that the medium Mr. Conklin "was a guest at the Presidential Mansion." If the newspaper expected a denial from Lincoln, surely they were taken aback, for when shown the story, he answered: "The only falsehood in the statement is that the half of it has been told. This article does not begin to tell the wonderful things I have witnessed." It was one of the few times Lincoln would publicly state his belief in spiritualism, although he never denied it.

After the attack on Fort Sumter, there was considerable optimism in the North the war would be short-lived, perhaps over in a matter of months. After all, the population in the North was more than double that in the Confederate states that seceded and the nation's manufacturing and matériel centers were located in the North. However, with the prescience he often revealed, Lincoln strongly disagreed. In fact, Lincoln knew more than most people about the Union Army's state of readiness, especially in the first few months of the war when McClellan's army was incapable of moving out of its encampments and defending Washington, D.C. Had the Confederate Army decided to occupy Washington in the early weeks after secession, Lincoln would have had to flee, and the Union Army would have had to launch an invasion to retake the nation's capital. Such a bold move by the Confederate general staff could easily have tilted the balance of the war in the first few months and perhaps even forced Lincoln's government to seek a negotiated cessation of hostilities.

A Confederate occupation of Washington would have also forced England, officially neutral at the outset of the war, to rethink its own policy so as to protect one of its vital sources of cotton. As it was, there was great debate in England over intervening on behalf of the Confederacy. Only after Prince Albert convinced Queen Victoria's government that slavery, already banned in England and Europe, was a crime against humanity did the English decide not to intervene. Their participation, hoped for by the Confederacy, would have swung the balance of military power away from the North because a British blockade of Northern seaports would have prevented the U.S. Navy from blockading Confederate ports. In this way, the early months of the Civil War were not just about the North losing the Battle of Bull Run, but the possibility of an Atlantic war that Lincoln didn't believe he could win. Thus, President Lincoln's pessimism was a matter based on facts as well as prescience.

As the worries and burdens of the bitter and bloody war weighed heavily on the president, his world seemed to collapse in early 1862 when young Willie Lincoln had taken ill with "bilious fever," likely typhoid, the result of pollution in the White House water system. This was an especially devastating blow to the president because Willie was the son the president had most doted on, especially after the death of Eddie, and was also a release from the grinding depression Lincoln endured every day as a result of the war. In fact, among the president's few pleasant diversions from the day-to-day prosecution of the war were those times spent with his sons, Willie and Tad, and their pets, a pony and two little goats. Now that Willie lay ill, growing weaker with each day, the president and Mary Todd Lincoln kept an anxious vigil at their stricken son's bedside, too distraught to concentrate fully on anything else. Through agonizing days and nights, Lincoln broke away from the often-contentious meetings with his cabinet, particularly during the open conflicts between Secretary of State William Seward and Treasury Secretary Salmon P. Chase, to visit Willie's sickroom, while Mary Todd sat with the boy for hours at a time.

Finally on the afternoon of February 20, 1862, eleven-year-old Willie Lincoln, his lungs filled with fluid, could hold on no longer and passed from this world. Lincoln, choked with grief, told his secretary, John Nicolay, "Well, Nicolay, my boy is gone. He is actually gone!" Then the president broke into tears. Mary Todd burst into hysterics in the White House hallway outside the family quarters and became inconsolable. She never again set foot in the room where Willie died or in the East Room, where his body was embalmed. Nor could she summon the strength to attend her son's funeral in the White House on a dismal and stormy winter day. As the president gazed at the face of his dead son, who had been his favorite, he said, with great emotion, "He was too good for this earth . . . but then we loved him so."

After Willie's passing, Lincoln sought comfort from the Almighty to a greater degree than he ever had before. "Without the assistance of [a] Divine Being . . . I cannot succeed," he said. He also ruminated increasingly on the reality of life after death and believed that Willie's spirit was a presence close to him. "Do you ever find yourself talking with the dead?" the president asked his friend and treasury secretary Salmon P. Chase, who was at a loss to answer. Lincoln told Chase, "Ever since Willie's death, I catch myself involuntarily talking to him, as if he were with me, and I feel that he is."

On another occasion, Lincoln asked an aide, "Colonel, did you ever dream of a lost friend, and feel that you were holding sweet communion with that friend, and yet have a sad consciousness that it was not a reality? Just so I dream of my boy, Willie." Whether he realized it or not, that was no dream. The president had experienced an afterdeath communication, a visitation from a deceased loved one through the dream state. Its purpose was to bring a message of comfort from Willie to his father, a means of communicating that his spirit was still close by.

The president found brief measures of solace in Shakespeare's *Macbeth* and *King Lear*. He also read from Constance's elegy for her dead son in *King John*: "And, father cardinal, I have heard you say/That we shall see and know our friends in heaven:/If that be true, I shall see my boy again."

One night, several months after Willie died, fire erupted in the White House stables. Frantically, the president raced to the scene of the blaze. "Have the horses been taken out?" he screamed. Guards escorted him back to the safety of the White House, where, from a second-floor window, he watched as the fire was extinguished. Then Lincoln cried, for there was Willie's pony, dead in the charred ruins of the stable. It was a sad irony and bitter postscript to Willie's death.

As desolate as Lincoln's personal life had become, it was even worse for his wife. The grief-stricken Mary Todd at times became almost delusional in her denial of the finality of death and turned to mediums and séances to communicate with her deceased sons, Eddie and Willie. She grasped at whatever branch she could as she slid deeper into depression. And with every new medium she heard about, she held out the hope it would bring her into communication with Willie and Eddie as if to bring them back to life. She relied on her husband as her only link to day-to-day reality, fighting with him at night when she felt he paid too much attention to the war and not enough to their shared grief. It was all Lincoln could do to keep his domestic life from unraveling before his eyes. Meanwhile, as the War Between the States and the war between the Lincolns dragged on, the president maintained his belief in predestined events. "In the present civil war, it is quite possible that God's purpose is something different from the purpose of either party." Lincoln's thoughts overlapped religious belief with the supernatural: "He permits [the war] for some wise purpose of His own, mysterious and unknown to us."

Mysticism was also an anchor for the president because, like his belief in predestination, it gave him hope that there was a greater intelligence behind the chaos that seemed to beset him on every side. Many historians have wrongly attributed Lincoln's interest in mysticism and spiritualism entirely to his wife. While she certainly persuaded him to join her at séances after Willie's death, Lincoln wrote to his friend Joshua Speed expressing "his tendency to mysticism" in 1842, several years before the spiritualist crazes swept America in 1848.

The Lincolns, Nettie Colburn, and the White House Séance Table

Although the president had made clear his belief in spiritualism, it is also clear that the specific driving force behind President Lincoln's visits to the séance table was Mary Todd, who sought consolation over the deaths of Willie and Eddie. The Lincolns' first séance to communicate with Willie was conducted by the medium Mrs. Cranston Laurie, who practiced from her private home in Georgetown. Apparently, Mary Todd was so satisfied with the session that the Lincolns subsequently invited the Lauries to the White House or visited them at their home several times between 1862 and 1865. Shortly after their first sessions, Mrs. Laurie urged Nettie Colburn, a gifted twenty-year-old medium, to offer her services to the Lincolns. When the Lincolns agreed to meet her, spiritualist Thomas Foster introduced Nettie to Mary Todd, who then requested a sitting with the young woman. She "never charges for her séances," Mary Todd was told. "They are free."

Nettie's first sitting for Mary Todd was held at the Lauries' home, where, for an hour, she demonstrated her abilities while in trance. The first lady was impressed: "This young lady must not leave Washington. I feel she must stay here, and Mr. Lincoln must hear what we have heard. It is all-important, and he must hear it." Mary Todd arranged employment for Nettie in the Agricultural Department. With her new job paying her a salary, she was then able to accommodate the growing number of Washington's top society eager to receive the benefits of her mediumistic gifts.

Notwithstanding his lingering grief over Willie's death, the president still had the pressing concerns of war weighing on him. As the year 1862 ground over the lives of the soldiers under his command, it was becoming clear that the nation needed a moral reason for the prosecution of the war. Was it justification enough that these troops fight only to prevent secession? Was there a moral value to that? Lincoln decided not.

Prior to his presidency, Lincoln made clear his belief, rooted in the Founders' own beliefs as they set them forth in the Declaration of Independence, that all men were equal. Still, he admitted, the Constitution itself restricted the notion of equality by counting slaves as three-fifths of a man. Moreover, Lincoln conceded that he had no idea how to eliminate slavery, given the contentious nature of the issue, the rights of the states as set forth in the Constitution, and his own campaign promise not to interfere with slavery in the South. Despite his belief in the principles of the Declaration of Independence, Lincoln had not been an outright abolitionist and remained sympathetic to the South. Mary Todd was a Southerner, and although antislavery, her sympathies, too, remained with the sovereign rights of the slave-owner states. More to the point, from the beginning of his term in office, Lincoln's overriding goal had been the preservation of the Union at all costs, which meant leaving slavery untouched in the Southern states despite the pleas of the abolitionists to rid the Union of slavery once and for all.

Then, during the progression of the war and in the face of clear indicators that the Union would not enjoy an easy victory with minimal casualties, public opinion in support of the war began to waver. At this point, a marked transformation occurred in the president's thinking. Might the nation rally around the cause of emancipation? As the president considered an emancipation proclamation—a decision that sharply divided his advisors and was stretched across moral and political arguments—he faced a dilemma of enormous proportions. Abolitionists urged him to "sign it now. Take a firm stand. Tell the slaves they are free. Let come what may." On the other side—the side that argued that states' rights were at the heart of our Federalist Union—he was reminded of his campaign promise not to intervene in the South and counseled, "Do not sign the [proclamation]. You'll be making our position worse than ever. It may even turn the Border States against us to the side of the South. You'll be most bitterly hated."

Lincoln wrote a draft of a proclamation of emancipation in September, then held back, awaiting, he said, a Union victory before issuing such a sweeping and controversial document. In fact, he informed his cabinet that he'd "made a vow, a covenant, that if God gave us the victory in the approaching battle, [he] would consider it an indication of Divine will, and that it was [his] duty to move forward in the cause of emancipation." In other words, the president was waiting for a divine sign or portent to help him make his decision. All the while, Lincoln wrestled with the question of whether it was God's intention that the slaves be freed. But Lincoln had no palpable sign to guide him. "The Almighty gives no audible answer to that question, and his revelation— the Bible—gives none," he said. But a full decade before that fateful night of decision on the second floor of the White House, young Nettie Colburn had already set forth on a course that would ultimately intersect with the very choice Lincoln was struggling with himself to make.

In the 1850s, a teenaged Nettie had become aware of her mediumistic abilities when she discovered she could induce spirit rappings. Her ability manifested itself quite dramatically during the 1856 James Buchanan and John C. Fremont presidential contest, in which Nettie's father, a staunch Fremont supporter, found out just how accurate his daughter's talent was. Too young and inexperienced to comprehend the political differences between the candidates, on the day before the election she nevertheless "was seized by a power I could not control." Grabbing a piece of paper, Nettie scrawled the name "Buchanan," and as she did, "loud raps came upon the table." Her startled father asked, "Do you mean . . . that Buchanan will be elected tomorrow?" Nettie nodded. The next day, her prediction proved accurate. Her father was convinced that his daughter could help others with her predictions.

With her father's approval and support, Nettie went on to become a "spiritual lecturer," mainly in New England towns and villages. When the Civil War erupted in April 1861, despite Northern expectations of a quick victory, she predicted otherwise: "Our spirit friends . . . reply . . . it would continue four years, and require five practically to end it." She moved to Washington to be by the side of her youngest brother, who had been wounded in the war and hospitalized. In a trance, Nettie said the spirits directed her to go to President Lincoln to seek aid for her brother, but she demurred, fearing she would be thought an "escaped lunatic." In December 1862, however, a furlough was granted to the brother. Meanwhile, Nettie had made the acquaintance of a number of mediums who believed her to be a genuine psychic.

One evening, after Nettie had first demonstrated her abilities to Mary Todd at the Lauries' home, Mrs. Laurie was invited to the White House and asked to bring "Miss Nettie" along with her to meet the president. Nettie was frightened, approaching the event with the "natural trepidation of a young girl . . . about to meet some superior being . . . [I] was almost trembling [as] I entered . . . the . . . White House." Mary Todd ushered Nettie into the Blue Room, where they waited for the president to join them. President Lincoln soon arrived to meet Nettie and greet his friends the Lauries and their daughter, Mrs. Miller, a physical medium. Nettie was "led forward and introduced. He stood before me, tall and kindly, with a smile on his face. Dropping his hand upon my head, he said, 'So this is our little Nettie, is it, that we have heard so much about?' "

"Yes, sir," Nettie smiled and answered.

The president led her to an ottoman at the foot of his chair, bade her sit, then proceeded to question her about the details and practice of mediumship. Throughout, she said, "His manner . . . was genial and kind." A spirit circle was formed, and finally Lincoln asked her, "Well, how do you do it?"

Soon Nettie was in a trance. "I lost all consciousness of my surroundings and passed under control," she would write years later. For the next hour, she offered spirit messages, which the president appeared to understand, and then turned to the subject of the forthcoming Emancipation Proclamation. From the spirit world, Nettie received and relayed a message for Lincoln "not to delay . . . [its] enforcement beyond the opening of the year [1863]." Her spirit control assured the president it would be "the crowning event of his administration and his life; and that while he was being counseled by strong parties to defer . . . [or] . . . delay action, he must in no way heed such counsel, but stand firm to his convictions and fearlessly perform the work and fulfill the mission for which he had been raised up by an overruling Providence." Those present in the room during the medium's trance state observed that "some strong masculine spirit force was giving speech to almost divine commands," rather than the voice of a young woman barely out of her teens. After Nettie's delivery of the message to Lincoln, one guest queried, "Mr. President, did you notice anything peculiar about the method of address?" Lincoln stood up "as if shaking off his spell," then glanced at a full-length portrait of Daniel Webster, which hung above the piano, and emphatically answered, "Yes, it is very singular, very!"

Former congressman Daniel Somes asked, "Mr. President, would it be improper for me to inquire whether there has been any pressure brought to bear upon you to defer the enforcement of the proclamation?"

Lincoln replied, "It is taking all my nerve and strength to withstand such a pressure."

"When I regained consciousness," Nettie later wrote about the event, "I was standing in front of Mr. Lincoln, and he was sitting back in his chair, with his arms folded . . . looking intently at me." The group gathered around the room sat in "perfect silence." They watched the young girl and the melancholy president eye each other as if trying to figure out what hidden force was behind the message. Ultimately, Nettie's reading was summed up this way: "The Civil War will not end until the president issues an Emancipation Proclamation to set free the millions of slaves in the United States." She confirmed it was the spirit of Northern patriot, great orator, and politician Daniel Webster who communicated the emphatic message to her, a message Webster himself might have delivered because in life he "articulated a near-mystical devotion to the Union." Like Webster, Lincoln reflected the same devotion to the Union in his speeches.

When Nettie's channeling session was finished, the president turned to her, placed his hand upon her head, and said, "My child, you possess a very singular gift; but that it is of God, I have no doubt. I thank you for coming here tonight. It is more important than perhaps anyone present can understand. I must leave; but I hope I shall see you again." He shook Nettie's hand, bowed to the others present, and took his leave. Nettie remained for another hour, talking with Mary Todd and her friends, then returned to Georgetown.

Nettie's was not the only voice who had communicated messages to President Lincoln from the Other Side concerning the Emancipation. Another paranormal influence brought to bear on the president to issue the proclamation came from U.S. Senator Thomas Richmond, who disclosed in his 1870 book *God Dealing with Slavery* letters that had been received psychically, which were then sent to the president, hoping to persuade him to issue the order. It took another few months of wavering before Lincoln issued the proclamation, but on January 1, 1863, it went into effect and changed the course of the Civil War.

While Lincoln's stewardship of the country and his leading the Union to victory in the Civil War probably were his greatest accomplishments as a statesman, history regards the Emancipation Proclamation as Lincoln's most significant political accomplishment. Not only did the proclamation make clear a moral purpose for pursuing the war, but it established the groundwork for the ongoing American civil rights movements a century later.

Still, Lincoln initially questioned whether the proclamation would succeed as a political and social document. If it did not accomplish its purpose in rallying the Union around a moral cause, the president worried, would it actually result in the freedom of the slaves were the Confederacy to have survived? And would the moral message of the proclamation serve the purpose of saving the Union when the proclamation itself represented a broken promise Lincoln-the-candidate made to the nation in 1860 when he promised not to interfere in the slave-holding states? Clearly, Lincoln's doubts and anxiety seem to have been mitigated, in part, by his reliance on advice from the spirit world as communicated to him by Nettie. And, of course, once he resolved his hesitancy, Lincoln said, "I never, in my life, felt more certain that I was doing right, than I do in signing this paper." The president had sought a divine portend to guide him morally along the right path. And the message from Daniel Webster's spirit may well have been the sign that convinced Lincoln to issue the proclamation. Many close friends and colleagues confirmed this, and years later, Mary Todd acknowledged it herself. Finally, Nettie, who wrote that she had looked directly into Lincoln's face when she awoke from her trance state after delivering Daniel Webster's message, believed with all her heart that the president was influenced by her séance.

On another occasion, in December 1862, Philadelphia railroad magnate Colonel Chase witnessed the Lauries' younger daughter, who possessed mediumistic abilities, induce a trance, walk up to President Lincoln, and say, "A congress of wise spirits hold the welfare of [the] nation in their keeping. You, sir, have been called to . . . serve a great and mighty purpose. . . . Thou art the man. Issue a proclamation of emancipation giving freedom to the slaves and from that hour victory will crown the Union Army and humanity will be served." Chase later told a newspaper reporter, "We listened spellbound to her burning words, and when she ended there was not a dry eye in the room." The young girl claimed to be controlled by the Roman philosopher Seneca. Chase described the spirit address as an "inspiration. It was one of the most powerful pleas for human rights I have ever heard." The president said, "I am deeply impressed."

When Chase was asked by the incredulous reporter, "Do you contend that the Emancipation Proclamation was issued as a result of communication with the world of the spirits?" Chase answered, "There is not the least doubt that the communications turned the scales and was the pivot upon which one of the most important events in American history revolved." From the time of

Miss Laurie's trance reading, Union forces won more than two dozen battles, precisely as the young girl predicted.

Lincoln's interest in the paranormal and spiritual had only been whetted by the events preceding his announcement of the Emancipation Proclamation. They continued through 1863, an especially active period of White House séances and the assemblage of spirit circles. On February 5, there was another séance at the Laurie home, requested by Mary Todd for herself and several friends. At the last minute, the president decided to attend. Nettie thought Lincoln "appeared tired and haggard," more so than only several weeks earlier. "Well, Miss Nettie, do you think you have anything to say to me tonight?" the president asked. "Suppose we see what they will have to tell us."

Nettie's psychic communiqués were translated to her through entities called "spirit controls," one of whom was known as "old Dr. Bamford." He was Lincoln's particular favorite. Once the spirit took hold of Nettie and her waking personality was transformed into the medium for the stentorian Dr. Bamford, it announced its message in prophetic tones, denouncing the current state of the army and military strategy and demanding that the president take action. "The army [is] totally demoralized," began the Jeremiad. "Regiments are stacking arms, refusing to obey orders to do duty; threatening a general retreat." Then, "a vivid picture was drawn of the terrible state of affairs." The others present were surprised, but not the president.

"You seem to understand the situation," he said. "Can you point out the remedy?"

"Yes, if you have the courage to use it," the spirit control answered.

Lincoln smiled and replied, "Try me."

Dr. Bamford proceeded. "It is one of the simplest. The remedy lies with yourself. Go in person to the front, taking with you your wife and children, leaving behind your official dignity and all manner of display. Resist the importunities of officials to accompany you. Avoid the officers and seek the tents of the private soldiers. Inquire into their grievances. Show yourself to be what you are, the Father of your People! Make them feel that you are interested in their sufferings . . . the many trials which beset them . . . whereby both their courage and numbers have been depleted."

"It shall be done," Lincoln answered unhesitatingly.

"It will do all that is required," Dr. Bamford continued. "It will unite them to you in bands of steel. And now, if you would prevent a serious, if not fatal, disaster to your cause, let the news [be] disseminated throughout the camp of the Army of the Potomac. Have it scattered and broadcast that you are on the eve of visiting the front. . . . This will stop insubordination and hold the soldiers in check . . ."

"If that will do any good, it is easily done," the president said.

In the ensuing conversation, the spirit control told the president he would be reelected, particularly on the wings of a Union victory in the war. After the séance, Lincoln, while confirming the gravity of the army's situation, asked those present not to speak publicly about it. Lincoln took seriously the urging of Nettie's spirit control that he personally visit the Union troops. The day after the séance, newspaper headlines proclaimed: "The President Is About to Visit the Army of the Potomac."

At the battle line, "the ovation tendered him showed the spontaneous uprising of a people to receive a beloved ruler . . . he was literally borne on the shoulders of soldiers through the camp, and everywhere the 'boys in blue' rallied around him . . . and [he left] a united and devoted army behind him when he returned to Washington." Nettie wrote, "The wisdom of [the president's] action told the result." The soldiers saw Lincoln as a "man . . . in all his simplicity," not the "president," and with him he carried "a personal influence which would be felt throughout the camp."

Lincoln realized that although he might be a spiritual believer in the privacy of the family quarters of the White House, he could not let the population at-large think that matters of national policy and war strategy were discussed with advisors from an ethereal world on the Other Side. In particular, he wanted no one to know that he'd received advice from the ghost of Daniel Webster. Nettie, too, was frequently cautioned not to discuss her psychic sessions with reporters because the presidential séances were strictly a private matter. It was nearly thirty years later that she wrote a book about her experiences and disclosed some of the private and sensitive information she shared with Lincoln.

In April 1863, the president paid another visit to the world of the paranormal when he observed the abilities of the medium Charles Schockle at a White House demonstration that included spirit rappings and levitations. Also present that evening were several friends and two Lincoln cabinet officials, Secretary of War Edwin Stanton and Secretary of the Navy Gideon Welles. The audience watched tables move, a portrait of Henry Clay shift back and forth, and two candelabra that were gifts to John Adams lift themselves almost to the ceiling. The president also heard loud rappings under his feet, which, Schockle explained, came from the spirit of an Indian who wished to make his presence known. "I should be happy to hear what his Indian Majesty has to say," Lincoln replied. Following more rappings, a message from the spirit of Henry Knox, Lincoln's first secretary of war, was delivered to the medium through a demonstration of mechanical writing. Knox advised the president to "use every means to subdue; make a bold front and fight the enemy."

The president asked Schockle, "I should like to ask General Knox if it is within the scope of his ability to tell when this rebellion will be put down."

Schockle answered, "Washington, Lafayette, Franklin, Napoleon . . . and myself have held frequent consultations on this point. This is something which our spiritual eyes cannot detect. . . . Franklin sees the end approaching. Other spirits have conflicting opinions."

"Opinions differ among the spirits as well as among humans," Lincoln remarked, perhaps as much to the spirit of General Henry Knox as to his living White House guests. "They don't seem to understand running the machines among the celestials much better than we do. Their talk and advice sound much like the talk of my cabinet." The president seemed clearly disappointed in the medium's evasive answer, but there was little he could do to elicit a consensus from the assembled spirits.

Next came a series of loud rappings, which Schockle was able to decipher through an alphabetic code. Room lights dimmed and "a supernatural picture, on a large mirror . . . was witnessed," of the Confederate steamer *Alabama* being chased by another large vessel, then floating idly with no sign of life on board. The picture seemed to answer Lincoln's question about how best to capture the *Alabama*, which had devastated Union shipping on both sides of the Atlantic and had sunk the USS *Hatteras* off the coast of Texas. When the séance ended, the president told Schockle the supernatural pictures persuaded him they were of a "heavenly nature."

In fact, the CSS *Alabama* was chased across the Atlantic and into Cherbourg Harbor by the American steam sloop-of-war USS *Kearsarge*, which patrolled the outer entrance to the harbor until the *Alabama* came out to fight and opened fire on the Union sloop. A furious firefight ensued in French territorial waters, with each vessel circling the other, trying to rake the other's bow. About an hour later, after both warships had exchanged over two hundred rounds, the *Alabama*, unable to cripple the *Kearsarge* because of bad powder and shot and hit below her waterline, began to sink. When water began rushing through her lower decks in torrents, the *Alabama*'s captain, Raphael Semmes, struck his colors to the U.S. Navy sloop and transferred most of his crew by lifeboat to the *Kearsarge* and a nearby British vessel. In the few remaining moments just before she slipped under the waves, however, the Confederate warship, with her load lightened after her crew had abandoned her, appeared to the crews watching over the gunwales of both rescue ships as an idle lifeless vessel, perhaps exactly as it had appeared to Lincoln in his vision. The

CSS *Alabama* sank in French waters outside Cherbourg on June 11, 1864, after having captured over sixty Union prizes of war with an estimated value of more than six million dollars. The wreck of the *Alabama* resting in two hundred feet of water was located by a French minesweeper in 1988 and has been recognized as an historical artifact of marine archaeology.

As the war progressed, there was no lack of mediums who claimed contact with Lincoln. J. B. Conklin told of receiving a telepathic message from Edward D. Baker, a longtime friend of the president, who had been killed in battle. According to Conklin, Baker's message two months after his death was, "Gone elsewhere. Elsewhere is everywhere." Other mediums introduced to the president included Charles Foster, Charles Colchester, Lucy Hamilton, and Charles Redmond. Redmond once warned Lincoln of enemy danger as he traveled from Philadelphia to Washington, which, the medium claimed, saved the president's life. At a Colchester séance, Mary Todd, while holding hands with others gathered around the table in a darkened room, heard tapping sounds and noises she believed were from Willie in the spirit world. Colchester, however, was of dubious reputation and ability and was subsequently exposed to be a fraud after it was discovered that he, not spirits, produced the rapping sounds.

On one occasion, the president was part of the audience when the Lauries' daughter, Belle Miller, played a piano that began to vibrate intensely, levitated, then lurched and shifted across the floor toward Nettie Colburn. Those present in the fully lit room searched for an explanation by examining every part of the grand piano, but found no evidence of chicanery or deception. Someone suggested, "Let's sit on the piano and see if the spirit force can still raise it." Lincoln, along with three others, quickly seated himself on the large instrument. The combined weight of four full-sized men planted firmly atop the concert grand should make it impossible for the piano to raise itself from the floor. However, moments later, Nettie said she felt a huge burst of energy jolt through her body and asked Mrs. Miller to play the piano once more. Again, the instrument levitated with all four upon it, and those gathered watched in awe as the piano sat suspended in midair, then finally returned to the floor. Sworn statements given by witnesses attested to the veracity of the experience.

In May, Nettie was again asked to visit Mary Todd. This time, the Confederates were winning the Battle of Chancellorsville, and the president was distraught over the communiqués received from the front. "Oh, Miss Nettie, such dreadful news. They are fighting at the front. Such terrible slaughter. All our generals are killed and our army is in full retreat. Such is the latest news," said a distressed Mary Todd. "Oh I am glad you have come. Will you sit . . . and see if we can get anything from 'beyond?' " Nettie quickly complied and instantly her spirit control, this one named Pinkie, took over and "assured Mrs. Lincoln that her alarm was groundless." Nettie predicted there "would be better news by nightfall, and the next day would bring still more cheering results." The messages calmed Mary Todd somewhat. Lincoln, looking anxious and careworn, later entered the room, and Mary Todd immediately shared what the medium said. Nettie repeated the spirit control's communication that the news would brighten—which it ultimately did—and the assurances seemed to boost the president's mood.

In early 1864, several private séances were held for the Lincolns, usually at one p.m. when the president took his lunch. One day, Lincoln himself summoned Nettie to the White House and cautioned her *this* séance was in strictest confidence. She was ushered into a room where two military officers were seated. Nettie induced a trance and when she again became conscious of her surroundings, an hour later, she was standing near a long table "upon which was a large map of the Southern states." She was also holding a pencil. While the two military men quickly stepped back and stared at her, the president continued to study the map. Not certain what had occurred or what her spirit control had said, Nettie was able to catch several remarks from those assembled around the table. "It is astonishing, how every line she has drawn conforms to the plan agreed upon," she heard the president say.

"Yes, it is very astonishing," the older of the two military officers agreed.

Former congressman Somes joined the others in the room. "Well, was everything satisfactory?" he asked.

"Perfectly," answered Lincoln. "Miss Nettie does not seem to require eyes to do anything."

Apparently, Nettie had traced lines upon the map and, although she never learned the purpose, concluded that what she had drawn was of the utmost importance. "Those . . . were not days of indulgence or idle curiosity in any direction, nor was Mr. Lincoln a man to waste his time in giving exhibitions in occult for the amusement of his friends," she later wrote.

Still, Somes cautioned the president that there are those who will say, "You did not see what you in reality *did* see." To which the president gave no response.

Later that same evening when Nettie called on the president to thank him and say good-bye before she returned home, the president took both her hands in his and asked, "When you return next year you will come and see us again, won't you?"

"Yes, I will return if you are here," Nettie answered. This time, Lincoln's forlorn expression made clear that he understood the significance of her reply. "Do your spirit friends warn me, too? Colchester has been telling me that for months." Nettie could only tell him that the spirits she had contacted warned her of danger hanging over the president's life.

Almost a year later, prior to Lincoln's second inauguration in March 1865, Nettie again repeated the ominous message that the spirits "reaffirm the shadow they have spoken of still hangs over you."

"Yes, I know," the president answered impatiently. "I have letters from all over the country from your kind of people—mediums, I mean—warning me [of] some dreadful plot against my life. But I don't think the knife is made, or the bullet run, that will reach it. Besides nobody wants to harm me."

"Therein lies your danger, Mr. Lincoln, your overconfidence in your fellowmen," Nettie answered.

"Well, Miss Nettie, I shall live till my work is done, and no earthly power can prevent it. And then it doesn't matter so that I am ready, and that I ever mean to be," the president replied. And that was the last time Nettie saw Lincoln alive. "Never again would we meet his welcome smile," she wrote.

How much of an adherent was Lincoln to the new spiritualist movement that had swept across nineteenth-century America? The evidence indeed suggests that he was a strong believer because of his relationships with several mediums during his presidency, and he never disavowed the movement publicly. Nettie wrote, "He would not have connected himself with it, especially in peculiarly dangerous times, while the fate of the nation was in peril. A man does not usually follow or obey dictation in which he has no faith, and which does not contain information of active present value *to him*." In his times of greatest anxiety, particularly as he wrestled the issuance of the Emancipation Proclamation, he drew upon spiritual guidance to strengthen his resolve that he had already made the morally right decision.

But Nettie also made clear that despite the president's openness and interest, "Mrs. Lincoln was more enthusiastic regarding the subject than her husband, and openly and avowedly professed herself connected with the new religion." Had the president "declared an open belief in [spiritualism], he would have been pronounced insane and probably incarcerated," Nettie concluded.

The Prophetic President

Throughout his life, Lincoln took his dreams very seriously, many of which were psychic and frequently demanded that he interpret their meaning. One night, in

June 1863, in a particularly disturbing dream, Lincoln saw his son Tad with a pistol that he'd given the boy, "big enough to snap caps, but no cartridges or powder." At the time, Mary Todd and Tad were on a shopping trip in Philadelphia, but the apparent dream warning so concerned the president that he hurriedly telegraphed his wife at the hotel where she stayed: "Think you had better put Tad's pistol away safely. I had an ugly dream about him."

In 1864, while Mary Todd worried that "poor Mr. Lincoln is looking so brokenhearted, so completely worn-out," another of his strange dreams shook her. While the Lincolns were away from the nation's capital, the president dreamed the White House was on fire, motivating Mary Todd to send two telegrams to Washington to be certain all was safe in the Executive Mansion.

Were the president's dreams born of anxiety or clairvoyant to the point of having had premonitions whose outcomes were altered by intervention? We know that Lincoln believed himself to be clairvoyant. For example, one telling comment by Lincoln revealed his dependence on precognitive abilities. Predicting the unfavorable outcome of one Union loss in battle, he admitted, "I believe I feel trouble in the air before it comes." Even among those who dismissed Lincoln's psychic ability as "superstition," there was unanimity of opinion that "he was a very sensitive man," noted his Springfield law partner, William Herndon.

In 1864, Lincoln was reelected to a second term. While the population of the North cheered, the South and their sympathizers in Northern states seethed. Lincoln knew that winning the war between the states was not enough, and in his second inaugural address on March 4, 1865, he vowed to bring the nation back together, "With malice toward none; with charity for all; with firmness in the right, as God gives us to see the right, let us strive on to finish the work we are in; to bind up the nation's wounds." He saw himself as a divine instrument, carrying out a Providential intent to heal what had been torn apart. He'd once told his friend Ward Hill Lamon that he was certain ". . . the star under which he was born was at once brilliant and malignant; the horoscope was cast, fixed, irreversible. . . ."

Now, in his second term, there were more concerns for Lincoln's safety as the number of threats increased. He once showed a newspaper editor visiting the White House a cubicle in his desk that contained more than eighty threatening letters: "I know I am in danger, but I am not going to worry over threats like these." Lincoln knew that his wartime policies had made him lots of enemies, some of whom still fervently believed the military outcome of the war could be reversed politically were Lincoln to be removed from office. Lincoln also believed that a determined assassin would find a way to get to him no matter what the level of protection. Ever the fatalist, the president ordered the most threatening letters to be discarded: "No vigilance could keep them out . . . a conspiracy to assassinate, if such there were, could easily obtain a pass to see me for any one or more of its instruments." He even told friends he could see images in his dreams that were portents of a violent end to his life. But he believed that if fate had meted out for him a violent end, then it would be a destiny he could not escape.

Some feel the strongest evidence of Lincoln's psychic ability was his precognitive dreams, some of which were painfully obvious, while others required interpretation. One particularly significant recurring dream occurred to Lincoln prior to almost every major Union triumph over Confederate forces, including the victories at Antietam, Gettysburg, and Vicksburg. In April 1865, the dream reappeared. "I had a warning dream again last night," Lincoln told colleagues and family. "It related to water. I seemed to be in a singular and indescribable vessel that was moving with great rapidity toward a dark and indefinite shore. I have always had this dream preceding every great event of the war. Victory has not always followed this dream. . . . I think the dream must apply to General Sherman who is campaigning in Virginia, for there is no other great event that I know of which is apt to happen." When General Ulysses Grant expressed skepticism in such prophetic dreams, the president insisted his dream surely must be interpreted as good news. "I think it must be from Sherman."

On April 9, 1865, Confederate General Robert E. Lee surrendered to General Grant at Appomattox Court House, Virginia. The long and costly Civil War that claimed 600,000 lives was finally over, and the celebrations throughout the North quickly began. However, that same month, the president experienced an unusually vivid dream, as dream premonitions nearly always are, which he described to his wife and closest friends in great detail.

"I retired very late," the president said. "I had not been long in bed when I fell into a dream. There seemed to be a deathlike stillness about me. Then I heard subdued sobs, as if a large number of people were weeping. I thought I left my bed and wandered downstairs. I went from room to room in the White House. No living person was in sight. But the same mournful sounds of distress met me as I passed along. It was in all the rooms, every object was familiar to me, but where were all the people who were grieving as if their hearts would break? I was puzzled and alarmed. What could be the meaning of all this?

"Determined to find the cause of a state of things so mysterious and so shocking, I kept on until I arrived in the East Room, which I entered. Before me was a catafalque, on which there was a form, wrapped in funeral vestments. Around it were soldiers who were stationed as guards. There was a throng of people, some gazing, mourning upon the corpse, whose face was covered, others weeping pitifully. 'Who is dead in the White House?' I demanded of one of the soldiers. 'The president!' was the answer. 'He was killed by an assassin!' Then came a loud burst of grief from the crowd, which woke me from my dream. I slept no more that night; and although it was only a dream, I have been strangely annoyed by it ever since."

Mary Todd thought the dream "horrid," and regretted having been told. The president reassured her, "Well, it is only a dream, Mary." Yet for Mary Todd, who had endured the deaths of her two sons and who had seen firsthand proof that premonitions and predictions did come true, her husband's sorrowful dream filled her with dread no matter how he tried to minimize it. Forces from her darker side engulfed her and for the next few days after her husband's report of his dream, she sought constant reassurances from him that everything would be all right. But she believed none of them, fearing the worst was about to happen. Days later, those fears came true.

The president seemed to have brushed aside the memories of his nightmare days earlier and with the war over, Lincoln sought respite from the arduous task of rebuilding the South that lay ahead. He agreed to attend a play with his wife at Ford's Theater on the evening of Good Friday, April 14, 1865, to see if he could lift her spirits as well. Mary Todd liked diversions as much as anyone, and when she had fallen into one of her moods, as she had as a result of her husband's report of his nightmare, attending the popular comedy *Our American Cousin*, starring the actress Laura Keene, might bring her a little levity, the president thought. And since the invitation had been made by the theater manager himself and had so pleased the usually dour Mary Todd, the president acquiesced. At least that was what he had told friends. But why, despite dream warnings of danger, threats to his life, and the advice of friends, would Lincoln so tempt fate?

His former law partner, William Herndon, remembered being told often by Lincoln, "I am sure I shall meet with some terrible end." Mary Todd said her husband's "only philosophy was, what is to be, will be, and no prayers of ours can reverse the decree." Herndon recalled, "He always contended that he was doomed to a sad fate." It is characteristic of premonitions that those who experience them often cannot tell exactly when they will come true. Perhaps, as Herndon said, the president, "felt the nearness of the awful hour." And that was why, perhaps, the president put himself into the hands of fate that Good Friday and allowed his destiny to play itself out.

Friday, April 14, began with breakfast that Lincoln shared with his eldest son, Robert. There followed meetings with government officials, his cabinet, the victorious General Grant, and various friends. At the cabinet meeting, the premonitions were on Lincoln's mind: "Gentlemen, something extraordinary is going to happen, and that soon." Then he described his recurring water dream: "I am on a great, broad, rolling river, and I am in a boat . . . and I drift . . . and I drift." Those present thought him unusually distracted and morose. Nonetheless, later in the afternoon, the president and Mary Todd enjoyed a carriage ride.

Lincoln confided to W. H. Crook, his bodyguard, that he'd dreamed for three consecutive nights that he would be assassinated. "Crook, do you know, I believe there are men who would want to take my life. And I have no doubt they will do it. It would be impossible to prevent it." Crook pleaded with the president not to attend Ford's Theater that evening. But it was to no avail. Uncharacteristically, as if sensing impending tragedy, he said to Crook, "Good-bye" rather than "Good night," his usual farewell.

The president and his party arrived at the theater at 9:20 P.M., and as they ascended to the "state box" reserved for them, the large audience "rose and cheered enthusiastically." At the same time, however, in what can only be called another unfortunate twist of fate, the police officer assigned to protect the president left his post outside the president's box. And so, John Wilkes Booth, the actor and Southern sympathizer who so vehemently hated Lincoln he planned to kill him with his own hand, gained ready access to the theater and lurked nearby. Undetected, he hid in the shadows outside the theater box, where he waited for his chance to carry out "the last and greatest tragedy of the war," as Herndon so aptly said.

Meanwhile, in the White House, at about the same time as the curtain was rising at Ford's, the Lincolns' dog, as animals sometimes do before catastrophic events, psychically sensed something terrible about to happen and became frantic. The usually quiet and gentle pet inexplicably started barking uncontrollably as if seized by a sudden fear for its life, and began running around the family quarters in a frenzy, looking for its master, the president. Try as they might, the White House personnel could not calm the dog, who continued to run through the hallways until it stopped, threw its head back, and began to wail as if its own life were in danger. There was no quieting the dog, whose yelps aroused servants from all over the White House. Somehow everyone knew that the dog had sensed something terribly wrong that had either just happened or was in progress. They feared for the president.

With the police officer absent from his guard post, John Wilkes Booth was free to wait outside the box until the sound of laughter and applause filled the theater. Even Mary Todd, who always looked around corners for signs of foul play, had lowered her guard and was engrossed in the actors' performances. Now, Booth, seeing his chance, stealthily sneaked into the president's box and moved up behind the president, who was seated in a rocking chair, smiling, laughing, and winking at Mary Todd seated to his right. To their right were Miss Clara Harris and Major Henry R. Rathbone. Booth was as silent as a shadow inside the president's box as he quickly pulled a tiny derringer and pointed it directly at the back of Lincoln's head. Without announcing his presence, Booth immediately fired a single round that penetrated Lincoln's skull, mortally wounding him. It was nearly 10:15 P.M.

The shot startled Mary Todd, who began screaming. However, it all happened so quickly that the audience, completely unaware of what happened, thought it part of the play. Then, with Mary Todd shrieking, "They have shot the president," the audience turned in their seats to see Major Rathbone struggling with the assassin until Booth pulled out his knife and stabbed him repeatedly. Still Rathbone held on, hoping he could prevent Booth from escaping until help came, but he was too weakened from the wounds and loss of blood. Booth, now desperate to get away, pushed Rathbone aside and leaped out of the presidential box, catching his spur in the folds of an American flag that draped the box as he fell to the stage below. Hobbled and in pain from the sprained ankle he received in the fall and waving his knife as if to strike at phantom spirits around him, the demented actor declaimed to the audience, *Sic semper tyrannis!"* ("Ever thus to tyrants!") as he "quickly limped across the stage" and escaped behind the proscenium. Meanwhile, as the president's life's blood ebbed away, pandemonium broke out in the theater.

The unconscious president was carried to a house across the street as onlookers hoped that the doctor, who had already been summoned, might be able to stanch the flow of blood and remove the tiny bullet. But it was already too late. The wound had been fatal. Although he struggled through the night, stubbornly rallying even as his life signs faltered, at 7:22 on the morning of April 15, Abraham Lincoln stopped breathing, his heart failed, and he passed over from this world to the next. Secretary of War Edwin Stanton uttered the memorable words, "Now he belongs to the ages." And a pall fell over the entire country.

Just as he'd seen in his dream premonition, within a day after his death, Lincoln's casket was positioned on a platform in the White House East Room, protected by soldiers. Then after lying in state for crowds of mourners, a special train took his body home to Springfield, Illinois, for burial. Along the route of the sorrowful journey as the train slowly made its way through towns and cities were grieving citizens who tearfully paid their final respects to the Great Emancipator. Even the train tracks themselves, observers wrote, seemed silenced by the overwhelming sadness of Lincoln's sudden passing. The president's death was, Herndon said, "an indescribable shock," which plunged the nation into deep and unprecedented mourning.

While the nation mourned in the days following the assassination and funeral, the police pursued Booth and his fellow conspirators. Booth, trapped in a Virginia barn, was shot to death eleven days after his crime. His confederates were captured and ultimately tried and convicted. Three of them were hanged. As it turned out, the plot to assassinate Lincoln was more elaborate than it had first seemed, involving other members of his administration and cabinet and General Grant as well. It was a true assassination plot aimed at overthrowing the leader who had prosecuted the War Between the States, emancipated the slaves, and ultimately defeated the Confederacy. It was certainly not borne out of the delusions of a lone gunman, and to the extent that Vice President Andrew Johnson was unable to pursue Reconstruction, the plot succeeded. For the next one hundred years, until Hubert Humphrey's first Civil Rights plank in the Democratic Party platform in the 1948 election, the South seemed to have gained politically what it had lost on the battlefield, its own version of apartheid.

Although the president was dead, his ghost seemed to live on in various manifestations. For several successive years, only on April 27, a "phantom funeral train" traveled the same route taken by the "official funeral train," from Washington, D.C., through New York State, west to Illinois. However the ghost train never reached its journey's end. The Albany, New York, *Evening Times* reported the phantom train's journey:

"Regularly in the month of April, about midnight the air on the tracks becomes very keen and cutting. On either side of the tracks it is warm and still. Every watchman, when he feels the air, slips off the track and sits down to watch. Soon the pilot engine of Lincoln's funeral train passes with long, black streamers and with a band of black instruments playing dirges, grinning skeletons all about.

"It passes noiselessly. If it is moonlight, clouds come

over the moon as the phantom train goes by. After the pilot engine passes, the funeral train itself with flags and streamers rushes past. The track seems covered with black carpet, and the coffin is seen in the center of the car, while all about it in the air and on the train behind are vast numbers of blue-coated men, some with coffins on their backs, others leaning upon them.

"If a real train were passing its noise would be hushed as if the phantom train rode over it. Clocks and watches would always stop as the phantom train goes by and when looked at are five to eight minutes behind. Everywhere on the road about April 27 watches and clocks are suddenly found to be behind."

For a number of years, the phantom train continued to appear, right on schedule. Then one year it failed to materialize. Eventually, after missing several more years, the ghost train was no longer seen.

Lincoln's Ghost

Lincoln's impact on American history was immeasurable. In 1864, when he sought reelection, he said, "I want to finish the job." When he was murdered, his plans for reconciliation between the states were abruptly interrupted, and his work left incomplete. Perhaps that is why his spirit has been seen and reported in the White House more often than any other president's. Did his enormous psychic energy continue in the afterlife? Does that explain why Lincoln has been the White House's most conspicuous ghost?

Imagine spending a night in the Lincoln bedroom of the White House, answering a knock on your bedroom door, and opening it to find standing there the apparition of a tall, gaunt figure in a stovepipe hat whom you recognize as Abraham Lincoln. Or perhaps you are walking down a White House hallway when coming in your direction is a specter, a mere shadow, which you soon realize is none other than President Lincoln himself. Do you report the sighting or do you simply wipe the image from your eyes and pretend it was only an illusion?

Although there are scant records of Lincoln's apparition in the Executive Mansion during the last half of the nineteenth century, it doesn't suggest his spirit wasn't present. In the years immediately after his death, White House personnel reported mysterious footsteps in the hallways; however, it is likely records were lost or witness accounts went unreported, since many parapsychologists feel his spirit never left the White House. Years later, shortly after the turn of the century when President Theodore Roosevelt occupied the White House, T. R. admitted, "I think of Lincoln, shambling, homely, with his sad, strong, deeply furrowed face, all the time. I see him in the different rooms and in the halls."

During the terms of President Calvin Coolidge (1923–29), his wife, Grace, was the first to report actually seeing Lincoln's ghost, dressed "in black, with a stole draped across his shoulders to ward off the drafts and chills of Washington's night air." She explained that, one day, as she passed by the Yellow Oval Room, she was startled to see Lincoln's apparition staring out a window in the direction of the Potomac, his hands behind him. The specter momentarily looked in her direction, then turned and departed. During his life, the room was Lincoln's library, and he often gazed intently through the window, deep in thought and contemplation, agonizing about the course of the war. At the same window in the Yellow Oval Room, adjacent to the Lincoln Bedroom on the second floor of the White House, the late president's spirit has been seen or felt by others including Carl Sandburg, the poet and noted Lincoln biographer, who acknowledged that on a visit to the White House he sensed Lincoln near him at the Oval Room window. President Herbert Hoover also admitted to hearing mysterious noises in the Executive Mansion. Although he never acknowledged it was Lincoln's ghost, Hoover left no doubt that he'd heard *something* he could not explain.

By the time Franklin Delano Roosevelt began his long

tenure as president, Lincoln had been dead for nearly seventy years. However, his specter remained, unwilling or unable to leave the White House. Earthbound spirits are frequently drawn to places of intense emotion in life, and in Lincoln's case, there was the additional regret and frustration of unfinished business. During FDR's administration, Lincoln's ghost was at its most active, perhaps because of his steadfast concern about the perilous state of the nation during the Great Depression and World War II.

First Lady Eleanor Roosevelt never officially acknowledged that she'd seen Lincoln's ghost, but she used Lincoln's bedroom as her study, and admitted that when she worked late at night she sensed Lincoln's presence as though he was "standing behind her, peering over her shoulder." She also acknowledged that she'd heard Lincoln's "footsteps in the second-floor hallways." One day as Mrs. Roosevelt's secretary, Mary Eben, walked by Lincoln's bedroom, she came upon the specter of a gaunt form sitting on the bed "pulling up his boots." The frightened young woman did not remain one moment longer than she had to. Shrieking in fear, she quickly fled out of the room and down the corridor. Mary Eben was but one of many people, including, according to the *Washington Star*, President Roosevelt's valet, who once ran from the White House, screaming in fear that he'd just witnessed Lincoln's ghost.

One of the most intriguing accounts came from Queen Wilhelmina of the Netherlands, who visited the White House during the war years, while in exile from the Nazis. Late one night, an insistent knocking on the Rose Room door awakened her from a fitful sleep. Thinking it might be an important message, she said, "Come in." When no one entered, the queen opened the door, and there stood the apparition of none other than Lincoln in his familiar stovepipe hat. Stunned, Queen Wilhelmina promptly fainted from fright. The next day, when she told President Roosevelt what happened, he said he wasn't surprised. Although he'd never seen Lincoln's specter himself, he said he had no doubts about Queen

Wilhelmina's vision because Mrs. Roosevelt often told him about reports of the ghost, especially in the Lincoln Room. However, when the queen shared the details of her ghostly encounter with guests the following evening at a White House function, they were decidedly more amazed.

For Winston Churchill, England's wartime prime minister who displayed unflagging courage against the Nazi peril, visitations from ghosts were apparently another matter. Churchill, who had visited FDR at the White House on more than one occasion, slept in the Lincoln Bedroom only one night. After that, although he refused to discuss his reasons, he never slept in that room again. What caused Churchill's discomfort? Churchill never admitted it, but many people thought he'd been frightened by Lincoln's apparition, especially after Queen Wilhelmina's story circulated through Washington social circles.

Even President Roosevelt's dog, Fala, might have sensed the ghost. White House staff told of Fala's suddenly barking at something apparently only the dog could see, perhaps Lincoln's presence. What Fala might have seen also might have frightened Lillian Rogers Parks, the White House seamstress during the Roosevelt administration, who years later would also be a witness to the ghost of Andrew Jackson. Mrs. Parks was working in a second-floor room one day when she heard someone repeatedly approaching the door, although she knew no one was there. The White House was quite empty at the time with the Roosevelts at Hyde Park along with most of their maids. Soon, Mrs. Parks went looking for the cause of the noise. On the third floor, she found a male servant she assumed was responsible for the footsteps. The servant had no idea what Mrs. Parks was talking about since he'd just arrived and hadn't been on the second floor. Then he realized what she'd heard. "That was Abe you heard," he told her.

Roosevelt's vice president, blunt-speaking Harry Truman, never claimed he'd witnessed Lincoln during his terms as president (1945–53). However, according to his daughter, Margaret, who acknowledged she'd sensed Lincoln's presence, Harry Truman did not deny the presence of ghosts in the White House, "so I won't lock my doors to bar them either," he said. He wrote his wife, Bess, who often stayed at their family home in Independence, Missouri, because she didn't like Washington, "I sit in this old house, all the while listening to the ghosts walk up and down the hallway. At four o'clock I was awakened by three distinct knocks on my bedroom door. No one was there. Damned place is haunted, sure as shootin'!"

Truman had been "much taken with the stories of Lincoln's ghost," wrote White House chief usher J. B. West. One night the president decided to play a prank and frighten his daughter and three of her friends who were to sleep overnight in Lincoln's bed. Truman asked his doorman and barber John Mays, a tall, thin gentleman, to don a stovepipe hat and "lurk in the corner of the bedroom." But on the day of the planned mischief, Mays declined, saying, "I didn't feel right about impersonating Mr. Lincoln." Perhaps he was also uneasy about the possibility that he might have bumped into the *real* ghost of Lincoln. It was the real ghost of Lincoln who also gave Rex Scouten, a Secret Service agent during the Truman years, the chills at night. "I go down that long hall and into the Lincoln Bedroom. I get a strange feeling," he admitted.

Margaret Truman frequently heard knocking on her bedroom door late at night. However, every time she checked, she found no one. When she told her father about the clamor, he first suspected a "natural" explanation, perhaps some structural problem with the building, and directed the White House be reinspected and, if necessary, shored up. Truman's decision proved to be no overreaction. The chief architect informed him that he hadn't acted a moment too soon, for the White House was in serious danger of a structural collapse. Was Lincoln's ghost responsible for the rappings as a way to caution the Trumans that the White House was close to falling down?

After the Truman years, there were fewer reports of Lincoln's ghost in the Executive Mansion. Some psychic researchers speculated that Lincoln's spirit became unsettled by the many changes and renovations the White House had undergone during the Truman administration.

During his terms in office, President Eisenhower made no effort to deny the experiences he'd had with Lincoln's ghost. Ike told his press secretary, James Haggerty, that he frequently sensed Lincoln's spirit in the White House. One day, Eisenhower explained, he was walking through a White House corridor when approaching him from the opposite direction was the specter of Lincoln. Ike took the encounter in stride. Perhaps after the horrors of World War II, the apparition of the Great Emancipator was a comforting sight. Surprisingly, Haggerty disclosed President Eisenhower's ghostly experience on a network TV program, despite the long-held White House position disavowing the presence of ghosts.

Jacqueline Kennedy, who occupied the White House exactly one hundred years after the Lincolns lived there, admitted that she sensed Lincoln's presence during her White House years, although there is no record of John F. Kennedy ever reporting the famed ghost. Jackie told reporters in 1961 that she thought the White House was "cold and drab," and disliked much of its furnishings. Feeling that "everything in the White House must have a reason for being there," she undertook a major restoration. When she'd completed the widely publicized project, the White House was freshly painted and replete with exquisite furnishings. That was when Lincoln's ghost began to stir once again. Likely, Lincoln's spirit was unsettled by the massive alterations in White House decor because it was during the restoration that Jackie was startled to encounter Lincoln's ghost. When he occupied the White House, Lincoln largely ignored such matters as interior decorating, and exploded in anger when his wife overspent refurbishing what he called "this damned old house."

Lincoln returned to haunt JFK's successor in office as

well. One night in the old Lincoln Bedroom on the second floor of the White House as President Lyndon Johnson's wife, Lady Bird, watched a TV program about the Lincoln assassination, she sensed the Great Emancipator's presence. Mrs. Johnson suddenly found herself drawn to a plaque on the mantel that described Lincoln's association with the room. As she read the inscription, she experienced a shudder, likely the result of Lincoln's ethereal presence. Most sightings of Lincoln have taken place in the so-called Lincoln Bedroom, which was actually his Cabinet Room, and where he signed the historic Emancipation Proclamation. It was dubbed the Lincoln Bedroom years later when his bed was moved there.

Mary Todd Lincoln had purchased the carved rosewood bed in the Lincoln Bedroom for some ten thousand dollars, a wildly enormous sum at the time. President Lincoln, at odds with Congress over Mary Todd's spending for the White House, was furious at his wife's extravagance, especially in wartime, and refused to sleep in the bed, calling it a "flubdub." When eleven-year-old Willie died in that very bed in 1862, the president found yet another reason to avoid it.

Notwithstanding official denials, members of first families continued to report Lincoln's ghost, while some had no desire to coexist with it. When Gerald Ford was in office, his daughter, Susan, publicly acknowledged her belief in ghosts and made it clear she would never sleep in "that room." According to one account, Susan actually witnessed Lincoln's specter.

During the Reagan years, the president's eldest daughter, Maureen, and her husband, Dennis Revell, often slept in the Lincoln Bedroom when they visited the White House. Maureen, who died of cancer in 2001, claimed that, in the early-morning hours, she and her husband sporadically witnessed "an aura, sometimes red, sometimes orange," which they believed was Lincoln's spirit. The couple once awakened in the Lincoln bed to witness his transparent specter at the window. Maureen later wrote about her experience: "I know it sounds hard to believe and weird as all get-out. Dad thought we were

Loony Tunes." In 1987, Maureen confirmed to *Newsweek*, "I'm not kidding—we've really seen it."

Despite President Reagan's initial skepticism, he later remarked in a Lincoln's Birthday address that he'd begun to ponder the possibility of Lincoln's ghost in the White House. "Now, I haven't seen him myself, but I have to tell you, I am puzzled, because every once in a while, our little dog, Rex, will start down that long hall toward that room [Lincoln's Bedroom], just glaring as if he's seeing something, and barking. . . . Funny thing, though, I have to feel, unlike you might think of other ghosts, if [Lincoln] is still there I don't have any fear at all. I think it would be very wonderful to have a little meeting with him and very probably very helpful."

When Reagan's youngest daughter, Patti Davis, asked her father if he'd ever encountered Lincoln's ghost, " 'No,' my father answered, a bit sadly, I thought. 'I haven't seen him yet. But I do believe he's here.' "

First Lady Nancy Reagan's contact with Lincoln's spirit was less direct than that of her daughters or predecessors. Mrs. Reagan had to constantly straighten Lincoln's portrait, which she repeatedly found had tilted itself, a result of psychic energy manifested by the unseen entity. She once said, "If Ronnie is away for a night or something, I can be here alone. I'm not afraid. I don't hear Abe Lincoln knocking on my door."

There were no reports of Lincoln's ghost during the Bush administration. Both President and Mrs. Bush flatly denied ever seeing Lincoln or any other spirit in the White House. However, tongue in cheek, Mrs. Bush touched on the question in *Millie's Book*, which was supposedly narrated by the Bush's dog: "Although this is the room where the White House ghost is supposed to appear, the Bushes have not seen it nor do they believe in ghosts. I must confess that I have not seen one either."

During the Clinton years, there were at least two sightings of Lincoln's spirit. One encounter was admitted by President Clinton's brother, Roger, who claimed he'd sensed Lincoln's presence in the White House. In the second—perhaps it was a slip of the tongue when a Clinton aide admitted witnessing Lincoln's apparition—the story, reported briefly in the news, was quickly denied by the White House, and dismissed as a joke. During Clinton's second term, however, a scandal emerged concerning more than four hundred guests who, in many instances, made campaign contributions in exchange for overnight stays in the Lincoln Room. How many of those guests who slept in the famed carved rosewood bed sensed or saw Lincoln's apparition? How many of them will admit to a ghostly encounter? When Mary Todd purchased the famed bed, the angry president said, "It stinks in the nostrils of the American people!" How many visitors in the Lincoln Bedroom during the Clinton administration felt Lincoln's seething anger at the presence of that infamous bed or the sadness at having slept in the spot where Willie Lincoln died?

Many psychic researchers believe President Lincoln never left the White House, and interestingly, only a few of those who've confronted his specter were frightened. Rather, most said the presence was comforting. Does he endure to finish his work, interrupted by assassination? It seems certain that the melancholy but magnanimous spirit of Abraham Lincoln, one of our greatest presidents, maintains his vigil over the Union he so selflessly sacrificed his life to preserve.

CHAPTER TEN

Recent Hauntings

Modern man . . . has not ceased to be credulous. . . .
The need to believe haunts him.

—William James

There is a gifted medium whose ability to communicate with the spirit world manifested when he was still a boy in Catholic school. He had made contact with the spirit world and believed not only in the existence of a world most people could not see and did not know was there, but in his own ability to communicate with it. When he innocently told his teacher about it, the nun said, in no uncertain terms, she did not believe he had such abilities. The child protested, "But the saints long ago did those things. They had all kinds of psychic experiences." The teacher flushed with anger and shot back, "Those things happened centuries ago. They don't happen anymore!" But she was wrong. They do.

The Eisenhowers

After moving countless times during their married life, Mamie and Dwight Eisenhower were understandably excited by the prospect of finally settling down in a permanent home of their own. During her husband's long and distinguished military career, Mamie lived in thirty-seven residences, from simple army housing for junior officers to the stately mansions provided for the general staff, as her husband moved up the ranks to become the Supreme Allied Commander leading the war effort in Europe. But as Mamie had often said, no residence was ever really hers. Most of the places in which they lived were billets, either government-owned or -provided, and their nomadic life was typical of many couples in the military. When, after Ike's retirement and short tenure as president of Columbia University, they bought a dilapidated nineteenth-century farmhouse in Gettysburg, Pennsylvania, in 1950 and renovated it, Mamie's dream of her own home finally came true. It took them only thirty-four years of marriage, Mamie joked to friends after finally taking ownership of the property.

The farmhouse, adjacent to the famed Gettysburg battlefield, was ultimately restored by the Eisenhowers into a twenty-room Georgian-style residence. Mamie adored her new home, which she lovingly called her "dream house," on its 189 acres in the gentle rolling hills of the southern Pennsylvania countryside, and filled the living room with furniture, family photos, and other cherished mementos and keepsakes she'd accumulated during their many years of marriage. They especially enjoyed their sun porch, which looked out to the east and the Gettysburg battlefield. For an old soldier like General Eisenhower, this place, not too far from the Army War College in Carlisle, would have also been his dream retirement home, except that he wasn't about to retire.

Ike was a genuine war hero and one of America's most popular figures. His confident smile had flashed across motion picture screens on the Movietone news from the first dark days after the American defeat at the hands of Rommel's Panzer Division tanks at Kaserine in North Africa to the D day Invasion to the collapse of the Nazi Reich in 1945. Now, in 1952, after the unpopular Truman had decided not to run and Communist Chinese troops had ground the UN advance up the Korean peninsula to a halt, sending the entire war into the kind of trench warfare not seen since World War I, the Republican Party turned to Ike. At the 1952 Republican National Convention, Eisenhower supporters overwhelmed the Taft and Dewey delegates, and marching down the aisles to the tune of "Onward Christian Soldiers," they drafted Eisenhower for president.

The 1950s were a watershed in American politics, and Ike, so popular he carried the Republicans into the normally Democratic South, became the decade's hero. He was elected president twice—in 1956 by such a large electoral margin that some commentators even predicted the demise of the Democratic Party—and turned his Gettysburg estate into the "little" White House. This was more Mamie's choice than his because when the Eisenhowers did not have to be in Washington, Mamie preferred they stay in Gettysburg. This, she told friends, was her real home. In 1955, while Ike recovered from his first heart attack suffered during his presidency, Gettysburg became the temporary White House, where, doctors suggested, the best cure for the recovering, but still critically ill, president was Mamie's cuddling with her husband in bed to relax his heart and keep it from going into fibrillation. Thus the Eisenhowers' Gettysburg home became the place where Ike's health was restored.

After two terms in office, Ike left the presidency in 1961, and the Eisenhowers wasted no time returning to Gettysburg, driving the eighty miles themselves in Mamie's car from Washington to the farmhouse, where they spent their remaining years together. Ike became the Republican Party's elder statesman during the ensuing decade, giving his blessing to the candidacy of his former vice president, Richard Nixon, in 1960 and again in 1968 and overseeing his presidential library. In 1969, Ike died of complications of congestive heart failure at the age of seventy-nine, the last president of the United States born in the nineteenth century.

Mamie Eisenhower spent the next, and final, ten years of her life bereft. Without her husband, she described herself as "a lost soul," and when her son, John, wanted her to move in with his family, she would hear none of it. She continued to live at her farmhouse, spending much of her time in her bedroom suite on the second floor. In 1978, Mamie repeated what she'd so often said about Gettysburg, "We had only one home, our farm." The next year, she died of a stroke at the age of eighty-three and was laid to rest next to her husband and first-born son in their hometown, Abilene, Kansas.

After Mamie passed on, the Eisenhowers' Gettysburg home was designated a national historic site. Following Mamie's death, reports began of unexplained footsteps, voices, and a frequent rustling noise, which rangers assigned to the house could not identify, although they attempted to locate the source of the strange goings-on to no avail. Lights in the front hall of the farmhouse blinked on and off, according to park rangers, and the engineers they called to inspect reported there was nothing wrong with the electrical wiring. Neither the engineers nor the rangers, however, could explain why the lights flickered at strange times for no apparent reason.

Rangers also told of hearing music inexplicably drifting through the hall from an unused guestroom in the building. At night, they reported "thumping noises." On other occasions, doors opened and closed, seemingly under their own power, one of which, in particular, was a large stable door with hinges that made it impossible to open and shut quickly or suddenly. Yet witnesses saw the door loudly bang open and then slam by itself. Needless to say, the incidents frightened some personnel, and two of three rangers assigned to the house threatened resignation if these strange phenomena didn't stop. But they didn't stop. In fact, they got worse.

As if the ghost were drawing power from the house itself, Mamie's spirit materialized to one of the rangers, who reported she'd witnessed the ghost on a number of occasions in a corner of the first lady's living room. The sight of the apparition, manifesting itself and becoming almost corporeal right before her very eyes, alarmed her, she said. The ghost seemed to know who she was and had appeared specifically in her presence.

Staff members weren't the only ones who reported

strange phenomena in the Eisenhower house. Visitors also told of similar incidents in which objects seemed to move under their own power, and try as the visitors might, they could not explain them away. However, the Federal Park Service officials who were asked about the occurrences flatly dismissed them as nothing more than hallucinations or pure fiction. Initially the Park Service considered the ghost stories a joke fit for Halloween and not meant to be taken seriously. But those rangers who'd witnessed the unearthly incidents knew better, admitted they'd been made uneasy, and complained to their bosses about what they could not explain.

Eventually the unsettling paranormal activity in the Eisenhower home came to the attention of National Park Service official Priscilla Baker, special assistant to the director. Baker, open to the possibility of such paranormal phenomena, was not against bringing a psychic into the house to help solve the mystery. However, she lacked the support of her superiors, who made it clear they would just as soon ignore the supernatural activity. Although Baker was criticized for her interest and curiosity about ghost stories and apparitions, she persisted and, after learning about a respected and nationally recognized medium named Anne Gehman, invited her to the Eisenhower home. Gehman's reputation was impeccable, her experience extensive, and she agreed to visit Gettysburg. Baker was careful to do all her research and investigations about ghostly reports on her own personal time, so as not to run afoul of disapproving management.

In 1982, Gehman arrived at the Eisenhower farm for a two-day visit. She entered the main door in the front of the house, accompanied by a small entourage of Park Service employees, other official attendees, and the park historian. Looking toward the stairwell, Gehman quickly determined the cause of the blinking lights by establishing a psychic connection with the spirit, who identified herself as Rose Wood, Mrs. Eisenhower's personal maid for many years and an author who'd written about her years at the White House. In life, Mrs. Wood had been a witness to Abraham Lincoln's ghost and the apparition of President Andrew Jackson. The maid told Gehman she'd been at her happiest on earth when she worked for Mamie. In fact, Mrs. Wood said, she never wanted to leave the house. But why had she turned the lights on and off? Her spirit communicated that she simply wanted people working there to know she was still present, but promised to stop playing with the lights. True to her word, there were no further problems reported with electricity in the Eisenhowers' home.

Electrical disturbances are a common form of communication from the departed. Upon physical death, the spirit or soul survives as a form of energy, which we have yet to quantify. Since energy operates according to electromagnetic principles, it is reasonable that spirits are able to influence electrical equipment, such as lights, as a means of communicating to us, which Mrs. Wood did.

Gehman also tried to find some evidence of the presence of Mamie Eisenhower's spirit. She walked around the house, both downstairs and upstairs, sensing spirit presences in various rooms. Finally she confirmed that Mamie's ghost was, indeed, present, especially in the living room and in an upstairs bedroom, where her apparition gazed out the window, as she often did in life. The ranger who'd witnessed Mamie's specter had no knowledge or expertise in psychic phenomena. She only knew that she'd seen Mamie's ghost several times in a corner of the living room. Gehman assured the park ranger that she was not suffering from an overactive imagination. Another ranger who'd seen Mamie's spirit, a veteran who'd served in Vietnam, literally thought he was losing his mind from posttraumatic stress disorder. No, Gehman assured him, he was fine. What he'd witnessed was not a hallucination, but a genuine apparition.

A short time after Gehman's arrival in the house, Mamie's spirit materialized, and communicated at least one reason why her ghost persisted in making its presence known to Park Service personnel. Mamie explained that she was concerned with the structural safety of the back stairs, which were used as an exit from the house. Her spirit insisted that the stairs "were not safe," and that by materializing she hoped to draw attention to the need for repairs. However, not all her supervisors at National Park Service management were as open-minded as Priscilla Baker. It took some time before she could convince her skeptical bosses to send structural inspectors to the house on the word of a psychic. But Baker persisted, and when, finally, carpenters were assigned to check the back staircase they, indeed, found it in need of repair, just as Mamie's spirit had warned.

Mamie's ghost also explained the rustling noise that park personnel had been unable to decipher. They couldn't figure out where it was coming from because every time they looked for its source, they found nothing. Mamie told Gehman that the noise park rangers heard was the crinkling sound of her taffeta dress, which she'd favored wearing when on earth. In addition, the former first lady's spirit revealed she was upset about plans to rip up a portion of her yard for additional parking. This was something Mamie said she could not bear, and so her ghost materialized to discourage workers from making any change by frightening them. Quite possibly the Park Service heeded Mamie's admonition again because, as a result of Mamie's materializing—although no one in an official capacity would admit it—the Park Service at the time did not replace that part of the yard with a parking lot.

Gehman also discerned the spirit presence of President Eisenhower, although not with the same degree of intensity as his wife's. Ike's ghost sat in his favorite chair in his study on the first floor of the house surrounded by many books. This was the room where Eisenhower in life had spent a great deal of time, especially after leaving office. It was clear to Gehman that Ike's specter looked directly at her and acknowledged her presence because—still an officer and a gentleman—Eisenhower's spirit rose briefly from its chair, smiled, nodded, seemed to greet her, and then sat down again. But despite its polite behavior, the spirit of Eisenhower communicated little else.

Another spirit presence Gehman sensed in the Gettysburg house was Mamie's mother, Elvira Dowd, who died in 1958, but for some reason was connected to the property. Still another entity detected was that of a man who'd once been a military aide to Eisenhower. Officials later explained the aide's affinity for the house: his widow, at the time, was an employee of the Eisenhower's granddaughter, Susan.

Gehman also discerned several other presences, including one she identified as "Clinton," which raised far more questions than answers. Fortunately, the park historian was able to explain that the first settler who'd built the original farmhouse on the property in the 1840s was named Quentin Armstrong. Perhaps, Gehman thought, she had psychically confused two similar-sounding names she'd heard clairaudiently by taking "Clinton" for "Quentin."

Another communication to Gehman was from American Indian spirits who explained the land had "considerable religious significance" before the appearance of white settlers and hoped the Park Service would respect that fact. Reportedly, following the messages from the Indian spirits, officials heeded the advice and began early stages of research into the history of the land before the Pennsylvania colonists settled it. In their follow-up, the park officials used another message from Gehman in which she said that "human remains" were buried beside a well in the garden behind the house. The medium pointed to what she said were the bones of an American Indian who'd been put to death by his own tribe for some infraction of their rules, but rangers were unaware of long-ago buried bones on the property. It wasn't until more than a year later that a park employee excitedly called Priscilla Baker to report that an oral history of the house, including tape recordings and long-forgotten files, had been found. Incredibly, one of the historical reports told of a gardener years earlier, who'd found human remains when he worked for the Eisenhowers. When he asked Mamie what she wanted done with them, she instructed the gardener to rebury the remains so they might rest in peace. Gehman's psychic impressions were confirmed.

Outside the Eisenhower house, which adjoins the famed Gettysburg battlefield, Gehman psychically observed a line of ghosts. They were the apparitions of Civil War soldiers in tattered blue uniforms who had fought and died in the bloody battle and whose bodies, she thought, were buried at the national cemetery at Gettysburg. As Gehman watched the specters mournfully march by, she said the ghost soldiers rattled off their names to her, a roster of the walking dead. Gehman repeated aloud, as quickly as she could, what she'd heard clairaudiently to the park historian who was accompanying her, but who did not see the ghostly procession. He later checked the names of the soldiers Gehman had announced and verified the accuracy of her report. This bit of sensational information, although witnessed by a government official who followed up on data he'd received on the spot as it was being communicated to Gehman, did not make it into the historical record. Nor could Baker, who worked at the Eisenhower farmhouse at Gettysburg for seventeen years, persuade officials of the National Park Service that ghosts exist. She was a firsthand witness to the paranormal events that took place at Gettysburg and in the Eisenhower farmhouse and is convinced she was in the presence of ghostly apparitions. "Of course the spirits can come back. I have no doubt anymore. It's been proven to me," she said.

It's often easier to describe reports of apparitions than explain why they appear, but in Mamie's case, her spirit was drawn back to where she'd been happiest in the physical world, her Gettysburg home. Through Gehman, Mamie also explained that "she liked to check from time to time and make sure everything was O.K. in the house."

John F. Kennedy

In 1962, Dr. Stanley Krippner, a psychologist and parapsychology researcher, was taking part in a hallucinogenic drug experiment when he experienced an unsettling premonition about President John F. Kennedy. In his psychedelic vision, Krippner said, "I found myself gazing at a statue of Lincoln . . . the head was bowed. There was a gun at the base of the statue and someone murmured, 'He was shot. The president was shot.' Lincoln's features slowly faded and those of . . . Kennedy appeared. The voice repeated . . . [and] . . . my eyes . . . filled with tears."

On November 22, 1963, Kennedy told friends in Dallas, "If anyone really wanted to shoot the president . . . it is not a very difficult job. All one has to do is get on a high building someday with a telescopic rifle and there is nothing anyone can do to defend against such an attempt." Three hours after JFK said this, that's exactly what happened. As Kennedy almost casually described it, he was assassinated as he rode in his open limousine in a motorcade past the multistory Texas School Book Depository building. The assassination was a shock to the nation who had elevated the young president and his first lady to the status of heroes.

Following his murder, Jackie Kennedy, herself afraid for her life because she believed there was a larger conspiracy at work inside the government as she told author William Manchester years later, wrote letters to her departed husband, seeking to communicate with him spiritually and emotionally. Skeptics argue that such activity, while cathartic, is entirely grief-induced. That may be partially true, but not the full explanation, for Mrs. Kennedy was seeking afterdeath communications. She no doubt believed that by writing to her husband he would psychically connect with her deeply felt emotions and thoughts. It was not unlike prayers, which departed loved ones receive.

Several years later, when Robert Kennedy announced his presidential candidacy, Mrs. Kennedy, shaken by his intention to run for president in 1968, described her terrible premonition: "You know what will happen to Bobby, the same thing that happened to John," she said. She was right, and in 1968, Robert Kennedy was assassinated in Los Angeles just moments after he gave his victory speech after defeating Vice President Hubert Humphrey in the California primary.

Lyndon Johnson

Lyndon Johnson completed JFK's term, then was elected in his own right in 1964, just as the noted medium Arthur Ford through his spirit control Fletcher predicted. In 1968, Johnson refused to run for a second term after American public opinion turned against the Vietnam War, especially after the success of the North Vietnamese Tet offensive.

Johnson was a New Deal Democrat, a social progressive who during his years in Washington amassed a huge fortune in communications, one of the most carefully regulated industries in America. Just before the Kennedy assassination in 1963, LBJ was in real danger of being thrown off the 1964 Democratic national ticket and possibly of going to jail because of the Bobby Baker scandal in the Senate, which took place under LBJ's stewardship as majority leader. Baker also worked for Johnson. It was Johnson who, after the assassination, reversed the Kennedy policy of pulling U.S. military advisors out of Vietnam and increased the American presence there. Some scholars say that had it not been for the Vietnam War and his policies to prosecute the war, Johnson could have been one of this nation's greatest presidents, ranking alongside Lincoln and Roosevelt. In many ways, Johnson's legislative campaign to enact civil rights legislation, the Voting Rights Act, and the War on Poverty legislation was the most aggressive domestic policy assault on social inequity in the United States since Roosevelt's New Deal. Yet today, suspicions still linger about Johnson's role in covering up the JFK assassination with the Warren Commission. What most people don't know is that, second to Lincoln, Johnson was one of our nation's most psychic presidents.

Since his childhood in Texas, Johnson was plagued by

frightening dreams and nightmares, which, as president, he often shared with Doris Kearns, who worked for him and later wrote *Lyndon Johnson & the American Dream*. In one recurring dream, he saw himself "sitting . . . in a big straight chair." Then a "stampede of cattle" headed toward him as he struggled to move, but he discovered his muscles were frozen and couldn't budge.

The paralysis dream worsened in 1968 after the North Vietnamese Tet offensive. In the dream, Johnson said he was transformed into the late president Woodrow Wilson. Although LBJ said his head was his own, "from the neck down his body was paralyzed." One night, to be certain that he was alive and Wilson was the one who was deceased, Johnson ran his hands over Wilson's portrait. LBJ became intensely fearful that his dream was a portent that he would suffer a stroke in his next term. "He could not rid himself of the suspicion that a mean God had set out to torture him in the cruelest manner possible," Kearns wrote.

By late 1967, Johnson faced growing public pressure to deescalate the Vietnam War, find a solution to an inflationary economy that was spinning out of control, and address the danger of race riots in the inner cities. As he watched war casualties mount and presided over a nation divided by issues of war and race, he increasingly considered leaving politics for good. If he had made a devil's bargain to escape justice in 1963, it was now coming back to haunt him, and the vision he had of eliminating poverty in America was all but buried beneath the statistics of body counts, aerial sorties, and the rising number of American POWs. In 1968, antiwar advocate Senator Eugene McCarthy scored impressive numbers in the New Hampshire Democratic primary, numbers that would have embarrassed any incumbent president in the same party as the challenger. At that point, although he realized he could not remain in office, stubborn pride interfered. Johnson didn't want to be thought cowardly by leaving the presidency or serving a second term and becoming politically impotent by the deepening social morass. His feelings of hopelessness worsened as he sought an honorable way out. His situation, Kearns said, was a "total impossibility."

Then, as often happens, Johnson's answer arrived in a dream that was different from any he'd ever had before. LBJ "saw himself swimming in a river." He swam from the middle of the water toward one shore, and then toward the other. However, no matter how much he swam, he could not reach the shore, but was simply swimming round and round. LBJ concluded the dream's message was that he must free himself from politics. So the beleaguered president changed his strategy and ordered an end to bombing north of the twentieth parallel, a major shift in Vietnam War policy. A short while later, Johnson announced to the nation that he would not seek reelection in 1968.

Thus, Johnson's "decision to withdraw from . . . Vietnam . . . was influenced by a dream that clarified for him the impossible no-win situation he was in," wrote Peter and Elizabeth Fenwick in *The Hidden Door: Understanding and Controlling Dreams*. Had Johnson experienced a problem-solving dream that was drawn from his subconscious mind—as skeptics would argue— or was it psychic? One paranormal theory suggests the dream state "makes the mind more receptive to outside input," such as telepathy or afterdeath communications. Psychics suggest that LBJ might have experienced a psychic dream in which a departed loved one, or a former president, communicated to him the course of action he needed to take in his desperate circumstance. Interestingly, while many military figures throughout history gained advice for battle from paranormal dreams, Johnson's dream helped initiate the pursuit of a negotiated solution to the Vietnam War even though the final peace would elude him and its pursuit would destroy the administrations of the two presidents who succeeded him.

As a young member of the House of Representatives who came to Washington as a Roosevelt Democrat and a supporter of FDR's New Deal, Johnson was passionately committed to the causes of civil rights and the elimination of poverty in the United States. Today, his landmark legislation programs stand as a testament not only to Johnson's principles, but to his skills as a great negotiator who worked with the Republican Congressional leadership to move his bills through the House and Senate. Yet Johnson will always be associated with the disaster of the Vietnam War, a war he described in the audiotapes he secretly recorded in the Oval Office as one America could not win no matter what the military did. Even his own secret negotiations to end the war foundered because his generals wanted him to pursue a victory and the North Vietnamese demanded reparations to allow the Americans to withdraw with honor. Is it no wonder his beleaguered psyche sought answers in the visions of dreams.

These were visions that came to him at night, torturing his soul. First, he suffered from the overwhelming guilt concerning his involvement in what he admitted to Senator Richard Russell, whom he'd named to the Warren Commission, was a conspiracy to cover up the murder of President John F. Kennedy. And second, he was tormented over his involvement in the Vietnam War as the price he had to pay for remaining in office and avoiding prison. He fully believed that this war he'd pursued on the ground in Southeast Asia had cost him his ultimate victory in the war against poverty, disease, and racial discrimination. He would leave office unfulfilled. His was truly a remorse of conscience.

Johnson was a psychic individual living in a residence filled with the active spirits of those who had come before him. Thus, it's not surprising that the spirits of the departed who occupied the White House were especially active during LBJ's tenure there. Many times spirits may not be seen nor heard, even though their presence, very much with us, can be sensed. "You just know they're around" is a typical comment from someone who senses a ghost close by, feeling as it were a surge of energy crawling along one's skin or arousing the hairs on the back of the neck. As it happened, among the spirits most agitated by the presence of the Johnsons' family in the

White House were Abraham Lincoln and his young son Willie.

During the Johnson years, one of his daughters, Lynda, lived in the same room where young Willie Lincoln died in 1862. John Alexander in *Ghosts Washington Revisited* said that Lynda never claimed to see or hear Willie; however, she was "very much aware . . . that it was in her room that the Lincoln boy breathed his last breath," according to Liz Carpenter, who never went further in her comments on the subject. Alexander noted, however, that Liz Carpenter made her statement about Willie Lincoln's presence "with a smile." Since neither Lynda nor anyone else in the White House ever spoke further about Willie's presence, the cryptic reply likely meant she experienced some sense of the child's spirit in the room, just as Willie's specter was reported in the earlier presidential administrations of Ulysses Grant and William Howard Taft. In yet another experience, Lynda answered a late-night knock on her door. When she opened it, no one was there. When she inquired about it the next day, no one she asked admitted to having come to her door. Had it been the ghost of Lincoln or some other unseen entity that still inhabited 1600 Pennsylvania Avenue?

Also reported during the LBJ White House years were "phone calls from the departed." According to one author and paranormal researcher, presidential family members received telephone calls but found no one at the other end of the line. When questioned, White House operators said they'd not been responsible for ringing the phones on those occasions. During the Johnson era in the 1960s, the White House phone system was not the digital system of today; it was controlled completely by operators, who routed calls to the president or other family members by hand according to a strict set of rules. If the operators had not rung the phones of family members and an investigation uncovered no malfunctions to the phone system, who was responsible? Phone calls from the deceased may sound far-fetched, but are actually quite common. It takes only a tiny electrical charge to make a phone ring; and the spirit is actually some form of energy. It is not so unreasonable for the spirit to use electronical means to communicate with the living.

Richard Nixon and Lincoln's Ghost

Publicly, Richard Nixon professed no interest in the paranormal or supernatural. Privately, the self-described "rock 'em, sock 'em" campaigner had more contact with the supernatural than most people ever realized. Earlier we reported that when Nixon was besieged by the Watergate scandal he roamed White House corridors at night talking to portraits of late presidents, perhaps hoping for advice from their spirits. Nixon, a man with an enigmatic and complex personality, had, since the 1950s, been in analysis with psychotherapist Dr. Arnold Hutschnecker, a personal relationship and friendship that endured through the Watergate crisis, even though by then Nixon was no longer in actual therapy. Hutschnecker, who practiced in New York, embraced the "psychic beliefs" of Jeane Dixon, and Nixon was open to Dixon's psychic and astrological prophecies, according to Anthony Summers in *The Arrogance of Power: The Secret World of Richard Nixon*. However, if Nixon was aware of any of several predictions made about his political downfall, he ignored them, including the prognostications of British psychic Malcolm Bessent and astrologers Noel Tye and Joan Quigley. Still, he considered supernatural intervention a direct cause of his political demise and told Rabbi Baruch Korff on his final day in the Oval Office that he felt he was being "punished by God."

Nixon always believed he was destined for great things. Other people realized this about him as well. When Nixon was just nine years old, for example, his Sunday school teacher in Yorba Linda made an unusual prediction. According to Nixon biographer Anthony

Summers, she said that someday the young Richard Milhous Nixon would be President of the United States. Following his graduation from college, Nixon had his palm read. Summers quoted the teenaged palmist Dorothy Welch, who said, "I got quite a shock. What I saw was a path of incredibly brilliant success . . . then the most terrible black cloud like a disaster or accident. . . . I told him what I read, but in a toned-down version. . . . He was such a serious sort of guy . . . the full version would have made him distraught. He wouldn't have known how to cope."

Always a man of contradictions, as Eisenhower's vice president he was badly frightened when a well-known astrologer predicted an assassination attempt. Richard and Pat Nixon had been in dangerous situations during the eight years he served as vice president, most notably in South America, where rock-throwing pro-Communist mobs attacked his limousine. Nixon, though shaken, toughed it out and challenged the crowd to "know the truth." Perhaps Nixon was worried about assassination attempts throughout the rest of his term, but after he had left office and John F. Kennedy was murdered in 1963, Nixon was quoted as having said, "I think it would not have happened to me."

In the summer of 1974, Nixon's son-in-law Edward Cox revealed the president's state of mind as Nixon's final weeks in the White House played themselves out. Nixon had been "walking the halls . . . talking to pictures of former presidents [and] giving speeches." Turning to the spirits of presidents past for advice, Nixon asked whether he should fight on against his enemies or resign from office. The unraveling of the president's emotional condition, which Bob Woodward and Carl Bernstein said probably occurred during the late spring and early summer of 1974, did not negate his psychic experiences. In fact, even though his grip on his political reality might have been fragile, that did not imply that his paranormal encounters were hallucinatory. If anything, Nixon's psychic powers would have been enhanced during this period as he retreated into himself.

U.S. News & World Report called Nixon a "strangely solitary man" and claimed his secretive personality would never have allowed him to reveal something so open to disparagement as a psychic experience. However, there is circumstantial evidence to connect Nixon with the ghost of Lincoln in the White House. Nixon had a strong affinity for Lincoln, which dated back to age twelve when he was given a picture of the Great Emancipator that he placed above his bed. Later in his life, "Nixon believed he was the contemporary Lincoln," according to *Richard Nixon, a Psychobiography*. As a case in point, one night in 1970 when he was besieged by crowds of anti–Vietnam War protesters angered by his invasion of Cambodia, Nixon was too troubled to sleep. The country had been coming apart since the Cambodia invasion, and Nixon had called the antiwar activity on college campuses the work of "bums." The ROTC building at the University of Wisconsin was burned down, the National Guard had been called out to Kent State, and colleges across the country were conducting teach-ins on the war to calm the sheer fury of their student populations.

That night in the ominous silence that fell over Washington, D.C., before the next day's demonstrations, a fitful Nixon lay awake. Instead of forcing himself to stay in bed, he wandered through the White House to Lincoln's Sitting Room, where he listened to classical music. When his valet, awakened by the president's activity, inquired whether he needed anything, Nixon asked if he'd ever visited the Lincoln Memorial after dark. When the man said no, Nixon asked the valet to accompany him to the magnificent monument, where, in a historic conversation, Nixon confronted some of the antiwar activists camping there. In one of the more sensitive moments of Nixon's tenure in the White House, he talked openly with protesters about the Vietnam War and why his invasion of Cambodia was intended to shorten the war, not expand it. What motivated his late-night walk to the steps of the Lincoln Memorial? Was it inspired by Nixon's affinity for the Great Emancipator or contact he'd had with Lincoln's ghost?

The Lincoln Sitting Room was often a refuge for Nixon during other times of crisis, especially during his final days. Perhaps, just like First Lady Jacqueline Kennedy, who often reported sensing Lincoln's presence in that same room, Nixon perceived Lincoln's spirit there as well. During the Watergate crisis, Nixon knelt and prayed at the table upon which Lincoln signed the Emancipation Proclamation. He also instructed that when he died he was to lie in state "beneath the dome of the Capitol," as had presidents since Lincoln. Taken together, these and other incidents form a pattern that suggests Nixon, as had many White House predecessors, experienced some form of psychic communication with Lincoln.

Nixon, whose model of a warrior-president was Theodore Roosevelt, had an aversion to admitting defeat and intensely disliked quitting in the face of adversity or disappointment. That was exactly what he told a national television audience in the 1952 Checkers speech, when he fought to sway public opinion in his favor as Eisenhower pondered whether to keep him on the ticket. So as the Watergate crisis spread like a cancer through the heart of his administration and even his staunchest Republican supporters in the Senate began to turn against him, he agonized about whether to fight on or resign the presidency. He fought to keep control of the infamous Oval Office tapes that contained the "smoking gun" statement indicating his knowledge of the break-in and his need to cover it up. But he lost that battle. He circled the wagons around the Oval Office and even put the United States on a high Defcon alert in 1973 when he believed the Soviets were about to intervene on Anwar Sadat's behalf during the Yom Kippur War. But just like the events that befell Bill Clinton during the Monica Lewinsky scandal and subsequent impeachment hearings, whatever the president did was considered a disingenuous attempt to deflect public attention away from charges pending against him. Yet the warrior inside Nixon fought on.

In the privacy of his own heart as he walked along the empty corridors of a White House under siege, Nixon sought solace from the spirits of those presidents who had fought their private wars inside these very same walls. Wasn't Harry Truman, his old nemesis, beset by a hostile Congress and country as he desperately tried to extricate the United States from Korea? How did JFK manage to wiggle out of the Cuban missile crisis when everybody knew that Kennedy had knowledge in advance of what the Soviets were up to and tried to bury the evidence until the newspapers got ahold of it? And Kennedy came out of it a hero. Now here Nixon was, alone with the ghosts of former presidents, seeking their advice. Attorney General John Mitchell was gone. John Erlichmann and Bob Haldeman were gone and fighting their own battles. John Dean had been turned by Nixon's own enemies. And Henry Kissinger and Alexander Haig were already pushing him out the door. There was nobody he could turn to except the spirits of the dead. So, alone in his own panic and frenzy, Nixon looked inward to channel the spirits of those who abided unseen in the White House alongside the living. Only a short while after his "conversations" with the portraits of former presidents, Nixon made the difficult and unprecedented decision to leave office on August 9, 1974. There are many who argue that Nixon's resolution had been arrived at through supernatural intervention, the actual spirit of Lincoln convincing him that for the good of the country and the sanctity of the Constitution it was time for him to go.

Lincoln's ghost has long had a reputation for materializing during times of national difficulty or distress. What more appropriate time for the Great Emancipator to resolve the crisis caused by Watergate? When Nixon finally made his decision, he said he was acting for the good of the nation. Had he been advised by Lincoln's spirit, which psychically connected with him at that moment? Paranormal research suggests that powerful emotion will often draw a spirit close in time of need. Lincoln would have strongly disapproved of Nixon's behavior and dishonesty. Why then might his spirit help Nixon? Considering Honest Abe's integrity, his goal would be to help the nation rather than the discredited and dishonored Nixon. The evidence is circumstantial, but considering Nixon's behavior and the history of Lincoln's ghostly appearances in the White House, the scenario is plausible. Nixon may have been his own worst enemy, and responsible for his own ruin, but it appears his downfall was karmically predestined although moderated, to a degree, by the benevolent spirit of Lincoln who hovered over Nixon during Nixon's days in the White House. Lincoln was still watching over his dangerously divided nation and protected it, even from its own president.

Jimmy Carter

Before Jimmy Carter was Governor of Georgia or President of the United States, he and his wife, Rosalynn, called Plains, Georgia, their home. It was where they were born and lived as children. When Jimmy resigned from the navy in 1953, following his father's death, he returned home to this tiny town to run the family's peanut farming business. Three years after he returned to Plains, the Carters and their three young sons moved into an old house, which already had a long reputation for being haunted, and lived there until 1960. It was not until May 1979, during what turned out to be her final year in the White House, that First Lady Rosalynn Carter would share with the media her experiences about living in the haunted house. She was especially guarded about the family's paranormal experiences in Plains because her husband had once seen a UFO, reported it as an official sighting to NICAP, and then after his presidential inauguration promised the nation that he would find out what secrets the government kept about UFOs so he could disclose it to the world. It was a promise he never fulfilled because shortly after his inauguration he was paid a visit in the Oval Office by an agent from his own National Security Agency, who actually threatened him and the lives of his family should he ever talk about UFOs to the nation. That was why Rosalynn was especially careful about talking about the paranormal.

However, in an interview with *Good Housekeeping* magazine about the haunted house in Plains, Rosalynn revealed, "I knew about the ghost before Jimmy and I moved in," she said. "But I wasn't really afraid of it. I just never disturbed it by going into the 'haunted room' alone at night."

The plantation-style frame house, situated in a thicket of magnolia trees, was built sometime around 1850. It had "a wide center hall, twin living rooms and many fireplaces," as well as "its original hand-planed floorboards." The ghost who lived there mainly centered its actions in the spacious front room on the house's west side. Inez Laster, employed in the house as a cook in the early 1950s, said, "Things would happen in that room. I could hear knocking on the door. Then it would open and shut and I'd hear walking. I'd see a woman with a long white dress coming from the cemetery. Dr. Wise, the man I worked for, could see her too. He'd say it was our imagination. But when he spoke to the woman, she and the light she carried both vanished. Sometimes I'd hear her walking on the attic stairs."

Rosalynn recalled her childhood recollections of the old house: "When I was a little girl, my best friend was Jimmy's sister, Ruth [Carter Stapleton]. We had to pass the 'haunted house' to visit each other. We were about eleven and so afraid of the house that we took the long way around." It required a great leap of faith, therefore, for the Carters to move into a house they knew was occupied by a ghost.

In 1973, when Jimmy was Governor of Georgia, Rosalynn and several friends returned to the house hoping to discover "the mystery of the ghost." She said, "When we lived here, our living room furniture was in this room. But there was no heat, so we didn't use it very often. One night we heard a crash in there. We waited a bit. Then the whole family trooped in together, thinking a window had fallen shut. But the window was still wide open." Rosalynn added, "I wasn't afraid of living in the house, but I would not have gone into the room at night by myself!" However, others who lived in the house were "too frightened" to remain and moved out. One tenant was horrified when someone—or something—pulled the sheets from the bed in the dead of night. Rosalynn also remembered a story she'd been told about a small white dog that would bound onto the porch, then vanish when anyone bent down to pet it.

On their return to the house in 1973, Rosalynn went up to the attic with its two fireplaces. Between the attic floor and the "haunted room" was a small space approximately three by five feet in which three men could lie down, but not stand up. The cubiclelike space had remained hidden for more than a century until it was uncovered by the Carters' young sons. "When we lived here, Jack was ten, Chip, seven, and Jeffrey, five," Rosalynn said. "They liked to play in the attic and one day they noticed a loose brick in the hearth. They discovered that the bricks and the boards under them would lift out to reveal this room. Chip thinks he remembers seeing a small chair down there. The boys often played in the hidden room."

The secret room and the ghostly doings were somehow connected. No one can be certain, but it is likely the tiny compartment was a hiding place for soldiers during the Civil War, a stop along the Underground Railroad, or, even earlier, a place to take cover from Indian attacks.

During Rosalynn's 1973 visit, a boy in the group discovered why the room remained well-hidden for so long. It had been secreted within a closed closet. Another closed closet was found "on the other side of the house," and there, under the floorboards, was another secret room. The purpose of the small hidden rooms remains an enigma as does the identity of the ghost who presumably knows, but hasn't yet revealed what happened in those rooms a hundred fifty years ago. Curiously, in spite of her haunted house experience in Plains, when First Lady Rosalynn Carter was asked about ghosts in the White House, she issued a terse "no comment."

In January 1977, United Press International reported that the Carters' daughter, Amy, then in the fourth grade, when asked to choose a book in school, selected one about ghosts. In *Ghosts Washington Revisited*, author John Alexander told of young Amy inviting several girlfriends to sleep over in the White House. Out of curiosity, the girls decided they would attempt to summon the ghost of Lincoln by bringing a Ouija board to the Lincoln Bedroom. However, they never communicated with his spirit, for Rosalynn told her daughter and friends to end their adventure contacting the spirit world. Still, Rosalynn was inquisitive enough about the paranormal to permit a spoon-bending demonstration by Israeli psychic Uri Geller, a veteran of the government's Remote Viewing operation who'd become famous for his feats of psychokinesis.

George H. W. Bush

Was President George Bush candid when he said that he'd never confronted or even glimpsed a ghost in the White House? In 1993, a national tabloid reported that Bush might not have revealed the entire story because he'd actually witnessed the apparition of President Lyndon B. Johnson. According to the newspaper, LBJ's spirit returned to the White House in 1991 when the United States was engaged in the Persian Gulf War. The timing of a ghostly visit by LBJ was no surprise, coming when it did, because Johnson's presidency was besieged by the bitter and fractious Vietnam conflict. The Gulf War, the largest U.S. military action since Vietnam, drew his spirit back.

According to a "White House source," which was not identified by the tabloid, Bush was with Secretary of

State James Baker and Defense Secretary Richard Cheney in a late-night Oval Office meeting about the Gulf War when an inexplicable chill whisked by, blowing papers and documents from the president's desk. Then the lights flickered off and LBJ's voice was heard, laughing heartily. The tabloid said Bush confided that he'd also heard "footsteps at night and [saw] a tall, gruff, big-eared ghost resembling LBJ."

Johnson's ghostly return to the White House during the Persian Gulf War, no doubt, recalled troubling memories of Vietnam. However, it is also possible that Bush mentally connected with LBJ's spirit and drew it back to commiserate at a tense time during his presidency. Either way, Bush flatly denied to the media that he'd seen or heard Johnson's spirit, or any other White House ghost. This is the same Bush who was director of the Central Intelligence Agency in the 1970s, the period during which the CIA had conducted covert psychic research into psychokinesis, teleportation, out-of-body experiences, and remote viewing. In 1999, Israeli psychic Uri Geller told *USA Today*, "George Bush, then head of the CIA, was very open-minded to the field of the paranormal. I'm sure you didn't know that." The CIA's response to Geller's revelation: "No comment."

George W. Bush

On Friday November 3, 2000, *Vanity Fair* astrologer Michael Lutin taped a TV interview program for the Fox News Channel, which aired the next two days, and thus before Election Day, November 7. Lutin said, "The loser is going to be the winner and the winner is going to be the loser. This election has so many sides to it and so many weird twists to it, I don't think we're going to know anything Wednesday morning what the situation is going to be."

Lutin could not have been more correct. The contest between Al Gore and George W. Bush—in which the vice president won the national popular vote and the

Texas governor was officially ahead in the Florida vote and thus the vote in the Electoral College—dragged on for a full five weeks of Florida recounts and court battles during which time no one was sure who would ultimately be the victor. The contest ended when the Republican-appointed majority of the U.S. Supreme Court shut down the Florida recount, effectively designating Governor George W. Bush the forty-third President of the United States. Six months after the election, final recount tallies in Florida were still mixed, according to the method of the recount, with Al Gore winning according to some methods and George W. Bush winning according to others. Both sides in Florida claimed victory, but the Supreme Court had already ruled five-to-four, and George W. Bush, elected, effectively, by a single vote, was inaugurated on January 20, 2001. Thus, according to which method of recount one believed was correct, Lutin's prediction actually came true.

This forces the question, was one of the nation's closest and most controversial presidential elections predestined? Psychic and astrological predictions for political leaders have come a long way in our modern computer-driven, satellite-fed, digital, technological age since the prophecies of Nostradamus.

Or have they?

CHAPTER ELEVEN

The Reagans

It is the stars/The stars above us,/govern our conditions.

—William Shakespeare, *King Lear*

With the exception of the Lincolns, no other first family was more fascinated by the workings of the paranormal than were the Reagans. This fascination became public with the revelation of Nancy Reagan's relationship with an astrologer, and it was greeted by a media firestorm. Perhaps first ladies before Nancy Reagan were more discreet or lived in simpler times, when media coverage was less sensationalistic and intrusive. By the 1980s, however, the media loved sensationalism, and the relationship between Nancy Reagan and astrologer Joan Quigley began a feeding frenzy when it hit the news wires. The secret of how astrology influenced the daily routine of the Reagan administration burst onto the front pages in 1988 when former White House chief of staff Donald Regan authored *For the Record*, in which he claimed that the dictates of astrological predictions were a constant issue in planning Reagan's schedule. The flood of derision and criticism quickly followed:

"Good heavens! An astrologer dictating the president's schedule?" blared *Time* magazine, adding, "New book tells of first lady's reliance on . . . seer."

A *New York Post* headline screamed: "Astrologer Runs the White House."

The Nation magazine accused President Reagan of being "nurtured in . . . [a] . . . rich loam of folk ignorance [and] historical figment. . . ." The article accused Mrs. Reagan and her astrologer of "peering into a crystal ball, guiding the policies of the U.S.," which the magazine charged was an "abdication of executive responsibility."

The Economist described "A star-crossed White House" and claimed "Americans are torn between shock and amusement at this bizarre revelation. It is the source of endless jokes and some chagrin. The religious right, thundering idolatry, is single-minded in its dismay." The article continued, "Both Mr. and Mrs. Reagan were known to be superstitious . . . but reliance on an astrologer to determine the American president's calendar is less endearing: it makes the administration look odd and rather silly."

The Federation of American Scientists, including five Nobel laureates, wrote Reagan to complain they were "gravely disturbed." "In our opinion," they said, "no person whose decisions are based, even in part, on such evident fantasies can be trusted to make the serious— and even life-and-death—decisions required of American presidents."

In his book, Donald Regan charged that "the president's schedule—and therefore his life and the most important business of the American nation—was largely under the control of the first lady's astrologer." Regan said the astrologer's timing of events reeked havoc with White House and presidential schedules. Although he insisted his book was not written with any animus or out of revenge or vindictiveness, not everyone agreed, especially Nancy Reagan. "I wrote about astrology because it was an essential truth about the way the Reagans operated," he insisted.

It was President Reagan's first chief of staff, Mike Deaver, Regan said, "who integrated the horoscopes . . . into the presidential schedule." When Regan learned about astrology in the White House, he thought it was a joke, until it was made clear to him that it was not. Deaver's advice: humor Mrs. Reagan. Although a skeptic, Regan said he tried, but remained troubled by the influence of horoscopes on the president's scheduling. But Regan approached the entire issue of the paranormal from the perspective of a political operative, an inside-the-Beltway professional, for whom anything smacking of anything less than the smooth-running gears of a well-engineered administrative machine was something to be feared. Besides, he was right about one thing: you can't convince the president's sharp-toothed enemies just waiting for the opportunity to pounce that one can time the mechanism of a political administration to what he believed were the vagaries of a prognosticator's tossing of the celestial dice.

Regan didn't know it, nor might he have been able to appreciate it even if he did, but the Reagans' long interest in astrology dated back to the 1950s, not surprising considering their Hollywood background. Hollywood is a place where sure things usually fail and only the most improbable, if not impossible, succeed. In other words, Hollywood is home to an industry in which success is almost often built on the margins, not on the mainstream. Success in Hollywood has the architecture of a bumblebee, which, from an engineering perspective, is not supposed to fly. But it does. That's what Hollywood is like, and people who succeed in Hollywood, like Ronald Reagan and Nancy Davis Reagan, know this as if it's their mantra. They look for an edge to achieve success any way they can, even when it comes from the alignment of the planets.

Accordingly, Hollywood, even as far back as the silent movie era, became a place where celebrities, desperate for success, sought their career advice and answers in all sorts of extranormal venues, especially in the planets and stars. That's why, throughout most of the twentieth century, alternative cultures flourished in California, where many astrologers, psychics, and mediums have long thrived. Reagan biographer Kitty Kelly wrote, as a case in point, that in the late 1960s when Reagan became

Governor of California he took "his oath in the middle of the night, acting on advice from an astrologer who said that was the most propitious time." The Reagans were "devoted clients" of Hollywood astrologer Carroll Righter, whose zodiac parties they regularly attended, and secretly consulted psychic-astrologer Jeane Dixon, until Mrs. Reagan lost faith in her abilities. Thus, it made perfect sense that Nancy Reagan would bring astrology to the White House from her background in the entertainment industry in Los Angeles just as it made perfect sense for Mary Todd Lincoln, lonely and isolated and looking for some sign that her beloved sons were nearby, to have brought formal séances into the Lincoln White House.

Regan, who only knew Joan Quigley as Mrs. Reagan's "friend" from San Francisco, admitted he was greatly frustrated coping with circumstances in which the president's schedule was decided by "occult prognostications." The astrologer "believed that the zodiac controls events and human behavior and that she could read the secrets of the future in the movements of the planets." It was a conviction Regan did not share, claiming Quigley was not always accurate, and complained that by humoring the first lady, "we had given her control."

Regan found it useless to challenge the astrologer's advice because each time the president set foot out of the White House for an appearance or press conference, Mrs. Reagan insisted the times were to be approved by her "friend." Regan argued in vain that the president needed to be out meeting and talking to people, an opinion not appreciated by the first lady. When he asked whether it was possible that the astrologer was mistaken, Mrs. Reagan adamantly answered that "her friend" correctly predicted the assassination attempt on the president in March 1981, as well as several other major circumstances, even a premonition of "dire events" in November and December 1987. These "events" turned out to be the Iran-Contra scandal, which was an interesting spin on the concept of "events" inasmuch as DEA investigators later learned, even though their files were deep-sixed by the CIA and NSA, that the Iran-Contra scandal didn't overtake the White House because it was planned from inside the Oval Office itself. Insofar as the Hinckley assassination attempt was concerned, Quigley's critics point out that her assassination "prediction" was actually made after the event had already occurred.

In the Reagan White House, even the reactions to world crises fell under planetary influences. For example, concerning the president's dealings with and comments about Soviet leader and party chairman Gorbachev, Mrs. Reagan's "friend" formulated horoscopes to help gain insight into Gorbachev's personality and likely actions. President Reagan's demand that Gorbachev "take down that wall," was subject to astrological timing, too. Joan Quigley also scheduled the president's meetings with Gorbachev, particularly in Reykjavik, Iceland, after which Reagan revealed to the assembled press that he and Chairman Gorbachev discussed UFOs and threats from hostile extraterrestrials. "I asked Mr. Gorbachev," President Reagan said, "what if we were threatened by aliens from outer space? Wouldn't we resolve our differences to resist a common enemy?" President Reagan later made a very similar speech about UFOs and ETs to the U.N. General Assembly, whose timing was also scheduled by Mrs. Reagan's "friend." It is noteworthy that Ronald Reagan was only one of two former governors and eventually presidents who publicly reported having seen a UFO. The other governor was Jimmy Carter, whom Reagan defeated in the 1980 presidential election.

Other political events, such as press conferences and major speeches, were scheduled according to Quigley's advice and held on what Quigley deemed to be "good days," even if a date had to be changed at the last minute, per the first lady's orders. Regan offered a glance at what were considered astrologically appropriate or good days as opposed to "bad days" for the president:

Late December thru March bad
January 16–23 very bad

January 20 nothing outside White House—possible attempt
February 20–26 be careful
March 10–14 no outside activity!
March 19–25 no public exposure
April 3 careful

And so it went: the days best for presidential activity, and those when caution was to be exercised. Regan complained that the number of "dangerous or forbidden dates" permitted little leeway for scheduling. Still, astrology was an unspoken rule when Regan talked about the president's planned events. If there was a cover-up of the paranormal in the Reagan administration, it went far beyond the subject of UFOs or ghosts in the White House; it was to hide from the public that an official first prognosticator was casting the president's specific chances for success based on the alignment of celestial bodies. At least, some commentators said years later when the story finally came out, the pharaohs and other monarchs who reigned according to advice of diviners or wizards looking at the stars, were open about it. In the case of the Reagan White House, it was as if there were a black hole at the center of all events, distorting them according to an unseen physical force. That force was the advice of Joan Quigley.

There are many specific examples of such last-minute schedule changes. In 1981, as Reagan and his top aides worked to free American hostages held by Lebanese terrorists, it became necessary for the president to address reporters. However, when Mrs. Reagan learned the date, she forbade him to do so, insisting that her "friend" deemed the timing wrong to talk to the press. When the president's surgery to remove a polyp in his intestinal tract was delayed in July 1985, Regan suspected it might have been because of astrological advice, a suspicion he never confirmed. Similarly, when Reagan and Gorbachev were to meet in Reykjavik, Iceland, for critical talks on arms reductions, the date of the president's departure was scheduled by the astrologer. Regan wanted to bring these scheduling issues up with the president, but he could never establish to what extent the president himself knew of or relied upon his wife's dependence on astrology. However, the horoscope became so much a part of White House decision-making and scheduling that, for a time, Regan had on his desk a "color-coded calendar" with dates numbered this way: green marked good days, red indicated bad ones, and yellow for questionable days.

Once when, by chance, Vice President George Bush raised the question of the president's many and seemingly arbitrary schedule changes, Regan revealed that the first lady's astrologer had determined them. Vice President Bush, surprised and dismayed, exclaimed, "Good God, I had no idea."

If Regan stuck to working the president's schedule around the good days, as indicated by his color-coded calendar, he was able to avoid any conflicts with the first lady. However, if Quigley indicated that a particular day or week was "bad" for the president, his timetable was thrown into "a state of chaos," and any presidential appearances were subject to cancellation or strict limitations. As a result, the relationship between the first lady and Regan was often contentious, and when Regan left as White House chief of staff, no love was lost between the two. That's the story Donald Regan told about the first lady's astrologer. What was Mrs. Reagan's version of events?

When Regan surprised Mrs. Reagan with public revelations of the White House astrologer, the escalating criticism and ridicule forced the first lady to defend herself. In her book, *My Turn: The Memoirs of Nancy Reagan*, she wrote "astrology was simply one of the ways I coped with the fear I felt after my husband almost died," a reference to the March 1981 assassination attempt by Bush family friend John Hinckley. She also admitted to her fear of the "twenty-year death cycle for American presidents," and was deeply worried that the attempt on the president's life might be an "omen" of even worse tragedy ahead. Could a future attempt on

Reagan be prevented? Mrs. Reagan said that in her emotional turmoil she turned to astrology, but in her spin on the controversy and in marked contrast to Regan's version, she minimized her dependence on Quigley's advice.

It was talk show host and entertainer Merv Griffin, a longtime Reagan Hollywood friend, who initially introduced Mrs. Reagan to Joan Quigley, a frequent return guest on Griffin's popular TV show in the 1970s. Griffin told Mrs. Reagan that Quigley said, "The president should have stayed home [on March 30, 1981]. I could see from my charts that this was going to be a dangerous day for him." That explanation, which Quigley later repeated to the first lady, led Mrs. Reagan to believe she could have kept the president from heading to the site of the assassination attempt. Quigley also said she'd seen in her charts that Richard Nixon would easily win reelection in 1972. However, she also saw "trouble" ahead in his horoscope, which proved to be the Watergate scandal.

"My relationship with Joan Quigley began as a crutch," Mrs. Reagan said, pointing out Quigley's claim that she had predicted the assassination attempt before it occurred. After the Hinkley shooting, Mrs. Reagan was very worried about her husband's safety; she said that Quigley's predictions and advice on good and bad days were just "one of several ways I tried to alleviate my anxiety about Ronnie." From her first conversations with Quigley, she said, astrology "had become a habit." While Donald Regan painted a picture of astrology as a pervasive influence in the White House, at least from his perspective, Mrs. Reagan downplayed Quigley's impact on presidential decisions.

Still, the relationship with Quigley deepened considerably after the astrologer said she could determine the president's "good" and "bad" days for travel plans and public appearances. Soon the two women were in regular telephone contact, and Quigley would tell the first lady which days were "safe or dangerous" for presidential activities. The information given to Mrs. Reagan was forwarded to White House Chief of Staff Michael Deaver who would change a date or time if necessary. When Regan took Deaver's place, the same procedure was in place. According to Mrs. Reagan, if a schedule change could not be made, she acquiesced to Deaver or Regan.

"While astrology was a factor in determining Ronnie's schedule, it was never the only one, and no political decision was ever based on it," Mrs. Reagan maintained. Don Regan certainly didn't share that opinion and, in fact, saw the astrologer's role in the White House quite differently. While Mrs. Reagan and Donald Regan agreed that Mike Deaver accepted Quigley's scheduling, Regan never condoned the astrologer's influence and saw it at best as a disruption and at worst as the very kind of torpedo that could sink the entire administration. After all, at the core of Ronald Reagan's constituency were rock-ribbed religious conservatives whose leaders would bolt the Reagan majority if they thought their president were being controlled by a diviner.

Mrs. Reagan was obviously aware of the potential controversy if her use of astrology to influence the president's schedule became known so she took pains to cover it up. For one thing, since Mrs. Reagan didn't "think an astrologer should be sent checks signed by the first lady," Quigley was paid through a third person, chosen by Mrs. Reagan. While Nancy realized news of a White House astrologer would be "embarrassing" to the president, she claimed she never realized "*how* embarrassing." But she said she never felt help from an astrologer was "particularly strange."

Mrs. Reagan insisted that "Joan's recommendations had nothing to do with policy or politics, ever. Her advice was confined to timing, to Ronnie's schedule, and to what days were good or bad, especially with regard to his out-of-town trips." To that, Donald Regan answered, "But he—or in this case she—who controls the president's schedule controls the workings of the presidency. It is the national chart of influence."

In 1985, after having conferred with one another over

the phone or through intermediaries, Mrs. Reagan saw Joan Quigley in person for the first time when the fifty-something attractive blonde was invited to a White House state dinner and she and the first lady met privately for tea. At the time of the first lady's meeting with Quigley, did the president know about his wife's ongoing relationship with the astrologer? Probably not, according to Mrs. Reagan; however, he later discovered what was going on and accepted the fact.

One thing Mrs. Reagan said she never considered was that Donald Regan, despite their differences, would "take this information about my interest in astrology and twist it to seek his revenge on Ronnie and me." She said she was "shocked and humiliated" by the public revelation of Quigley, which Mrs. Reagan had done her best to keep secret. The first lady became, in her own words, a "national laughingstock . . . the butt of countless jokes." At some point, she said she no longer paid attention to critics, while describing the ordeal as a "long nightmare." The relationship between the first lady and the astrologer was bound to come out because it was just the kind of Beltway tidbit that reporters loved. Therefore, if Mrs. Reagan believed such news could be kept secret, she was naive, although the American public itself was far more accepting of Mrs. Reagan's consultations with an astrologer than were the media. Out in the public, psychic hotlines, professional astrological advice, and books on the paranormal were hot sellers, especially back in the 1980s when many mediums had their own shows on cable television. For the Reagans, who were a very popular couple with American families, the revelations about Joan Quigley were not even an item. If anything, that was what people in La-la Land did.

In response to the media stories, the first lady said flatly the United States was never run by Joan Quigley, and insisted the horoscope was a personal way of dealing with her "trauma and grief . . . the pain of life." Even Donald Regan does not say astrology guided policy, per se; however, by timing presidential events, Quigley obviously influenced policy. Mrs. Reagan claimed the accusations of Quigley's impact were "distorted" by Regan. For her part, Quigley told *Time* magazine, "I don't make decisions for [the Reagans]. An astrologer just picks the best possible time to do something that someone else has already planned to do. It's like being in the ocean: You should go with the waves, not against them."

What Joan Said

After books by Donald Regan and Nancy Reagan on the subject, the third description of the controversy came from Quigley herself. In *What Does Joan Say?,* Quigley told her version of seven years as astrologer to the Reagans: "What Mrs. Reagan omitted about the way she used astrology and my ideas would fill a book." It is a different story from what Mrs. Reagan presented, and some critics felt Quigley overstated her role, taking too much credit for Reagan's presidential accomplishments. According to Quigley, it was Mrs. Reagan who adamantly insisted the media must never know that the first lady had an astrologer: "This must never come out!" Realizing the potential media hostility and political fallout, the message to Quigley was clear: she was not to talk to reporters, and if any sensitive issue should be asked of her, Quigley was told, "Lie if you have to. If you have to, lie." Quigley said she did not follow those instructions. She would exercise discretion in her answers, but she would not lie.

Mindful of the twenty-year presidential curse, Quigley was aware that if she did her job correctly—that is, if the president's horoscopes were accurate—Reagan would be the first president elected in a "zero year" to live through his term in office since James Monroe was elected in 1820. The fact is that after the March 30, 1981, attempt on the president's life, there never was another. "Was astrology one of the reasons?" Mrs. Reagan was asked. "I don't *really* believe it was, but I don't *really* believe it wasn't. But I do know this: it didn't hurt, and I'm not sorry I did it," she answered. Quigley said she understood her awesome responsibility and placed the Reagans uppermost: "Nancy and I did work well. She trusted me completely and followed my advice absolutely."

Quigley also wrote that Mrs. Reagan's "intuitions about the people surrounding [her husband] were almost preternaturally acute." It was as if "she had a sixth sense about the people around the president. Nancy, protective of her husband at every turn, was almost psychic in her awareness of his best interests and the motives of those surrounding him."

Although Quigley understood that she would never receive acknowledgment from the first lady, she also realized the obvious: "I felt that doing astrology for a president would be a unique experience, insofar as we know, in American history. I would be able to contribute to protect and, at times, to influence this most powerful man."

And exactly how did she help and influence the Reagans at the very outset of their relationship? The first lady's reputation was an immediate source of controversy because many people viewed her sometimes-imperial manner with disdain. The hyperbole reached the point where some compared her to Marie Antoinette, the reviled Queen of France, when, during the rampant inflation of the early 1980s, she seemed to spend lavishly on personal items for the White House. As portrayed in a suspicious and openly hostile media, Mrs. Reagan appeared vain and haughty, concerned mainly with expensive china and her chic wardrobe. Stung by media criticism of her ostentatious style and tastes, in 1981 she asked Quigley to create "a new image" for her.

According to Quigley, she set about creating a new and improved persona for the first lady by giving her advice based on aspects of her astrological chart that stood the strongest possible chance of succeeding. The effects were almost instant and dramatic. Within the year, Mrs. Reagan began attending a number of charitable functions and became involved in a variety of public service projects, particularly antidrug efforts. As the AIDS crisis began to build and the federal government was accused of being close-minded about the medical issues surrounding the growing epidemic, Mrs. Reagan championed the plight of AIDS-infected children. Quigley suggests that, following the astrologer's very specific instruction, the first lady generally softened her image by being more accessible and sympathetic to causes ranging from the arts to broader health issues, and even poked fun at herself. The image transformation worked.

But Quigley was far more specific in her book about what she did and what brought her to the first consultations with the first lady. Quigley said she had been following Reagan's fortunes long before he became president. In 1976, Reagan unsuccessfully sought the Republican presidential nomination, and Quigley foresaw that Gerald Ford would lose the election to Jimmy Carter by making an incorrect statement that would seriously strain his credibility. It happened in a dramatic moment during one of the nationally televised debates when Ford suggested that the Soviet domination of its Warsaw Bloc nations was less of an issue than the media made it out to be. Governor Carter jumped on President Ford, demanding that he "ask the people of Poland about that." Inside the spin rooms, the political aides and reporters could smell the blood. And the next day it spilled all over the front-page headlines from the *Washington Post* to the *San Francisco Chronicle*, screaming, "Ford Denies Moscow Dominates Eastern Europe." With inflation kicking toward double digits, the dollar not even worth the "Whip Inflation Now" button the president wore on his lapel, the Nixon pardon still an issue, and an American chief executive apparently not capable of taking a free swipe at the Soviets during an electoral debate, the voters threw Ford out after only a partial single term. Now it would be Reagan's turn, and in secret, Quigley began planning how she could help him.

When Quigley went to work on Reagan's horoscope, without his exact time of birth, she had to determine it astrologically, a process known as "rectification." Following that, to prepare the hundreds of astrological charts necessary, Quigley employed computers, without which she said, "The amount of in-depth work I did would have been impossible."

Reagan was born February 6, 1911, in Tampico, Illinois, one of five presidents born under the sign of Aquarius, including Abraham Lincoln and Franklin Delano Roosevelt. It is an astrological sign, Quigley explained, distinguished by "humanitarian vision." From Reagan's charts, Quigley recognized the president's traits and leadership abilities. Without delving into details, one example, oversimplified here, is the presence of "Mercury in Capricorn, in conjunction with his Capricorn in Uranus," which Quigley explained accounted for Reagan earning the title, "the Great Communicator."

"As with every human being, it was [Reagan's] destiny to undergo certain experiences," Quigley said. "Whenever . . . possible, astrology enabled him to avoid danger, to appear always at his best," she explained. "I believe that God intends certain experiences for each of us. Astrology is God's way of letting us read the overall plan for our lives."

Quigley said she forwarded to the first lady her husband's horoscope with a detailed astrological forecast beginning August 1, 1980, and determined the best days and times for such activities as trips and campaign debates right up until Reagan's landslide win that November. She also claimed that Reagan's chart "indicated that he was vulnerable to assassination." However, his horoscope showed he had the strength to mend from the bullet wound suffered in the assassination attempt, as well as recover from two cancer surgeries and the stresses of the presidency.

After Merv Griffin put them in contact with each other, Quigley and Mrs. Reagan consulted on a regular basis, sometimes as often as several times a day. According to the astrologer, for the seven years she served the administration, she gave Mrs. Reagan the best times for presidential press conferences, speeches, and public appearances and other "routine" appointments and activities, usually down to the minute, by using a "very complicated astrological technique . . . to predict what is happening." She also determined the best times and arrangements for long journeys, including "departure times of Air Force One when the president was aboard," and in the event of emergencies, was ready with astrological advice for the first family. "Astrology operates on many levels: physical, emotional, mental, and philosophical or spiritual. The Reagans took complete advantage of all these forms of assistance and advice," Quigley said.

Quigley was also forced, during the publicity that followed the release of her book, to defend an issue many astrologers and professional spiritualists find unfair. Can advice based on a supernatural or nonquantifiable source become addictive? Since you can't test it in a laboratory or point to a set of statistics to prove a point, is supernatural advice taken more on faith than on logic? And, if taken on faith, might it not run the danger of becoming addictive? How different is an astrological advisor from one of the pharaoh's sorcerers? Accordingly, in defending Mrs. Reagan, Quigley confronted frequent accusations that the first lady couldn't make up her own mind or that she relied on the stars for everything. "In all fairness," Quigley said, "Nancy was in no way addicted to astrology," although she took it more seriously than her husband did. Quigley explained that the first lady only contacted her when it was "necessary." She did not seek help about "frivolous matters," and only occasionally asked for help with personal and family problems. The hand on the nation's tiller, Quigley tried to make clear, was not that of a soothsayer, but that of the president.

Did Quigley know whether President Reagan was aware of her advice? She believed he "had to have known about me and the advice I was giving Nancy. He must have been aware and acquiesced when I gave instructions concerning the timing for certain congressional arm-twisting." Quigley claimed that she also advised the president he needed to order a thorough investigation into the space shuttle *Challenger* disaster, which exploded shortly after takeoff on January 28, 1986, killing the seven crew members aboard.

When Reagan said he was looking for information in advance that would help him prepare for a 1986 summit meeting in Reykjavik, Iceland, with Gorbachev on the thorny and sensitive issue of an arms agreement, Quigley was again consulted. She advised Reagan to press hard for negotiations to every extent he could. She also took credit for urging the president to stop referring to the Soviet Union as the "Evil Empire." His softening his tone toward the Soviet chairman was one of the ways the two leaders were able to create a path of trust between them that ultimately wound up easing the way toward the end of the Cold War.

The Iceland trip was particularly important and required that Quigley also cast Gorbachev's horoscope. Quigley said she also charted Gorbachev's horoscope so the president would have a better sense of the man he was negotiating with. She astrologically determined Gorbachev was "very tough" and because of the influence of Gemini, a talkative individual, "highly intelligent," with the "Aquarian vision of the brotherhood of man that he shared with Ronald Reagan." In their horoscopes, Quigley said she saw a chemistry between the two leaders, "one which I then believed could change the face of modern Russia and relieve the world of the threat of nuclear disaster between the superpowers." Suggesting a past life connection between the two, Quigley wrote, "The friendship that developed between Reagan and Gorbachev in this life is the continuation of a friendship from the past." Gorbachev, also interested in the paranormal, was believed to have secretly consulted a clairvoyant in the Kremlin to learn his future.

Quigley said she also became involved in advising the president on the most difficult and possibly the most dangerous scandal during his administration, the Iran-Contra scandal. This potentially devastating affair, which some people believed began inside the White House and led all the way up through Vice President Bush to President Reagan himself, pit cabinet members and federal law enforcement agencies against one another and involved the U.S. government in the middle of a drug-trafficking network and money-laundering ring. The danger of a continuing investigation existed right through all of the remaining years of the Reagan administration and was put to an end only when President George H. W. Bush pardoned Casper Weinberger, thereby eliminating the possibility that Weinberger's notes—notes that might have incriminated Bush—would find their way into court. Through it all, President Reagan seemed a man at the mercy of events. Caught up in the affair and amid damaging revelations involving his National Security staff and the CIA, Reagan sought to learn when the scandal would end and, perhaps in desperation, asked Mrs. Reagan, "What does Joan say?"

Although not involved in the Iran-Contra scandal, Quigley claimed she predicted it "in a roundabout way," and gave Mrs. Reagan advice on the best way to handle the embarrassment that Quigley said was in the president's chart when Uranus and Saturn "turned against him." Quigley said Reagan's problems in the scandal were fated and thus could not be prevented, explaining, "when the cosmic forces turn against one, it is best to run for cover, and insofar as is possible, to conceal oneself until the fury abates." At some point, "malevolent planets had turned against Reagan, and there was no way for him to prevail," she said. Therefore, Quigley's advice centered on making sure that whenever the president spoke, which should be as infrequently as possible, it be only on good days. Much of the work had to be left to subordinates, and the affair would eventually play itself out. Quigley's advice and predictions were accurate, and when Iran-Contra was finally over, the president phoned to thank her.

Ronald Reagan's tenure has been dubbed the "Teflon presidency," for despite Irangate and verbal blunders, his popularity remained largely intact through two terms. Did the astrologer deserve much of the credit for this feat? "Until I took over the task of guarding President Reagan's tongue by astrology, he had a tendency to come out not infrequently with real bloopers and other remarks better left unsaid."

Answering Donald Regan's charge that she'd chosen good days and excluded from consideration bad ones, Quigley said her task was far more complicated, for she also had to provide the exact time an event should take place. For example, Quigley provided times and locations for two debates between Reagan and Democratic presidential candidate Walter Mondale in 1984. She admitted to an error in her advice for the first debate, giving the advantage to Mondale, who, according to the media analysts, handled Reagan quite well. However, she corrected her information for the second debate, to Reagan's benefit. Quigley also astrologically timed Reagan's presidential addresses, including his State of the Union addresses, to the exact second they had to begin.

Quigley found: "Reagan had configurations in his horoscope very much like Lincoln's in several important respects." Reagan, like Lincoln, was elected in a "zero year," so there always existed a danger. "While Reagan had times when he could have been assassinated, I was always able to protect him," Quigley said. By contrast, Lincoln's murder was "absolutely fated." Not "even the finest astrologer could have prevented [it]. Astrology, like life, is a rather fascinating combination of fate and free will."

When Reagan was required to attend performances, Quigley checked "his special indicators with extra care." Had there been imminent danger, she would have forcefully insisted the Reagans not go. Where the president's safety was concerned, Quigley said she "stood guard astrologically."

Reporters who covered Reagan were curious why the presidential plane, Air Force One, departed at "unusual times." For example, it might have been twenty after or before the hour, but no one knew why. Quigley said the times were astrologically determined with Reagan's safety in mind.

In addition to the president's safety, protecting his health was also a major issue for Quigley. For example, in July 1985, when Quigley prepared the president's charts, she realized the horoscope revealed surgery in his future. With a "Scorpio ruler," Reagan had a tendency for tumors, she explained. A polyp had been removed in 1984. The next year doctors discovered a second polyp. Surgery was set for July 10. However, Quigley informed Mrs. Reagan that July 13 at noon was a better time: "It was because of me that the operation was successful and there was no recurrence of cancer between July 1985 and the time Reagan left office in 1989." What would have been the result if surgery had been performed before the day and time Quigley suggested? She said doctors would have chanced not fully excising the cancerous growth. To base medical procedures on astrological timing seems extremely unscientific in today's high-tech medical environment. However, for centuries astrology and medicine were inextricably related, as in the case of Nostradamus, who was both a physician and astrologer.

"Long, complex trip[s]" were an especially important responsibility for Quigley, she revealed. One such trip was Reagan's tour of the Philippines, Japan, and South Korea in November 1983, which also took the president on a number of "side trips and appearances." His travels required precise timing by Quigley, particularly where meetings might have touched on issues that related to the president's foreign policy. Among other presidential journeys was Reagan's visit to the Tokyo Economic Summit in 1986, for which Quigley also carefully chose the president's departure time. When Reagan and Gorbachev met for their historic Geneva Summit, Quigley advised the best times for sensitive meetings between the two.

Quigley determined the absolute best time for Reagan to announce his reelection plans for a second term in

1984. When the Reagans wanted to make the announcement in December 1983, she convinced them that late January 1984 was a better time: "I felt if he declared his intention to run at the time I chose, he was a cinch to win the election." She determined 10:55 P.M., Sunday, January 29, 1984, was best. "The planets were grouped in the part of the chart that referred to the person making the declaration to run. It was sort of like sitting in a poker game and holding a royal flush," Quigley explained. Did anyone know just how much the president's astrologer determined the exact timing of his reelection announcement? "It was common knowledge among those in the astrological community and others," she said.

In spring 1985, shortly after the beginning of his second term, Reagan became embroiled in controversy when he laid a wreath at Bittburg, a cemetery in Germany where soldiers from the infamous and dreaded Waffen SS unit were buried. Reagan's ill-conceived and ultimately awkward visit to the Nazi cemetery was bitterly criticized by Jewish organizations, especially Holocaust survivors who were victims of the SS. Quigley proudly took credit for timing Reagan's stop so the dispute would be minimized. "The Bittburg visit was brief, and the controversy soon died down. I had defused Bittburg for all intents and purposes," Quigley said. As well, she timed another presidential visit to the Nazi death camp at Bergen-Belsen.

Quigley also studied the chart for Reagan's controversial Supreme Court nominee Robert Bork after he failed to obtain confirmation. "Bork was destined to be beaten," she concluded. When Anthony Kennedy's name was submitted next, Mrs. Reagan forwarded his name, birth date, and where he was born to Quigley. The first lady also asked the astrologer for the best time to announce that Kennedy was being proposed for the Supreme Court. Quigley chose November 11 at exactly 11:32:25 A.M. Kennedy's horoscope accurately predicted his confirmation by the U.S. Senate, which occurred on February 3, 1988. In an ironic way, President George W.

Bush owes Quigley some gratitude as well because it was Justice Kennedy who joined the majority in selecting Bush to become the forty-third President of the United States when he voted to shut down the Florida recount, effectively handing Florida's twenty-five votes to the Governor of Texas.

"Choosing the appropriate time for an important beginning" is usually "the most difficult task" for an astrologer. "The times I set are always very exact. Presidential astrology has its advantages. The president can often command that things be done at a certain time in a way other people cannot," Quigley explained, adding, "An astrologer is not a magician. There are always limitations. An enlightened astrologer can help a great leader . . . harness the cosmic forces to his purposes, but only for a time. No one masters [them] forever. Sooner or later they turn against us, if only at the end." As examples, consider the fates of Lincoln, the Kennedys, Martin Luther King, Jr., and Gandhi—all assassinated; Napoleon, who spent his last years in exile on St. Helena and died as the result of poison; FDR, who died in the arms of his mistress; and Nixon, who suffered an ignominious fall during Watergate.

Quigley admitted that her efforts for the Reagans were extremely time-consuming, and the seven years she served Reagan is something she would not do for a president again. When it was over, Quigley said, she "breathed a sigh of relief."

Did astrology help or hinder the Reagan presidency? The fact is that Reagan pulled through an assassination attempt and two cancer surgeries, broke the "zero year presidential death cycle," withstood the Iran-Contra scandal, negotiated the successful dismantling of the Soviet nuclear threat, and at age sixty-nine (the oldest man ever elected president), served two full terms. He was only the second Republican in the modern presidency to do so, after Dwight Eisenhower (1953–1961).

Was Mrs. Reagan an overprotective wife who meddled in presidential policies, or was she so astute in her use of an astrologer that she strengthened her husband's presidency? Whichever conclusion one reaches, it seems undeniable that many Reagan decisions were shaped by Quigley's advice, perhaps, in a way, not unlike the astrological advice given to rulers from the time of the pharaohs through the Middle Ages.

Mrs. Reagan wasn't the first of the first ladies to consult an astrologer, and she probably won't be the last. Edith Wilson and Florence Harding both consulted regularly with Washington, D.C., astrologer Madame Marcia Champney, who accurately predicted Warren Harding would die in office. President Teddy Roosevelt tacked an astrological chart to the underside of his chessboard, of all places, so he could refer to it. *People* magazine reported that Chicago astrologer Laurie Brady advised Betty Ford, who "mostly asked about her husband." In the 1984 presidential campaign, Democratic candidate Walter Mondale had an aide consult San Francisco astrologer Terrie Brill for guidance on choosing a running mate. However, Mondale dismissed the advice and selected Geraldine Ferraro against the astrologer's recommendation.

Skeptics contend that whatever successes Reagan achieved as president were in spite of astrological advice. But it appears his presidency was helped more than it was damaged, if we take Quigley at her word. Some have also raised ethical questions about the propriety of an astrologer in the White House, while supporters argued that it amounted to no more of an issue than any other paid consultant.

What would have been the outcome of the Reagan presidency without Joan Quigley? Of course we can never be certain, any more than we can be sure how history would have turned if President Lincoln had not heeded the medium Nettie Colburn's advice to issue the Emancipation Proclamation. Apparently forgetting the spiritualist influence on the Lincolns, a political analyst on the Web site Parascope.com said about Quigley's work for the Reagans, "It is perhaps the only instance of paranormal forces having an undeniable impact on the course of U.S. history."

That some presidential decisions may have been based on paranormal advice does not lessen their impact or importance, and if certain events were predestined, then astrologers and psychics were simply discerning that which was already fated. Perhaps without supernatural intervention, American history would have unfolded differently and not as well. Of course, there remains the risk that if some psychic or astrological advice was erroneous, or even dangerously wrong, mistaken policies were formed in much the same way as presidents and advisors err without paranormal assistance. Still obdurate skeptics deny even the remotest possibility that in our high-tech, scientific age, an astrologer or medium— regarded as forms of superstition or pseudoscience— might have helped or guided the country just as seers and stargazers had throughout the centuries.

Once, after a remarkable demonstration of astrology on Joel Martin's radio talk show, a respected astronomer was asked to scientifically explain how planets and stars can influence and affect our lives. Astrology, he said flatly, should not work. The only problem, he confessed, is that it *does* work.

CHAPTER TWELVE

Eleanor and Hillary

Don't believe what your eyes are telling you, all they show is limitation. Look with your understanding, find out what you already know, and you'll see the way to fly.

—Richard Bach, *Jonathan Livingston Seagull*

Nancy Reagan's astrologer Joan Quigley was not the last spiritual advisor to a first lady. Hillary Clinton also caused headlines across the country to signal another paranormal flap at the White House. Just in time for Bill Clinton's campaign for a second term, the question of whether Hillary Rodham Clinton was having personal conversations with the spirit of the late Eleanor Roosevelt broke in the press. Was it true? Was there another medium channeling spirits or divining the future at the White House? Absolutely not, thundered the Clinton spokespeople. But the source of the story had broken major news before, and he stood behind what he was saying.

It was in the spring of 1996 when Americans first learned that Mrs. Clinton had delved into the New Age with the help of "psychic philosopher" Jean Houston. Reporter Bob Woodward, who investigated the story of Watergate for the *Washington Post* and then wrote *All the President's Men* with Carl Bernstein, first disclosed

Mrs. Clinton's "talks" with the late Mrs. Roosevelt in his book *The Choice*, a behind-the-scenes story of the Clintons. It had been no secret that Mrs. Clinton admired Mrs. Roosevelt, who not only lived with her husband's great burden during the Depression and World War II but also bore the burdens of FDR's relationships with other women. There were other major similarities between Mrs. Clinton and Mrs. Roosevelt, which extended to their husbands' administrations, their political agendas, and the types of enemies who confronted them.

Like President Clinton and to a lesser extent President Carter, President Roosevelt was the target of a well-financed group of radical conservatives who sought to thwart his domestic economic and social programs at any cost. Roosevelt's detractors, some of whom were investing in the reindustrialization of Germany in the 1930s, ferociously blocked any U.S. attempts to oppose Hitler's and Mussolini's moves in Europe. Most people still believe that congressional reluctance to side with England and France against Hitler was simple isolationism after the disillusionment with the failed peace of World War I and the League of Nations. It wasn't. There were bankers, Wall Street law firms, and American industrialists already doing business in Germany. Some members of Congress who saw Hitler as a lucrative customer, and were secretly supporting him saw Roosevelt's social programs as a form of creeping socialism that would undermine their American way of life.

At the same time as the American industrial and financial communities were investing heavily in German weapons industries under the Nazi regime, their allies in Congress were attacking Roosevelt's New Deal. In fact, rather than reinvesting in an America suffering during the early years of the Depression, many industrialists saw a fascist-dominated Europe as a better deal and were taking their money out of the American economy. From industry's perspective, this was simply good business. As Peter Grose described in his biography of Allen Dulles, Germany was willing to borrow to get money to spend, and the U.S. industrial and banking communities were in the best position to satisfy the need. But there was another agenda as well. Many industrialists saw in Hitler and Mussolini a buffer to the growing threat of Stalin and the Soviet Union and its agenda to create an international workers' state. Accordingly, rearming Germany to keep Stalin inside his borders was surely an important element of the industrialists' strategy as well as providing them with what they saw as an investment opportunity they didn't have in the United States. All of this lay behind the formation of a cabal to thwart FDR and get him out of office by any means possible.

What most people don't know, however, is that opposition to President Roosevelt went far, far beyond simple rhetoric or legislative strategies. Roosevelt was the target of a well-planned assassination attempt in 1933, right before his inauguration, that left the Mayor of Chicago dead when he took a bullet for the president. The following year, President Roosevelt was almost removed from office by a planned coup d'état financed by a group composed of the leaders of American industry and led by none other than General Motors president William S. Knudsen, Irenee du Pont, and the members of the Morgan Bank. These and other industrialists, including Henry Ford, were among those who had been doing business with Hitler's Third Reich. The leaders of the military coup had raised three million dollars to overthrow the U.S. government, but the coup failed when a Marine Corps general who refused to take part in it exposed it.

Mrs. Roosevelt was a witness to all of this just as Mrs. Clinton was a witness to the radical right-wing conspiracy of innuendoes, half-truths, and outright lies to drive her husband from office. Mrs. Roosevelt was an articulate and steady partner to her husband and helped him focus on the plight of the real victims of the Great Depression. Although she was born into New York's privileged class in 1884, Anna Eleanor Roosevelt evolved into a powerful advocate for the poor, women, and minorities. After her husband's death, Mrs. Roosevelt became one of the founding motivators behind the embryonic United Nations and helped define the organization's focus on the rights of the underprivileged, the oppressed, and the victims of war and despotism. Mrs. Roosevelt could easily have become a U.S. Senator from New York had the Democratic Party offered her the nomination.

Eleanor and Franklin were actually distant cousins, born into a wealthy patrician family and married in 1905. World War I spurred her social consciousness, but personally, she said, "The bottom dropped out of my own particular world" when she found her husband engaged in an affair with his secretary. With an irreparable rift in her marriage, Mrs. Roosevelt knew that she would have to build her own life, which took another unexpected twist when FDR contracted polio in 1921 during a retreat at Campobello and fought to rehabilitate himself. Emotionally suffocated by his mother during this period, Franklin would have abandoned his political aspirations had it not been for Eleanor, who fought her mother-in-law for what amounted to Franklin's freedom to pursue a political career. Soon, Mrs. Roosevelt was also involved in political activities, and when the wheelchair-bound FDR was elected governor of New York in 1928, she often represented him at events.

Franklin Roosevelt only served one term as governor. He watched as the Hoover administration seemed frozen with confusion in the wake of the collapse of American financial markets on Wall Street. As banking institutions failed and people lost their homes and businesses, Governor Roosevelt was outraged at the inactivity of the Republican administration in the White House. Roosevelt championed what he called a "New Deal for the American people" and won the Democratic nomination for president.

In 1932, FDR was elected president and, as he set into motion what would become the most extensive agenda of social legislation in the history of the United States, Mrs. Roosevelt began to redefine the role of first lady. With the nation in the grips of a wrenching economic Depression, she developed for herself a difficult set of humanitarian causes aimed at easing the misery of the unemployed and hungry. Her visibility was unprecedented for a first lady. She became a speaker and writer, appeared on network radio, traveled on lecture tours, and wrote a popular syndicated newspaper column. She added to her causes women's rights and civil rights, and shortly after becoming first lady, wrote *It's Up to the Women*, encouraging women to participate in politics. To be sure, she was controversial and many abhorred her positions. Still her popularity and influence grew, and when she traveled—which was quite often—she became her husband's eyes or ears, his "nagging conscience" telling him what she thought, whether he wanted to hear it or not.

World War II posed another challenge for Mrs. Roosevelt. The U.S. Congress had not wanted the country to get involved in World War II. Even Ambassador Joseph Kennedy had actively campaigned against America's siding with the English, suggesting instead that the United States would be better off in an alliance with Hitler's Germany. In this argument, Joseph Kennedy was joined by members of Congress and other industrialists who had been investing in Germany, a group that also included Connecticut senator Prescott Bush and his father-in-law, George Herbert Walker, through the Union Banking Corporation. But Mrs. Roosevelt, acutely aware of the abuses of human rights taking place under the Nazis and the wave of genocide sweeping across Europe, prodded her husband to do whatever he could, not only to help Churchill during the very dark days after the evacuation from Dunkirk and the air war over Britain, but even during the Japanese invasion of China.

Roosevelt's secret "Flying Tiger" air war, denying the Burmese oil fields to the Japanese Army, combined with the U.S. embargo of oil to Japan, angered the Japanese and no doubt set in motion events that led to the bombing of Pearl Harbor. But our secret air war in Burma accomplished its mission by foreclosing Japan's abilities to wage a trans-Pacific war because they couldn't acquire the petroleum resources to do so. It was Pearl Harbor that got the United States into the war in the Pacific because it provided FDR with the basis for asking a stunned Congress to declare war on Japan. Then FDR got exactly what he was after when Hitler declared war on the United States. Now, despite the industrialists, the banks, and Hitler's supporters in Congress, the United States was in World War II to the finish. Once we were in the war, Mrs. Roosevelt traveled tirelessly, visiting hundreds of thousands of GIs and countless hospitalized servicemen here and abroad.

After FDR's death in 1945, Mrs. Roosevelt persevered, and was involved in the newly formed United Nations. An active Democrat, she never sought elected office, but continued to travel and speak out on issues until her passing in 1962 at the age of seventy-eight, having earned a worldwide reputation as the most controversial, idealistic, and socially conscious first lady in the nation's history.

Mrs. Roosevelt fought her husband's enemies just as Mrs. Clinton confronted what she called the "vast right-wing conspiracy" out to destroy her husband. Thus, there was an enormous similarity between the situations of Mrs. Roosevelt and Mrs. Clinton. But there were also enormous differences.

In an article published in *Talk* magazine as Hillary was beginning her campaign for the New York Senate seat of the outgoing Pat Moynihan, the writer correctly pointed out that both Eleanor Roosevelt and Hillary Clinton had very expansive social agendas at the outset of their husbands' administrations. But where Eleanor was constrained by the social restrictions imposed upon women in politics and business, Hillary, a Yale Law School graduate, was not. Yet Hillary found out that there were more subtle restrictions, especially when it came to getting her universal health care legislation through Congress. She was pilloried in the press for the mismanagement of the legislative campaign and what was perceived as her bullying members of her own party. By the time the Democrats lost both the House and the Senate in the 1994 elections, Hillary's health care legislation was dead. Then, in 1996, there was the smell of more scandal when the stories of secret "channeling" at the White House surfaced in print. However, Hillary was a child of her own generation, and the channeling as a way to think about something from a different perspective made sense.

When Hillary Rodham was still in college in the 1960s and 1970s, there was a renewed interest in spiritualism, which was now being dubbed "New Age." By the 1990s, the term "New Age" embraced many disparate interests, including alternative health and healing, the belief in the immediate presence of angels, the channeling of spirits, and a host of other metaphysical topics that filled countless books, films, TV programs, and self-help tapes. In 1998, *Life* magazine reported that eighty percent of Americans believed in an afterlife. A 1993 National Opinion Research Council survey from the University of Chicago found four in every ten Americans "reported having experienced some form of communication or contact with the dead." The *New York Times* revealed in 1997 that "nearly half of Americans believe in ESP. A hundred forty-five million think they've had a psychic experience." A 1993 *Time*/CNN poll found that sixty-nine percent of them thought "special guardian angels" exist, and from 1991 to 1995, more than five million copies of angel books were sold. This number doesn't include books about near-death experiences and other stories about what might lie beyond the curtain of death. Many described their interest in such phenomena as "nontraditional spiritual searching." Despite the growing popularity, however, disparaging comments in the press weren't hard to find. One newspaper editorial pronounced the first lady's activity, her reported attempts to work with spiritual advisor Jean Houston to channel the departed spirit of Eleanor Roosevelt so as to communicate with her, "a harmless bit of New Age nonsense."

Houston had been one of a group of well-known self-help authors invited to Camp David by the Clintons, who were seeking advice to strengthen the presidency by examining different approaches to problems. Houston, whose approach to solutions was clearly out-of-the-box thinking, soon became an influence in Mrs. Clinton's life and ultimately a source of controversy. Probably because Houston was able to explain to Mrs. Clinton how the first lady "was carrying the burden of 5,000 years of history when women were subservient," the two women quickly developed a rapport and explored ways the Clinton presidency could improve society.

To help Mrs. Clinton define more sharply who she was as first lady amid the ongoing Whitewater investigation and the ruins of her failed national health care plan, Houston was invited to the White House, where, in Mrs. Clinton's office, a large portrait of Eleanor Roosevelt suddenly caught her attention. It was a powerful reminder that when she was still in her teens she'd personally met Mrs. Roosevelt on several occasions. Houston shared those experiences with Mrs. Clinton, and the two began to talk increasingly about Mrs. Roosevelt's tireless efforts on behalf of numerous social causes, civil rights, and women's issues. Houston quickly realized that Mrs. Clinton was "really a serious Eleanor Roosevelt aficionado." Mrs. Clinton had long compared herself to Mrs. Roosevelt, and in his book, Bob Woodward noted that, to Mrs. Clinton, Mrs. Roosevelt was her "archetypal, spiritual partner."

In confidence, Mrs. Clinton told Houston that "she had always felt the presence of Eleanor Roosevelt in the White House," wrote Christopher Andersen in *Bill and Hillary: The Marriage*. "I was a huge admirer of [her]—I wanted so much to be like her, to make a real contribution as first lady. But after three years in the White House I felt stymied. I wanted to know what this brilliant woman would have done if she were alive today," Mrs. Clinton said.

And so, Houston urged Mrs. Clinton to "search further and dig deeper for her connections to Mrs. Roosevelt," by engaging in what Houston called "reflective meditation." Mrs. Clinton was encouraged to sit and "talk" to Mrs. Roosevelt, ask questions, and then imagine what her answers would be. Following Houston's instructions, Mrs. Clinton focused on Mrs. Roosevelt's passion, tenacity, and championing of the poverty-stricken. In her dialogues with the late first lady, Mrs. Clinton talked about "the obstacles, the criticism, the loneliness [Mrs. Roosevelt] felt. Hillary's identification with Mrs. Roosevelt was intense and personal," Woodward said. Houston also urged Mrs. Clinton to play the role of Mrs. Roosevelt, to answer as if she was the former first lady. Before long, according to Christopher Andersen, White House staff members heard Mrs. Clinton, "behind closed doors, having animated—if one-sided—conversations with Eleanor's ghost." Mrs. Clinton said she wanted to know what Mrs. Roosevelt would have done in her situation, how she would have handled matters. "She usually responds by telling me to buck up or at least to grow skin as thick as a rhinoceros."

Houston told Mrs. Clinton she needed to understand that Mrs. Roosevelt was more than a historic figure. "She was someone who also was hurt by all that happened to her . . . yet Mrs. Roosevelt could go on doing her work. Hillary needed to unleash the same potential in herself," Woodward wrote. Houston also urged Mrs. Clinton to engage in conversations with other great historical figures, such as Gandhi. One figure Mrs. Clinton declined to converse with was Jesus, saying it "would be too personal." Houston also tried to explain that she employed a visualization technique with Mrs. Clinton that teaches how to get in touch with "the wonder of the inner and outer worlds that is our legacy." "There was no séance! There were no spooks!" she declared emphatically. *New Republic* magazine agreed, "Eleanor Roosevelt was not raised from the dead." And the sessions with Houston were "not a spiritual event," a point that could be argued, considering Houston's long belief and interest in the spirit world and "channeling," the New Age term for mediumship, and the nature of the "reflective meditations" Mrs. Clinton engaged in.

Houston was among the many New Age or human potential movement figures who believed that a channeler, while in a trance, was in contact with the "collective unconscious," as Carl Jung called it. Houston asserted that a "finely tuned mind [could] reach back in time, tapping into the vestiges of our evolutionary ancestors that she says still exist in our brains," said *Newsweek*. She also believed those in a trance could increase their ESP abilities, including clairvoyance, precognition, and telepathy. In fact, earlier in her career, Houston carried out dream telepathy experiments. And she had connections to Edgar Mitchell, the Apollo 14 astronaut and a respected figure in parapsychology research, who founded his own institute to study extrasensory phenomena. Her denials notwithstanding, Houston clearly had a long history of paranormal interest. Whether Mrs. Clinton, a Methodist, embraced all or only some of Houston's beliefs is uncertain.

For her part, Mrs. Clinton explained that the visualization exercises or "conversations" with Mrs. Roosevelt were simply ways "to help spark my thoughts; it was a brainstorming session for my book" [a reference to *It Takes a Village*, which Mrs. Clinton was writing at the time]. Likely embarrassed, she did her best to play down her "talks" with Mrs. Roosevelt, even joked about them, and issued a written denial that Houston or anyone else was her spiritual advisor. Nor did Mrs. Clinton attempt to use anything she gained from her "conversations" with Mrs. Roosevelt to influence the president, as Nancy Reagan had done with her astrologer.

The denials hardly calmed the debate. Right-wing television commentator John McLaughlin, himself a former Jesuit, blasted Mrs. Clinton's "meditative dialogues" with Mrs. Roosevelt's spirit as "spooky, kooky, and dorky." He hollered at whomever was paid that week to listen to him, "New Age, quote-unquote, theology is . . . really very un-Christian, very un-Jewish, very untraditional in its genesis and expression."

Taking a surprisingly softer position was the respected Jesuit magazine *America*, which came to Mrs. Clinton's and Houston's defense. "They mock what they do not understand," the magazine wrote about critics of the "conversations" with Mrs. Roosevelt. The Jesuits certainly don't consider themselves New Age, nor would they ever consider engaging in séances, yet they are taught to pray "with an active imagination." *America* also suggested that in raising questions about talking to the departed, critics overlooked the long history of such dialogues within the context of traditional religion. Catholics, particularly, have a centuries-old legacy of saints with whom the faithful petition for special intentions. Asking St. Anthony to help find a lost article or object, praying to St. Jude in a hopeless or desperate situation, calling upon St. Thérèse of Lisieux for blessings or help are but a few examples.

Afterdeath communications research has revealed numerous reports of individuals praying to departed loved ones for help or for signs they can communicate with the living. Such signs can be anything: a headline in a newspaper, seeing a familiar acquaintance, or even hearing a favorite song over the radio at an appropriate moment. To make an analogy, conversations with the souls of the departed may represent a secular equivalent to conversing with the saints or other great religious teachers in any other faith. The only difference, the devout will argue, is that religious figures are more spiritually evolved. However, many New Age commentators and writers on spiritualism suggest that the only difference between talking to the departed and talking to saints is that an organized church has sanctioned the existence of saints.

On one level, Mrs. Clinton had engaged in a visualization or role-playing exercise to "think more creatively." But at another level, might a strong emotional connection have developed that resulted in actual contact with Mrs. Roosevelt's spirit? It is not surprising that Mrs. Clinton, as have generations of women, admired and even emulated Mrs. Roosevelt as a role model. But was Mrs. Clinton the only documented case of someone having had contact with Mrs. Roosevelt? Probably not, according to the story of noted sculptor Penelope Jencks, who in the late 1980s, several years before Mrs. Clinton's dialogues with the late Mrs. Roosevelt, was commissioned to create a first-ever statue of Mrs. Roosevelt for New York City, which would stand at the southern end of Riverside Park in upper Manhattan.

Jencks's project had been chosen from hundreds of submissions by a committee led by a New York man. Working in her studio on Cape Cod, Jencks, an attractive woman in her fifties, surrounded herself with hundreds of pictures of Mrs. Roosevelt in many poses: sitting, standing, smiling, serious, front view, profile, hat on, hat off. As well, there were several small models of the proposed eight-foot bronze statue, each showing Mrs. Roosevelt in a different position. Jencks told *The New Yorker* magazine in October 1994, "They are a tremendous help in my attempt to make the sculpture believable. I study them continually." She also read many works about the late first lady, and visited the Roosevelt Library in Hyde Park.

Jencks long had a huge affection for Mrs. Roosevelt, and she "always felt [she] could identify with her as a woman. I felt a special, intimate empathy," Jencks told writer Philip Hamburger in *The New Yorker* article. She was effusive in her respect and admiration for Mrs. Roosevelt's achievements and political positions.

Not surprisingly, creating an appropriate likeness of Mrs. Roosevelt became an "all-consuming passion." Jencks said she worked tirelessly to portray both Mrs. Roosevelt's "sense of peace and strength" in a pose that showed her positioned against a granite rock with her hand under her chin and looking deep in thought.

During the course of her work, Jencks became friendly with Mrs. Roosevelt's grandson Franklin Roosevelt III. She admitted to him that she was having difficulty sculpting the body in the proper proportions. When Jencks remarked that she wished she'd had a human model to work from, Frank Roosevelt suggested his daughter Phoebe might be agreeable since she resembled her famous great-grandmother. Now that Jencks had Phoebe as a model, she carefully measured the young woman, seeking the same body proportions she sought for the sculpture. In his *New Yorker* article, Hamburger told of visiting Jencks's studio, where, he said, "Eleanor Roosevelt's presence is almost palpable."

While still wrestling with the anatomy and proportions of Mrs. Roosevelt's body, Jencks had a "strange dream" that proved to be of enormous aid in solving her problem. In the dream, Jencks was in her studio, kneeling and sculpting, when she heard a voice say, "Oh here comes Mrs. Roosevelt!" Now her distress was alleviated, for she thought there'd be no further need for a model. Then, through the door walked Mrs. Roosevelt, except that she was "twenty feet tall." Mrs. Roosevelt smiled at Jencks, who contemplated how she would configure the sculpture, and that smile erased Jencks's concerns. Then the dream vision of Mrs. Roosevelt vanished. Jencks said she was "secure in the knowledge that I found Eleanor Roosevelt in my dreams." It was a dream that helped Jencks complete the torso of the statue, just as she hoped it would be, despite her earlier struggle. But was it merely a dream or an afterdeath communication?

Penelope Jencks and Hillary Clinton crossed paths when Jencks had the opportunity to visit the first lady in the White House, and Mrs. Clinton made no secret of her affinity for Mrs. Roosevelt. Jencks had made a small version of the statue she was readying for installation in Manhattan, approximately fourteen inches tall, which she gave to Mrs. Clinton. Copies of the maquette were later sold to raise money for Jencks's project.

Does Jencks's experience strengthen the argument that Mrs. Clinton's so-called "imaginary conversations" with Mrs. Roosevelt were actually something more than visualizations? Might Mrs. Clinton and Penelope Jencks have both been in contact with the spirit of the late first lady they so admired? The most succinct argument that Jencks's experience was paranormal in nature is that the dream visitation provided her with information she did not otherwise have. In other words, the vision solved Jencks's problem of how best to sculpt Mrs. Roosevelt's anatomy.

Bob Woodward concluded, "Hillary's session with Houston reflected a serious inner turmoil that she had not resolved." He also took a swipe at Mrs. Reagan, calling astrology a "kind of pseudoscience that could be fun or worth a laugh." If we were to accept Woodward's argument, then why disparage Mrs. Clinton's efforts to resolve her conflicts? Had Mrs. Clinton gone the conventional route of conflict resolution, psychotherapy or counseling from mainstream religion, there would have been little if any criticism. However, once she stepped beyond the narrow strictures of established practices to seek help, tolerance was in short supply. But if Houston's process helped, why not accept it? Might not there be many spiritual paths through which we can learn and grow?

And what if the "conversations" were interactive and not one-way or imaginary? What if Mrs. Roosevelt's spirit heard Mrs. Clinton's heartfelt questions and returned answers telepathically? Might Penelope Jencks's strong need for a solution to the problem of sculpting Mrs. Roosevelt have been solved by the dream visitation from the late first lady? Mrs. Clinton once pondered, "I do wonder what Eleanor might think of all this." Perhaps, one day, her spirit will answer.

The Jean Houston commotion was not the Clintons' only brush with paranormal or supernatural phenomena, and Houston may not have been the only spiritual teacher Mrs. Clinton consulted. A published account said Mrs. Clinton was believed to have quietly visited Sai Baba, a well-known Indian Avatar, and was said to have "come away from the experience feeling that [she] was not in the presence of an ordinary human being."

Mrs. Clinton also had a near-brush with the Hope Diamond curse that cost so many lives, possibly including the life of President Warren Harding. In November 2000, Neal Travis in the *New York Post* reported Hillary Clinton knew enough of the infamous 45-carat blue gem's history that she refused to go near it when it was on display at the Smithsonian, worried that the diamond's reputed bad luck might rub off on her. Mrs. Clinton's instincts might have been correct because in November 2000, she was elected U.S. Senator from New York, becoming the first presidential spouse in American history to be elected to Congress. Whatever advice she received from Mrs. Roosevelt must have worked because Mrs. Clinton, in an administration of firsts, became the first first lady to win office in her own right. Maybe she will be the first woman to run on a presidential ticket and perhaps the first woman to win the presidency.

CHAPTER THIRTEEN

The Haunted Capital

The spiritual world lies all around us and its avenues are open to the unseen feet of the phantoms that come and go.
—Henry Wadsworth Longfellow

When darkness falls over the nation's capital at the end of each day, thousands of federal officials and employees from the most powerful heads of Senate committees to mail clerks and typists leave their offices for home. Late at night, most government buildings become dramatically still except for the sound of an occasional cleaning cart or the footsteps of a security guard echoing through a deserted corridor. But, though the workers have gone home, it doesn't mean the buildings are devoid of activity because deep in the night another world materializes, this one of ghosts and spirits, turning Washington, D.C., into one of the most haunted cities in the country. There are substantial numbers of credible witnesses who have seen, heard, or sensed the ghosts that still call the nation's capital their home, drawn back to this earthly plane by power, ego, unfinished business, or because their lives on earth were tragically cut short. And the buildings they haunt stand as laconic witnesses to the human tragedies that took place inside their walls.

The White House

In 1953, a couple visiting the newly installed Eisenhowers at the White House reported with considerable consternation and fright that they'd witnessed the specter of a British soldier bearing a fiery torch. Rarely do haunting spirits pose a menace. However, this ghost attempted to set the couple's beds on fire in a guestroom on the second floor of the White House. About that the wife was quite adamant.

That same apparition had been seen at other times. He is believed to be the ghost of a young British soldier under the command of Alexander Cochrane. He was one of the invading soldiers who died on the grounds of the White House that infamous August night in 1814 after he participated in setting the building on fire during the British torching of the capital city. Apparently the British soldier's restless and obviously disturbed earthbound spirit was unable to resolve the animosity he long carried that his life had been cut short at an early age.

Haunting in a destructive way, although atypical of most ghosts, is not unheard of. However, since the soldier's specter has not been reported since the 1950s, perhaps he has finally dispelled his negativity and found peace in the afterlife, realizing the War of 1812 and all his earthly battles are long past.

The Octagon House

The stately Octagon, as it's called, is a beautiful Georgian-style mansion with six, not eight, sides, that stands on New York Avenue and Eighteenth Street, only two blocks from the White House. It was in the Octagon that President and Mrs. Madison resided for a year while the White House was rebuilt following its torching by the British in 1814. The Octagon is famous not only because it once housed the Madisons, but because it was one of the first private residences in the new nation's planned capital.

Washington, D.C., had already been designated as the seat of America's federal government when Colonel John Tayloe, a wealthy Virginian who owned a huge plantation in Mt. Airy, Virginia, looked for a place to build a town house. President George Washington, Tayloe's close friend, urged him to build in the nation's new capital city that Washington himself had helped to plan. Tayloe took to the suggestion, and in 1800, he constructed the Octagon for his family of fifteen children, seven daughters and eight sons. The mansion became popular for social functions, and among the famous who visited were the Marquis de Lafayette, Baron Von Steuben, Captain Stephen Decatur, Henry Clay, Daniel Webster, and such presidents as Adams, Jefferson, Madison, Monroe, and Jackson. The mansion itself became instantly as celebrated as its guests because it was an architectural masterpiece that featured an elegant center hall, which, in turn, was the landing for an impressive elliptical-shaped staircase spiraling its way up to the building's third floor. Since Colonel Tayloe first opened the doors of the Octagon House to his rich and powerful guests, the mansion has become the home to a number of spirits.

The most famous ghosts among the apparitions witnessed in the Octagon House were President and Mrs. Madison, who continued to haunt the mansion through the nineteenth century as if the balls they were attending would never come to an end. But the story of spiritual manifestations in the Octagon goes much farther. After the Madisons no longer lent their presence to the mansion, witnesses reported having seen several specters materialize on the towering staircase. In particular, people noticed the ghost of an exceedingly pretty young woman falling or, worse, leaping over the second-floor banister and plunging twenty feet to her death. This ghost might have been Colonel Tayloe's youngest daughter who incited her father's wrath by falling in love with a British officer whom he had forbidden her to see. The angry colonel confronted his distraught daughter on the staircase, where she was standing, and they argued. Then they fought, and finally with a bloodcurdling scream, she either accidentally fell or deliberately jumped over the railing to her death right before the eyes of her horrified father. Many believe her apparition haunts the Octagon House because her life was cut short at a moment of intense energy or frustration.

Hers is not the only macabre phenomenon around the area of the staircase. Witnesses have reported hearing the plaintive cries of a grief-stricken woman and the scuffle of unexplained footsteps, seeing mysterious footprints suddenly appear on the floor, or watching doors that seem to open and close by themselves. Others have stood terrified as lights inexplicably switched themselves on or have watched in fear as the carpeting at a particular spot at the foot of the stairs draws itself back to expose the bare floor. That same spot at the bottom of the great oval staircase is also the focus of a report, in recent years, concerning a burst of frigid air that chills visitors to their very bones even on warm or hot summer days. Cold spots are sometimes called "psychic winds," breezes or gusts from another dimension that can be produced by a nearby spirit presence.

Some psychics who'd visited the Octagon concluded that this was the very spot at the foot of the stairs where Tayloe's other forlorn daughter plummeted to her untimely death from the upper-floor landing. The tragedy may have been accidental, although one version claims this daughter despaired after her father thwarted her attempt to elope. Colonel Tayloe's grief and guilt over his daughters' deaths was overwhelming. Although many historians consider the stories of the Tayloe daughters' deaths to be legend, witness accounts have long persisted. Tayloe's own granddaughter wrote that, after he died, house bells rang on their own, and "everyone said that the house was haunted."

Could the ghost on the staircase be someone other than one of Tayloe's daughters? Perhaps it is the spirit of a teenage servant girl who had caught the eye of a lascivious British officer. Frightened after the soldier's repeated advances, the girl fled the officer who had entered the house to chase her down and then, in a panic, either fell or jumped over the banister to her death three floors below. Or maybe the officer, furious that his attentions had been spurned, simply murdered the girl and threw her over the railing, leaving her ghost to haunt the scene of her bloody death.

The Tayloe family resided in the Octagon until Mrs. Tayloe's death in 1855. However, that did not stop later claims of phantom footmen flagging down coaches for notable visitors. These visions seemed to end by the close of the nineteenth century, during which period the Octagon was first occupied by a school and then later by government offices. Today the building is the property of the American Institute of Architects who purchased it in 1899. In the 1950s, a caretaker reported witnessing an apparition in early 1800s military dress. Then in the 1960s, an invisible presence turned lights on and off. In more recent years, witnesses and employees told of seeing or sensing spirits in the vicinity of the famed staircase as well as on the upstairs floors. Institute officials have been reticent about the subject of hauntings, but many people have no doubt that the ghosts in the Octagon are still active.

The Capitol Building

Not only do the living members of the legislature and their support staffs occupy the Capitol Building, where the U.S. Congress sits, but the spirits of the departed also roam the halls and offices, silent watchers from the Other Side. In 1898, the *Philadelphia Press* reported no fewer than fifteen ghosts actively haunting the Capitol Building, among whom, famed architect Major Pierre L'Enfant, chosen by George Washington himself to design the new "Federal City" at the end of the eighteenth century, was the most frequently sighted. It is probably for good reason that L'Enfant still stalks the halls because Congress, despite its many promises, never paid the architect for his work, and in his last years he unceasingly tried to get the money owed him, efforts that ended in futility and desperation. The deeply embittered L'Enfant died in poverty, his spirit unable to resolve the government's refusal to pay him, and so his ghost remains bound to this earth, still seeking its recompense. His apparition, when seen in the Capitol, holds a parchment, the bill for the monies so long due him. But there are many other ghosts who keep the angry L'Enfant company.

The ghosts of Presidents John Quincy Adams and James Garfield—as well as Garfield's assassin—have all been witnessed in the Capitol Building. As well, in Statuary Hall, inexplicable footsteps have been heard, and the apparitions of several lesser-known political figures have appeared to startled tourists. There, at least one congressmen and two speakers of the House have also been seen.

In the Capitol's Rotunda, witnesses reported seeing the specter of a worker who fell to his death in the 1860s when the Rotunda was being built, still holding his wooden tray of tools. Keeping him company is the apparition of a stone mason, whose terrible fate was to be shut within a wall when the Senate was being constructed in the 1790s. Witnesses have noticed him slipping through a Senate basement wall. John Lenthall, an engineer crushed to death when bricks fell from a passageway that tumbled down in 1808, is another spirit whose manifestations have terrified witnesses. He placed a curse on the entire Capitol Building when he died, and years later, Lenthall's malevolent ghost caused the Capitol's walls to crumble, columns to split, and the building's foundation to become unsteady—a rare and frightening instance where an angry ghost exerted actual physical influence over a structure and exacted revenge for his fate after death. Over the years, several other phantom employees also returned, victims of the many accidents that have befallen craftsmen and laborers at the site.

In addition to workers, there are reports of soldiers from wars long past who may haunt the Capitol, marching from time to time in solemn procession in the dead of night. Witnesses have seen the ghost of a Revolutionary War soldier, in full uniform, pass by the now-empty Washington crypt where our first president may originally have been laid to rest before his body was moved to Mt. Vernon. Also, the specter of a World War I infantryman, believed to be the young soldier whose body was placed in the Tomb of the Unknown Soldier at Arlington National Cemetery, has been seen. But when spotted by living witnesses, the ghost hurriedly saluted and then vanished.

One of the most celebrated spirits at the Capitol might be that of Henry Wilson, Grant's vice president, who had such a passion for baths he spent inordinate amounts of time in his tub even when he should have been tending to the duties of office. In November 1875, Wilson died from pneumonia after becoming severely chilled when he emerged into the icy air straight from a steaming hot bath. It has been said that strong emotional connections often draw spirits back to earth. If that's true, then there is logic to the manifestation of Wilson's soapsuds-covered apparition, which startled more than one witness when it appeared near his old office still hacking and sneezing from the effects of a severe cold.

One of the most bone-chilling specters ever reported in the Capitol was the Demon Cat, which for years was said to haunt the basement, piercing the dank night air with shrill and horrifying howls. In the 1950s, the hellish entity swelled to the size of a tiger, according to a frightened guard who saw the entity grow before his very eyes, until it vanished into the darkness. Terrified security men also saw the Demon Cat fifty years before in 1898 and, earlier still, in 1862. When once a sentry shot at the phantom, it disappeared. Some thought the chilling specter was an omen that foretold bad news.

Rathbone House

Although President Lincoln's apparition may well be the most sighted ghost in Washington, both at the White

House and the Lincoln Memorial, the ghosts of his cabal of assassins still roam the earth, their tortured souls, no doubt, condemned to linger among the living where they may repent their terrible crime. They are the guilty, but what of the innocent people present the night of Lincoln's murder whose spirits also returned, unable to find any more peace in the afterlife than they did here on earth? Are they to suffer along with the guilty simply because they were in President Lincoln's company in his final hours? This is the fate of Henry Rathbone.

On the night the president was shot and killed at Ford's Theater, Mr. and Mrs. Lincoln were joined in the official box by Major Henry Rathbone and his fiancée Clara Harris. As John Wilkes Booth made his escape, Rathbone attempted to tackle the assassin and in the struggle was stabbed in the head and neck. Although Rathbone physically recovered from his serious wounds, the psychological damage was permanent, and as a result, he suffered from depression and severe mood swings. Rathbone resigned his military commission soon thereafter, married Clara in 1867, and moved with her to Germany, where he'd hoped to start a new life. But the change in residence from Washington, where they'd lived on Jackson Place in Lafayette Square, did nothing to erase the traumatic memories of the president's assassination. Rathbone continued to plummet emotionally, and in 1883, as the family prepared for a trip back to the United States, he fell into a fit of madness, shot Clara to death, and attempted to murder their children before he was stopped by a nurse. Rathbone attempted to take his own life, but survived his self-inflicted gunshot wounds and spent the rest of his life in an insane asylum. His crime was one of the earliest attempts at mass murder and suicide in the annals of true crime.

After Rathbone's death, many people living near his former home in Washington told of hearing an unusual wailing emanating from inside the house. The cries were so frightening that passersby crossed the street, fully aware of the tragedy of the Rathbones, and petrified that somehow they would be touched by it if they dared venture near the house. The moaning from the tormented ghosts eventually became too much to bear, and the house on Lafayette Square was torn down.

Mary Surratt's Boardinghouse and the Plot to Assassinate Lincoln

John Wilkes Booth did not act alone in his plot to kill President Lincoln. Nor was he simply a crazed gunman. In fact, he'd formed a band of conspirators with the intention of assassinating several top government officials, including Vice President Andrew Johnson, Secretary of State William Seward, and if he'd been in Lincoln's box at Ford's Theater on the night of the murder, General Grant. This was a well-planned and nearly executed coup d'état, whose purpose went beyond the removal of the president. Its intent was to derail Reconstruction and undo the results of the Emancipation Proclamation even if it couldn't actually reverse Union victory in the Civil War. In part, because of the Jim Crow laws in the latter part of the nineteenth century and the U.S. Supreme Court's legalization of segregation under Plessy v. Ferguson, Booth and his conspirators got what they wanted. However, with the exception of the killing of Lincoln, all of Booth's assassination attempts went awry, and it wasn't long before the traitors in Booth's gang were caught. Booth and coconspirator David Herold were trapped in a barn on Garrett's Farm in Virginia. Soldiers hoping to force Booth from the barn set it on fire. However, Booth never got the chance to surrender, as Herold had done, because he was shot and killed by the soldiers despite orders to capture him alive.

Authorities also had two of Booth's other coconspirators under arrest: George Atzerodt and Louis Payne, also known as Louis Powell. There was never any question about their complicity in the president's assassination because the evidence of their guilt was apparent. However, there was a fourth individual whose guilt was truly in doubt: Mary Surratt, who owned the boardinghouse on H Street where Booth and his crew secretly met to plot the assassination. Because the authorities believed her to be a coconspirator and an accomplice, Mrs. Surratt was arrested and charged despite her vehement protests that she had no knowledge of what the men were furtively talking about and, thus, no prior knowledge of the crime. Although Mrs. Surratt admitted that Booth had often been to her boardinghouse, she claimed she hardly knew him or understood his intentions. However, despite her pleas of innocence, she could not deny that her son, John, was heavily implicated in the assassination conspiracy. This turned out to be another piece of damning evidence against her.

Mrs. Surratt's claims of innocence were overwhelmed in the climate of fever-pitched emotions that gripped Washington and the nation after the president's murder. Mrs. Surratt was convicted along with the three other conspirators. Meanwhile, her son eluded authorities by escaping to Canada and then to Europe. Two years later when John Surratt was returned to stand trial, passions had calmed and he received a light sentence. His mother, however, suffered quite a different fate. The court sentenced her to be executed.

Less than three months after Lincoln was assassinated, the death sentences imposed on the four were carried out. On July 7, a sweltering day in Washington, the coconspirators were hanged on a scaffold built within the grounds of the old Arsenal Penitentiary. Up to the very end, Mrs. Surratt vociferously insisted she was innocent. Later, many agreed with her, believing she had been unfairly executed. Even if she knew more than she admitted to police, once tempers cooled, many felt the punishment for her conviction—her foreknowledge of the conspiracy—was grossly disproportionate to her crime itself. Given the tragic and emotion-charged circumstances of Mrs. Surratt's death, it is no wonder that her disconsolate ghost had been seen or heard in several locations, one of which was the tavern she and her husband once owned in Maryland.

After Mrs. Surratt's execution, her daughter, Annie, tried to sell the three-story boardinghouse. It stayed on the market for a while, but because of the stigma of guilt attached to it, the building sold for much less than it was worth. The new owners did not remain long, nor did subsequent owners, apparently driven away by inexplicable groaning, long doleful cries, and voices that drifted from an upper floor. It was assumed the mournful phantom was Mrs. Surratt, bemoaning her fate, unable to find peace in the next stage of life because of the injustice done to her in this life.

Old Brick Capitol

Not only did Mrs. Surratt's ghost haunt her old boardinghouse—it also haunted the Old Brick Capitol, where she was held when it was used as a prison. The building was demolished in the early 1900s and became the location of the U.S. Supreme Court. But back when the Old Brick Capitol stood, there were reports that every July 7, the anniversary of her execution, Mrs. Surratt's specter was seen in the window of her jail cell, where, the witnesses reported, she could be seen crying bitterly while she gripped the iron bars as tightly as she could as if to shake them loose. Since the day she was falsely accused, wrongfully convicted, and hanged, Mrs. Surratt's tormented ghost has also been reported visiting the grounds of the Arsenal Penitentiary, walking to the very spot where she was executed.

Fort Lesley McNair

Mrs. Surratt's apparition has also been seen drifting through the courtyard of Fort Lesley McNair, not far from Capitol Hill and the Arsenal Penitentiary. Originally the four bodies were buried under the gallows, but later they were moved to grave sites. Where Mrs. Surratt was first buried there grew a boxwood tree that, because the growth was so quick and the foliage so robust, many people believed it to have been a sign that Mrs. Surratt was not guilty and had herself been the victim of a rush to judgment.

Whether it appears at the old boardinghouse, the Old Brick Capitol, Fort McNair, or the Arsenal Penitentiary, Mary Surratt's ghost is indeed a restless spirit. Perhaps still searching for peace through vindication, Mrs. Surratt's tortured specter is condemned to walk the earth, bitter and frustrated, until her innocence is proven and her good name restored.

Annie Surratt's Ghost

Distraught and desperate about her mother's imminent execution, on July 6, the evening before the hanging, Annie Surratt attempted to appeal directly to President Andrew Johnson by pushing her way onto the White House grounds, where she futilely banged on the front door and sobbed in a heartrending plea to save her mother's life. Security officers pulled her away, and the president never heard her appeal directly. For many years thereafter, witnesses claimed that on every July 6, Annie's ghost returned to the White House to plead for her mother's life, just as she had the night before Mary went to the gallows.

Ford's Theater

Ford's Theater on Tenth Street, the scene of President Lincoln's assassination, was a place so emotionally charged from the heinous and violent act that it could not escape from becoming haunted. Ford's closed following Lincoln's death, its reputation horribly defamed. But more than a hundred years later, in 1968, when it was reopened as both a theater and museum, actors reported sensing a bitter cold sensation on one part of left center stage. Some performers complained they'd become nauseous and frightened, and they shivered to the point where they couldn't remember their lines. Well-known actor Hal Holbrook, who performed at Ford's following its reopening, was among those who acknowledged he'd felt something he could not explain. Mediums who'd visited the theater determined the disturbances were the result of psychic energy that still remained there a hundred years later after Lincoln's death. It was, perhaps, a legacy, a pure force of hatred and evil that still hung in the air from the villainous John Wilkes Booth after he fired the fatal bullet, jumped to the stage in fury, and hobbled across the floorboards to escape.

Mathew Brady, the most famous photographer of the Civil War era, took pictures of the ill-fated box at Ford's where Lincoln sat on the night of his assassination. When the daguerreotype was developed, it was said to reveal the near-translucent presence of none other than John Wilkes Booth peering through the curtain at the moment before he crept behind the president and fired the fatal round into Abraham Lincoln's head. Whether this story is true or a legend, it has been said that the intense energy exuded by people at the moments of their greatest calamity can actually be recorded on a photographic medium. If, indeed, Mathew Brady captured the ghostly apparition of John Wilkes Booth on a photographic plate, this might explain why.

The malevolent spirit of John Wilkes Booth not only burned its image into Mathew Brady's photographic plate—it also manifests itself in Ford's Theater itself. From time to time since the theater's reopening, according to some reports, actors, stagehands, and even audience members have told of being startled by the apparition of Booth, whose soul is doomed to wander as a result of the heinous murder he committed as well as his treason and conspiracy. Considering the enormity of the tragedy, and the many unanswered questions concerning the circumstances and the conspirators, it is not surprising that Booth along with the other figures involved in the assassination should remain earthbound where they relive their unresolved agony. Many spirits, whose commission of terrible crimes binds them to the earth, are unable to move on to the Other Side until, after many years, they've endured their portion of the pain they inflicted on their victims.

Holt House

As if Booth, his coconspirators, and Mary Surratt were not enough, even Judge Advocate General Joseph Holt, who pronounced the death sentence for the three conspirators and Mrs. Surratt, was doomed to become a wandering spirit. The federal justice was so troubled by the possibility that he'd sent an innocent woman to the gallows that he tortured himself until his death over how he had sealed her fate. Following the hangings of the four, Holt secluded himself, remaining in his house like a hermit, obsessively rereading the trial transcripts as if he were looking for one piece of information that might allow him to exonerate himself for the verdict he pronounced upon Mrs. Surratt. But his efforts did not avail him, and he died an unhappy and guilt-ridden man whose fate was to haunt the house he once lived in.

In the years following Holt's death, the new residents reported hearing inexplicable footsteps as if someone troubled were repeatedly walking back and forth, sometimes for hours. Was it the restless ghost of Judge Holt fomenting over the death sentence he meted out to Mrs. Surratt? Did he still agonize about her guilt or innocence? Maybe his spirit is a victim of the injustice done to Mary Surratt in the wake of the public fury following, not only the assassination of the president, but the realization that it had been a part of a larger conspiracy in response to which the retribution of justice consumed the innocent as well as the guilty.

Even after the judge's house was demolished, his solitary apparition was seen dressed in his Civil War uniform and great cape, carefully making its way through the foggy night along First Street in Washington. Some thought the ghost was heading for the jail in the Old

Brick Capitol to put, yet again, questions to the imprisoned Mary Surratt, still trying to resolve the perplexing mysteries about her role—if any—in the assassination.

John Calhoun's Residence

After the British torched the halls of Congress during the War of 1812, the Legislature met for several years in the Old Brick Capitol at the intersection of First and East Capitol streets, which later became a residence and then a Civil War prison. At the site of the Old Brick Capitol building today is the U.S. Supreme Court. This is indeed an important intersection replete with history.

For example, when the celebrated Southern orator John C. Calhoun lived in the Old Brick Capitol building, he was visited by George Washington's spirit, which warned him against the South's secession from the Union. Following Calhoun's death in 1850, his ghost eventually returned, deeply troubled by secession and the resulting Civil War. Among other spirits who'd made their presence known in the former prison were the infamous Confederate spy Belle Boyd, who was once confined there and, of course, Mary Surratt.

Decatur House

U.S. Navy Captain Stephen Decatur was the commander of the American attack on the Barbary pirates in Tunis and Algiers in 1815 that succeeded in ending pirate attacks on American merchant shipping in the Mediterranean. Upon his return from that engagement in 1815, in a now-famous toast, he was quoted as wishing that our country might always be in the right in its dealings with foreign nations: "But right or wrong, our country." He is still revered today as a great naval hero who led the marines "to the shores of Tripoli" in 1804, when, in one of the most successful and daring lightning expeditions in U.S. Navy history, he burned the frigate USS

Philadelphia, which had fallen into the hands of North African pirates. Decatur became a navy commissioner and lived in a three-story brick building in the Lafayette Square area of Washington, D.C., which has come to be known as the Decatur House. Prior to the War of 1812, Decatur urged that Captain James Barron be court-martialed for failing to resist a British warship at sea, allowing his frigate, the USS *Chesapeake*, to be boarded, and his crew to be detained when British officers searched for navy deserters who, they said, were serving under Barron's command. Barron was convicted and dismissed from the navy, after which Decatur became captain of the *Chesapeake*. Not surprisingly, the animosity Barron felt toward Decatur festered until it swelled to such violent anger that Barron challenged Decatur to a duel years after the War of 1812 had ended.

Not wanting to worry his wife, Decatur did not tell her about the duel and, unbeknownst to her, quietly slipped away for his ill-fated appointment after a sleepless night. The two men met on the morning of March 14, 1820, in nearby Badinburg, Maryland, and Decatur, fatally wounded from a single shot by Barron, was taken by carriage back to his home where he died soon after. As one might expect, Mrs. Decatur was overcome by the terrible turn of events and spent the rest of her life in mourning.

Those passing by Decatur's house after his untimely death reported seeing the forlorn apparition of the late naval hero gazing from a first-floor bedroom window, just as he had the entire night before the duel, likely still regretting the folly of his agreeing to fight a duel with a deadly marksman like James Barron. Subsequent owners of the house did their best to keep Decatur's ghost from the window by having the glass panes blocked off and covered with an unmovable shutter to disguise the wall. Thus, they hoped, the troubled specter would be prevented from staring out the window. But spirit phenomena aren't bound by physical strictures, and so Decatur's wraith simply resumed its tortured existence elsewhere in the house. In recent years, his specter has been witnessed as it exited through the rear door of his former home, carrying a small black velvet box that held his dueling pistols. Mrs. Decatur's disconsolate spirit has also been heard crying, no doubt unable to resolve the tragic circumstances that ended her husband's life on earth.

Halcyon House

In 1813, the nation's first secretary of the navy, Benjamin Stoddard, passed on, his final years having been spent alone and in misery after he'd become both incapacitated and indigent. Ironically, Stoddard had named his home near M Street in the fashionable Georgetown section the Halcyon House, after the mythical bird who could calm the oceans. Following Stoddard's death, however, his house was anything but peaceful as witnesses reported hearing inexplicable groans, whispered words that could not be understood, and persistent knocking sounds. Frightened visitors also talked about an apparition that materialized out of the walls.

Once a stop on the Underground Railroad for escaped slaves during the Civil War, in the 1930s, Halcyon House became the property of Albert A. Clemens, an eccentric and emotionally unstable man who proceeded to reconstruct the house in a most bizarre fashion. He added doors that opened only to walls, the attic became a "religious shrine," and he built a stairway that led nowhere. The Halcyon's coach house was converted into a crypt, and the garden became a burial ground for mummies. Among his other peculiar additions and changes, Clemens disconnected the house's electrical supply and capped off the internal wiring. Apparently he believed his alterations would allow him to live forever. However, as all mortals must, Clemens passed on in 1938, unable to cheat death.

Following his passing, subsequent owners of the property reported strange incidents throughout the 1940s and 1950s, including inexplicable electrical disturbances in the now rewired house. Then, in the 1960s and the early 1970s after the building had been converted to an apartment building, a rare phenomenon was reported: levitations of at least three people who slept in an upstairs bedroom. Also in the 1970s, the apparition of a woman was seen on several occasions. In more recent years, residents in one particular apartment in the Halcyon House said they'd heard someone walking in the unoccupied attic above them.

The ghosts of both unhappy and troubled men, Stoddard and Clemens, still call the Halcyon their home. They've been sighted on the staircase, close by an old worn chair in a drawing room, and in several other unlit rooms. In a city where finding a decent apartment has always been difficult, the ghosts of Stoddard and Clemens made life intolerable indeed for the building's residents.

The Old Pension Building

When President Grover Cleveland held his inaugural ball, he chose the huge Pension Building on Judiciary Square, which was originally the location of a jail and insane asylum. The large, ugly brick edifice, erected in 1885 at a price of fifteen million dollars, ultimately became the government's office of Veterans Affairs. The concept for the building was suggested by U.S. Quartermaster General Montgomery Meigs whose design included eight Corinthian solid onyx columns to be built in the huge hall of the building. However, to Meigs's extreme displeasure, the government, in an effort to save money, only allowed hollow columns to be erected and covered them with an imitation onyx facade. Meigs decided to make use of the empty pillars by placing invaluable papers that had belonged to the nation's Founding Fathers inside them. Among the documents was possible evidence about the assassination of President Lincoln, which Meigs was given by Lincoln's eldest son, Robert, who was certain that he'd found explosive material about his father's murder that could "tear the country apart." To prevent the information from becoming public, the documents were securely stored in the unfilled columns.

In 1917, a guard rubbed his eyes in disbelief when he noticed that an image of the head of an Indian accompanied by the outline of a buffalo had somehow suddenly appeared amid the raised relief on one of the columns. It was the strangest thing he'd ever seen. The next day, famed Buffalo Bill Cody died. Had the appearance of the image signaled a portent of events to come? Was General Meigs's spirit responsible for the sign? Many thought so. Several months later, there were more changes when the onyx columns bore the image of a skull with an evil sneer. In the next few years, more faces were seen, among them those of George and Martha Washington.

So intense and frequent had the strange faces become that in the late 1920s, government officials had the supernatural countenances painted over so they couldn't be seen. The building then became the property of the District of Columbia Supreme Court. But whoever painted over the faces underestimated the power of ghostly presences, for they remained and reappeared in the form of "wandering shades." One night during the Depression years, a terrified guard fled the building after he claimed he was pursued by a soldier's specter riding a horse.

Throughout the ensuing years, many more ghosts were seen. One was James Tanner, who'd been the official court recorder of the Federal Court and had transcribed testimony from those who'd been eyewitnesses to President Lincoln's assassination. Tanner had long been hopeful that someday more would be told about the crime. Later in life, he worked in the Pension Building and then went on to lecture publicly about the murder.

One night in 1972, a guard in the Old Pension Building noticed and pursued a shadowy form in the corridor. When he looked more closely, he saw a man with an unusual manner of walking. The guard cautiously moved behind the stranger, hoping to ask him why he was in the building, when suddenly the man spun and looked straight into the guard's face. Terrified, the guard let out a chilling cry and quickly fled the building. When next seen wandering on Pennsylvania Avenue, the shaken guard told police he'd seen a man with no eyes who "smelled of the stench of the dead." It was surely the ghost of William Tanner who'd lost both his feet from a Civil War injury, which explained the specter's odd walk.

Francis Scott Key House

Francis Scott Key, who composed "The Star-Spangled Banner" while watching the burning of Fort McHenry from the deck of a British warship in Baltimore Harbor, lived for more than thirty years in a house on M Street in Georgetown, which he built in 1802. Key adored his home so much that throughout the late nineteenth century, long after he died, his ghost returned to haunt the place, likely because the owners wanted to renovate the property. Once they did, a ghostly torment began with terrifying moans, mysterious bloodstains on the attic ceiling, and floorboards that creaked from an invisible entity moving across them. As years went by, the house fell into disrepair, the haunting worsened, and by the 1920s, no one wanted to live there. Finally the house was renovated and restored to its original appearance during the years when Key called it home. Mysteriously as it had begun, the ghostly phenomena stopped. However, when the house on M Street was demolished for a freeway ramp to be constructed, Francis Scott Key's spirit materialized to construction workers, obviously still emotionally attached to his former home and unsettled about its demise.

Fort McHenry

Fort McHenry, in Baltimore harbor, is best known as the site of the British nighttime naval bombardment during the War of 1812 that inspired Francis Scott Key to compose the lyrics to "The Star-Spangled Banner." Key had been detained on board a British frigate during the attack on the Baltimore forts defending the city, and the day after Fort McHenry successfully resisted the attack from mortar-lobbing bomb ketches, naval cannon fire, and Congreve's rockets, Key was released. He returned to a Baltimore hotel, where he wrote a poem about the valiant defense of Baltimore, which became the national anthem.

Years after the War of 1812, there were frequent accounts of hauntings at Fort McHenry, including inexplicable heavy footsteps, electrical disturbances, windows flinging themselves open and shut, the sound of furniture moving itself across the brick floor, and doors that unlocked themselves. During the War of 1812, the building where the ghostly incidents occurred was a soldiers' barracks, and while the Civil War raged, Confederate prisoners were confined there.

According to authors Richard Winer and Nancy Osborn in *Haunted Houses*, "Shadowy figures have been seen prowling the walls and ramparts of Fort McHenry for as far back as anyone can remember."

According to at least one theory about the hauntings, one of the ghosts is the spirit of an American soldier killed by the British in September 1814; he now lurks in a part of the fort where he hid when the invaders stormed into the compound. A second specter is thought to be that of a Union soldier who fell asleep while at his sentry post during the Civil War. For neglecting his duty, the soldier was court-martialed and sentenced to a firing squad. However, before the sentence could be carried out, the condemned prisoner found a way to commit suicide with a smuggled gun. Since his death, his disconsolate spirit must march eternal rounds along the parapets of the fort as its perpetual penalty for the sentry's dereliction of duty in life.

In 1976, for the celebration of the American Bicentennial, President Gerald Ford selected Fort McHenry, now a national monument administered by the National Park

Service, as the location for the kickoff ceremony. The night before the gala event, the White House Secret Service detail and federal park rangers swept through the fort to clear each building, a necessary security measure in advance of the president's arrival. The festivities were scheduled to begin at "the dawn's early light."

Each building was examined, then locked by security personnel while guards were positioned on the fort walls. At the moment the men went to close and lock two large doors, a park ranger glimpsed a shadow in the window of one of the buildings and quickly notified the Secret Service agents, some of whom also admitted to witnessing the shadow. Weapons at the ready and accompanied by guard dogs straining at their leashes, they ran down the corridor to check the identity of the intruder. But they found no one. Had the "shadowy" form at the window been the specter of the young Union soldier whose spirit was atoning for his neglect of duty by acting as a sentry in 1976 to protect President Ford from danger? Whoever or whatever it was, it simply slipped back to the Other Side and disappeared into history.

Daniel Sickles House

Theresa Sickles was a beautiful young woman unhappily married to Representative Daniel Sickles, a former aide to President James Buchanan. In the years just before the Civil War, the couple, who lived on Lafayette Square and were members of Washington's exclusive social circle, entertained the city's power elite at parties in their home. But Sickles was so involved in politics he had left little time for his wife, who grew lonely and turned her affections to an attractive widower named Philip Barton Key, the son of Francis Scott Key. The affair between Theresa and Philip couldn't be kept secret for long, and it was soon a lively topic of gossip inside what people today call the Beltway. Sickles learned of his wife's infidelity through an anonymous letter and was properly outraged.

Theresa Sickles tearfully admitted the truth when her husband confronted her with the accusation, devastating him and ultimately driving him into a jealous fury. It wasn't just the image of his wife in the arms of another man that made Sickles seethe with rage; it was the public humiliation he felt at the slap to his honor and reputation his wife's extramarital affair had caused. He'd been played the fool, and all of Washington knew it. But how could he exact revenge?

Several days later, Sickles noticed the well-dressed Philip Key walking by his house on his way to the Washington Club across the street. When Key waved a white handkerchief, possibly a sign of submission and a peace offering to the outraged husband, Sickles believed it was a signal to his wife for another clandestine rendezvous. That was all the enraged Sickles could stand. He ran down the street after Key—now with his pistols in hand—to the Washington Club and waited by the door until Key came out. Shouting, "Key, you scoundrel, you dishonored my house. You must die," Sickles aimed the weapons, pulled the triggers, and shot Key to death on the doorstep of the Washington Club. Sickles was arrested and charged with murder. However, he was found not guilty by reason of "temporary aberration of mind," a verdict that marked the first time the temporary insanity defense was used successfully in a U.S. murder trial. But the affair didn't end with Key's death and Sickles's verdict of insanity. Key's ghost returned, and many witnesses in the subsequent months reported seeing Key's ghost in front of the Washington Club pacing back and forth at the spot where he'd been shot to death.

By the time of the Civil War, the once-fashionable Washington Club had closed its doors as a commercial establishment and become a private residence, where one of the old club's most important residents was President Lincoln's secretary of state, William Seward. Seward, who had purchased the territory of Alaska from Russia, was also one of the intended targets of John Wilkes Booth's conspiracy to kill top government officials. Booth had ordered Louis Payne, one of the members of his group of assassins, to kill Seward, who was recuperating at home from serious injuries suffered in a carriage accident. Booth's plan was simple. Payne was to sneak into Seward's house as if he were a common thief, stab the secretary of state to death, and phony up a crime scene to make it look like a cat burglary gone awry.

On the night of the assassination attempt, although Payne's furtive break-in was meant to proceed silently, something went wrong when an inexplicably loud noise awakened Seward's son and a servant. Alarmed that either Seward himself had fallen or there was an intruder, they arose, ran to the secretary of state's bedroom, and saved him from Powell, whose dagger blade was poised only inches above Seward's chest, seconds away from the killer's final plunge. All agreed that had it not been for the mysterious crash, they would have discovered Seward's murdered body the next morning instead of an assassination in progress during the night. But what could have explained the noises? Many paranormal experts believe to this day that the loud crash was caused by the ghost of the patriotic Philip Barton Key, sending out a dire warning of the assassination attempt by psychokinetically causing the clamor and thus saving Seward's life.

And what fate awaited Daniel Sickles, whose murder of Philip Barton Key may well have saved the life of Secretary of State Seward? After being found temporarily insane by the court and remanded to the care of his doctors, Sickles was eventually judged fully recovered from his bout of insanity and in no further need of medical treatment. Thereupon he was freed from all further culpability in Key's murder. Sickles received an officer's commission in the U.S. Army and became a commander of a volunteer regiment during the Civil War, in which he served with honor. Leading his men against a Confederate position at the Battle of Gettysburg, Sickles was seriously wounded by flying shot; in order to save his life, the field surgeons amputated his leg. Sickles then proudly donated his severed leg to the Medical Museum of the Armed Forces Institute of Pathology in Washington, where it was put on display in a glass case. After his death, Sickles's ghost returned to the museum, where an employee said she saw a stout shadow with one leg—an accurate physical description of Sickles after the war—hovering near the case that contained his amputated limb.

Washington Club

After the affair between Sickles and Philip Key and after the assassination attempt on Seward, the building that housed the Washington Club and Seward's residence became a stage for the playing out of other tragedies in the years that followed. After he survived Payne's assassination attempt and tried to console himself after the death of President Lincoln, Seward suffered personal calamity again when his wife and daughter died, one right after the other. In 1869, a broken and dispirited Seward moved out, and soon stories circulated that a diabolical spirit still resided in the house, churning up nothing but evil. As a result, people were fearful of living there. In the 1880s, the YMCA moved in, but also left after supernatural disruptions attributed to Seward's tortured spirit. Because no one would reside in the haunted edifice it was demolished in 1895. Once the building where he'd known so much tragedy was gone, Seward's troubled ghost was not heard from again.

St. John's Church

The legend of St. John's Church, on Lafayette Square, says that each time a renowned American leader passes on, the specters of six famed Washingtonians materialize at exactly midnight in the church's Pew of the Presidents. Erected in 1821, many U.S. presidents attended the historic brick church with its distinctive three-leveled steeple and columns.

Old Stone House

Old Stone House, a popular museum on M Street, was once a haunted farmhouse dating back to 1795, where no less than eleven ghosts were reportedly sighted by witnesses. One notorious entity earned such a reputation for violence against women that merely entering the room where the evil presence lurks is perilous for any female. The spirit is said to be capable of harassment, sexual assault, and other forms of violence.

Other and gentler spirits in the house include a young woman's wraith seen on the stairs and the specter of another woman in eighteenth-century dress near a fireplace. Another ghost is that of a heavyset woman in nineteenth-century attire. There is also the specter of a man wearing what appear to be eighteenth-century knee breeches. The ghost of another man with long hair has been spotted near a window in the front room. Many believe one of the apparitions is the original owner, Christopher Layman, who built the house in 1795. Still other spirits are those of a young boy who runs through a hallway and a small African-American child. The ghost of a man in Colonial clothing has appeared on the second floor of the three-story building.

Why so many hauntings in one house? Each had some strong emotional connection to the building that he or she has yet to release. Today the Old Stone House is still a museum, run by the National Park Service, but there are no scheduled evening hours.

Henry Adams House

One evening in the 1880s, noted historian Henry Adams came home to find his ailing wife, Marion, dead, lying near the fireplace in their house on H Street in Lafayette Square. Because Adams was strangely silent about her death, rumors quickly spread that he'd neglected her or was somehow responsible for her death. Still behaving strangely, Adams ordered that her gravestone make no reference to her name or dates of her birth and death. Later, in his autobiography, Adams also omitted any reference to his wife. But Marion Adams would soon have her revenge.

Not long after Henry Adams died, neighbors said the house was haunted by the ghost of Mrs. Adams. When sunset came, they reported hearing a woman's sobs, which many were certain came from her unhappy spirit. Those who later lived in the house said they'd experienced a "cold spot" in front of the fireplace where Mrs. Adams' body had been found. Her specter was also seen sitting in a rocking chair in her former bedroom. Witnesses said the apparition gazed into the eyes of those who saw her, and would not stop staring until the person shrieked in fright. Only then did the ghostly presence of Marion Adams vanish.

National Theater

The National Theater on E and Thirteenth Streets was erected in the 1830s. Shortly after it opened, a good-looking young actor was killed by a jealous fellow performer. Years later, after the theater was remodeled, witnesses said the murdered actor's spirit returned. Theater employees told of seeing the young actor's ghost, and a night watchman also claimed he confronted the specter in the theater's basement.

Fort Monroe

Although Fort Monroe is not located in Washington, but in Virginia, so many ghosts of prominent Americans have been seen there that the site bears mention. In 1834, when the huge fortress was built facing Chesapeake Bay, it was the only one in the country entirely surrounded by a moat. During the Civil War, even though the sturdy stone fort was located in Virginia, the capital state of the Confederacy, it remained under the control of Union forces; as many as fourteen hundred personnel and dependents once lived there. The Confederates did not dare attack, although they surely would have liked to take the fort to protect their own navy from blockading Union warships.

Fort Monroe's phantom visitors over the years form an impressive list of apparitions of the famous, among whom are Captain John Smith, the Marquis de Lafayette, and Edgar Allan Poe, who briefly served at the fort and returned there to give a poetry reading only a month before his death. The ghosts of both President Lincoln and General Grant have also been encountered there perhaps because Grant was believed to have planned his final military campaign of the Civil War with members of his general staff inside the fortified compound.

When the war ended, the President of the Confederate States, Jefferson Davis, was captured and imprisoned within Fort Monroe, where he was shackled in a casemate cell. Davis's ghost has returned to that cell, still shackled to his earthly pain. Across from his cell, witnesses told of seeing the apparition of Davis's wife, Varna, gazing in his direction, her portly ghost despairing about his humiliating imprisonment and the mistreatment she believed he'd suffered.

By far, the fort's most famous apparition is known as the "Luminous Lady," Camille Kirtz, the wife of Captain Wilhelm Kirtz, who lived there during the Civil War period. Camille was a young woman who wanted more from life than her jealous and abusive husband could give her, so she began a love affair with a dashing young officer. Kirtz learned of the illicit liaison when he unexpectedly returned from a military trip and to his shock found his wife and the soldier in one another's arms. The furious Kirtz immediately drew and fired his service revolver at the young officer, but blinded by his rage, he missed his target. He mortally wounded his wife instead. Kirtz was arrested for her murder, served time in prison, and years later went back to the fort, where, once, at the end of a darkened narrow alley, he was stopped by what he thought was a lighted lantern. However, the glowing figure was the apparition of Camille. Later, the place where her luminous being materialized was unofficially dubbed "Ghost Alley."

Vice President's Residence

Normally, most people outside of Washington, D.C., pay little attention to the office residence of the vice president on the grounds of the U.S. Naval Observatory. In the 2000 election, however, the residence hosted platoons of news crews who hoped for photo opportunities with Al Gore, the Democratic candidate for president. The vice president's residence also made the news recently when its current occupant, Dick Cheney, chairman of the president's Energy Resources Review Committee, complained that the house uses up too much energy and wanted the bill for the heat and electricity picked up by the U.S. Navy instead of by the vice president's budget.

In recent years, the vice president's residence has been the site of at least one haunting. During President Jimmy Carter's term in office, Vice President Walter Mondale's daughter, Eleanor, complained about a phantom that appeared in her bedroom one night when she was sleeping over in the mansion. Eleanor Mondale wrote about her paranormal experience in *Swing* magazine, describing the apparition that she saw in the moonlight shadows near the window. "I was so scared," she wrote, "I fainted. Upon coming to, I reached for the phone and picked up the 'hot line' to the Secret Service command post. I whispered that there was a man in my room and hung up. Minutes later, two agents busted in the room, guns drawn." However, they found no intruder in the room. Eleanor told them she'd seen a ghost. But the Secret Service men were not sympathetic to that answer and asked her very forcefully and in no uncertain terms that she "never do that again!"

Someone once said that Washington, D.C., has "so

much to see—so many monuments, memorials, museums, sites—that if you spent one day visiting each, it would take more than forty years to see them all." Many of those places were, or still are, the homes of the unseen: the spirits of the famous and infamous, the greats, the near-greats, and the ingrates. Washington, D.C., is a focus of energy, the city where power, ego, pride, revenge, and the unfinished business of personal and political strife loom as major reasons why the nation's capital may be haunted by the spirits of those whose lives were either tortured or unfulfilled. Many who lived and died in Washington, D.C., did not wish to surrender the positions they'd had on earth or forgive and forget the tragedies they suffered here. Still others, however, choose to remain on this earthly plane to watch over the capital and the nation's leaders, acting as guardian angels when they can.

In 1891, the *Washington Star* called the capital "America's most haunted city," and the stories of Washington's ghosts are as much a part of the country's history as the stories of the living. So if you visit, listen for the ghosts, look for them, and sense them around you. Don't be unduly frightened; they are there for their own reasons. Although you may well be startled, stay calm. Experts advise that if you do confront a ghost, pray for the soul to move on and to find peace in the next stage of life where it belongs. You may not encounter an apparition in Washington—then again, you just might.

CHAPTER FOURTEEN

The Channeling of the Presidents

The thought of death leaves me in perfect peace, for I have a firm conviction that our spirit is a being of indestructible nature.

—Johann von Goethe

Historically, mediums have channeled communications from departed leaders, kings and queens, and spiritual prophets. Mediums appear in almost all literatures, religious and secular, delivering messages from a world we cannot see to people desperately seeking guidance. Revered as message bearers of great truth or reviled as frauds or charlatans, mediums continue to be at the center of controversy even in the twenty-first century, both on television and in the tabloid newspapers. In the United States, a relatively young country by world standards, mediums have told of receiving messages from departed presidents and first ladies. The medium Ina Twigg made contact with the spirit of John F. Kennedy. And Kennedy's Democratic predecessor, Harry Truman, still as feisty and outspoken as he was on earth, communicated through well-known medium and writer Kenny Kingston. Via automatic writing, Ruth Montgomery received messages telling her Eleanor Roosevelt's spirit was as busy in the next stage of her existence as she was here. Meanwhile, Franklin Delano Roosevelt's spirit came through Irish medium Geraldine Cummins to say that he'd observed his own funeral.

In fact, FDR was no stranger to the paranormal. In addition to his conversations with Jeane Dixon toward the end of his life, he also attended séances with several talented mediums to obtain advice from the spirits of deceased presidents, military leaders, and others he'd respected. Nathan Miller in *FDR: An Intimate History* told of an incident in which Roosevelt discovered that the wife of Mrs. Roosevelt's valet believed in reincarnation. FDR was sufficiently curious to talk about the subject with the valet's wife, a heavyset woman who weighed nearly two hundred pounds and moved around with some difficulty. When she told the president she hoped to reincarnate as a canary, FDR laughed loudly, "I love it! I love it!"

Hoping to receive messages from the spirits of several departed presidents for the purposes of answering questions raised in this book, we called upon two respected and experienced channelers, Dorothy Maksym and Alexander Murray, whose work has been familiar to psychics and paranormal researchers for many years. Some differentiate mediums from channelers, while others use the terms interchangeably. Both Dorothy and Alexander prefer to be identified as "channelers" because of their well-developed facility to receive messages from discarnate entities, even the "higher self."

We structured the sessions so as to rule out any opportunity for either channeler to engage in prior research into the spirits of the presidents they were asked to contact, although we hasten to add that both are individuals of impeccable integrity. Remember, summoning a discarnate entity to communicate is not like pressing a button and expecting an instant response. In other words, you cannot always make contact with the spirit you hope to hear from, nor can you be certain that the answer will be the one you expect. Such are the vagaries of channeling. Both Dorothy and Alexander told us in advance that they could not guarantee we'd contact those from whom we hoped to receive answers. That caveat notwithstanding, neither channeler placed any restrictions whatsoever on our sessions.

Dorothy and Alexander—who do not know each other—have different methods of channeling. Asked how she receives messages from the spirit world, Dorothy replied, "There is only one mind and we can reach every mind that ever existed," paraphrasing Ralph Waldo Emerson. Her technique is to call upon the spirits, listen to their responses, then repeat what she hears. She does not enter a trance state as many mediums and channelers do in order to contact the spirit world. In our sessions, I offered no clues, hints, or other information to the two channelers than was absolutely necessary for them to do their jobs.

Dorothy Maksym on the Nature of Channeling

I asked Dorothy several questions relating to the process of channeling:

JOEL: What explains why you're able to access this information?

DOROTHY: You're always one with the universe.

J: Are you hearing voices clairaudiently?

D: Something pops into my head. I'm channeling. I repeat aloud the words I hear, except when I indicate that it could be my own thoughts or personality. It's actually more difficult when I have opinions. If I receive an answer to something I know nothing about, then I know it's directly from the [spirit world].

J: Can you ever see the spirits materialize?

D: I see them in my mind.

J: In the nonphysical world, do the spirits of the late presidents communicate with each other, and do they meet or hold council?

D: Yes, definitely. We have a government here, and they have a spiritual government. They're active in on the Other Side.

J: Does it ever interact with our government here on earth?

D: What they're dealing with in the spiritual government [the ideals] might not become ours for many, many years, even centuries. Eventually those [ideals] drift down to the physical plane.

We had several specific questions to ask Dorothy. The following is a transcript of the channeling session. The only editing was for purposes of clarity and eliminating repetition, simply to make the material easier to read, but without changing its meaning. During the actual channeling, Dorothy frequently paused to listen for answers to our questions, an aspect of the spirit communication process that is not reflected in the written transcripts.

Dorothy Maksym Talks to JFK

Dallas

One of the unanswered questions about the Kennedy assassination was why the president, who'd been informed that there were plots against his life, chose to ride through Dealy Plaza with the top down on his limousine. Was it Vice President Lyndon Johnson who, as some historians say, convinced Kennedy to keep the bubble top off because it would be an insult to the residents of Dallas to assume that the President of the United States could not ride through an American city with the top in place? Johnson was the only person who directly benefited from the Kennedy assassination because the investigation into Johnson's relationship with aide Bobby Baker was stopped and Johnson, whom Bobby Kennedy wanted off the 1964 ticket, became the president.

J: Can you communicate with the spirit of President John F. Kennedy and ask him why on the day he was

assassinated, he rode in the Dallas motorcade in an
open limousine with its protective bubble top down?

D: He really believed that he was invincible and immortal. He believed he was chosen by God, and he
thought that he would eventually control the whole
world.

J: Even though he had the normal conscious fear of assassination that any president would have?

D: No. He thought he was above everything.

The Marilyn Monroe Suicide

Dorothy was asked about the still-controversial scandal surrounding the suicide of Marilyn Monroe and her
relationship with the Kennedys. Marilyn Monroe died in
1962 after what doctors said was an overdose of the sedatives she was taking as her career continued to spiral
into oblivion and as she was being passed around between Jack Kennedy and Bobby Kennedy. Shortly before her death, in her desperate attempts to capture the
attention of the Kennedy family, Marilyn Monroe threatened to disclose the secret that there had been a UFO
crash near a southwestern city (Roswell, New Mexico)
and that not only had JFK told her about it, but he also
told her that the army had captured the bodies of the
creatures who had been inside the crash. Monroe's telephone threat to Bobby Kennedy was captured by the
CIA surveillance on her phone line and filed under the
names of the ongoing space retrieval operations "Moon
Dust" and "Bluefly."

J: Another controversy about JFK that's never been
fully answered concerns the death of actress Marilyn
Monroe. There have been rumors ever since she died
in 1962 from an overdose of sleeping pills that the
Kennedys were somehow involved. Is there any truth
to that?

D: John F. Kennedy was not involved. But his brother
Robert was. Actually I feel that she did take her life,

but she did not intend to. The stress she was under was a result of her fear and knowledge of things [about] the government, and she was involved in a lot, so the Kennedys became very concerned about her.

J: When she threatened to reveal her affair with Bobby Kennedy, didn't that contribute [to his worry]?

D: No. She had much more knowledge than that.

J: About things going on in government?

D: Yes.

J: So did the Kennedys kill her? Or was it stress that led her to take her own life?

D: In a roundabout way they killed her, but she did not intend to die.

J: But Marilyn took the pills? A Kennedy or anybody else didn't feed them to her?

D: Yes, she took the pills. But it was in desperation. She was just trying to find peace.

J: Did Bobby Kennedy or [someone working for him] sneak into her house and drug or poison her?

D: No, no. She took the pills, but it was more than she was used to taking. She took a lot of them. Again, she was just trying to find peace. She did not intend to kill herself.

J: But she was afraid or intimidated by someone?

D: Yes, yes. She was in fear.

J: In fear of the Kennedys?

D: Not of John Kennedy. But his brother [Robert] and his political connections.

Dorothy Maksym with Richard Nixon

We didn't tell Dorothy Maksym in advance of our session that we wanted her to contact Richard Nixon because we wanted to make sure all her information was received psychically. Nor did Dorothy have any opportunity to do any research about Richard Nixon, his family, or his presidency. Therefore, what Dorothy told us about

Richard Nixon and what he communicated to her was startling indeed.

The stories of Richard Nixon and his resignation, Watergate, the infamous tapes, and the impeachment hearings still influence politics today. But there are more questions than there are answers. Why would a president whom the polls indicated would overwhelmingly defeat any candidates the Democrats put up authorize his secret group of operatives to break into the Democratic headquarters? What information or documents were they looking for that Nixon feared? Were they, as G. Gordon Liddy has said, looking for incriminating photos or evidence against Maureen Dean, wife of Nixon's counsel John Dean? Were they looking for evidence that would incriminate Nixon's friend Bebe Rebozzo? Despite rumors, the answers still elude us. Nixon's spirit, as we found out, offered no answers as to what was in the headquarters, but was frustrated that the Watergate story lingers on.

J: What can you tell us about Richard Nixon?

D: President Nixon never left earth. His spirit is working through a much younger man who is now in his late forties and was very dedicated to him and looked upon Richard Nixon as a martyr.

J: Can you keep talking as he talks to you?

D: Nixon admits his ego and power overwhelmed his reasoning. He knows he was hardworking, bright, and dedicated. He says he wanted to be the best president there ever was. "I wanted to be very strong especially in the area of the military and national defense," he is telling me right now. He insists his downfall was the result of listening to advisors and against his own better judgment. He's insistent about that. He is "obsessed with Watergate," he admits. How could something so insignificant have brought him down with what he stood for and all the good he did? That's how he puts it to me.

J: Was Nixon's spirit at Yorba Linda, as has been reported?

D: Yes, it was. Whoever saw Nixon's spirit must have been open to his energy. He says his soul visited many places, including his summer retreat at San Clemente. After he left office, he was a broken, completely broken man. These are the words he uses. He cried all the time, he admits. In private, he lost control, emotionally, which was completely opposite his public persona of always wanting to appear in control. He knows he did wrong and followed advice that was completely against his judgment.

J: What is he thinking now about his predicament?

D: My mission now is to clear my name through those on earth, he says. He's very emphatic. He's very strong-willed. He is completely obsessed with clearing his name, and he's still very troubled, frustrated, and bitter. "I returned to earth to clear my name," he says. That's his purpose. "I am the president," he says. He won't let go. His ego—which is an emotional state—won't let go.

J: Why did Nixon's spirit appear at Yorba Linda?

D: An investigator or researcher was delving into his political career. At the time, it was someone who was actually writing something quite positive. Nixon made his presence felt, hoping to be able to put into the mind of the writer, through telepathy, favorable ideas about himself that he wants to get across to the public.

J: Did it work?

D: The researcher found the ideas, "just flowing like magic," he says. But the researcher never knew that the origin of the ideas he thought were his own were actually being communicated by Nixon's spirit. The writer just thought he was having a lucky day. The man would pick up a book, open to the right page, and just keep going. Actually Richard Nixon's ghost was guiding him, but he didn't know it.

J: Who is Nixon's spirit working through in this life?

D: That man is someone who was on Nixon's payroll years ago. He really looked up to Nixon. He's tall

and thin with sandy blond hair. This individual began
as a volunteer when he was quite young. He was very
dedicated and later went on the payroll. He is still
trying to clear Nixon's name. But this person does
not know that Nixon is working through him psychically. This person admired Nixon so much that he is
open to Nixon's psychic energies and thoughts, which
have been able to come through to him.

J: How is it possible that communications from a spirit
can enter the mind of someone still in the physical
body?

D: There is only one mind, and all of us share it. Therefore any one mind can communicate with any other
mind. It's in all our power. There is also a particular
reason for each individual to show up on earth at a
particular time.

J: Who is this person who wants to restore Nixon's
legacy?

D: The man is someone now in politics and has written
articles about Nixon. He is loyal to Nixon to the very
end and wants to clear his name. It's an obsession.
He wants everyone to understand Nixon as he knew
him and think of Nixon as a great man. This man
actually has many of Nixon's possessions, such as his
books and even some of his clothing. This individual
is a collector. He reads President Nixon's books. He
also has a desk that Nixon used. In fact, the desk is
his most prized possession. Patricia Nixon gave the
Nixon mementos to him.

J: Does Nixon's spirit identify the person he is now
working through on earth?

D: Nixon won't give me the man's name. He says this
person always has been one who worked behind the
scenes in politics. He has no interest in running for
political office or being known by the public. If Nixon
gives his name and it becomes known, President
Nixon feels it would call attention to the man and
interfere with what he's doing to help restore Nixon's
name and reputation. Also, this man does not know

Nixon's spirit is working through him. He would be shocked to see and hear his name coming from a psychic.

J: Where does President Nixon's spirit travel?

D: When Congress is in session, his spirit is there. It has to be there, he says. He is still deeply interested in politics and hasn't been able to let go. Nixon sometimes had a terrible temper here on earth. The stronger the temper and will, the stronger the power of the soul to manifest and interact on the physical plane.

J: Does Nixon's spirit mind that visitors to the library at Yorba Linda can hear the Watergate tapes? [We were careful not to inform Dorothy about reports that tape players at Yorba Linda malfunctioned from time to time.]

D: He does not want people to hear the Watergate tapes. That's why the tape machines break down sometimes. He's interfering with them. His spirit has used its energy to interrupt the tapes from playing. "Why can't people let that business go?" he asks me. "How did it all get so out of control?" He doesn't understand why there is so much interest in it. "I want the American people to forgive and forget all the negativity and instead remember the good I did," he says.

J: What explains the mysterious tapping noises coming from the Watergate display room?

D: He is responsible. It's his way of trying to unnerve visitors, to distract them from concentrating on Watergate materials and to let people know that he is still there.

J: What does he say now?

D: He's agitated. He's talking about the accomplishments he wants people to remember, like ending the Vietnam War. He's reminding me to say that he was the president who went to China. He's mentioning arms treaties he signed and says people should remember he was tough on crime. He is saying: "I'm the president who began the EPA to protect the environment. While I was president, man walked on the moon. It was during my administration that the Consumer Product Safety Commission began. Do you remember that I started the war on cancer? It was while I was president that affirmative action got going. I lowered the voting age. For God's sake, I served in the navy for four years. Why don't people remember any of that? Why is that damned Watergate break-in the only thing people want to remember about me? I was confident about my place in history until that damned Watergate."

J: He sounds very emotional.

D: Nixon's spirit is terribly upset. I can hardly keep up with all the accomplishments he's rattling off. It almost sounds like he's still running for office. He says when he was on earth, he knew what he did would be glorified in heaven. That's why he feels what happened to him politically is even worse than people can imagine. He feels no sense of worth about himself. He said that's why his spirit is still here. That's why he remains. He says, "The price of glory was not worth this. To reach so high, and to have to fall so low." He admits he'll remain in emotional turmoil until Americans recognize him for what he believes he achieved. He disappointed the American people, he admits. "I let them down." These are his exact words I'm hearing now.

J: What about his wife, Pat?

D: "Pat never much liked the White House," he says. "But she did try to make the best of it. Pat was heartbroken by my resignation. She was hurt by the scandal and humiliation hurled at us. But she always stood by me. I think Tricia took it all worse than Julie. Tricia, you know, was always the quieter, more sensitive one." Now he's telling me that when things were darkest for him, during Watergate, his mother's spirit came to help him. That's what kept him strong. "My mother was a saint." Those are his words.

J: What about reports of the luminous green mist seen floating above Nixon's grave?

D: The grave itself has an energy, and the green light

can be the energy of Nixon's physical body's memory or the energy of people sending thoughts and prayers to him.

J: Is there an end to his turmoil?

D: Nixon's emotional turmoil won't end until Americans recognize his achievements and forgive and forget Watergate. That's why he won't let go, he keeps telling me, insisting. His spirit can't leave now. He's especially upset that people are able to hear those Watergate tapes. He's totally obsessed with those White House recordings. He says that if he could generate enough energy, he'd destroy all those tapes. He wishes people wouldn't go to Yorba Linda just for the tapes or the Watergate display.

J: How can he release the emotion that is holding him back?

D: His mission is now to clear his name. Eventually he will let go of his earthly anguish and move on to the Other Side. But he has to transcend the emotional state he's in. Right now, he's trapped, he says, in an emotional state of consciousness.

J: Will Nixon's spirit continue to make its presence felt at his childhood home and Presidential Library?

D: Definitely!

Dorothy Maksym on President Truman

The Roswell Incident

In July 1947, newspapers across western United States reported on a press release sent out by Lt. Walter Haut, the public information officer at Roswell Army Air Field, that a special detail from the 509th, stationed at the airfield, had retrieved the debris of a crashed flying saucer out in the desert near Roswell, New Mexico. The next day, the army denied the report that it was a flying saucer they found, saying instead that it was the debris from a crashed weather balloon. This story appeared in the *New York Times* and other newspapers across the country. With these two press releases and the testimony from scores of witnesses over the years from 1947 to the present, the Roswell Incident has become one of the most important stories in UFO lore. At the time of the Roswell crash, Harry Truman was president. Ultimately his name became involved with stories about the crash and the decisions in the years that followed to establish a high-level top-secret unit within the federal government to cover up the story of the crash while at the same time finding out as much as possible about the spacecraft and the creatures found inside, whose bodies were recovered and brought back to the Roswell Army Air Field.

J: Can we talk to President Harry Truman? He was president during the famous "flying saucer" crash in Roswell, New Mexico, in July 1947, in which it's widely believed several extraterrestrial beings were killed. Ever since, there's been controversy about the government hiding the UFO after they captured it. Did Truman know more about the incident than the public was ever told?

D: Truman was given a lot of information, but much of it was tainted.

J: By whom?

D: I'm [psychically] getting that there were religious fanatics who didn't want anything of that nature to be disclosed or exposed. But those in high offices controlled the information.

J: Were they military officials?

D: Yes. But they were also very fearful of the devil and that kind of thinking.

J: So you're saying they were religious fundamentalists. But President Truman knew more than he announced or admitted?

D: Yes. But he was also given wrong or tainted information, and intelligence, which they made him keep secret.

J: So they never wanted the truth about the crashed saucer revealed?

D: No.

J: Truman never spoke about whatever he knew? Was he afraid?

D: Well, they—the higher-ups—convinced him that for the sake of the country it wouldn't be wise. [Plus] he'd been given wrong information.

J: So Truman knew less than we thought? Would you call it disinformation?

D: Yes.

J: Are you saying that he was convinced not to speak because of national security reasons?

D: Yes, he was convinced that he had to keep quiet.

Dorothy Maksym with FDR

There are at least two intriguing conspiracy stories associated with the presidency of Franklin Delano Roosevelt that came out in Dorothy's channeling session. One involves the attempt by powerful American industrialists and their friends in the military to stage a coup to remove Roosevelt from power. The coup was born out of the fears of industrialists that FDR's domestic policies bordered on socialism and would align the United States with the Soviet Union and Josef Stalin. Roosevelt was also the target of an assassination attempt in early 1933 that missed.

The attempted coup and assassination attempt were part of a general malaise on the part of American conservative politicians, including Ambassador Joseph Kennedy, JFK's father and Meyer Lansky's rum-running partner during Prohibition, who had urged the United States to support Hitler and the Third Reich. There were American industrialists, along with institutions in the banking community, who were involved in financing the rearmament of Germany under the Third Reich. Roosevelt's policies were perceived as a threat to American profits generated from Hitler's attempts to rearm Germany as were Roosevelt's policies toward Japan, which was engaged in expansionist policies in the Far East. Roosevelt's embargo on oil sales to the Japanese because of their invasion of China and the president's clandestine deployment of American air power under Claire Chenault and his "Flying Tigers" to interdict the Japanese Army so as to prevent them from reaching the Burmese oil fields also angered American industrialists and their banker friends in the investment community.

The second great conspiracy theory involves Roosevelt's foreknowledge that the Japanese were planning an attack on Pearl Harbor. It was a well-known fact that the Americans had broken the Japanese codes and knew that a Japanese Imperial Navy fleet led by aircraft carriers was on its way to attack Pearl Harbor. The Japanese were demonstrating in force what American general Billy Mitchell had argued years earlier at his court-martial: bombers launched from aircraft carriers could destroy enemy shipping. Mitchell had also predicted that Japan would launch just such an attack against the U.S. Pacific fleet at Pearl Harbor. Also, the Japanese had telegraphed their intentions by recalling their delegation during last-minute talks in Washington to try to reach a settlement on the American refusal to sell oil to Japan during the Japanese invasion of China. Even FBI Director Hoover had personally warned FDR that an attack on Pearl Harbor was in the final implementation stages and would be carried out in a matter of days or weeks.

But FDR believed he had a card up his sleeve that could solve both his problems with the Japanese and with those Americans financing and supporting the rearmament of Hitler's Reich. Because the president had, by December 1941, successfully prevented the Japanese from reaching the Burmese oil fields, he believed that even if America were attacked, Japan wouldn't have the material resources to prosecute a war across the Pacific. They just didn't have enough fuel. At the same time, after Montgomery had broken the back of Rommel's Panzer divisions at the Battle of El-Alamein in North Africa, Roosevelt also believed that the Germans wouldn't have the capacity to produce the petroleum fuel they needed to complete their conquest of Eastern Europe. Hitler's invasion of Russia, already in the planning stages, would end up just like Napoleon's, only this time with Stalin absorbing the blows from the Nazi *Wehrmacht*. By waiting until Hitler and Stalin had beaten each other into the ground, Roosevelt's intelligence analysts told him, he might be able to see both of America's enemies in Europe destroy themselves. All FDR had to do, therefore, was to get Hitler to declare war on the United States first so as to get America into the world war. And the Japanese would do it for him by attacking Pearl Harbor.

Thus, Roosevelt, who had also been trying to get the U.S. Congress to declare war against the Axis to spend America out of the Depression as well as to destroy the fascist regimes that threatened to enslave the planet, now saw his opportunity to play his hidden card as the Japanese aircraft carrier fleet, unaware that they were playing right into FDR's hands, steamed across the Pacific toward Pearl Harbor in December 1941. As the story goes, the navy sent the aircraft carriers with their planes on board out of Pearl on exercises but left the battleships and destroyers in place so the Japanese wouldn't be tipped off that we knew what was coming. The navy also did not disperse our aircraft at the army airfields in Hawaii, similarly to deceive the Japanese into believing that we were sitting ducks. The last thing our military intelligence services wanted to reveal was that we had already decrypted the Japanese codes. By taking our aircraft carriers out of Pearl before the bombardment, the navy saved the weapons that would project the U.S. military power to victory. The aircraft carrier became the most important weapon that helped the U.S. Navy wrest control of the Pacific from the Japanese fleet from 1942 to 1945 and win the war. At the same time, by absorbing the attack on Pearl Harbor and then asking Congress for a declaration of war on Japan, FDR got his three-for-one when Germany declared war on the United States, and the government had to pump the economy with money to manufacture the weapons the military needed. Once we were in it, FDR knew we could win it.

J: Can we try to communicate with President Franklin Delano Roosevelt?

D: Okay.

J: When FDR became president in 1933 during the Great Depression, the unemployed and impoverished may have seen him as a hero, but he had many enemies.

D: Yes.

J: There were secret plans for a coup against Roosevelt by some very powerful people—industrialists and corporate leaders. Many in big business despised FDR's "New Deal" and social programs for the poor, fearing government interference would hurt their profits and ability to make money. Some big names wanted to be rid of FDR. People like DuPont, Ford, and George Herbert Walker who was President George W. Bush's great-grandfather opposed FDR's policies and saw investment opportunity for the United States and Nazi Germany. Does President Roosevelt have any thoughts or opinions about what his political enemies wanted to do to him?

D: He's telling me that he [was] very much like John F. Kennedy. He was destined to be president. He felt that he had divine intervention on his side during his presidency, and he was untouchable as long as he really tried to better the country.

J: So political enemies, even an attempted coup, didn't trouble him?

D: I feel he had a faith in God that he couldn't be touched.

J: Does he have any animosity or resentments? What did he do to thwart political adversaries who wanted him out of office at almost any price?

D: When you asked me that question, what psychically came to mind was Hawaii. That's his biggest regret because he knew the attack [on Pearl Harbor] was going to happen, and he was given false or misleading information about it.

J: You're talking about Pearl Harbor?

D: Yes. And he's never forgiven himself for that.

J: You're saying FDR knew about the attack on Pearl Harbor before it happened?

D: Oh yes! Sure. And he felt with the information he'd been given, the best thing [was to say nothing]. But it is his biggest regret.

J: What is?

D: That he knew in advance Pearl Harbor would be attacked by the Japanese and he did nothing about it.

J: Why didn't he do something?

D: Because of misinformation given to him that he should sit back and let [the attack] happen. He said he should have handled it very differently.

J: Who gave FDR misinformation about Pearl Harbor? Who misled him?

D: Military and political leaders. What he's saying now is that knowing about the attack in advance, he should have gone in and protected the men. It would have still served the same purpose to get us into the war, which he felt we had to do. But he says he shouldn't have sat back and let [so many Americans die].

J: So his not giving advance warning to the troops that would have saved more lives at Pearl, that's more troubling to him than a coup or any attempts against him personally?

D: Yes. His handling of Pearl Harbor is his one regret.

J: But what about any attempts against him?

D: The more he believed he was doing the right thing for people, the more he thought those opposing him would [understand]. He thought that if he showed he was really making this a better country, it would awaken a sense of caring within his enemies, and he would win them over.

J: There was an assassination attempt on his life in early 1933 when he was still president-elect. But the assassin shot and killed Mayor Anton Cermak of Chicago instead. To this day, there are questions about whether FDR or Cermak was the target. What does he say about that close call?

D: What you just described—the failed attempt on his life—convinced him that he was [protected by] divine guidance. That was proof to him. They're also telling me that the more knowledgeable and intelligent our great leaders are, the more highly evolved they are, and the more [they have] the ability to change.

J: Is it possible that presidents who were very powerful, the very well-known ones like Washington, Lincoln, and FDR, were under some kind of divine protection, more than most other people?

D: God's plan works constantly. They are not outside God's plan for one second.

J: So when some presidents come back to earth as spirits, are the ones who return predisposed to some higher degree of spirituality? Or do they return for some specific purpose?

D: They feel they are instruments for guiding this country. It's their baby. And whether in body or in soul, they have a tremendous attachment here.

J: What explains why some presidential spirits are never heard from? Do some not come back to walk the earth?

D: They said that's not true. It's just that nobody was listening, or nobody was listening to the ones who heard them.

J: So even the ones we don't hear from are present?

D: Oh yes. Once you're in spirit, you are free to travel, just as we're free to travel from this dimension to other dimensions, which we do in astral projection. They are constantly between dimensions.

J: Might some presidents have been so satisfied on the Other Side, feeling their life's work on earth was done, they saw no reason to come back here?

D: I get a great big no. Not at all.

J: Why is that?

D: None of them are satisfied. We're too primitive.

J: And do they spiritually evolve on the Other Side?

D: Well, we lose the limitations the physical world imposes on us once we're no longer part of the three-dimensional [world].

Dorothy Maksym with Abraham Lincoln

J: What about Abraham Lincoln? Is he capable of answering a question?

D: Sure.

J: What are President Lincoln's thoughts about the terrible Civil War he led the country through? And what does he say about the Emancipation Proclamation, which really was an abandonment of his campaign promise to preserve the Union at all costs, even if it meant guaranteeing no interference in the slave holding states?

D: He said the Emancipation Proclamation was his [greatest achievement]—the greatest thing he ever did for this country to bring [it] freedom. Unless we have freedom, we are not a civilized country. I'm channeling. He says that was the most important act in his eyes, to free this country, to become a more spiritual world or dimension to live in.

J: There's a story that President Lincoln may have received encouragement to issue the Emancipation Proclamation from one or more mediums who did readings for him and Mrs. Lincoln. Does he say anything about that?

D: He's saying that he had many spiritually attuned people around him here [on earth].

J: So is it possible that he was especially influenced by a young medium named Nettie Colburn?

D: Well, he didn't look at her or the others as mediums. Rather he thought of them as knowledgeable people who were attuned to the universe.

J: About the Civil War. What does President Lincoln think regarding the fact that this country had to go through a Civil War in order to preserve the Union? How does he view his leadership throughout the war?

D: He says the war was an act of purification. In the physical world, we have to eliminate negative energy, and the only way we have been able to do it up until now is through physical actions. The Civil War was one of the best things that ever happened to this nation.

J: Despite the tremendous loss of life, bloodshed, and tragedy?

D: Yes. It was a fight between right and wrong. In the physical world that is the only way you win.

J: And how regretful is he that his life was cut short before he could heal the wounds between the North and South?

D: He says very knowingly and with satisfaction, "My job was done."

Dorothy Maksym with George Washington

J: What messages might there be from George Washington?

D: He was very tall and extremely intelligent. He was an extraterrestrial as were Jesus, Lincoln, and Buddha.

J: What do you mean when you say extraterrestrial?

D: These people were all fathered by a great intelligence.

J: More so than the average person?

D: Yes.

J: Would Washington have any guidance for future presidents? As "Father of Our Country," wouldn't he have some excellent advice to offer?

D: In today's politics, spirituality and right do not [have a place]. He says it's your crooked politicians who are out to win, to control, and, in their greed, ruin America.

J: Is there any way we can overcome these circumstances or improve them?

D: Make your voice [heard]. He was disturbed by the confusion surrounding the election for president in 2000, and the delay in who was chosen the winner.

J: Is President Washington optimistic about the future of the country?

D: No.

J: Does he consider both major political parties a danger?

D: Yes. More so the Republican Party. But they are [both] out for themselves. They're out for money, the mighty dollar, and they [seek] more control. Citizens—the people of this country—are just pawns being used by politicians to obtain what they want.

J: Wasn't that true when he was our leader? Wasn't it that way in the days of the Founding Fathers and the early presidents: Washington, Adams, Jefferson, Madison, and Monroe?

D: Oh no, no. They said we were all here to make this country a beautiful place that would work. With all their heart and soul, all their energy, they wanted a perfect nation for the people.

J: So why can't they help us? If they're so powerful in the spirit world, why haven't they psychically influenced recent presidents to [steer] us to a better moral track?

D: Because the American people do not deserve individuals like them [the Founding Fathers]. He says we have the [leaders] we deserve. Crooks, he called them. I didn't say that.

J: That's what George Washington said?

D: Well, that's what I heard. I'm not giving my own opinions.

J: So they won't help us? Is it our nation's karma or destiny to have to go through one political mess after another? Does it have to get worse and worse?

D: I'm being told that if we have a crooked government, it's because we are crooked in our hearts. We cheat and lie and don't look out for the other person. This is what I'm channeling. This is not me. Until a nation of people live, breathe, and express ideals and integrity, it cannot have [honest government].

J: Did George Washington communicate that to you?

D: Yes.

J: Did any long-past or recent president ever ask him to return and help? Have any presidents prayed to him for advice or counsel?

D: I don't usually remember messages I give. But I do remember mentioning that [former] President Clinton would often try to tune into their minds. He would go off and meditate and ask them for help, mainly from Thomas Jefferson for some reason. Clinton had an affinity for Jefferson. He might even have thought he was a reincarnation of Jefferson. That's what I'm hearing.

J: When Hillary Rodham Clinton was first lady and was having so-called imaginary conversations with the late Eleanor Roosevelt, might they not have been imaginary?

D: Yes. What an intelligent thing for Mrs. Clinton to do. Don't forget Emerson's words that there is only one mind, and everyone's mind is accessible to everyone else, no matter where they are.

J: Does George Washington see the Bushes as good or bad?

D: As he said earlier, corruption runs through our political system today.

J: Will the Founding Fathers—the early patriots and presidents—continue to watch over the country?

D: Yes.

J: But they're not intervening?

D: No, they can't.

J: Why not?

D: Because we haven't asked them to. Nor is our time deserving of that kind of help. Washington says that we have to raise our own consciousness [in order] to obtain a better government.

J: But on the other hand, if a president, say, George W. Bush, were to call on George Washington for advice, would his spirit communicate help?

D: Of course! But he says, "Have no worry. Bush would never do that."
J: So what's Washington's last word of advice for presidents and the country?
D: Save your money and become involved in politics and change them!

Alexander Murray

Alexander Murray is one of New York's most respected channelers with a remarkable facility for receiving spirit communications from notable figures in history. He utilizes automatic writing, a type of mediumship or channeling in which he takes down information that originates in sources other than his conscious mind, and records the data that courses through him, very similar to a court reporter who writes down exactly what is said in the courtroom.

As Alexander began channeling, we noticed a slight alteration in the articulation and cadence of his voice. The phrasing and intonation became more deliberate. There were also long pauses as he wrote down the spirit's response to each question. Those are not reflected in his verbatim transcript, which follows:

JOEL: We were hoping that a presidential spirit who has relevance for our time will communicate with us.
ALEXANDER: Not every spirit is available at the moment. So you kind of have to put it out there. I'm also asking my [spirit] guides to help me. We'll find out who's willing to communicate with us. They're aware that we're doing this.
J: I understand.
A: Well, I'm getting goosebumps. And I'm getting the name [John] Quincy Adams. They're starting to write. All right, I have the first sentence. It reads, "I can see there is a great need for the nation to find a spiritual reality, which is personal." This is going to be

quite extensive. And it's quite interesting. He writes, "I am convinced that religion has done a greater disservice to the nation and national unity than is understood. All people are innately spiritual beings. But religion is something learned from exterior sources, rather than developed from an inner personal connection with the Truth and Wisdom that guide all who open themselves to it. The new era holds a potential for regression into the worst habits of the past. I hope that the nation can put aside the provincialities and preferences that have been in the past the basis of depriving certain citizens of their divinely bestowed rights. Our Declaration and Constitution refer to these as inalienable. Let them not be alienated who most deserve to be welcomed and respected. I give myself to the task of helping in whatever way I can those who would have a friendly assistance. From your faithful, John Quincy Adams."

J: Does that imply that he is still here with us [in spirit]? Does it suggest that he still serves and watches over or somehow guides elected officials even now, and in the years since his death? In other words, did his spirit influence later presidents?

A: The answer to that question is, "Wherever I may and whenever I can, I have done and will continue to do."

J: So he is helping somehow and watching over the country?

A: Exactly. The answer is yes.

J: Has he ever returned anywhere as an apparition? If he's in the spirit world does he have the facility to return here to be seen in an apparitional form?

A: He says, "I have appeared to President Lincoln."

J: May I ask why?

A: "President Lincoln sought help and guidance."

J: Did Lincoln seek the help of [John] Quincy Adams specifically? Or is that just who responded?

A: The answer is, "Not of me in particular, but of those who might help and guide." I think it must mean that Lincoln asked [for help] in a general way.

J: And this is who responded?

A: Right. He [Quincy Adams] was available.

J: Does he recall what advice he gave to President Lincoln? I assume it must have concerned slavery and the Civil War?

A: "Yes." I'm getting such an electrical tingle. It's amazing!

J: Is it from him [John Quincy Adams]?

A: I think so. I'll read you what's here so far, apropos of something he said to Lincoln: "That there was no cause so great and no time so critical to the resolution of the slavery issue, that he must not fear the consequences of war." Lincoln feared the consequences, but Adams must have advised him there was apparently a time [when it] was critical to act.

J: Right.

A: It continues, "Had Lincoln backed down, it would have split the nation and allowed slavery to continue for another hundred years. The loss of soldiers' lives and civilian casualties was a necessary sacrifice, though regrettable in the extreme. Yet so many more would have been lost in the time thereafter. What terrible choices God presents us with!"

J: What was John Quincy Adams's position and thoughts on slavery?

A: He answered, "You may know that I detested it and was on record against it always."

J: Can he tell us a little about what he does on the Other Side? What is his role or function in the afterlife? Is he still in the company of other early patriots and the Founding Fathers?

A: Here's your answer: "You may know that I was and am a restless rather than a restful spirit. I have always had a great need to be active, not necessarily busy. I do indeed embrace my dear father [John Adams] and even his old rival [Thomas] Jefferson, whose views are most congenial to mine. We sometimes operate in concert, but mostly know what each other is doing by our constant communion."

J: What about his mother [Abigail Adams]? She's regarded as one of our [strongest] first ladies, for her outspoken nature and near-equality with her husband, considering the [era] they lived in. Many have regarded her as an early feminist, although somewhat possessive and severe.

A: The answer is, "My dearest mother, Abigail, has been always our beloved companion and guide. She is of that angelic aspect which makes her radiant love a thing of constant refreshment and sustenance. She has a wisdom which commands respect from us and might truly enlighten those on earth who sought it."

J: But Mr. President, you had a reputation in life, unlike your mother, of being rather lonely and sharp-tongued. History tells us that you were not happy as President of the United States. Why was that so? Has history recorded this correctly?

A: His answer, "You may know that I disliked the political life, and the deals and compromises which were a daily feature of the office. I also had such difficulty in convincing those about me to take the high road rather than follow the seductions at every hand. I was happier in the Congress, where I left the earth. But happiness is not a thing the presidency or any office can bestow. I found my happiness in the contemplation of finer and higher things. I was and am a happy spirit."

J: So he was much more [satisfied] as a legislator than he was as president?

A: Right.

J: So in view of the fact that he was considered very eloquent, and in many ways brilliant and precocious, has history treated him fairly?

A: He answers, "I believe that there are those who understand a person such as me, and have the capacity to empathize with and recognize in me a mind and heart whose perspective parallels their own. Some historians have honored me. Whereas most have ignored rather than forgotten me. You be the judge of it."

J: [John] Quincy Adams's father had been [the second] president, then Quincy Adams was elected [the sixth] president. Since his father [John Adams] died in 1826 and John Quincy [Adams] was elected in 1824, his father would have been alive for more than a year while his son was in office. Was there a tremendous pride from father to son at the time? Or was there resentment or indifference? What was the father's reaction to his son also becoming president? I guess there's a parallel to President George W. Bush and his father President George Herbert Walker Bush, particularly inasmuch as both John Quincy Adams and George W. Bush were minority presidents, whose fathers had been one-term presidents and were selected not as the first choice of the voters, who elected their opponents, but took office only after the intervention of other government agencies. John Quincy Adams lost the raw popular vote and was selected by the House of Representatives. He defeated a candidate from the state of Tennessee. Similarly, George W. Bush lost the raw popular vote, and possibly the raw vote in Florida, which would have thrown the electoral vote to his opponent, and might have lost the presidential election had it not been for the U.S. Supreme Court's favorable ruling on a petition from the Republican Party to stop the Florida recount. He, too, defeated a candidate from the state of Tennessee. What does your father think about this?

A: Your answer: "My father was most honored and I believe it brought him greater satisfaction than anything I had accomplished in our lifetime. You might imagine some parallels with the former and current Presidents Bush." So I guess he's saying—he's imagining that former President Bush is very proud of his son.

J: Does he have any reaction to the election of George W. Bush? Or does he pay attention to such things any more?

A: He answers less about himself, and I sense more about the administration. He refers to more than a single person here. "When we see such a division in the electorate and national sentiment, it is cause for great concern. As I stated earlier, divisiveness may polarize into hostility or even conflict with scarcely any relationship between the issues and the deeper fundamental causes. Economic recessions are the climate for discontent. Something must be done quickly to avert the downward spiral, which will undermine not only the economy, but the nation as a whole. Prosperity can evaporate all too quickly if this problem is ignored."

J: John Quincy Adams was an advocate of free speech. Does he feel that we are compromising, in any way, our freedom of speech today because of the politically correct attitudes we have, the divisiveness in this country, and the fear people have of offending each other? Does he, in any way, think we are going backward [regarding] freedom of speech or is that a misperception?

A: I've gotten this answer: "I do believe it is fundamental to free speech that one has the right to offend. Free speech cannot, however, encompass or countenance libel, which is to say, one has the right to his opinions, whatever they may be. But facts are facts and cannot be misstated to attack another's honor. Concerning your present tendencies, let not the fear of disapproval dissuade those who hold eccentric views. The United States was founded by those whose opinions radically disagreed with those which were accepted at the time."

J: Speaking of those who founded the country, there is a perception today and in recent generations that we had great patriots early in the nation's history, and that the Founding Fathers and the early presidents were probably far more ethical and better than any politician we've had in recent years. Is that myth or is that true?

A: He replies, "I believe the founders of our nation were idealists, though their ideals may have differed in their pursuit of their common goals for the new nation. That, I believe, lent a certain moral tone to their quest. Surely they were human folk, not demigods, with all the human weaknesses accorded to ordinary beings. Yet they had vision and were guided. So in the handling of power, they conceived of themselves as custodians of a sacred trust. Remember they had suffered many hardships for their freedom, so it was clear to them what has over time become somewhat obscured. When presidents became dealmakers rather than leaders, the tone and tenor of the office changed."

J: What does [John] Quincy Adams think about the people some would today call "revisionists" who refer back to the early presidents—even Abraham Lincoln—as racist or sexist? In other words, they apply today's values to judging people who lived a hundred or two hundred years ago.

A: "I believe it is a kind of folly to imagine that the wisdom [which] experience has provided subsequently can be applied to former times, persons, and situations. All have lived in error at some point in their lives. Life lessons are often only clear and learnable because of the errors of others in the past."

J: Is there a greater objectivity that one views from the spirit world than when individuals, including [John] Quincy Adams, were on earth? Do you see things more clearly from the Other Side? Is the view better [from there]?

A: He answers, "I see from a mostly subjective and personal perspective. The objective is sometimes like a maze where one can become lost in the facts. So I note what appears to be real and inquire of myself if it really is."

J: Does he agree that, as historians say, Abraham Lincoln was our greatest president? Or was it perhaps Washington or Franklin Delano Roosevelt? Does it even matter?

A: He says, "I would not wish to name one," I suppose referring to a president. "But certainly Lincoln was a man of greatness. The presidency did not make him what he was."

J: But when [John] Quincy Adams looked on from the spirit world and saw Richard Nixon or Bill Clinton embroiled in scandal, what was his reaction? Are we making too much of them [scandals] or are we correct in our condemnation? What is [John] Quincy Adams's opinions of those kinds of blots on the presidency, if in fact they matter?

A: "Learn from these reflections of the national psyche. They have represented the country better than you realize, [considering] the way they were selected by their parties and how they were promoted. I believe that the position of president is one which can only be described in practical terms as transparent."

J: John Quincy Adams, a one-term president like his father, was defeated in his run for a second term after a bitter campaign, and left this earth in 1848 after suffering a stroke while delivering a speech to Congress. Did he have any regrets and what were they? Finally, does he have any advice to give us for the future and for the country's well-being?

A: The answer is, "I died happily doing what I loved to do. I recommend it to all. Die happily doing what you love most. I say to the nation, do not waste the older, aging generation. In your haste to have the new, do not forget that they were once young rebels who now have white hair. And they may yet be your best hope and greatest resource. Give to your future the possibility of happiness and fulfillment by creating a future for yourselves that includes a useful and productive old age."

After the channeling session with Alexander Murray, we asked him several questions to clarify the process.

J: Were you in a trance when you were channeling John Quincy Adams's spirit?

A: I was in a light trance state but I've developed the ability to remain conscious during the channeling.

J: Was there any physical sensation you experienced?

A: I had an electrical feeling.

J: Did your handwriting change at all during the channeling?

A: My handwriting became a little different—a mixture of mine and the channeled spirit.

J: What did you think of [John] Quincy Adams?

A: He liked words. He's intelligent, but I didn't find him prickly or stuffy.

J: Did you see or sense his presence?

A: I felt him around. I could feel his presence and his personality. It was nice, really. I could actually see an image of him. This was very lucid.

Not since John Quincy Adams had a son followed his father to the White House until George W. Bush. The Bushes and the Adamses have been the only two father-son presidents in the nation's history. Beyond that there are other synchronicities or similarities between them. Both John Quincy Adams's and George W. Bush's fathers were once diplomats and vice presidents. Both were from wealthy old-line Northeastern families. Both had mothers with "strong personalities" and influence over their husbands and sons.

Most remarkably, both became president in hotly contested and contentious elections. In 1824, Quincy Adams received fewer popular and electoral votes than closest rival Andrew Jackson in a four-way contest. But since no candidate received a majority of the electoral vote, the election was decided in the House of Representatives, where Quincy Adams, in a brokered vote, was elected by a majority of the House members. In 2000, George W. Bush won with fewer popular votes than Al Gore. After five weeks of disputed vote recounts in Florida, Bush won the presidency by a single vote in the controversial 5–4 U.S. Supreme Court decision in which Anthony Scalia, the justice who voted to stay the Florida recount, refused to recuse himself even though his son was a member of the law firm representing Governor Bush.

After just one term in office, John Quincy Adams was turned out by the voters who elected Andrew Jackson from Tennessee, the man Adams had defeated four years earlier. John Quincy Adams then served in the

House of Representatives. He was obviously on George W. Bush's mind for, shortly before being sworn in as president in January 2001, Bush revealed that he'd begun reading a biography of none other than John Quincy Adams. It was a book former president George H. W. Bush suggested that his son read.

Certainly reasonable people can debate over the reality of the spiritual world, the presence of spirits of the departed among us, and over our ability to communicate with those who have passed to the Other Side. People who have described what we call near-death experiences have reported certain commonalities, such as the long tunnel, the white, all-embracing light, and the presence of loved ones who help the newly departed make the transition to the next plane. Is it not possible, therefore, that the descriptions of near death that people have given us are a clue to what awaits us on the Other Side?

Every religion gives us some insight into the nature of the reality that awaits all of us after we leave this earthly plane. These are insights that we live by and that have helped guide our nation from the days of the first fiery speeches for independence in Philadelphia, Boston, and Virginia. Now, as the power of the United States extends into its third century, it will undoubtedly be tested in the years ahead as it was during previous national crises and wars. Therefore, is it so far-fetched to believe that there are souls on the Other Side willing and able to give advice and guidance to those who need it? Perhaps, instead of running from the spirits who haunt the White House and other locations of great power, we, and especially our leaders, should seek them out to communicate with them?

People may have laughed derisively at the Reagans and at Hillary Rodham Clinton for their respective interests in the paranormal and the messages they might have received from the spirit world, but there's no question that their open-mindedness and abilities to consider new information without rejecting it out of hand because it was New Age helped them to be more responsive and to reach a higher consciousness. Both the Reagans and Hillary Rodham Clinton achieved great things during their stays in the White House, and perhaps someday Senator Clinton will return to the White House as Madame President Clinton.

Maybe the next time you're on a tour of the White House and walk down some of the public corridors, you should keep your eyes, ears, and spirit wide open. Who knows? Maybe you'll be one of the fortunate individuals who turn a corner, look down a hall, see a strange light coming out of the Rose Room, or hear a voice that's not the tour guide's telling you to move along. Maybe you will, indeed, become one of the fortunate few who sees a bit of the Other World that inhabits the haunted White House.

Cause I've learned this and I'm gonna tell ya: there's a time for live things and a time for dead, for ghosts and for flesh 'n bones: all life is just a sharing of ghosts and flesh. Us humans are part ghost and part flesh—part fire and part ash—but I think maybe the ghost part is the longest lastin, the fire blazes but the ashes last forever.

—William Goyen
"Ghosts and Flesh, Water and Dirt"

APPENDIX A

Presidential Haunted Places: A Travel Guide

If you would like to visit some of the places written about in *The Haunting of the Presidents,* we've included this selected travel guide. Because pertinent information, such as telephone numbers, visiting hours, admission prices, and opening and closing times, is subject to change, we suggest you call before you visit any of these locations. Some have Web sites that provide information. Many are open to the public. However, those that are now private residences might not be readily accessible to visitors. We can't guarantee you'll see a ghost—but we can't be sure you won't.

California

Richard Nixon Library and Birthplace
18001 Yorba Linda Boulevard
Yorba Linda
714-993-3393

District of Columbia

Capitol Building
National Mall
202-224-3121

Decatur House
748 Jackson Place NW
202-842-0920

Dolley Madison House
Madison and H Streets NW

Ford's Theater National Historic Site
511 Tenth Street NW
202-426-6924 or 202-347-4833 (box office)

Fort Lesley McNair
Main gate: P Street between Third and Fourth Streets
SW

Halcyon House
3400 Prospect Street NW
Private residence

Henry Adams House
202-638-6600
Now the site of a hotel, the house was on Lafayette
Square at H Street NW, across from St. John's Church.

Key House
Demolished. The house was located on M Street in
Georgetown, where the northeast ramp of the Key
Bridge is presently located.

McLean Mansion
2020 Massachusetts Avenue NW
202-775-5200
Now is the Indonesian Embassy

National Theater
1321 Pennsylvania Avenue NW
202-628-6161

Octagon House
1799 New York Avenue NW
202-638-3221
Now the American Institute of Architects Museum

Old Stone House
3051 M Street NW
202-426-6851

Pension Building
440 G Street NW

Rathbone House
Demolished. The house was at 8 Jackson Place on Lafayette Square.

St. John's Church
Sixteenth and H Streets NW
202-347-8766

Mary Surratt's Boardinghouse
604 H Street NW

U.S. Supreme Court
First and East Capitol Streets NW
Once the site of the Old Brick Capitol

Washington Club
Demolished. It was located on Lafayette Square between Fifteenth and Sixteenth streets NW.

White House
1600 Pennsylvania Avenue NW
Contact the White House Visitors Center, 1450 Pennsylvania Avenue NW, at 202-456-7041 for a 24-hour recording about tour information, or visit www.whitehouse.gov.

Woodrow Wilson House
2340 S Street NW
202-387-4062
Now is a museum.

Florida

Harry S. Truman Little White House Museum
111 Front Street

Key West
305-294-9911

Georgia

Lion's Club
Junction of Highways 62 and 37
Leary
Location of Jimmy Carter's UFO sighting

Little White House State Historic Site
401 Little White House Road
Warm Springs
706-665-5870
Franklin D. Roosevelt's vacation home

Illinois

Lincoln's Tomb State Historic Site
Oak Ridge Cemetery
Springfield
217-782-2717
For more information, contact the State Historical Sites
Division, 313 Sixth Street, Springfield, IL 62701, at 217-
785-1584.

Old Courthouse
Junction of I-55 and I-72
Springfield
217-782-2424
Site of Lincoln's ghost

Indiana

Tippecanoe Battlefield
Tippecanoe County Historical Association
909 South Street
Lafayette
765-476-8411
Site of 1811 battle where General William Henry Harrison defeated Indians led by Tenskwatawa.

Tippecanoe River State Park and Prophetstown. South of Beardstown. Take U.S. Highway 35. Prophet's Town is on the west bank of the Wabash River, near the mouth of the Tippecanoe River at Oswego.

Maryland

Fort McHenry National Monument and Historic Shrine
End of East Ford Avenue
Baltimore
410-962-4290

Montpelier Mansion
Maryland National Park
9401 Montpelier Drive
Laurel
301-953-1376

Surratt House and Tavern
9110 Brandywine Road
Clinton
240-868-1121
Museum

Massachusetts

John Adams National Historic Site
1250 Hancock Street
Quincy
617-770-1175

Missouri

Harry S. Truman National Historic Site
223 North Main Street
Independence

Truman Home
219 North Delaware Street
Independence
816-254-7199, 816-254-9929, 816-254-2720

New York

Fox Sisters' Home
South of Lily Dale, off I-90
716-595-2505
Burned to the ground in 1955. House was rebuilt and moved from Hydesville to Lily Dale Assembly.
Original site of Fox home is noted by a marker in Hydesville, approximately thirty miles east of Rochester.

Martin Van Buren National Historic Site (Lindenwald)
State Route 9H
Kinderhook (Twenty miles south of Albany)
518-758-9689

Sagamore Hill National Historic Site
Theodore Roosevelt Home
20 Sagamore Hill Road
Oyster Bay
516-922-4447
Sagamore Hill Visitors Center
516-922-7866

North Carolina

Andrew Johnson Birthplace
Mordecai Historic Park
1 Mimosa Street
Mordecai Square
Raleigh
919-834-4844

Ohio

James Garfield Home
Garfield Road
Hiram (Twenty-five miles south of Cleveland)
Private residence

Pennsylvania

Eisenhower National Historic Site
97 Taneytown Road

Gettysburg (Adjacent to the Gettysburg Battlefield)
717-338-9114

Gettysburg National Military Park
Taneytown Road
Gettysburg
717-334-1124
717-337-0445 (information about ghost tours)

Valley Forge National Historical Park
I-76 and U. S. Highway 422
Valley Forge
610-783-7700

Tennessee

John Bell Farm
Adams, Robertson County
U. S. Highway 41, 36 miles north of Nashville.
615-696-3055
(The farmhouse was demolished, but the property remains, so does the Bell Witch Cave. There is a Tennessee historical marker on U.S. Highway 41 in memory of the Bell family.)

Virginia

Ash Lawn Estate
James Monroe Parkway (Highway 795)
Charlottesville (Five miles southeast of Charlottesville)
434-293-9539

Carter's Grove Plantation
Part of Colonial Williamsburg
Route 60 East
James City
Mansion outside city limits
Location of "refusal room"
757-220-7453

James Monroe Museum and Memorial Library
908 Charles Street

Fredericksburg
540-654-1043
Site of Monroe's law office from 1786 to 1789

La Lafayette Restaurant (also known as Chimneys
Tavern)
623 Caroline Street
Fredericksburg
540-373-6895

Monticello
Charlottesville (Two miles southeast of Charlottesville
on Highway 20)
434-984-9822, 434-977-1738

Mount Airy
East of Tappahannock, near Warsaw (Across the river
on U.S. Highway 360)
Colonel John Tayloe home

Mount Vernon
George Washington Memorial Parkway
Mount Vernon
703-780-2000
Ghostly tours of Mount Vernon during last week of
October.

Old Fort Monroe and Casemate Museum
Mercury Blvd, Ingalls Road
Fort Monroe
(On Chesapeake Bay near Hampton. Take I-64 to Exit
268.)
757-788-3391

University of Virginia
Charlottesville
434-924-0311

Washington House
1200 Charles Street

Fredericksburg
540-373-1569
Home of George Washington's mother, Mary Ball Washington

APPENDIX B

Presidential Terms of Office and Dates of Births and Deaths

1. George Washington 1789–1797 (February 22, 1732–December 14, 1799)
2. John Adams 1797–1801 (October 30, 1735–July 4, 1826)
3. Thomas Jefferson 1801–1809 (April 13, 1743–July 4, 1826)
4. James Madison 1809–1817 (March 16, 1751–June 28, 1836)
5. James Monroe 1817–1825 (April 28, 1758–July 4, 1831)
6. John Quincy Adams 1825–1829 (July 11, 1767–February 23, 1848)
7. Andrew Jackson 1829–1837 (March 15, 1767–June 8, 1845)
8. Martin Van Buren 1837–1841 (December 5, 1782–July 24, 1862)
9. William Henry Harrison 1841 (February 9, 1773–April 4, 1841)
10. John Tyler 1841–1845 (March 29, 1790–January 18, 1862)
11. James Knox Polk 1845–1849 (November 2, 1795–June 15, 1849)
12. Zachary Taylor 1849–1850 (November 24, 1784–July 9, 1850)

13. Millard Fillmore 1850–1853 (January 7, 1800–March 8, 1874)
14. Franklin Pierce 1853–1857 (November 23, 1804–October 8, 1869)
15. James Buchanan 1857–1861 (April 23, 1791–June 1, 1868)
16. Abraham Lincoln 1861–1865 (February 12, 1809–April 15, 1865)
17. Andrew Johnson 1865–1869 (December 29, 1808–July 31, 1875)
18. Ulysses S. Grant 1869–1877 (April 27, 1822–July 23, 1885)
19. Rutherford B. Hayes 1877–1881 (October 4, 1822–January 17, 1893)
20. James Garfield 1881 (November 19, 1831–September 19, 1881)
21. Chester Alan Arthur 1881–1885 (October 5, 1829–November 18, 1886)
22. Grover Cleveland 1885–1889 (March 18, 1837–June 24, 1908)
23. Benjamin Harrison 1889–1893 (August 20, 1833–March 13, 1901)
24. Grover Cleveland 1893–1897 (Served nonconsecutive terms)
25. William McKinley 1897–1901 (January 29, 1843–September 14, 1901)
26. Theodore Roosevelt 1901–1909 (October 27, 1858–January 6, 1919)
27. William Howard Taft 1909–1913 (September 15, 1857–March 8, 1930)
28. Woodrow Wilson 1913–1921 (December 29, 1856–February 3, 1924)
29. Warren G. Harding 1921–1923 (November 2, 1865–August 2, 1923)
30. Calvin Coolidge 1923–1929 (July 4, 1872–January 5, 1933)
31. Herbert Hoover 1929–1933 (August 10, 1874–October 20, 1964)
32. Franklin Delano Roosevelt 1933–1945 (January 30, 1882–April 12, 1945)

33. Harry S. Truman 1945–1953 (May 8, 1884–December 26, 1972)
34. Dwight D. Eisenhower 1953–1961 (October 14, 1890–March 28, 1969)
35. John F. Kennedy 1961–1963 (May 29, 1917–November 22, 1963)
36. Lyndon B. Johnson 1963–1969 (August 27, 1908–January 22, 1973)
37. Richard M. Nixon 1969–1974 (January 9, 1913–April 22, 1994)
38. Gerald R. Ford 1974–1977 (July 14, 1913–   )
39. Jimmy Carter 1977–1981 (October 1, 1924–   )
40. Ronald Reagan 1981–1989 (February 6, 1911–   )
41. George H. W. Bush 1989–1993 (June 12, 1924–   )
42. William J. Clinton 1993–2001 (August 19, 1946–   )
43. George W. Bush 2001– (July 6, 1946–   )

APPENDIX C

Presidential Wives

In some instances, wives of presidents died before their husbands assumed or completed their terms of office. Thus, several first ladies were not presidential wives but were daughters or other relatives or friends who served in the position. Only one president, James Buchanan, never married. His niece served as official White House hostess. Following are the dates of births and deaths of presidential wives.

Martha Dandridge Custis Washington 1731–1802
Abigail Smith Adams 1744–1818
Martha Skelton Jefferson 1749–1782
Dolley Payne Todd Madison 1768–1849
Elizabeth Kortright Monroe 1768–1830
Louisa Johnson Adams 1775–1852
Rachel Donelson Robard Jackson 1767–1828
Hannah Hoes Van Buren 1788–1819
Anna Symmes Harrison 1775–1864
Letitia Christian Tyler 1790–1842
Julia Gardiner Tyler 1820–1889
Sarah Childress Polk 1803–1891
Margaret Smith Taylor 1788–1852
Abigail Powers Fillmore 1798–1853
Jane Means Appleton Pierce 1806–1863

Mary Todd Lincoln 1818–1882
Eliza McCardle Johnson 1810–1876
Julia Dent Grant 1826–1902
Lucy Ware Webb Hayes 1831–1889
Lucretia Rudolph Garfield 1832–1918
Ellen Lewis Herndon Arthur 1837–1880
Frances Folsom Cleveland 1864–1947
Caroline Scott Harrison 1832–1892
Ida Saxton McKinley 1847–1907
Alice Hathaway Lee Roosevelt 1861–1884
Edith Kermit Carow Roosevelt 1861–1948
Helen Herron Taft 1861–1943
Ellen Louise Axson Wilson 1860–1914
Edith Bolling Galt Wilson 1872–1961
Florence Kling DeWolfe Harding 1860–1924
Grace Anna Goodhue Coolidge 1879–1957
Lou Henry Hoover 1874–1944
Anna Eleanor Roosevelt 1884–1962
Elizabeth "Bess" Wallace Truman 1885–1982
Mary "Mamie" Geneva Doud Eisenhower 1896–1979
Jacqueline Lee Bouvier Kennedy Onassis 1929–1994
Claudia "Lady Bird" Alta Taylor Johnson 1912–
Patricia Ryan Nixon 1912–1993
Elizabeth Bloomer Warren Ford 1918–
Rosalynn Smith Carter 1927–
"Nancy" Robbins Davis Reagan 1921–
Barbara Pierce Bush 1925–
Hillary Rodham Clinton 1947–
Laura Bush 1946–

Bibliography

The following is a selected bibliography of books and other reference sources used. Because so many were referred to, it is impossible to list them all.

Books

Alexander, John. *Ghosts: Washington Revisited*. Atglen, Pennsylvania: Schiffer, 1998.

———. *Ghosts: Washington's Most Famous Ghost Stories*. Washington, D.C.: Washington Books, 1975.

Andersen, Christopher. *The Day John Died*. New York: HarperCollins, 2000.

———. *Bill and Hillary: The Marriage*. New York: William Morrow, 1999.

Anderson, Jean. *The Haunting of America*. Boston: Houghton Mifflin, 1973.

Berger, Arthur S. and Berger, Joyce. *The Encyclopedia of Parapsychology and Psychical Research*. New York: Paragon House, 1991.

Berlitz, Charles. *Doomsday 1999 A.D.* Garden City, New York: Doubleday, 1981.

Bingham, Joan and Riccio, Dolores. *Haunted Houses USA*. New York: Pocket Books, 1989.

———. *More Haunted Houses*. New York: Pocket Books, 1991.

Bishop, Jim. *The Day Lincoln Was Shot*. New York: Harper & Row, 1964.

Bliven, Bruce, Jr. *The American Revolution: 1760–1783*. New York: Random House, 1958.

Bodine, Echo. *Relax, It's Only a Ghost*. Boston: Element Books, 2000.

Boller, Paul F., Jr. *Presidential Anecdotes*. New York: Oxford University Press, 1996.

Bonnell, John Sutherland. *Presidential Profiles: Religion in the Life of American Presidents*. Philadelphia: Westminster Press, 1971.

Brandon, Jim. *Weird America*. New York: E. P. Dutton, 1978.

Brandon, Ruth. *The Spiritualists*. New York: Knopf, 1983.

Breur, William B. *Unexplained Mysteries of World War II*. New York: John Wiley & Sons, 1997.

Brodie, Fawn M. *Thomas Jefferson: An Intimate History*. New York: W. W. Norton, 1974.

Broughton, Richard S. *Parapsychology: The Controversial Science*. New York: Ballantine, 1991.

Brown, Raymond Lemont. *Phantom Soldiers*. New York: Drake, 1975.

Bumgarner, John, M.D. *The Health of the Presidents*. Jefferson, North Carolina: McFarland, 1994.

Canadeo, Anne. *Fact or Fiction: Ghosts*. New York: Walker, 1990.

Caroli, Betty Boyd. *First Ladies*. New York: Oxford University Press, 1987.

Carrington, Hereward and Fodor, Nandor. *Haunted People: Story of the Poltergeist down the Centuries*. New York: E. P. Dutton, 1951.

Cavendish, Marshall, ed. *Man, Myth & Magic*. North Bellmore, New York: Marshall Cavendish, 1995.

Cayce, Edgar. *My Life as a Seer: The Lost Memoirs*. New York: St. Martin's Press, 1999.

Christopher, Milbourne. *Houdini: A Pictorial Life*. New York: Thomas Y. Crowell, 1976.

Clark, Michael. *Reason to Believe*. New York: Avon Books, 1997.

Cohen, Daniel. *The Encyclopedia of the Strange*. New York: Avon Books, 1985.

——. *Civil War Ghosts*. New York: Scholastic, 1999.

——. *The World's Most Famous Ghosts*. New York: Dodd, Mead, 1979.

Collins, David R. *Shattered Dreams: The Story of Mary Todd Lincoln*. Greensboro, North Carolina: Morgan Reynolds, 1994.

Corso, Philip J. and Birnes, William J. *The Day After Roswell*. New York: Pocket Books, 1997.

Current, Richard N. *The Lincoln Nobody Knows*. New York: Hill and Wang, 1958.

Davis, Burke. *Old Hickory: A Life of Andrew Jackson*. New York: The Dial Press, 1977.

DeGregorio, William A. *The Complete Book of U.S. Presidents*. New York: Dembner Books, 1989.

Donald, David Herbert. *Lincoln*. London: Jonathan Cape, 1995.

Dossey, Larry, M.D. *Be Careful What You Pray For . . . You Just Might Get It*. New York: HarperSanFrancisco, 1998.

——. *Healing Words: The Power and the Practice of Medicine*. New York: HarperSanFrancisco, 1993.

——. *Reinventing Medicine*. New York: HarperCollins, 1999.

Dreller, Larry. *Beginner's Guide to Mediumship*. York Beach, Maine: Samuel Weiser, 1997.

Drosnin, Michael. *The Bible Code*. New York: Simon & Schuster, 1997.

Eadie, Betty J. *The Ripple Effect: Our Harvest*. Seattle: Onjinjinkta, 1999.

Ebon, Martin, ed. *Communicating with the Dead*. New York: New American Library, 1968.

Edmunds, R. David. *The Shawnee Prophet*. Lincoln: University of Nebraska Press, 1983.

Elwood, Ann. *Weird and Mysterious*. New York: Globe Book, 1979.

Fenwick, Peter and Fenwick, Elizabeth. *The Hidden Door to Understanding and Controlling Dreams*. New York: Berkley Books, 1999.

Ferris, Gary. *Presidential Places: A Guide to the Historic Sites of U.S. Presidents*. Winston-Salem, North Carolina: John F. Blair, 1999.

Fisher, Joe and Commins, Peter. *Predictions*. New York: Van Nostrand Reinhold, 1980.

Fitzsimons, Raymund. *Death and the Magician: The Mysteries of Houdini*. New York: Atheneum, 1981.

Flexner, James Thomas. *Washington: The Indispensable Man*. Boston: Little, Brown, 1969.

——. *George Washington in the American Revolution*. Boston: Little, Brown, 1967.

Fodor, Nandor. *Freud, Jung and Occultism*. New Hyde Park, New York: University Books, 1971.

——. *Between Two Worlds*. West Nyack, New York: Parker Publishing, 1964.

Freeman, Douglas Southall. *George Washington: A Biography, Leader of the Revolution*. Volume Four. New York: Charles Scribner's Sons, 1951.

Freeman, Eileen Elias. *Touched by Angels*. New York: Warner Books, 1993.

Freidel, Frank. *Franklin D. Roosevelt: A Rendezvous with Destiny*. Boston: Little, Brown, 1990.

—— and Pencak William, eds. *The White House: The First Two Hundred Years*. Boston: Northeastern University Press, 1994.

Freud, Sigmund. *Studies in Parapsychology*. New York: Macmillan, 1963.

Fuller, Edmund and Green, David E. *God in the White House: The Faiths of American Presidents*. New York: Crown, 1968.

Fuller, John G. *The Airmen Who Would Not Die*. New York: Berkley Books, 1979.

Gabriel, Mary. *Notorious Victoria*. Chapel Hill, North Carolina: Algonquin Books, 1998.

Gardner, Robert. *What's So Super About the Supernatural?* Brookfield, Connecticut: Twenty-First Century Books, 1998.

Glass, Justine. *They Foresaw the Future*. New York: G. P. Putnam's Sons, 1969.

Goldsmith, Barbara. *Other Powers: The Age of Suffrage,*

Spiritualism, & the Scandalous Victoria Woodhull. New York: Alfred A. Knopf, 1998.

Gould, Lewis, ed. *American First Ladies: Their Lives and Their Legacy.* New York: Garland Publishing, 1996.

Greenhouse, Herbert B. *The Book of Psychic Knowledge.* New York: Taplinger, 1973.

——. *Premonitions: A Leap into the Future.* New York: Bernard Geis Associates, 1971.

Guiley, Rosemary Ellen. *The Encyclopedia of Ghosts and Spirits.* New York: Facts on File, 1992.

Haas, Irvin. *Historic Homes of the American Presidents.* New York: Dover Publications, 1991.

Harrison, Maureen and Gilbert, Steve. *Abraham Lincoln: Word for Word.* San Diego: Excellent Books, 1994.

Harvey, Gail. *On the Wings of Angels.* Avenel, New Jersey: Gramercy Books, 1993.

Harwell, Richard, ed. *Washington.* New York: Charles Scribner's Sons, 1968.

Hauck, Dennis William. *Haunted Places: The National Directory.* New York: Penguin Books, 1996.

Hay, Peter. *All the Presidents' Ladies.* New York: Viking, 1988.

Healy, Diana Dixon. *America's First Ladies: Private Lives of Presidential Wives.* New York: Atheneum, 1988.

Heckler-Feltz, Cheryl. *Heart and Soul of the Nation: How the Spirituality of Our First Ladies Changed America.* New York: Doubleday, 1997.

Herndon, William H. and Weik, Jesse W. *Herndon's Life of Lincoln.* Cleveland: World Publishing Company, 1930. (Originally written 1888.)

Holzer, Hans. *Ghosts I've Met.* New York: Ace Books, 1965.

——. *The Ghosts That Walk Washington.* Garden City, New York: Doubleday, 1971.

——. *Where the Ghosts Are.* Secaucus, New Jersey: Citadel Press, 1997.

Houdini, Harry. *A Magician Among the Spirits.* New York: Arno Press, 1972.

Ingermanson, Randall, Ph.D. *Who Wrote the Bible*

Code? Colorado Springs, Colorado: Waterbrook Press, 1999.

James, Marquis. *Andrew Jackson: Portrait of a President.* New York: Grosset & Dunlap, 1937.

Jefferies, Ona Griffin. *In and Out of the White House: From Washington to the Eisenhowers.* New York: Wilfred Funk, 1960.

Jeffers, H. Paul. *An Honest President: The Life and Presidencies of Grover Cleveland.* New York: William Morrow, 2000.

Kaczmarek, Dale. *National Register of Haunted Places.* Oaklawn, Illinois: Ghost Research Society. (Pamphlet.)

Karpin, Michael and Friedman, Ina. *Murder in the Name of God: The Plot to Kill Yitzhak Rabin.* New York: Henry Holt, 1998.

Kaye, Marvin, ed. *Haunted America.* New York: Barnes and Noble, 1990.

Kearns, Doris. *Lyndon Johnson and the American Dream.* New York: Harper & Row, 1976.

Kingston, Kenny. *I Still Talk To . . .* New York: Berkley Books, 1994.

Kirkpatrick, Sidney. *Edgar Cayce: An American Prophet.* New York: Penguin Putnam, 2000.

Kunhardt, Philip B., Jr.; Kunhardt, Philip B. III; Kunhardt, Peter W. *The American President.* New York: Riverhead Books, 1999.

———. *Lincoln: An Illustrated Biography.* New York: Portland House, 1992.

Lattimer, John, M.D. *Kennedy and Lincoln: Medical and Ballistic Comparisons of Their Assassinations.* New York: Harcourt Brace Jovanovich, 1980.

Leemings, David and Page, Jake. *Myths, Legends and Folktales of America.* New York: Oxford University Press, 1999.

Lewis, David and Hicks, Daryl E. *The Presidential Zero-Year Mystery.* Plainfield, New Jersey: Haven Books, 1980.

Lewis, James R., ed. *Encyclopedia of Afterlife Beliefs and Phenomena.* Detroit: Gale Research, 1994.

——. *Astrology Encyclopedia*. Detroit: Gale Research, 1994.

—— and Oliver, Evelyn Dorothy. *Angels A to Z*. Detroit: Gale Research, 1996.

Lewis, Lloyd. *Myths After Lincoln*. New York: Harcourt Brace Jovanovich, 1973.

Liljencrants, Johan. *Spiritism and Religion: Can You Talk to the Dead?* New York: Devin-Adair, 1918.

Lyons, Arthur and Truzzi, Marcello. *The Blue Sense: Psychic Detectives & Crime*. New York: Warner Books, 1991.

Mack, John, M.D. *Abduction: Human Encounters with Aliens*. New York: Ballantine Books, 1994.

Magill, Frank, ed. *Great Events from History: American Series*. Englewood Cliffs, New Jersey: Salem Press, 1975.

Manchester, William. *The Glory and the Dream*. Boston: Little, Brown, 1973.

Mandelbaum, W. Adam. *The Psychic Battlefield: A History of the Military-Occult Complex*. New York: St. Martin's Press, 2000.

Markowitz, Harvey, ed. *American Indian Biographies*. Pasadena, California: Salem Press, 1999.

Martin, Joel and Romanowski, Patricia. *Love Beyond Life*. New York: HarperCollins, 1997.

——. *We Don't Die*. New York: G. P. Putnam's Sons, 1988.

Matheson, Richard. *Mediums Rare*. Baltimore: Cemetery Dance Publications, 2000.

Maynard, Nettie Colburn. *Was Abraham Lincoln a Spiritualist?* Philadelphia: Rufus C. Hartranft, 1891.

McCollister, John. *So Help Me God: The Faith of America's Presidents*. Louisville, Kentucky: John Knox Press, 1991.

McHargue, Georgess. *Facts, Frauds and Phantasms: A Survey of the Spiritualist Movement*. Garden City, New York: Doubleday, 1972.

McPherson, James M. *To the Best of My Ability*. New York: Dorling Kindersley, 2000.

Melder, Keith E. *Hail to the Candidate: Presidential*

Campaigns from Banners to Broadcasts. Washington, D.C.: American Institute of Architects Press, 1992.

Melton, J. Gordon, ed. *Encyclopedia of Occultism & Parapsychology*. Detroit: Gale Research, 1996.

Miller, Nathan. *F.D.R.: An Intimate History*. Garden City, New York: Doubleday, 1983.

Milton, Joyce. *The First Partner: Hillary Rodham Clinton*. New York: William Morrow, 1999.

Mitchell, Edgar D. *Psychic Exploration*. New York: G. P. Putnam's Sons, 1974.

———. *The Way of the Explorer*. New York: G. P. Putnam's Sons, 1996.

Monahan, Brent, ed. *The Bell Witch: An American Haunting*. New York: St. Martin's, 1997.

Montgomery, Ruth. *A Search for the Truth*. New York: Fawcett Crest, 1966.

———. *The World Before*. New York: Fawcett Crest, 1976.

———. *A Gift of Prophecy: The Phenomenal Jeane Dixon*. New York: Bantam Books, 1966.

Moody, Raymond, M.D. with Perry, Paul. *Reunions: Visionary Encounters with Departed Loved Ones*. New York: Villard, 1993.

Morehouse, David. *Psychic Warrior: Inside the CIA's Stargate Program*. New York: St. Martin's Press, 1996.

Morris, Edmund. *Dutch: A Memoir of Ronald Reagan*. New York: Random House, 1999.

Morse, Melvin, M.D. with Perry, Paul. *Parting Visions*. New York: Villard, 1994.

Muldoon, Sylvan. *Psychic Experiences of Famous People*. Chicago: The Aries Press, 1947.

Myers, Arthur. *The Ghostly Gazetteer: America's Most Fascinating Haunted Landmarks*. Chicago: Contemporary Books, 1990.

———. *Ghosts of the Rich and Famous*. Chicago: Contemporary Books, 1988.

Nesbitt, Mark. *Ghosts of Gettysburg*. Gettysburg, Pennsylvania: Thomas Publications, 1991.

Noonan, Peggy. *The Case Against Hillary Clinton*. New York: HarperCollins, 2000.

Olasky, Marvin. *The American Leadership Tradition*. New York: Free Press, 2000.

Ostendorf, Lloyd, ed. *Lincoln's Unknown Private Life*. Mamaroneck, New York: Hastings House, 1993.

Padover, Saul K., ed. *A Jefferson Profile as Revealed in His Letters*. New York: John Day, 1956.

Paletta, Luann and Worth, Fred L. *The World Almanac of Presidential Facts*. New York: World Almanac, 1988.

Parker, Derek and Parker, Julia. *Atlas of the Supernatural*. New York: Prentice Hall, 1990.

Parks, Lillian Rogers. *My Thirty Years Backstairs at the White House*. New York: Fleet, 1961.

Pressing, R. G. *Rappings That Startled the World: Facts about the Fox Sisters*. Lily Dale, New York: Dale News. (Pamphlet.)

Quigley, Joan. *What Does Joan Say?* New York: Birch Lane Press, 1990.

Randle, Kevin D. and Schmitt, Donald R. *The Truth about the UFO Crash at Roswell*. New York: M. Evans, 1994.

Reader's Digest Association. *Mysteries of the Unexplained*. Pleasantville, New York: Reader's Digest Association, 1982.

——. *Into the Unknown*. Pleasantville, New York: Reader's Digest Association, 1981.

Reagan, Nancy. *My Turn: The Memoirs of Nancy Reagan*. New York: Random House, 1989.

Regan, Donald T. *For the Record: From Wall Street to Washington*. New York: Harcourt Brace Jovanovich, 1988.

Roberts, Bruce and Roberts, Nancy. *America's Most Haunted Places*. Garden City, New York: Doubleday, 1976.

Roberts, Henry C. *The Complete Prophecies of Nostradamus*. Oyster Bay, New York: Nostradamus Company, 1982.

Roberts, Nancy. *Civil War Ghost Stories and Legends*.

Columbia, South Carolia: University of South Carolina Press, 1992.

———. *Haunted Houses: Tales from 30 American Homes*. Chester, Connecticut: Globe Pequot Press, 1988.

Sandburg, Carl. *Abraham Lincoln: The War Years. Volume One*. New York: Harcourt Brace, 1939.

Schull, Bill D. *Animal Immortality: Pets and Their Afterlife*. New York: Fawcett Gold Medal, 1991.

Scott, Beth and Norman, Michael. *Haunted America*. New York: Tom Doherty Associates, 1994.

Seale, William. *The White House: The History of an American Idea*. Washington, D.C.: American Institute of Architects Press, 1992.

Senate, Richard. *Ghost Stalker's Guide to Haunted California*. Ventura, California: Charon Press, 1998.

Seuling, Barbara. *The Last Cow on the White House Lawn and Other Little Known Facts About the Presidency*. New York: Doubleday, 1978.

Shebar, Sharon Sigmond and Schoder, Judith. *The Bell Witch*. New York: Julian Messner, 1983.

Sheldrake, Rupert. *Dogs That Know When Their Owners Are Coming Home*. New York: Crown, 1999.

Shenkman, Richard. *Legends, Lies & Cherished Myths of American History*. New York: William Morrow, 1988.

Smith, Susy. *Prominent American Ghosts*. Cleveland: World Publishing Company, 1967.

———. *Ghosts Around the House*. Cleveland: World Publishing Company, 1970.

Sotnak, Lewann. *Haunted Houses*. New York: Crestwood House, 1990.

Stebben, Gregg and Morris, Jim. *White House Confidential: The Little Book of Weird Presidential History*. Nashville: Cumberland House, 1998.

Steiger, Brad, ed. *Project Blue Book*. New York: Ballantine Books, 1976.

Stephens, Autumn. *Wild Women in the White House*. Berkeley, California: Conari Press, 1997.

Stevens, William Oliver. *Discovering Long Island*. New York: Dodd Mead, 1939.

Summers, Anthony. *The Arrogance of Power: The Secret World of Richard Nixon*. New York: Viking, 2000.

Swann, Don. *Colonial & Historic Homes of Maryland*. Baltimore: Johns Hopkins University Press, 1975.

Targ, Russell and Harary, Keith. *The Mind Race: Understanding and Using Psychic Abilities*. New York: Villard, 1984.

Taylor, L. B., Jr. *The Ghosts of Virginia*. Williamsburg, Virginia: Progress Printing Company, 1996.

——. *The Ghosts of Fredericksburg*. Williamsburg, Virginia: Progress Printing Company, 1991.

——. *The Ghosts of Williamsburg*. Williamsburg, Virginia: Progress Printing Company, 1983.

Thomas, E. H. Gwynne. *The Presidential Families: From George Washington to Ronald Reagan*. New York: Hippocrane Books, 1989.

Time-Life Books, eds. *Hauntings*. New York: Barnes & Noble Books, 1989.

——. *The Mysterious World*. Alexandria, Virginia: Time-Life Books, 1992.

——. *Visions and Prophecies*. Alexandria, Virginia: Time-Life Books, 1988.

Tremain, Ruthven. *The Animals' Who's Who*. New York: Charles Scribner's Sons, 1982.

Truman, Margaret. *First Ladies*. New York: Random House, 1995.

Twigg, Ena. *The Woman Who Stunned the World*. New York: Manor Books, 1973.

Twohig, Dorothy, ed. *George Washington's Diaries: An Abridgement*. Charlottesville, Virginia: University Press of Virginia, 1999.

Underhill, Lois B. *The Woman Who Ran for President: The Many Lives of Victoria Woodhull*. Bridgehampton, New York: Bridge Works Publishing, 1995.

U.S. Congress. *Bibliographic Directory of the American Congress, 1774–1996*. Alexandria, Virginia: CQ Staff Directories, 1997.

Van deCastle, Robert L., Ph.D. *Our Dreaming Mind*. New York: Ballantine Books, 1994.

Volkan, Vamik D.; Itzkowitz, Norman; and Dod, Andrew W. *Richard Nixon: A Psychobiography*. New York: Columbia University Press, 1997.

Waldrup, Carole Chandler. *President's Wives*. Jefferson, North Carolina: McFarland, 1989.

Ward, Geoffrey C.; Burns, Ric; and Burns, Ken. *The Civil War: An Illustrated History*. New York: Alfred Knopf, 1990.

Watson, Robert P. *The Presidents' Wives*. Boulder, Colorado: Lynne Rienner, 2000.

Webster, Orville. *The Book of Presidents*. Los Angeles: JBG Publishing, 1991.

West, J. B. *Upstairs at the White House*. New York: Warner Books, 1974.

White House Historical Association. *The White House*. New York: Grosset & Dunlap, 1963.

Winer, Richard and Osborn, Nancy. *Haunted Houses*. New York: Bantam Books, 1979.

Woodward, Bob. *The Choice*. New York: Simon & Schuster, 1996.

Zall, Paul, ed. *Lincoln on Lincoln*. Lexington: University of Press Kentucky, 1999.

Magazines

America, American Heritage, Christian Science Monitor, Christianity Today, Cosmopolitan, Discover, Economist, Good Housekeeping, Jerusalem Report, Journal of the American Society for Psychical Research, Journal of Parapsychology, Journal of Religion and Psychical Research, Life, MacLean's, The Nation, National Parks, National Review, The New Yorker, Ohio, People, Psychic World, Psychology Today, Reader's Digest, Skeptic, Skeptical Inquirer, Smithsonian, Time, TV Guide, U.S. News & World Report, Washingtonian.

Newspapers

Akron Beacon-Journal, Newsday, New York Daily News, New York Post, New York Times, USA Today, Washington Business Journal, Washington Post.

Personal Interviews Conducted

Priscilla Baker, Janet Edstrom, Peter Edstrom, Anne Gehman, Dorothy Maksym, Dorothy Mallone, Pamela Mallone, Alexander Murray, Alex Oberman.

Web sites

All the Presidents' UFOs
www.presidentialufo.com

Ghosts of the Prairie
www.prairieghosts.com

Haunted Places in the District of Columbia
www.theshadowlands.net

THE ASTROLOGY GIFT GUIDE

Constance Stellas

*Finding a great gift is as easy as
knowing someone's birthday...*

INTRODUCING
THE <u>FIRST</u> BUYING GUIDE FOR ALL
SIGNS, OCCASIONS, AND BUDGETS!

This unique gift-buying guide uses individual profiles for
each astrological sign to help you choose the perfect gift.
Includes:

• A vast array of gift ideas, in three price ranges
• Personality profiles for each sign: ruling passion, style,
colors, and more
• Shopping lists for men, women, children and teens
• Gift suggestions for every occasion: birthdays, weddings,
showers, housewarming, holidays, and much more

207262

To order call: 1-800-788-6262

S457/Stellas